Julian Miller   Marco Tomassini
Pier Luca Lanzi   Conor Ryan
Andrea G.B. Tettamanzi
William B. Langdon (Eds.)

Genetic Programming

4th European Conference, EuroGP 2001
Lake Como, Italy, April 18-20, 2001
Proceedings

 Springer

Series Editors

Gerhard Goos, Karlsruhe University, Germany
Juris Hartmanis, Cornell University, NY, USA
Jan van Leeuwen, Utrecht University, The Netherlands

Volume Editors

Julian Miller
University of Birmingham, School of Computer Science
E-mail: j.miller@cs.bham.ac.uk

Marco Tomassini
University of Lausanne, Computer Science Institute
E-mail: marco.tomassini@iismail.unil.ch

Pier Luca Lanzi
Politecnico di Milano, Dipartimento di Elettronica e Informazione
E-mail: lanzi@morgana.elet.polimi.it

Conor Ryan
University of Limerick, Computer Science and Information Systems
E-mail: Conor.Ryan@ul.ie

Andrea G.B. Tettamanzi
Università degli Studi di Milano, Dipartimento di Tecnologie dell'Informazione
E-mail: andrea.tettamanzi@unimi.it

William B. Langdon
University College London, Department of Computer Science
E-mail: W.Langdon@cs.ucl.ac.uk

Cataloging-in-Publication Data applied for

Die Deutsche Bibliothek - CIP-Einheitsaufnahme

Genetic programming : 4th European conference ; proceedings / EuroGP
2001, Lake Como, Italy, UK, April 18 - 20, 2001. Julian Miller ...
(ed.). - Berlin ; Heidelberg ; New York ; Barcelona ; Hong Kong ;
London ; Milan ; Paris ; Singapore ; Tokyo : Springer, 2001
 (Lecture notes in computer science ; Vol. 2038)
 ISBN 3-540-41899-7

CR Subject Classification (1998): D.1, F.1, F.2, I.5, I.2, J.3
ISSN 0302-9743
ISBN 3-540-41899-7 Springer-Verlag Berlin Heidelberg New York

Springer-Verlag Berlin Heidelberg New York
a member of BertelsmannSpringer Science+Business Media GmbH

http://www.springer.de

© Springer-Verlag Berlin Heidelberg 2001
Printed in Germany
Typesetting: Camera-ready by author, data conversion by Christian Grosche, Hamburg
Printed on acid-free paper   SPIN: 10782492   06/3142   5 4 3 2 1 0

Lecture Notes in Computer Science

Edited by G. Goos, J. Hartmanis and J. van Leeuwen

Springer
Berlin
Heidelberg
New York
Barcelona
Hong Kong
London
Milan
Paris
Singapore
Tokyo

Preface

In this volume are the proceedings of the fourth European conference on Genetic Programming (EuroGP 2001) which took place at Lake Como in Italy on April, 18–20 2001. EuroGP has become firmly established as the premier European event devoted to Genetic Programming. EuroGP began life in 1998 as an international workshop and was held in Paris (14–15 April, LNCS 1391). After that it was held in Göteborg, Sweden (26–27 May 1999, LNCS 1598). Its first appearance as a conference was last year in Edinburgh in Scotland (15–16 April, LNCS 1802). Each year EuroGP has been co-located with a series of specialist workshops (LNCS 1468, 1596, 1803). This year was no exception and EvoWorkshops 2001 were also held at Lake Como (18-19 April, LNCS 2037).

Genetic Programming (GP) refers to a branch of Evolutionary Computation in which computer programs are automatically generated over a period of time using a process that mimics Darwinian evolution. The 30 papers in these proceedings more than amply demonstrate the wide and varied applicability of GP. There are papers that apply GP to robotics, artificial retina, character recognition, financial prediction, digital filter and electronic circuit design, image processing, data fusion, and biosequencing. In addition there are many papers that address foundational and theoretical issues.

A rigorous double-blind refereeing system was applied to the 42 submitted papers. This resulted in 17 plenary talks (40% of those submitted) and 13 research posters. Every submitted paper was reviewed by a minimum of two members of the International Program Committee, and if there was disagreement by a third reviewer. The Program Committee was carefully selected for their knowledge and expertise, and, as far as possible, papers were matched with the reviewers' particular interests and specialist expertise. The results of this process are seen here in the high quality of papers published within this volume. Many of these are by internationally recognised researchers.

The 30 published papers came from many European countries with a noticeable proportion from the Americas.

We would like to express our sincere thanks especially to the two internationally renowned invited speakers who gave keynote talks at the conference: Professor Enrico Coen of the John Innes Centre, UK and Professor Lee Altenberg of the University of Hawaii at Manoa. Professor Coen's talk was also shared with EvoWorkshops 2001. We would also like to thank Dr. Riccardo Poli of the School of Computer Science at the University of Birmingham for kindly agreeing to give a tutorial on GP.

This conference would have been considerably poorer without the support of many people. Firstly we would like to thank the very busy members of the Program Committee for their diligence, patience, and dedication in the task of providing high quality reviews. We would also like to thank EvoNET, the Network of Excellence in Evolutionary Computing, for their support, in particular, Jennifer Willies and Chris Osborne for their help, especially their sterling work on the registration and the conference web site. Thanks also to Chris Osborne and Mij Kelly for their assistance with the production of the conference poster. Finally we would like to thank the members of EvoGP, the EvoNET working group on Genetic Programming.

April 2001   Julian Miller, Marco Tomassini, Pier Luca Lanzi, Conor Ryan, Andrea G.B. Tettamanzi, William B. Langdon

Organisation

EuroGP 2001 was organised by EvoGP, the EvoNet Working Group on Genetic Programming.

Organising Committee

Program co-chair:	Julian Miller (University of Birmingham, UK)
Program co-chair:	Marco Tomassini (University of Lausanne, Switzerland)
Publicity chair:	Conor Ryan (University of Limerick, Ireland)
Local co-chairs:	Pier Luca Lanzi (Politecnico di Milano, Italy)
	Andrea G.B. Tettamanzi (University of Milan, Italy)
Publication co-chair:	William B. Langdon (University College, London, UK)

Program Committee

Wolfgang Banzhaf, University of Dortmund, Germany
Forest Bennett III, FX Palo Alto Laboratory, USA
Shu-Heng Chen, National Chengchi University, Taiwan
Marco Dorigo, Free University of Brussels, Belgium
Terry Fogarty, South Bank University, UK
James A. Foster, University of Idaho, USA
Hitoshi Iba, University of Tokyo, Japan
Christian Jacob, University of Calgary, Canada
Maarten Keijzer, Danish Hydraulics Insitute, Denmark
Ibrahim Kuscu , University of Surrey , UK
William B. Langdon, University College London, UK
Sean Luke, University of Maryland, USA
Evelyne Lutton, INRIA, France
Nic McPhee, University of Minnesota, Morris, USA
Jean-Arcady Meyer, Université Pierre et Marie Curie, France
Julian Miller, University of Birmingham, UK
Peter Nordin, Chalmers University of Technology, Sweden
Simon Perkins, Los Alamos National Laboratories, USA
Riccardo Poli, University of Birmingham, UK
Joao C.F. Pujol, Centro de Desenvolvimento da Energia Nuclea, Brazil
Kazuhiro Saitou, University of Michigan, USA
Jonathan Rowe, University of Birmingham, UK
Peter Ross, Napier University, UK
Conor Ryan, University of Limerick, Ireland
Marc Schoenauer, Ecole Polytechnique, France
Moshe Sipper, EPFL, Switzerland

Michele Sebag, Ecole Polytechnique, France
Terry Soule, St Cloud State University, Minnesota, USA
Andrea G. B. Tettamanzi, Genetica - Advanced Software Architectures, Italy
Adrian Thompson, University of Sussex, UK
Marco Tomassini, Université de Lausanne, Switzerland
Hans-Michael Voigt, Center for Applied Computer Science, Berlin, German
Peter A. Whigham, University of Otago, New Zealand
Xin Yao, University of Birmingham, UK
Tina Yu, Chevron Information Technology Company, USA

Sponsoring Institutions

EvoNet: The Network of Excellence in Evolutionary Computing.

Table of Contents

Talks

Posters

Heuristic Learning Based on Genetic Programming

Nicole Drechsler, Frank Schmiedle, Daniel Große, and Rolf Drechsler

Institute of Computer Science
Chair of Computer Architecture (Prof. Bernd Becker)
Albert-Ludwigs-University
79110 Freiburg im Breisgau
ndrechsl@informatik.uni-freiburg.de

Abstract. In this paper we present an approach to learning heuristics based on Genetic Programming (GP). Instead of directly solving the problem by application of GP, GP is used to develop a heuristic that is applied to the problem instance. By this, the typical large runtimes of evolutionary methods have to be invested only once in the learning phase. The resulting heuristic is very fast. The technique is applied to a field from the area of VLSI CAD, i.e. minimization of Binary Decision Diagrams (BDDs). We chose this topic due to its high practical relevance and since it matches the criteria where our algorithm works best, i.e. large problem instances where standard evolutionary techniques cannot be applied due to their large runtimes. Our experiments show that we obtain high quality results that outperform previous methods, while keeping the advantage of low runtimes.

1   Introduction

Decision Diagrams (DDs) are often used in CAD systems for efficient representation and manipulation of Boolean functions. The most popular data structure is the *Binary Decision Diagram* (BDD) [Bry86]. Recently, several approaches in logic synthesis have been presented that make use of BDDs. (For an overview see [DB98].) One drawback of this data structure is that it is very sensitive to the variable ordering, i.e. the size may vary from linear to exponential. Finding the optimal variable ordering is a difficult problem [BW96] and the best known algorithm has exponential runtime.

This is the reason why in the last few years many authors presented heuristics for finding good variable orderings. The most promising methods are based on dynamic variable ordering [FMK91],[Rud93],[PS95]: BDDs for some Boolean functions have been constructed for which all other topology oriented methods failed. New methods based on non-deterministic algorithms have been proposed for BDD minimization, e.g. genetic algorithms [DBG95] and simulated annealing [RBKM92],[BLW95]. The major drawback of these approaches is that in general they obtain good results with respect to quality of the solution, but the running times are often much larger than those of classical heuristics. Due to the high complexity of the design process in VLSI CAD often fast heuristics are used. These heuristics are developed by the designer

J. Miller et al. (Eds.) : EuroGP 2001, LNCS 2038, pp. 1-10, 2001.

himself. But they also often fail for specific classes of circuits. Thus it would help a lot, if the heuristics could learn from previous examples, e.g. from benchmark examples.

A theoretical model for learning heuristics by *Genetic Algorithms* (GAs) has been presented in [DB95]. The new aspect of this model is that the GA is not directly applied to the problem. Instead the GA develops a good heuristic for the problem to be solved. First applications to multi-level synthesis and to 2-level AND/EXOR minimization have been presented. There the model has not been fully used, i.e. only a part of the features has been implemented. Extensions have been proposed in [DGB96] and [DDB99], where learning of BDD heuristics has been studied based on GAs. But due to the fixed length encoding these approaches also have some disadvantages:

- The length of the heuristic is limited resulting in limitations with respect to quality.
- Decision procedures, like if-then-else, could not be integrated in the heuristics.

In this paper we present an approach to heuristic learning based on *Genetic Programming* (GP) [Koz92],[Koz94]. Due to the more flexible encoding based on tree structures, the disadvantages of the GA approaches described above can be avoided, while keeping the advantages. To keep the heuristic under development as compact as possible, reduction operators are introduced. Compared to GAs more flexible operators are defined and integrated in the GP run. Experimental results demonstrate the efficiency of the approach.

The paper is structured as follows: In the next section the problem definition is given and the model of heuristic learning is described. Then the solution based on GP is outlined and the (genetic) operators are introduced. Experimental results are reported and finally the paper is summarized.

2   Problem Description

In [DB95] a learning model has formally been introduced for GAs. In this section we briefly review the main notation and definitions to make the paper self-contained. Since the definition of the model is based on the evaluation of the fitness function only, it becomes obvious that even though it has been developed for GAs, it can be transferred to GPs directly.

It is assumed that the problem to be solved has the following property: There is defined a non empty set of optimization procedures that can be applied to a given (non-optimal) solution in order to further improve its quality. These procedures are called *Basic Optimization Modules* (BOMs) in the following. The heuristics are sequences of BOMs. The goal of the approach is to determine a good (or even optimal) sequence of BOMs such that the overall results obtained by the heuristics are improved. From the flexibility of the tree-like data structure in GPs we are later even able to define more powerful operators.

In the following we assume that the reader is familiar with the basic concepts and notation of evolutionary approaches. In [DB95] and [DGB96], a multi-valued string encoding of fixed length has been used, but this already by definition limits the quality of the result. Due to the GP concept, there is in principle no limit on the size of the resulting heuristics.

The set of BOMs defines the set H of all possible heuristics that are applicable to the problem to be solved in the given environment. H may include problem specific heuristics but can also include randomized techniques.

To each BOM h we associate a cost function, i.e. a value that determines how expensive it is to call this module. This value can be chosen dependent on different criteria, like memory consumption or run time. Furthermore, the quality function determines the quality resulting from the application of this module. These two values determine the fitness of the BOM. Summation over all BOMs in a heuristic determines the overall fitness. The elements are evaluated on a set of benchmark examples, the so-called training set. The multiple objectives are optimized in parallel by the method described in [DDB99].

2.1   BOMs

Most of the algorithms that are used here as BOMs for heuristic learning are well-known BDD minimization techniques They are based on dynamic variable ordering. *Sifting* (SIFT) is a local search operation for variable ordering of BDDs which allows hill climbing. *Group sifting* (GROUP) and *symmetric sifting* (SYMM) additionally make use of symmetry aspects of the variables of the considered Boolean functions. The BOM *window permutation* of size 3 (4), denoted as WIN3 (WIN4), tests all permutations of 3 (4) adjacent variables, where the window of size 3 (4) "goes" through the whole BDD from the top to the bottom variables. For all these techniques there is an additional BOM that iterates the method until convergence is reached. These BOMs are denoted by the appendix *CO, e.g.* iterated sifting is denoted by SIFTCO. The next BOM is called *inversion* (I) and inverts the variable ordering of a BDD between two randomly chosen variables. Finally, the set of BOMs contains an "empty" element, denoted as NOOP. In the GA approach this operator was used to model strings of various sizes, while the underlying data structure was a fixed-length string. Using GPs this problem by definition does not occur. Nevertheless, NOOP is important to describe a condition, e.g. it is possible to describe an IF-condition without a statement in the ELSE-branch. These types of operators could not be introduced using Gas, underlining the flexibility of the approach introduced below.

For more details about the learning model, the definition of BDD, and BOMs see [DB95], [DGB96], and [DDB99].

3   GP Solution

For basic definitions of GP we refer to [Koz92],[Koz94]. In the following only the problem specific description is given.

3.1   Representation

For GP-based heuristic learning, heuristics are represented by trees with outdegree 2, i.e. each node has two outgoing edges. The heuristics are the individuals generated during the evolutionary process. The trees include BOMs that are located at the leaf nodes. There are three additional node types that cover all the inner nodes:

1. CONCAT: The left son is evaluated and afterwards the result is used to evaluate the right son.
2. IF: An IF node always comes with a value x that represents a condition. The left son of this node is evaluated if the ratio (# symmetric variables / # variables in total) is smaller than x. Otherwise, the right son is evaluated instead.
3. WHILE: The procedure of subsequent evaluation of the left and the right son is iterated as long as it reduces the size of the BDD.

There may be CONCAT nodes at the leaves as well, while the types IF and WHILE can only occur at inner nodes. To evaluate a heuristic, the root of the corresponding tree has to be recursively evaluated by a *depth first search*-based technique.
If the root node is a leaf, then the BOM covering this leaf has to be applied to the BDD. If the leaf is a CONCAT node, nothing has to be done. Notice, that algorithmic descriptions of a heuristic using IF- and WHILE-conditions are not possible with this learning model if a string representation in a GA is used. On the other hand, each string generated by a GA can also be constructed using the GP approach.

3.2   Operators

For recombination of individuals during evolution, two crossover operators are provided:

1. CAT: The root nodes of the parents are linked by a new CONCAT node c. Parent 1 becomes the left son and parent 2 becomes the right son of c. The node c itself is the root of the offspring.
2. MERGE: The operator extracts a sub-tree of parent 1 and one of parent 2 and combines these sub-trees by an additional CONCAT node in the same way.

By definition it is obvious that bloating can be observed if CAT is used, while MERGE generates offspring with sizes that are similar to the parents' size.

Additionally, four mutation operators are used:

1. B-MUT: A BOM leaf is selected at random and the BOM at this leaf is replaced by a different one.
2. CI-MUT: A randomly selected inner CONCAT node is replaced by an IF node. The value x is also determined at random.
3. CW-MUT: This mutation is similar to CI, but the CONCAT node is replaced by a WHILE node rather than an IF node.
4. IF-MUT: Value x is either incremented or decremented by 0.1.

3.3   Algorithm and Parameter Setting

In this section we describe the parameter settings used in our GP. For the overall flow standard techniques as described in [Koz92],[Koz94] are used.

First, 20 individuals are generated for the initial population. To keep the run time moderate, it turned out by experiments that it is clever to limit the number of BOMs in a heuristic. In contrast to the GA approach, where fixed-length strings are used, in the GP approach this is not a strict limitation, since more powerful operators are available that allow to describe complex constructs, like loops based on WHILE. The initial elements are generated as follows: A tree with unlabelled nodes is traversed in a breadth first search manner, and each node is labeled with either IF (probability 20%), WHILE (15%) or BOM (65%). If a BOM is chosen, the sub-trees of the node are eliminated and when the BOM limit is reached, all following nodes are labeled with CONCAT and their sub-trees are removed. The individual is complete when there are no unlabelled nodes any more.

In each generation, 10 offspring are generated. The probabilities for the operators are given in the following table:

operator	CAT	MERGE	B	CI	CW	IF
probability	5	45	20	10	10	10

Two parents are selected in the case of crossover and one in the case of mutation by roulette-wheel-selection. The operator is applied and afterwards, the fitness of the offspring is calculated. The concept of multi-objective minimization [DDB99] is used for that and the optimization criteria are the resulting BDD sizes on a training set of BDD benchmarks. Evolution is aborted if either there has been no improvement for 100 generations or a limit of 1000 generations has been reached.

3.4   Size Reduction

To prevent bloating, a limit on the number of BOMs in an individual is set. If this limit is exceeded by crossover, the offspring is removed immediately and selection and recombination are repeated. Furthermore, a reduction mechanism has been included. If the sub-tree of a node did not cause changes in BDD size for any of the benchmarks in the training set, the node and its sub-trees are removed from the tree and replaced by a single CONCAT node since obviously this sub-tree does not contribute anything to the minimization of one of the benchmarks. It can be determined efficiently during evaluation if there has been an influence of a sub-tree to minimization, and by this reduction mechanism, sizes of the individuals are reduced considerably on average. Furthermore, this has a positive effect on the quality of the generated heuristics, since only parts are kept that have an effect on the quality of the result. This guarantees that no run time is wasted by application of BOMs that might be expensive, but do not produce any (positive) change. In application in VLSI CAD this is an important factor, since most of the tools are interactive.

4   Experimental Results

In this section we describe our experimental results obtained by the methods above. For all experiments we used a SUN Sparc 20 and all run times are given in CPU seconds. The results are compared with the GA approach from [DDB99] and the experiments are carried out in the same software environment using multi-objective optimization. For this, after each run a *set* of optimal (non comparable) solutions - instead of a single element - is returned. The same training set as in [DDB99] is chosen during the learning phase of the GP.

As a first result it can be observed that already very simple solutions give very high quality results, e.g. the following tree was contained in the final solution after the learning phase, that took about 25 CPU minutes:

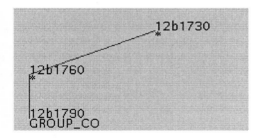

The * denotes a node of type CONCAT. Furthermore, at each node some program specific information about the pointer structure is provided. This simple heuristic obtains the following results:

| name | in | out | Genetic Programming | | [DDB99] | | |
			size	time	size	time	optimal
add6	12	7	28	0.25	28	0.10	28
addm4	9	8	163	0.18	163	0.10	163
cm85a	11	3	27	0.18	27	0.10	27
m181	15	9	54	0.27	54	0.20	54
risc	8	31	65	0.13	65	0.10	65
sum			337	1.01	337	0.60	
average			67.40	0.20	67.40	0.12	

The name of the benchmark is given in the first column followed by the number of inputs and outputs. Then the results for quality measured in the size of the BDD and the run time are given first for the GP approach and then for the approach of [DDB99]. As can be seen, on the training set both approaches obtain the same results with respect to quality, i.e. both determine the optimal values. The GP approach is slightly slower, but the situation changes, if the generated heuristic is applied to benchmarks that were unknown during the learning phase:

| Name | in | out | Genetic Programming | | [DDB99] | | |
			size	time	size	time	optimal
5xp1	7	10	41	0.11	50	0.10	41
alu4	14	8	353	0.49	354	1.40	349
cm151.a	12	2	16	0.16	16	0.10	16
cm162a	14	5	30	0.17	37	0.10	29
cm163a	16	5	25	0.20	26	0.10	25
Cmb	16	4	27	0.16	27	0.10	27
Cu	14	11	31	0.18	31	0.10	31
Sqn	7	3	48	0.12	56	0.10	48
Gary	15	11	289	0.38	306	0.20	289
s1494	14	25	386	0.30	383	0.40	368
Tial	14	8	579	0.50	611	1.00	563
Sum			1825	2.77	1897	3.70	
Average			165.91	0.25	172.45	0.34	

In all but one case, the GP approach is at least as good as the GA. On average the quality and run time are improved. This could already be observed for the simplest heuristic computed that even did not make use of the powerful operators, like WHILE and IF. Especially in the application of heuristic learning it is important to develop heuristics that are not only good for the training set, but to construct sequences of BOMs that generalize very well. Since in later application of the heuristic in general the benchmarks are not known in advance, the GP result is of very high quality: The BDD sizes measured in number of nodes and the run times are improved in parallel.

Due to space limitation, we cannot discuss all elements of the final solution in detail, but we will focus on some high-lights in the following.

An element very similar to the first one in the final set is:

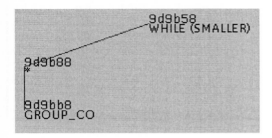

This element is nearly the same as the first one, but has the WHILE operator as top node. Thus, the sub-tree is called repeatedly and by this the quality can be further improved. Here it should be mentioned that the use of WHILE in the root node might be "dangerous", since on bigger benchmarks the run times can become very large. The WHILE implies that the complete sub-tree is repeatedly called as long as an improvement can be obtained. If the scenario is considered that the heuristics in the sub-trees always improve on the result of the previous iteration, but only very slightly, run times can explode. (In practice this has never been observed in our experiments, but this aspect should be considered when designing heuristics for application in VLSI CAD.)

The solutions can also become more complex:

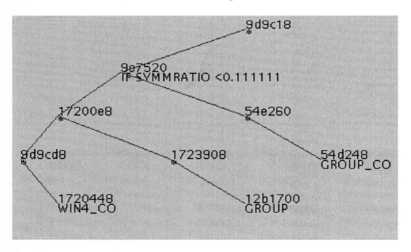

Then it is up to the user to decide for the specific application whether he is willing to invest more run time to get higher quality results. But as can be seen, all operators that are "GP specific", i.e. the powerful operators that cannot be described based on GAs really occur in the final solution (see examples above). The heuristics become very compact and by this also easy to analyze and easy to understand for the user.

The best solution with respect to quality measured in the number of BDD nodes found in this test run was:

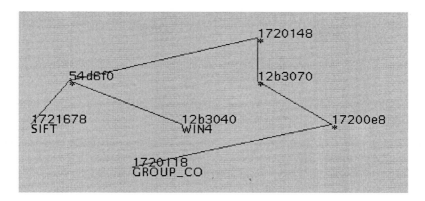

The sum over all nodes of the benchmarks that were unknown during the learning phase was 1805.

In summary, the GP approach clearly outperforms the (highly optimized) GA that has been developed over several years. The underlying data structure gives more flexibility and allows to define more powerful operators resulting in compact heuristics that obtain high quality results.

5   Conclusions

In this paper we presented an approach to learning heuristics based on GPs. It became possible to generate flexible high-quality heuristics that have very high performance in comparison to direct application of evolutionary techniques. Experimental results showed details about the learning phase and demonstrated the influence of the integration of decision procedures. This became possible due to the underlying encoding as trees typically used in GPs, while this turned out to be a limitation of the corresponding GA approach. It is focus of current work to study the multi-objective aspect of this application in more detail and to also apply the technique to further applications in the field of VLSI CAD.

References

[Bry86] R.E. Bryant. Graph-based algorithms for Boolean function manipulation. IEEE Trans. on Comp., 8:677-691, 1986.

[BW96] B. Bollig and I. Wegener. Improving the variable ordering of OBDDs is NP-complete. IEEE Trans. on Comp., vol. 45, num. 9, pages 993-1002, 1996.

[BLW95] B. Bollig, M. Löbbing, and I. Wegener. Simulated annealing to improve variable orderings for OBDDs. In Int'l Workshop on Logic Synth., pages 5b:5.1-5.10, 1995.

[DB95] R. Drechsler and B. Becker. Learning heuristics by genetic algorithms. In ASP Design Automation Conf., pages 349-352, 1995.

[DB98] R. Drechsler and B. Becker. Binary Decision Diagrams -- Theory and Implementation, Kluwer Academic Publishers, 1998

[DBG95] R. Drechsler, B. Becker, and N. Göckel. A genetic algorithm for variable ordering of OBDDs. In Int'l Workshop on Logic Synth., pages P5c:5.55-5.64, 1995.

[DDB99] N. Drechsler, R. Drechsler, and B. Becker. A new model for multi-objective optimization in evolutionary algorithms. In Fuzzy'99, LNCS 1625, pages 108-117, 1999.

[DGB96] R. Drechsler, N. Göckel, and B. Becker. Learning heuristics for OBDD minimization by evolutionary algorithms. In PPSN'96, LNCS 1141, pages 730-739, 1996.

[FMK91] M. Fujita, Y. Matsunga, and T. Kakuda. On variable ordering of binary decision diagrams for the application of multi-level synthesis. In European Conf. on Design Automation, pages 50-54, 1991.

[Koz92] J. Koza. Genetic Programming - On the Programming of Computers by means of Natural Selection. MIT Press, 1992

[Koz94] J. Koza. Genetic Programming II – Automatic Discovery of Reusable Programs. MIT Press, 1994

[PS95] S. Panda and F. Somenzi. Who are the variables in your neighborhood. In Int'l Conf. on CAD, pages 74-77, 1995.

[RBKM92] D.E. Ross, K.M. Butler, R. Kapur, and M.R. Mercer. Functional approaches to generating orderings for efficient symbolic representations. In Design Automation Conf., pages 624-627, 1992.

[Rud93] R. Rudell. Dynamic variable ordering for ordered binary decision diagrams. In Int'l Conf. on CAD, pages 42-47, 1993.

Evolving Color Constancy
for an Artificial Retina

Marc Ebner

Universität Würzburg, Lehrstuhl für Informatik II
Am Hubland, 97074 Würzburg, Germany
ebner@informatik.uni-wuerzburg.de
http://www2.informatik.uni-wuerzburg.de/staff/ebner/welcome.html

Abstract Objects retain their color in spite of changes in the wavelength
and energy composition of the light they reflect. This phenomenon is
called color constancy and plays an important role in computer vision
research. We have used genetic programming to automatically search the
space of programs to solve the problem of color constancy for an artificial
retina. This retina consists of a two dimensional array of elements each
capable of exchanging information with its adjacent neighbors. The task
of the program is to compute the intensities of the light illuminating the
scene. These intensities are then used to calculate the reflectances of the
object. Randomly generated color Mondrians were used as fitness cases.
The evolved program was tested on artificial Mondrians and natural images.

1 Introduction

The human visual system is able to correctly perceive the color of objects irre-
spective of the light which illuminates the scene. That is, the leaves of a tree still
look green to a human observer even if the tree is illuminated with red light and
the leaves actually reflect more red than green light. The task of computing color
constant descriptors for an image is known as the problem of color constancy.
One is able to somehow discount the illuminant and extract a measure of the
object's reflectance properties [26]. The same ability would also be useful for a
robot which has to work under different lighting conditions. To date, the lighting
still has to be carefully controlled such that the algorithms continue to work.
The problem of color constancy is also of particular importance for the task of
object recognition [7,10].

Numerous solutions to the problem of color constancy have been proposed,
i.e. Land's retinex theory [21], variants of the retinex theory [2,12,18], gamut-
constraint methods [1,8,9] recovery of basis function coefficients [13,14,17,23],
mechanisms of light adaptation coupled with eye movements [6], neural networks
[4,5,11,16,24], minimization of an energy function [25], comprehensive color normalization [7] or committee-based methods which combine the output of several
different color constancy algorithms [3]. We now summarize some background

J. Miller et al. (Eds.): EuroGP 2001, LNCS 2038, pp. 11–22, 2001.

on color image formation and discuss the two most widely known algorithms for color constancy: white-patch and the gray world assumption.

The response of a sensor at position $\mathbf{x}_s$ measuring the light reflected from a Lambertian surface at position $\mathbf{x}_o$ is given by

$$\mathbf{I}(\mathbf{x}_s) = \mathbf{n}_l \cdot \mathbf{n}_o \int_\omega R(\lambda, \mathbf{x}_o) L(\lambda) \mathbf{S}(\lambda) d\lambda$$

where $\mathbf{I}(\mathbf{x}_s)$ is a vector of sensor responses, $\mathbf{n}_l$ is the unit vector pointing in the direction of the light source, $\mathbf{n}_o$ is the unit vector corresponding to the surface normal, $R(\lambda, \mathbf{x}_o)$ specifies the percentage of light with wavelength λ reflected by the surface at position $\mathbf{x}_o$, $L(\lambda)$ is the intensity of light hitting the surface and $\mathbf{S}(\lambda)$ specifies the sensor's response functions [7]. The integration is over all wavelengths to which the sensors respond. Assuming ideal sensors for red, green and blue light ($S_i = \delta(\lambda - \lambda_i)$) with $i \in \{r, g, b\}$ and a light source which illuminates the surface at a right angle the equation simplifies to

$$I_i(\mathbf{x}_s) = R(\lambda_i, \mathbf{x}_o) L(\lambda_i)$$

where $I_i(\mathbf{x}_s)$ denotes the i-th component of the vector $\mathbf{I}(\mathbf{x}_s)$.

In this case the light illuminating the scene simply scales the reflectances. If there exists at least one pixel for each band which reflects all light for this particular band, one could simply rescale all color bands to the range $[0, 1]$.

$$R(\lambda_i, \mathbf{x}_o) = \frac{I_i(\mathbf{x}_s)}{L_{\max}(\lambda_i)}$$

with $L_{\max}(\lambda_i) = \max_{\mathbf{x}}\{I_i(\mathbf{x})\}$. This algorithm is called the white-patch retinex algorithm [10].

Another possibility would be to calculate space average color of the image and use this information to estimate the intensities of the light illuminating the scene. If one assumes that the reflectances of the surface are uniformly distributed over the interval $[0, 1]$, one gets

$$\frac{1}{N} \sum_{\mathbf{x}}^N I_i(\mathbf{x}) = \frac{1}{N} \sum_{\mathbf{x}}^N R(\lambda_i, \mathbf{x}) L(\lambda_i) = L(\lambda_i) \frac{1}{N} \sum_{\mathbf{x}}^N R(\lambda_i, \mathbf{x}) = L(\lambda_i) \frac{1}{2}$$

This is the so called gray world assumption. Thus, for a sufficiently complex image one can estimate the intensities of the light illuminating the scene as twice the space average color.

$$L(\lambda_i) = \frac{2}{N} \sum_{\mathbf{x}}^N I_i(\mathbf{x})$$

Both cues, space-average scene color as well as the color of the highest luminance patch are used by the human visual system to estimate the color of the light illuminating the scene [22].

Most work on the problem of color constancy has focused on finding an analytical solution. Some research has tried to learn the problem of color constancy using a neural network, e.g. [11,24]. We try to *evolve* the ability of color constancy for an artificial retina. In particular, we want to address the following questions. Is it possible to evolve a function for an artificial retina which estimates the intensities of the light illuminating the scene using a training set which only consists of randomly generated color Mondrians? The function is constrained to obtain and exchange information only locally but not globally. This property is very important in order for the retina to be scalable to arbitrary sizes. Will the results generalize to natural images? We now describe the architecture of the artificial retina.

2   An Artificial Retina

Our artificial retina consists of a two-dimensional array of elements. Each element is able to exchange information with its neighbors to the left and right as well as its neighbors above and below. The elements receive an image as input and their task is to compute the reflectances of the objects shown in the image. Each element may exchange information only locally in order to calculate the intensities of the light illuminating the scene. Thus, the artificial retina is scalable to any size.

For our experiment we assume that the viewed image is generated by multiplying the red, green and blue components of the pixel values with the intensities of the light illuminating the scene, that is,

$$\mathbf{p}_v(x,y) = (p_{r,r}(x,y) \cdot l_r, p_{r,g}(x,y) \cdot l_g, p_{r,b}(x,y) \cdot l_b)$$

where $\mathbf{p}_v(x,y)$ is the vector with color components of the pixel as it is perceived by the artificial retina, $\mathbf{p}_r(x,y) = (p_{r,r}(x,y), p_{r,g}(x,y), p_{r,b}(x,y))$ is the vector with reflectances, $\mathbf{l} = (l_r, l_g, l_b)$ is the vector which describes the intensities of red, green and blue light illuminating the scene.

The output $\mathbf{p}_o(x,y)$ of the element at position (x,y) is defined as

$$p_{o,i}(x,y) = \begin{cases} \frac{p_{v,i}(x,y)}{l_{e,i}(x,y)} & \text{if } l_{e,i}(x,y) > 0.001 \\ 1 & \text{otherwise} \end{cases}$$

where $i \in \{r,g,b\}$. Thus each element consists of three sub-elements, one for each color band. The output of each sub-element as well as the estimate of the intensities of the ambient light are restricted to the range $[0,1]$. The vector $\mathbf{p}_v(x,y)$ is available to the element at position (x,y). The intensities of red, green and blue light $\mathbf{l}_e(x,y)$ are calculated by a program which is evolved using genetic programming [19,20]. All elements are running the same program. The calculated intensities are stored locally as well as distributed to the neighboring elements.

Each element has the structure shown in Figure 1. It has access to the intensities estimated by the neighboring elements (left, right, up, and down) as

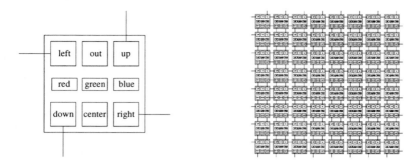

Figure 1. A single element of the artificial retina is shown on the left. Current knowledge of light illuminating the scene is stored inside the element (center) and is also distributed to the left, right, up and down. This knowledge is continually updated. Each element has access to the red, green and blue intensities of the viewed image. Using its knowledge about the light illuminating the scene, each element calculates the reflectances of its pixel (out).Each element only exchanges information locally, thus the individual elements may be combined easily to form a large $n \times n$ array (shown on the right).

well as to its own estimate of the light illuminating the scene. In addition to this information, it has access to the red, green and blue intensities of the viewed image. The intensities of red, green and blue light are calculated by iterating the following update equations:

$$
\begin{aligned}
\text{center}_i(x, y, t) &= l_{e,i}(x, y, t - 1) \\
\text{left}_i(x, y, t) &= l_{e,i}(x - 1, y, t - 1) \\
\text{right}_i(x, y, t) &= l_{e,i}(x + 1, y, t - 1) \\
\text{up}_i(x, y, t) &= l_{e,i}(x, y + 1, t - 1) \\
\text{down}_i(x, y, t) &= l_{e,i}(x, y - 1, t - 1) \\
l_{e,i}(x, y, t) &= \text{program}(\text{center}_i(x, y, t), \text{left}_i(x, y, t), \text{right}_i(x, y, t), \\
&\qquad \text{up}_i(x, y, t), \text{down}_i(x, y, t), \mathbf{p}_v(x, y), p_{v,i}(x, y))
\end{aligned}
$$

The intensities of the viewed image were used as an initial estimate of the light illuminating the scene.

$$
l_{e,i}(x, y, 0) = p_{v,i}(x, y)
$$

Our task is to find a program which calculates the red, green and blue intensities of the light illuminating the scene. To search the space of possible programs we have used genetic programming [19,20]. The function set consists of the binary arithmetic functions addition (+), subtraction (-), multiplication (*) and protected division (/), the unary functions multiply by 2 (mul2) and divide by 2 (`div2`). The set of terminal symbols consists of the constant one (`1`), red (`red`), green (`green`), and blue (`blue`) color channel, the sub-element's color channel (`band`), the element's current estimate of the illuminant (`center`) as well as the estimates of the illuminant calculated by the elements to the left (`left`), right (`right`), above (`up`) and below (`down`).

3   Experiments

A population of 1000 individuals was evolved for 50 generations. We did ten runs with different initial seeds for the random number generator. 1% of the next generation was filled with the best individual, 9% of the next generation was filled by applying the reproduction operator, 70% of the next generation was filled by applying the crossover operator and the remainder was filled by applying the mutation operator. We used tournament selection with size 7 to select individuals.

For each generation we randomly generated three Mondrians and evaluated the performance of the individuals on the different Mondrians. Each Mondrian was illuminated with random intensities for the red, green and blue components. The size of the Mondrians was 64x64 pixels with circular boundary conditions. The Mondrians were created by filling the background with a random color and then placing 64 filled rectangles with random colors on top of each other. The size of the rectangles was selected randomly in the range [8,24]. The position of the rectangles was also selected randomly.

Each evaluation consisted of iterating the update equations 100 times. For each Mondrian m we calculated the difference d_m between the output of the artificial retina and the known reflectances.

$$d_m = \frac{1}{3 \cdot \text{width} \cdot \text{height}} \sum_{x=1}^{\text{width}} \sum_{y=1}^{\text{height}} \sqrt{(\mathbf{p}_o(x,y) - \mathbf{p}_r(x,y))^2}$$

The largest difference over all Mondrians is used to calculate the fitness of the individual. Fitness is defined as

$$\text{fitness} = \frac{1}{1 + max_m\{d_m\}}.$$

The worst performance of an individual was used to calculate its fitness in order to reward generalists. Note that fitness is to be maximized and the error is to be minimized. Harvey et al. [15] have chosen a similar approach to evolve robust control algorithms for a simulated robot.

We also tried averaging the errors of several fitness cases instead of using the maximum error to determine fitness. However, if the number of fitness cases is large, then on average the red, green and blue intensities are 0.5 and a program which simply outputs $2\mathbf{p}_v$ might seem like a good solution. Obviously, this is not a solution we are looking for. Therefore we chose to use the maximum error over several fitness cases to calculate the fitness of an individual. In this case,

16   Marc Ebner

an individual has to produce very good results for all fitness cases in order to survive more than one generation. If an individual performs badly on even a single fitness case it is likely that this individual will be eliminated from the population. The individual with the highest fitness value at the last generation is our result.

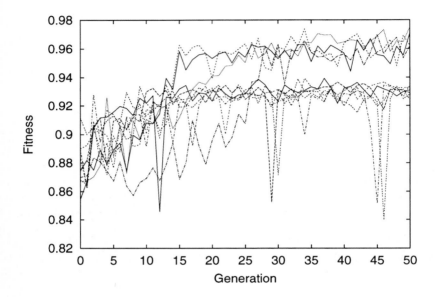

Figure 2. Ten runs were executed with different seeds for the random number generator. At the end of 50 generations, 6 of the runs were stuck in a local optimum. The best individual of all ten runs was analyzed in detail.

We performed 10 runs with different seeds for the random number generator. Figure 2 shows the maximum fitness for each of the runs. 6 of the runs were stuck in a local optimum. We now analyze the best individual of those 10 runs in detail.

4   Results

Run number 4 had the highest fitness value at generation 50. Figure 3 shows the output of the best individual found after 50 generations for three different fitness cases[1]. Each row shows the results for one fitness case. The first image in each

---

[1] The images can be viewed in color on the authors web page
http://www2.informatik.uni-wuerzburg.de/staff/ebner/research/color/
color.html

row shows the original image. The second image shows the light illuminating
the scene. The third image shows the image viewed by the camera. The fourth
image shows the estimated intensities and the fifth image shows the estimated
reflectances. The evolved individual uses mostly addition and division by 2 to
solve the task of color constancy.

The evolved individual uses the following code

```
(div2 (+ (+ (div2 (+ (div2 (+ (div2 down) (div2 (+ (div2 (+ (div2 (+ band
(div2 down))) (div2 (+ band (div2 (+ band (div2 center))))))) (div2 down)))))
(* (div2 down) (/ right (div2 (+ down (+ (div2 down) (div2 (+ (div2 (+ band
(div2 down))) (div2 (+ band (div2 (+ band (div2 center)))))))))))))))))) (div2 (+
(div2 (+ (div2 right) (div2 (+ band (div2 down))))) (* (div2 down) (/ right
(div2 (+ down (+ (div2 down) (div2 (+ (div2 (+ band (div2 center))) (div2 (+
band band)))))))))))))) down))
```

to estimate the intensities of the light illuminating the scene and thereby estimate
the reflectances of the viewed object ($d_1 = 0.0242$, $d_2 = 0.0343$, $d_3 = 0.0334$,
after 100 updates).

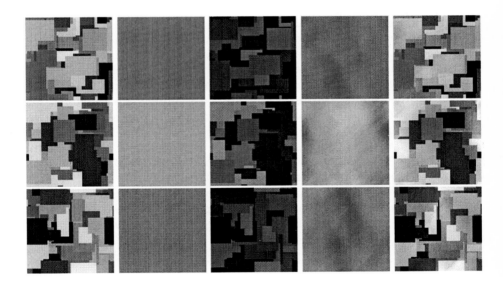

Figure 3. Results of one individual for three different fitness cases. The first image of
each row shows the original Mondrian. The second image shows the light illuminating
the scene. The third image shows the viewed image. The fourth image shows the estimated light intensities. The fifth image shows the reflectances which were extracted
from the viewed image by the artificial retina.

The same individual was also tested on natural images. The results of these
tests are shown in Figure 4. The images on the left show the results for an outdoor
photograph transformed in the same way as the artificially created Mondrians.

That is, we simply multiplied the pixel values with a randomly chosen color. The first image shows the original photograph. The second image shows the color illuminating the scene. The third image shows the colored photograph. The fourth image shows color estimated by the artificial retina. The fifth image shows the reflectances estimated by the artificial retina. Again the individual is able to restore the original colors (d=0.0246, after 300 updates, 190 × 128 image). Thus, we have shown that although the individual was only trained on color Mondrians it was able to estimate the reflectances of a color adjusted photograph.

The images on the right show the results for a test image created by Funt et al. [10]. The original image as well as the transformed image are part of a larger set for the problem of color constancy. The original image was taken with a camera under a uniform light model, the third image shows the same object viewed with colored light. We calculated the second image by dividing the pixel values of the third image by the pixel values of the first image to extract the color illuminating the scene. Note that in this case the assumption of a flat image does not hold. The fourth image shows the color estimated by the artificial retina and the fifth image is the output of our artificial retina (d=0.098, after 300 updates, 168 × 160 image). In this case the assumptions used during evolution, e.g. that the viewed object is flat, do not hold and the results are not as good as for the photograph. However the results show, that even in this case, the evolved individual is able to improve the appearance of the input image.

In order to compare the results we also applied the white-patch retinex algorithm and the algorithm using the gray world assumption to both images. The results for the white-patch retinex algorithm are shown in Figure 5 (d=0.032 for the photograph and d=0.063 for the ball) and the results for the algorithm using the gray world assumption are shown in Figure 6 (d=0.038 for the photograph and d=0.162 for the ball). The results for the photograph are comparable for all three algorithms. The images produced by white-patch retinex and gray world are a bit brighter than the output image of the evolved algorithm. In terms of the calculated error, the white-patch algorithm produced the best results for the ball image. The results for the ball seem to suggest that the evolved algorithm applies a mixed strategy.

5   Conclusion

We have evolved an algorithm to solve the problem of color constancy for an artificial retina using genetic programming. The retina was designed such that information is only exchanged locally, not globally. The artificial retina is thus scalable to arbitrary sizes. The individuals were trained on artificially created Mondrian images. The best program was tested on additional color Mondrians as well as natural images. Although the individual was only trained on Mondrian images it was also able to estimate the intensities of the light illuminating the scene for natural images and thereby estimate the reflectances of the viewed object.

Figure 4. Results of the evolved program for the artificial retina on two natural images. The images on the left show the results for an outdoor photograph. The images on the right show the results for an image which was created by Funt et al. [10] to test color constancy algorithms.

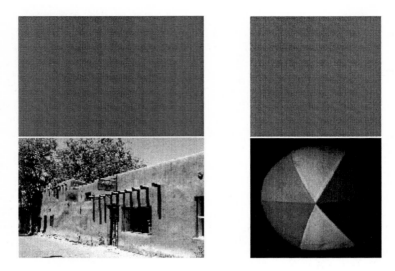

Figure 5. Results for the white-patch retinex algorithm. The first row of images shows the estimated color for the photograph and the image of the ball . The second row shows the output of the white-patch retinex algorithm for both images.

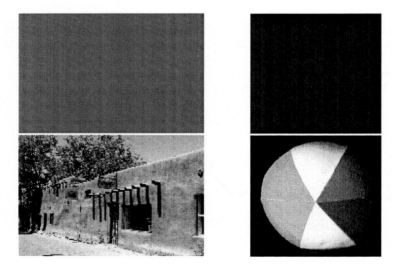

Figure 6. Results for the gray-world assumption. The first row of images shows the estimated color for the photograph and the image of the ball. The second row shows the output of the gray-world algorithm for both images.

Acknowledgements

We have used the lilgp Programming System Vers. 1.1 [27] for our experiments.

References

1. K. Barnard, G. Finlayson, and B. Funt. Color constancy for scenes with varying illumination. *Computer Vision and Image Understanding,* 65(2):311–321, February 1997.
2. D. H. Brainard and B. A. Wandell. Analysis of the retinex theory of color vision. In G. E. Healey, S. A. Shafer, and L. B. Wolff, editors, *Color,* pages 208–218, Boston, 1992. Jones and Bartlett Publishers.
3. V. C. Cardei and B. Funt. Committee-based color constancy. In *Proceedings of the IS&T/SID Seventh Color Imaging Conference: Color Science, Systems and Applications,* pages 311–313, 1999.
4. S. M. Courtney, L. H. Finkel, and G. Buchsbaum. A multistage neural network for color constancy and color induction. *IEEE Transactions on Neural Networks,* 6(4):972–985, July 1995.
5. P. A. Dufort and C. J. Lumsden. Color categorization and color constancy in a neural network model of V4. *Biological Cybernetics,* 65:293–303, 1991.
6. M. D'Zmura and P. Lennie. Mechanisms of color constancy. In G. E. Healey, S. A. Shafer, and L. B. Wolff, editors, *Color,* pages 224–234, Boston, 1992. Jones and Bartlett Publishers.
7. G. D. Finlayson, B. Schiele, and J. L. Crowley. Comprehensive colour image normalization. In *Fifth European Conference on Computer Vision (ECCV '98),* 1998.
8. D. A. Forsyth. A novel approach to colour constancy. In *Second International Conference on Computer Vision (Tampa, FL, Dec. 5-8),* pages 9–18. IEEE Press, 1988.
9. D. A. Forsyth. A novel algorithm for color constancy. In G. E. Healey, S. A. Shafer, and L. B. Wolff, editors, *Color,* pages 241–271, Boston, 1992. Jones and Bartlett Publishers.
10. B. Funt, K. Barnard, and L. Martin. Is colour constancy good enough? In *Fifth European Conference on Computer Vision (ECCV '98),* pages 445–459, 1998.
11. B. Funt, V. Cardei, and K. Barnard. Learning color constancy. In *Proceedings of the IS&T/SID Fourth Color Imaging Conference,* pages 58–60, Scottsdale, 19-22November 1996.
12. B. V. Funt and M. S. Drew. Color constancy computation in near-mondrian scenes using a finite dimensional linear model. In *Proceedings of the Computer Society Conference on Computer Vision and Pattern Recognition,* pages 544–549. Computer Society Press, 5-9 June 1988.
13. B. V. Funt, M. S. Drew, and J. Ho. Color constancy from mutual reflection. *International Journal of Computer Vision,* 6(1):5–24, 1991.
14. R. Gershon, A. D. Jepson, and J. K. Tsotsos. From [R,G,B] to surface reflectance: Computing color constant descriptors in images. In *Proceedings of the Tenth International Joint Conference on Artificial Intelligence,* volume 2, pages 755–758, 1987.
15. I. Harvey, P. Husbands, and D. Cliff. Issues in evolutionary robotics. In J.-A. Meyer, H. L. Roitblat, and S. W. Wilson, editors, *From animals to animats 2: Proceedings of the Second International Conference on Simulation of Adaptive Behavior, Honolulu, Hawaii, 1992,* pages 364–373. The MIT Press, 1993.

16. J. Herault. A model of colour processing in the retina of vertebrates: From photoreceptors to colour opposition and colour constancy phenomena. *Neurocomputing*, 12:113–129, 1996.
17. J. Ho, B. V. Funt, and M. S. Drew. Separating a color signal into illumination and surface reflectance components: Theory and applications. In G. E. Healey, S. A. Shafer, and L. B. Wolff, editors, *Color*, pages 272–283, Boston, 1992. Jones and Bartlett Publishers.
18. B. K. P. Horn. *Robot Vision*. The MIT Press, Cambridge, Massachusetts, 1986.
19. J. R. Koza. *Genetic Programming, On the Programming of Computers by Means of Natural Selection*. The MIT Press, Cambridge, Massachusetts, 1992.
20. J. R. Koza. *Genetic Programming II, Automatic Discovery of Reusable Programs*. The MIT Press, Cambridge, Massachusetts, 1994.
21. E. H. Land. The retinex theory of colour vision. *Proc. Royal Inst. Great Britain*, 47:23–58, 1974.
22. K. J. Linnell and D. H. Foster. Space-average scene colour used to extract illuminant information. In C. Dickinson, I. Murray, and D. Carden, editors, *John Dalton's Colour Vision Legacy. Selected Proceedings of the International Conference*, pages 501–509, London, 1997. Taylor & Francis.
23. L. T. Maloney and B. A. Wandell. Color constancy: A method for recovering surface spectral reflectance. *Journal of the Optical Society of America A3*, 3(1):29–33, January 1986.
24. C. L. Novak and S. A. Shafer. Supervised color constancy for machine vision. In G. E. Healey, S. A. Shafer, and L. B. Wolff, editors, *Color*, pages 284–299, Boston, 1992. Jones and Bartlett Publishers.
25. S. Usui and S. Nakauchi. A neurocomputational model for colour constancy. In C. Dickinson, I. Murray, and D. Carden, editors, *John Dalton's Colour Vision Legacy. Selected Proceedings of the International Conference*, pages 475–482, London, 1997. Taylor & Francis.
26. S. Zeki. *A Vision of the Brain*. Blackwell Science, Oxford, 1993.
27. D. Zongker and B. Punch. *lil-gp 1.01 User's Manual (support and enhancements Bill Rand)*. Michigan State University, 1996.

Adaptive Genetic Programming Applied to New and Existing Simple Regression Problems

Jeroen Eggermont and Jano I. van Hemert

Leiden Institute of Advanced Computer Science
Leiden University
{jeggermo,jvhemert}@cs.leidenuniv.nl

Abstract. In this paper we continue our study on adaptive genetic programming. We use Stepwise Adaptation of Weights (SAW) to boost performance of a genetic programming algorithm on simple symbolic regression problems. We measure the performance of a standard GP and two variants of SAW extensions on two different symbolic regression problems from literature. Also, we propose a model for randomly generating polynomials which we then use to further test all three GP variants.

1 Introduction

We test a technique called Stepwise Adaptation of Weights (SAW) on symbolic regression. We use a genetic programming algorithm and adapt its fitness function using the SAW technique in an attempt to improve both algorithm performance and solution quality. Also, we present a new variant of the SAW technique called Precision SAW.

Previous studies on constraint satisfaction [6] and data classification [4] have indicated that SAW is a promising technique to boost the performance of evolutionary algorithms. It uses information of the problem from the run so far to adapt the fitness function of an evolutionary algorithm.

In a regression problem we are looking for a function that closely matches an unknown function based on a finite set of sample points. Genetic programming (GP) as introduced by Koza [9] uses a tree structure to represent an executable object or model. Here we will use GP to search for functions that solve a symbolic regression problem.

The next section defines the symbolic regression problem and how this is solved using genetic programming. In Sect. 3 we provide information on the SAW technique and show how this technique can be applied to symbolic regression. In Sect. 5 we explain our experiments and we provide results. Finally we draw conclusions and we provide ideas for further research.

2 Symbolic Regression with Genetic Programming

The object of solving a symbolic regression problem is finding a function that closely matches some unknown function on a certain interval. More formally,

J. Miller et al. (Eds.): EuroGP 2001, LNCS 2038, pp. 23–35, 2001.

given an unknown function $f(x)$ we want to find a function $g(x)$ such that $f(x_i) = g(x_i) \; \forall x_i \in X$, where X is a set of values drawn from the interval we are interested in. Note that we normally do not know $f(x)$ precisely. We only know the set of sample points $\{(x, f(x))|x \in X\}$. In this study we use predefined functions and uniformly draw a set of 50 sample points from it to test our regression algorithms equivalent to the experiments with these functions in [10].

We use a genetic programming algorithm to generate candidate solutions, i.e., $g(x)$. These functions are presented as binary trees built up using binary functions and a terminal set. The precise definition of these sets and other parameter settings varies between the two experiments presented later. Therefore, we defer the presentation of these parameters until Sect. 5 where we conduct our experiments.

The selection scheme in an evolutionary algorithm is one of its basic components. It needs a way to compare the quality of two candidate solutions. This measurement, the fitness function, is calculated using knowledge of the problem. In symbolic regression we want to minimise the total error over all samples. This is defined as the absolute error in (1), which will be the fitness function for the standard GP algorithm.

$$\epsilon = \sum_{x \in X} |f(x) - g(x)| \tag{1}$$

Other fitness functions can be used. For instance, based on the mean square error. We use this simple approach and make it adaptive in the next section.

3   Stepwise Adaptation of Weights

The Stepwise Adaptation of Weights (SAW) technique was first studied on the constraint satisfaction problem (CSP). Solving a CSP can mean different things. Here the object is to find an instantiation of a set of variables such that none of the constraints that restrict certain combinations of variable instantiations are violated. This is a NP-hard problem on which most evolutionary computation approaches will fail because they get stuck in local optima. The SAW technique is designed to overcome this deficiency.

In data classification the problem is to find a model that can classify tuples of attributes as good as possible. When we observe this problem with constraint satisfaction in mind we can draw some analogies. For instance, in CSP we have to deal with constraints. Minimising the number of violated constraints is the object and having no violated constraints at all yields a solution. Similarly, in data classification, minimising the number of wrongly classified records is the object, while correctly classifying all records yields a perfect model.

The idea of data classification can further be extended to symbolic regression. Here we want to find a model, i.e., a function, that correctly predicts values of the unknown function on the sampled points. The object is minimising the error of prediction, consequently having no error means having found a perfect fit.

This is where SAW steps into the picture by influencing the fitness function of an evolutionary algorithm. Note that in all the problems mentioned above the fitness has to be minimised to reach the object. The idea behind SAW is to adapt the fitness function in an evolutionary algorithm by using knowledge of the problem in the run so far.

Algorithm 1 Stepwise adaptation of weights (SAW)

set initial weights (thus fitness function f)
set $G = 0$
while not termination **do**
   $G = G + 1$
   run one generation of GP with f
   if $G \equiv 0 \pmod{\Delta T}$ **then**
      redefine f and recalculate fitness of individuals
   fi
end while

The general mechanism for SAW is presented in Figure 1. The knowledge of the problem is represented in the form of weights. We add a weight w_i to every sample point $x_i \in X$. These weights are initially set to one. During the run of the genetic programming algorithm we periodically stop the main evolutionary loop every ΔT generations and adjust the weights by increasing them. Afterwards, we continue the evolutionary loop using the new weights incorporated into the fitness function as shown in (2).

$$saw\ fitness(g, X) = \sum_{x_i \in X} w_i |f(x_i) - g(x_i)| \tag{2}$$

The adaptation of weights process takes the best individual from the current population and determines the error it makes on each sample point. Each of the weights w_i corresponding to the error made on point x_i is updated using the error value $|f(x_i) - g(x_i)|$. We try two variants for altering weights.

- *Classic* SAW (CSAW) adds a constant value $\Delta w_i = 1$ to each w_i if the error on sample point x_i is not zero. This is based on the approach of violated constraints [6].
- *Precision* SAW (PSAW) takes $\Delta w_i = |f(x_i) - g(x_i)|$ and adds Δw_i to the corresponding weight w_i.

4   Problem Generator

Besides testing our two GP variants on two problems taken from literature we present here a method for generating symbolic regression problems. This enables us to study the performance of these techniques on a large set of polynomials of a higher degree. The regression of higher degree polynomials finds its use in different application areas such as computer vision and economics [2].

We generate the polynomials using a model of two integer parameters $\langle a, b \rangle$, where a stands for the highest possible degree and b determines the domain size from which every e_i is chosen. When we have set these parameters we are able to generate polynomials in the form as shown in (3). The values e_i are drawn uniform random from the integer domain bounded by $-b$ and b.

$$\sum_{i=0}^{a} \left(e_i x^i \right), \text{ where } e_i \in \{w | w \in \mathbb{Z} \wedge -b \leq w \leq b\} \tag{3}$$

The function $f(x)$ is presented to the regression algorithms by generating 50 points $(x, f(x))$ uniformly from the domain $[-1, 1]$. This method for generating X will also be used for the two Koza functions [10].

5   Experiments and Results

5.1   Koza Functions

To test the performance of the two variants of SAW we do a number of experiments using three algorithms. First, the genetic programming algorithm without any additional aids (GP). Second, the variant where we add SAW with a constant Δw (GP-CSAW). Last, the variant where we add SAW with $\Delta w_i = |f(x_i) - g(x_i)|$ (GP-PSAW).

We measure performance of the algorithms on two simple symbolic regression problems. Each algorithm is tested with two different population sizes as shown in Table 1. We use 99 independent runs for each setting in which we measure mean, median, standard deviation, minimum and maximum absolute error (ϵ). Furthermore we count the number of successful runs. Where we define a run successful if the algorithm finds a function that has an absolute error below 10^{-6}.

Besides comparing the three genetic programming variants we also provide results obtained by using splines on the same problems. This places our three algorithms in a larger perspective.

Here we present two experiments with functions taken from [10]. All genetic programming systems used the parameters shown in Table 2.

Quintic Polynomial. This quintic polynomial is taken from [10] and is defined by (4). The function is shown in Fig. 1. When we try to regress this function using standard cubic regression we get a total error (as measured with ϵ) of 1.8345.

$$f(x) = x^5 - 2x^3 + x, \ x \in [-1, 1] \tag{4}$$

Table 1. Experiment parameters: six different experiments where each experiment consists of 99 independent runs

experiment	populations size	number of generations
1	100	100
2	100	200
3	100	500
4	100	1000
5	500	100
6	500	200

Table 2. Parameters and characteristics of the genetic programming algorithms for experiments with the Koza functions

parameter	value
evolutionary model	$(\mu, 7\mu)$
fitness standard GP	see (1)
fitness SAW variants	see (2)
stop criterion	maximum generations or perfect fit
functions set	$\{*, \text{pdiv}, -, +\}$
terminal set	$\{x\}$
populations size	see Table 1
initial depth	3
maximum depth	5
maximum generations	see Table 1
survivors selection	keep best populations size offspring
parent selection	random
ΔT (for SAW)	5

Table 3 shows the results of the experiments on the quintic polynomial. Looking at the mean and the median for all experiments we conjecture that GP-PSAW produces the best solutions. GP-CSAW is not always better than GP, but it has the best results when we observe the maximum error, i.e., the worst result found. The best solution (1.704×10^{-7}) is found twice by GP-CSAW.

We look at the individual runs of experiment 4 (population size of 100 and 1000 generations) and determine all the successful runs and see that GP has 76 successful runs out of 99, GP-CSAW has 78 successful runs out of 99 and GP-PSAW has 85 successful runs of 99. These result are set out in Fig. 3 together with their uncertainty interval [13]. We use the usual rule of thumb where we need at least a difference two and a half times the overlap of the uncertainty interval before we can claim a significant difference. This is clearly not the case here. In experiment 6 (population size 500 and 200 generations) GP fails 2 times out of 99. The other two algorithms never fail. This is a significant difference, albeit a small one as the uncertainty intervals still overlap.

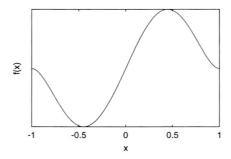

Fig. 1. The quintic polynomial on the interval $[-1, 1]$ (left)

Sextic Polynomial. This sextic polynomial is taken from [10] and is defined in (5). Figure 4 shows this function on the interval $[-1, 1]$. When we do a cubic regression on the function we get a total error (measured with ϵ) of 2.4210.

$$f(x) = x^6 - 2x^4 + x^2, \; x \in [-1, 1] \tag{5}$$

Table 4 shows the results of the experiments on the sextic polynomial. GP-PSAW has the best median in one experiment and best mean in three experiments. GP-CSAW never has the best mean but has the best median three times. If we are only interested in the best solution over all runs we have an easier job comparing. The best solution (1.013×10^{-7}) is found in experiment 2 by GP-PSAW in just 200 generations and by GP-CSAW in experiment 5 within 100 generations.

Similar to the quintic polynomial we examine the individual runs of experiment 4 (population size of 100 and 1000 generations) and determine all the successful runs. Here GP has 84 successful runs out of 99. GP-CSAW has 81 successful runs and GP-PSAW has 87 successful runs. These result are set out in Fig. 6 together with the uncertainty interval [13]. Although differences seem larger than with the quintic polynomial we still cannot claim a significant improvement. Tides turn compared to the quintic polynomial as here GP-CSAW fails twice, GP-PSAW fails once and GP always succeeds. This leads to a significant difference with overlapping uncertainty intervals between GP and GP-CSAW.

5.2   Randomly Generated Polynomials

Here we test our three GP variants on a suite of randomly generated polynomials. These polynomials can have at most a degree of twelve. The parameters of the underlying GP system are noted in Table 5

We generate polynomials randomly with the model from Sect. 4 with parameters $\langle 12, 5 \rangle$. We generate 100 polynomials and do 85 independent runs of each algorithm where each run is started with a unique random seed.

The previous simple functions had a smaller maximum degree and could therefore be efficiently solved with cubic splines. Here we need a technique that

Table 3. Experiment results for the quintic polynomial, all measurements taken with absolute error (ϵ)

experiment	median $(\times 10^{-7})$	mean $(\times 10^{-1})$	stddev $(\times 10^{-1})$	minimum $(\times 10^{-7})$	maximum
1. GP	4.610	1.351	2.679	2.640	1.050
GP-CSAW	4.605	1.339	2.599	2.445	1.102
GP-PSAW	4.391	1.286	2.972	2.598	1.559
2. GP	4.354	1.274	2.610	2.640	1.034
GP-CSAW	4.303	1.226	2.376	2.445	0.8525
GP-PSAW	4.200	1.049	2.254	2.543	1.317
3. GP	3.972	1.120	2.571	2.640	1.034
GP-CSAW	4.019	1.107	2.204	1.704	0.8525
GP-PSAW	3.855	0.7785	2.049	2.449	1.111
4. GP	3.763	1.161	2.547	2.324	1.034
GP-CSAW	3.693	0.8323	1.803	1.704	0.6969
GP-PSAW	3.669	0.6513	1.856	2.114	1.111
5. GP	3.465	2.045×10^{-1}	1.544×10^{-2}	1.965	1.433×10^{-1}
GP-CSAW	3.465	3.570×10^{-5}	8.463×10^{-8}	2.412	9.965×10^{-7}
GP-PSAW	3.395	3.382×10^{-5}	4.384×10^{-8}	1.974	5.071×10^{-7}
6. GP	3.343	2.045×10^{-1}	1.544×10^{-2}	1.965	1.433×10^{-1}
GP-CSAW	3.446	3.512×10^{-5}	8.337×10^{-8}	2.412	9.965×10^{-7}
GP-PSAW	3.325	3.331×10^{-5}	4.533×10^{-8}	1.937	5.071×10^{-7}

Table 4. Experiment results for the sextic polynomial, all measurements taken with absolute error (ϵ)

experiment	median $(\times 10^{-7})$	mean $(\times 10^{-1})$	stddev $(\times 10^{-1})$	minimum $(\times 10^{-7})$	maximum
1. GP	2.182	1.490	3.987	1.723	2.844
GP-CSAW	2.182	1.525	4.036	1.353	2.844
GP-PSAW	2.182	1.212	2.569	1.213	1.720
2. GP	2.182	1.179	2.882	1.172	1.730
GP-CSAW	2.098	1.244	3.626	1.244	2.491
GP-PSAW	2.115	1.135	2.495	1.013	1.720
3. GP	1.953	0.8001	2.318	1.171	1.730
GP-CSAW	1.916	0.8366	2.328	1.172	1.222
GP-PSAW	1.984	0.8403	2.226	1.013	1.720
4. GP	1.888	0.6963	2.258	1.135	1.730
GP-CSAW	1.824	0.6100	1.741	1.048	1.161
GP-PSAW	1.899	0.5084	1.418	1.013	5.467×10^{-1}
5. GP	1.385	1.507×10^{-6}	3.280×10^{-7}	1.087	2.912×10^{-7}
GP-CSAW	1.385	3.390×10^{-2}	2.500×10^{-1}	1.013	2.255×10^{-1}
GP-PSAW	1.385	2.485×10^{-2}	2.460×10^{-1}	1.125	2.460×10^{-1}
6. GP	1.260	1.417×10^{-6}	3.029×10^{-7}	1.087	2.912×10^{-7}
GP-CSAW	1.363	3.390×10^{-2}	2.500×10^{-1}	1.013	2.255×10^{-1}
GP-PSAW	1.260	2.485×10^{-2}	2.460×10^{-1}	1.115	2.4560×10^{-1}

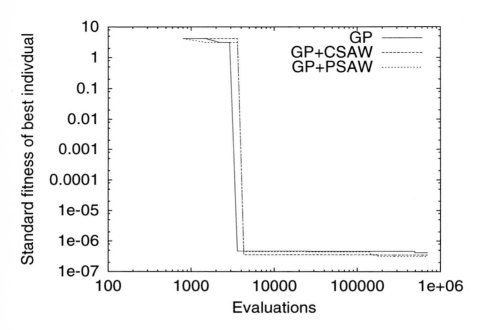

Fig. 2. Absolute error (ϵ) over evaluations for one run of the three algorithms for the quintic polynomial (right)

can handle a higher degree of polynomials. Hence, we try a curve fitting algorithm that uses splines under tension [3] on every generated polynomial. The results are very good as the average total error over the whole set of polynomials measured as the absolute error (ϵ) is 1.3498346×10^{-4}.

We present the results for the set of randomly generated polynomials in Table 6. Clearly, the new variant GP-PSAW is better than any of the others as long as we do not update the SAW weights too many times. This seems like a contradiction as we would expect the SAW mechanism to boost improvement, but we should not forget that after updating the weights the fitness function has changed so we need to re-calculate the fitness for the whole population. This re-calculateion can be performed by either re-evaluating all individuals or by using a cache-memory which contains the predicted value for each point and individual. Because we have used a general library we opted for the re-evaluation. Also, when we would extend the system in such a way that the data points would change during the run this would render the cache useless. But, in a GP system this will cost us fitness evaluations, leaving less fitness evaluations for the GP. Thus less points of the problem space are visited.

The comparison with the splines on tension only remains. The error of the splines on tension is incredibly low. As such our results are significantly worse. One reason could be the number of evaluations that are performed at maximum. Here we have set this at 20,000. If we look at the right hand of Figure 4 we notice

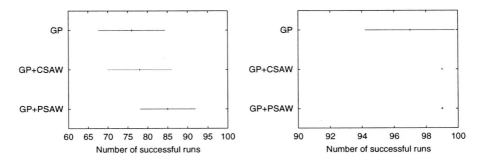

Fig. 3. Number of successful runs with uncertainty intervals for the quintic polynomial in experiment 4 (left) and experiment 6 (right)

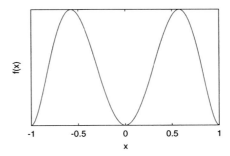

Fig. 4. The sextic polynomial on the interval $[-1, 1]$

that the absolute error suddenly drops after 10,000 evaluations. If we take into account that our current polynomials have a degree that is up to twice that of the sextic polynomial we can expect that a better solution will not be found before this 20,000 mark.

6   Conclusions

We have shown how the SAW technique can be used to extend genetic programming to boost performance in symbolic regression. We like to point out that the simple concept behind SAW makes it very easy to implement the technique in existing algorithms. Thereby, making it suitable for doing quick try outs to boost an evolutionary algorithms performance. As SAW solely focuses on the fitness function it can be used in virtually any evolutionary algorithm. However, it is up to the user to find a good way of updating the weights mechanism depending on the problem at hand. This paper shows two ways in which to add SAW to a genetic programming algorithm that solves symbolic regression problems. By doing this, we add another problem area to a list of problems that already contains various constraint satisfaction problems and data classification problems.

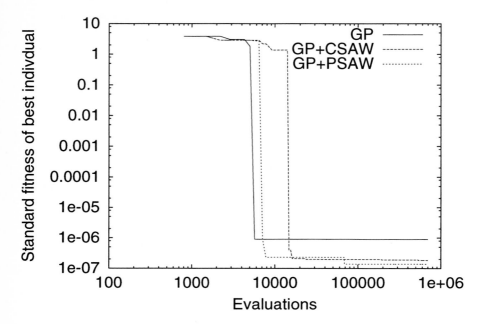

Fig. 5. Absolute error (ϵ) over evaluations for one run of the three algorithms for the sextic polynomial (right)

When we focus on a comparison of mean, median and minimum fitness it appears that our new variant of the SAW technique (Precision SAW) has the upper hand. In most cases it finds a better or comparable result than our standard GP, also beating the Classic SAW variant. Moreover, it seems that the SAW technique works better using smaller populations. Something that is already concluded by Eiben et al. [5].

When we restrict our comparison to the number of successes and fails we find that there is only a small significant difference when we run the algorithms with a populations size of 500. Then GP+PSAW is the winner for the quintic polynomial and GP for the sextic polynomial.

Our GP algorithms perform poorly on the suit of randomly generated polynomials compared to splines on tension. We suspect the cause to lie in the maximum number of evaluations. The Koza functions have showed us that the drop in absolute error can happen suddenly. We conjecture that our GP systems need more time on the higher degree polynomials before this drop occurs.

7   Future Research

We need to enhance our polynomial generator as we still have unanswered questions about which polynomials are easy to regress and which are not. Maybe we can alter or bias the generators parameters such that we can model polynomials

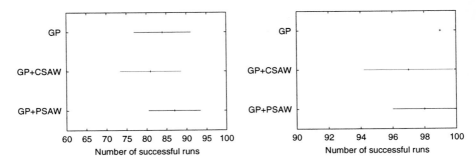

Fig. 6. Number of successful runs with uncertainty intervals for the sextic polynomial in experiment 4 (left) and experiment 6 (right)

Table 5. Parameters and characteristics of the genetic programming algorithms for experiments with the random polynomials

parameter	value
evolutionary model	steady state $(\mu + 1)$
fitness standard GP	see (1)
fitness SAW variants	see (2)
stop criterion	maximum evaluations or perfect fit
functions set	$\{*, \mathrm{pdiv}, -, +, \neg, y^3\}$
terminal set	$\{x\} \cup \{w|w \in \mathbb{Z} \wedge -b \le w \le b\}$
populations size	100
initial maximum depth	10
maximum size	100 nodes
maximum evaluations	20,000
survivors selection	reverse 5-tournament
parent selection	5-tournament
ΔT (for SAW)	1000, 2000 and 5000 generations

of which we have prior knowledge. A technique that is used in fields such as constrained optimisation [12] and constraint satisfaction [1].

The performance of genetic programming is seen as an interesting problem to overcome as many other techniques exist to boost performance of genetic programming [7, 15, 8]. These technique often are bias towards handling large data sets which is not the case for the problems we have described.

Looking at symbolic regression as used in this paper presents a problem that is viewed as a static set of sample points. That is, the set of sample points is drawn uniformly out of the interval of the unknown function and stays the same during the run. Therefore, the problem is not finding an unknown function, but just a function that matches the initial sample points. To circumvent this we could use a co-evolutionary approach [14] that adapts the set of points we need to fit, thereby creating an arms-race between a population of solutions and a population of sets of sample points.

Table 6. Experiment results for 100 randomly generated polynomials, results are averaged over the 85 independent runs. The error is measured as absolute error (1)

algorithm	ΔT	mean	stddev	minimum	maximum
GP		21.20	10.30	5.82	48.60
GP-CSAW	1000	21.55	10.33	5.79	48.05
GP-CSAW	2000	21.21	10.24	5.83	48.74
GP-CSAW	5000	21.25	10.47	5.75	49.31
GP-PSAW	1000	21.46	10.52	6.41	50.80
GP-PSAW	2000	20.45	10.05	5.90	48.06
GP-PSAW	5000	20.28	9.87	5.96	48.18

Acknowledgements

The program for the the Koza functions was created with the GP kernel from the Data to Knowledge research project of the Danish Hydraulic Institute (http://www.d2k.dk).

The program for the randomly generated functions was created with the Evolvable Objects library [11] which can be downloaded from http://sourceforge.net/projects/eodev.

References

[1] Dimitris Achlioptas, Lefteris M. Kirousis, Evangelos Kranakis, Danny Krizanc, Michael S.O. Molloy, and Yannis C. Stamatiou. Random constraint satisfaction a more accurate picture. In Gert Smolka, editor, *Principles and Practice of Constraint Programming — CP97*, pages 107–120. Springer-Verlag, 1997.

[2] With S. Ar, R. Lipton, and R. Rubinfeld. Reconstructing algebraic functions from erroneous data. *SIAM Journal on Computing*, 28(2):487–510, 1999.

[3] A. K. Cline. Six subprograms for curve fitting using splines under tension. *Commun. ACM*, 17(4):220–223, April 1974.

[4] J. Eggermont, A.E. Eiben, and J.I. van Hemert. Adapting the fitness function in GP for data mining. In R. Poli, P. Nordin, W.B. Langdon, and T.C. Fogarty, editors, *Genetic Programming, Proceedings of EuroGP'99*, volume 1598 of *LNCS*, pages 195–204, Goteborg, Sweden, 26–27 May 1999. Springer-Verlag.

[5] A.E. Eiben, J.K. van der Hauw, and J.I. van Hemert. Graph coloring with adaptive evolutionary algorithms. *Journal of Heuristics*, 4(1):25–46, 1998.

[6] A.E. Eiben and J.I. van Hemert. *SAW-ing EAs: adapting the fitness function for solving constrained problems*, chapter 26, pages 389–402. McGraw-Hill, London, 1999.

[7] C. Gathercole and P. Ross. Dynamic training subset selection for supervised learning in genetic programming. In *Proceedings of the Parallel Problem Solving from Nature III Conference*, pages 312–321, 1994.

[8] Chris Gathercole and Peter Ross. Tackling the boolean even N parity problem with genetic programming and limited-error fitness. In John R. Koza, Kalyanmoy Deb, Marco Dorigo, David B. Fogel, Max Garzon, Hitoshi Iba, and Rick L. Riolo,

editors, *Genetic Programming 1997: Proceedings of the Second Annual Conference*, pages 119–127, Stanford University, CA, USA, 13-16 July 1997. Morgan Kaufmann.

[9] J.R. Koza. *Genetic Programming*. MIT Press, 1992.

[10] J.R. Koza. *Genetic Programming II: Automatic Discovery of Reusable Programs*. MIT Press, Cambridge, MA, 1994.

[11] J. J. Merelo, J. Carpio, P. Castillo, V. M. Rivas, and G. Romero. Evolving objects, 1999. Available at `http://geneura.ugr.es/~jmerelo/EOpaper/`.

[12] Z. Michalewicz, K. Deb, M. Schmidt, , and T. Stidsen. Test-case generator for nonlinear continuous parameter optimization techniques. *IEEE Transactions on Evolutionary Computation*, 4(3), 2000.

[13] David S. Moore and George P. McCabe. *Introduction to the Practice of Statistics*. W.H. Freeman and Company, New York, 3rd edition, 1998.

[14] J. Paredis. Co-evolutionary computation. *Artificial Life*, 2(4):355–375, 1995.

[15] Byoung-Tak Zhang. Bayesian methods for efficient genetic programming. *Genetic Programming And Evolvable Machines*, 1(3):217–242, July 2000.

An Evolutionary Approach
to Automatic Generation of VHDL Code
for Low-Power Digital Filters

Massimiliano Erba[1], Roberto Rossi[1], Valentino Liberali[2],
and Andrea G.B. Tettamanzi[2]

[1] Università degli Studi di Pavia
Dipartimento di Elettronica
Via Ferrata 1, 27100 Pavia, Italy
erba@ele.unipv.it, roberto@ele.unipv.it
[2] Università degli Studi di Milano
Dipartimento di Tecnologie dell'Informazione
Via Bramante 65, 26013 Crema, Italy
vliberali@crema.unimi.it, tettaman@dsi.unimi.it

Abstract. An evolutionary algorithm is used to design a finite impulse
response digital filter with reduced power consumption. The proposed
design approach combines genetic optimization and simulation methodology, to evaluate a multi-objective fitness function which includes both
the suitability of the filter transfer function and the transition activity
of digital blocks. The proper choice of fitness function and selection criteria allows the genetic algorithm to perform a better search within the
design space, thus exploring possible solutions which are not considered
in the conventional structured design methodology. Although the evolutionary process is not guaranteed to generate a filter fully compliant
to specifications in every run, experimental evidence shows that, when
specifications are met, evolved filters are much better than classical designs both in terms of power consumption and in terms of area, while
maintaining the same performance.

1 Introduction

Although digital filter design methodology is well established, the technological
trend in silicon integration is now demanding for new CAD tools, to increase
designer productivity and to cope with increased integration density. The larger
and larger number of devices, integrated onto a single silicon chip, not only
leads to increased computational power and increased frequency performance,
but also increases power consumption, which is expected to be a major problem
for integrated circuit designers in the next decade. Since power consumption is
non-linear and input pattern dependent, its minimisation is a difficult task.

This paper illustrates an evolutionary approach to the design of digital filters
with reduced power consumption. Evolutionary algorithms [1] are a broad class
of optimization methods inspired by biology, that build on the key concept of

J. Miller et al. (Eds.): EuroGP 2001, LNCS 2038, pp. 36–50, 2001.
© Springer-Verlag Berlin Heidelberg 2001

Darwinian evolution [2]. After being successfully applied to physical design (partitioning, placement and routing), now bio-inspired electronic design methods are being considered in a variety of circumstances [3, 4]. Evolutionary algorithms for circuit synthesis are a powerful technique, which could provide innovative solutions to hard design problems, also when classical decomposition methods may fail [5].

In this work, circuits are evolved to compute a finite impulse response (FIR) filtering function. As explained in Section 2, the main objective is the reduction of power consuption through the minimization of transition activity of digital logic. Based on the behavioral description illustrated in Section 3, the evolutionary algorithm described in Section 4 is devised to evolve the FIR filter, which is described in VHDL and evaluated through the Synopsys synthesis and simulation tools, in order to obtain an accurate estimate of its power consumption. Section 5 presents a design case, comparing the filter obtained from simulated evolution with a conventional design.

2   Motivation and Problem Statement

Microintegrated technology enables the development of deep submicron CMOS circuits for digital signal processing (DSP) in a broad variety of applications. Low-cost and high-performance circuits are required to be competitive in a more and more demanding consumer market. Single chip solutions reduce costs, increase reliability, and can help to reduce weight and size of hand-held electronic products.

Being the real world steadily analog, interfaces between the digital processor and external variables must be used. This leads to mixed analog-digital integrates systems, including the DSP, the analog-to-digital and digital-to-analog conversion, and, in some cases, analog pre-processing and/or signal conditioning. In mixed systems, performance limitations come mainly from the analog section which interfaces the digital processing core with the external world. In such ICs, analog device performance can be severely affected by disturbances coming from switching digital nodes [6]. Therefore, low power digital design is a must, since it also helps to reduce the disturbance generated by the digital section of the circuit.

The power consumption P in a digital system is mainly due to the logic transitions of circuit nodes, and can be expressed as:

$$P = \frac{1}{2}CV^2 f\alpha \tag{1}$$

where C is the node capacitance, V is the power supply voltage, f is the clock frequency, and α is the transition activity, i.e. the average number of logic transitions in a clock period [7].

From (1), it is apparent that a low power design approach must account not only for minimisation of area and interconnections (to reduce C), but also for reduction of the transition activity of digital gates. The latter task is not

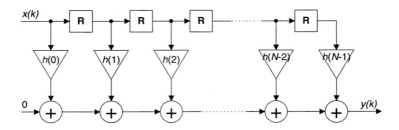

Fig. 1. Canonical direct form of a FIR filter

a straightforward one, because digital activity is a non-linear function of input patterns.

For this reason, an evolutionary algorithm based on genetic optimisation has been developed, with a twofold target. First of all, the digital filters randomly designed must be evaluated to check if their frequency response meets the mask requirements (band edges, pass-band ripple, stop-band attenuation). Then, filters meeting the mask constraints are evaluated to estimate their transition activity. The selection is done according to a global fitness function, combining both the mask fitness and the activity fitness.

The best result obtained with the simulated evolution is eventually encoded in VHDL and synthesized with Synopsys; the synthesis report provides information on the number of equivalent gates used for the design.

3   Genetic Representation of FIR Filters

A FIR filter implements a time-domain convolution between the input signal $x(k)$ and the filter impulse response, represented by the set of constant filter coefficients $h(k)$:

$$y(k) = \sum_{i=0}^{N-1} h(i)x(k-i) \tag{2}$$

The "canonical direct form" shown in Fig. 1 is a straightforward implementation of (2) [8]. It requires a set of $(N-1)$ registers (indicated with R in the figure) to store the previous samples of the input signal $x(k)$, a set of multiplier blocks to perform the multiplications of the (delayed) input samples and the filter coefficients, and an adder tree to obtain the weighted sum at the output $y(k)$.

Taking the $\mathcal{Z}$-transform of both input and output signals, we can write the frequency response of the filter in the z-domain:

$$H(z) = \frac{y(z)}{x(z)} = \sum_{i=0}^{N-1} h(i)z^{-i} \tag{3}$$

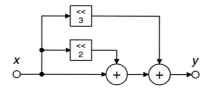

Fig. 2. Multiplication by 13 implemented with shifters and adders

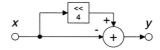

Fig. 3. Multiplication by 15 implemented with one shifter and one subtractor

which is still represented in the graphical form shown in Fig. 1, as the z-domain response of a register is z^{-1} [9].

To save area and to reduce power consumption, multiplier blocks are often replaced with shifters and adders [10]. As an example, multiplication by 13 can be implemented with two shifts and two additions, as illustrated in Fig. 2, where the block "$<< n$" means "left shift by n positions".

The canonical signed digit (CSD) representation [11] assigns a separate sign to each digit: 0, 1 and $\bar{1}$ ($= -1$). Its goal is to minimise the number of non-zero digits: by encoding the filter coefficients with CSD, the filter ouput can be computed using a reduced amount of hardware, since multiplications by zero are simply not implemented. As an example, consider the multiplication by 15: since $15 = 2^3 + 2^2 + 2^1 + 2^0 = (001111)_2$, this operation in binary arithmetics would require three shifts and three additions; while using CSD we can write $15 = 2^4 - 2^0 = (01000\bar{1})_2$, and we implement the same operation using only one shifter and one subtractor (Fig. 3).

Starting from these considerations, a digital filter can be described using a very small number of elementary operations, or *primitives*. All the operations can be arranged into a linear sequence, with the input signal $x(k)$ entering into the leftmost primitive ant the output signal $y(k)$ being the output of the rightmost primitive. Since a FIR filter does not have any feedback loop, the signal flow is always from left to right.

The primitives selected for FIR filters are listed in Table 1. Each elementary operation is encoded by its own code (one character) and by two integer numbers, which represent the relative offset (calculated backwards from the current position) of the two operands at the input. All primitives include a delay z^{-1}, to avoid possible problems due to timing violations during the synthesis process. The sequence of the encoded elementary operations is the genotype of the digital filter.

As an example, the following sequence is made of 6 primitives (6 genes):

Table 1. Primitives of the genetic algorithm

Name	Code	Op 1	Op 2	Description
Input	I	not used	not used	Copy input: $y_i = x$
Delay	D	n_1	not used	Store value: $y_i = y_{i-n_1} z^{-1}$
Left shift	L	n_1	p	Multiply by 2^P: $y_i = 2^P y_{i-n_1} z^{-1}$
Right shift	R	n_1	p	Divide by 2^P: $y_i = 2^{-P} y_{i-n_1} z^{-1}$
Adder	A	n_1	n_2	Sum: $y_i = (y_{i-n_1} + y_{i-n_2})z^{-1}$
Subtractor	S	n_1	n_2	Difference: $y_i = (y_{i-n_1} - y_{i-n_2})z^{-1}$
Complement	C	n_1	not used	Multiply by -1: $y_i = -y_{i-n_1} z^{-1}$

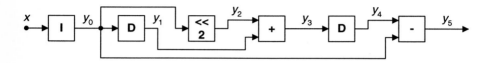

Fig. 4. Example of a signal flow graph in linear form

(I 0 2) (D 1 3) (L 2 2) (A 2 1) (D 1 0) (S 1 5)
It can be represented in the graphical linear form illustrated in Fig. 4 and it is interpreted as follows:

$$
\begin{aligned}
y_0 &= x \\
y_1 &= y_0 z^{-1} \\
y_2 &= 2^2 y_0 z^{-1} \\
y_3 &= (y_1 + y_2) z^{-1} \\
y_4 &= y_3 z^{-1} \\
y_5 &= (y_4 - y_0) z^{-1}
\end{aligned}
\tag{4}
$$

The last value is the output of the filter. By merging the equations (4), we obtain the input-output relationship:

$$
y = x(5z^{-4} - z^{-1})
\tag{5}
$$

We note that such representation of a filter has the same essence as a program in a simple imperative programming language, and we can apply genetic programming [12] or, more precisely, Cartesian genetic programming [13] to the task of designing FIR filters.

The design method proposed is this paper is completely different from the conventional design approach.

Classical filter designs are based on the minimization of a norm in the design space, e.g. on the determination of the minimum number of filter coefficients that allow to obtain a filter response within the given specifications. Such an appoach reduces the number of filter coefficients (the "taps" in Fig. 1), but it does not guarantee that the digital network is "optimal" in some sense at the end of the design process.

On the other hand, the evolutionary design approach uses a fine granularity of the primitives and, hence, of the filter structure. From the structure shown in Fig. 4), filter coefficients cannot be directly seen. The advantages of this approach is the simple genetic encoding, that allows the evolutionary algorithm to perform a fine search within the design space, exploring also possible solutions which are simply not considered in the classical method [14]. By taking into consideration a larger design space, we have a higher chance of finding a solution which is (in some sense) "better" than the conventional one.

Since the main target of this work is the reduction of power consumption, the evolutionary algorithm will have to estimate the transition activity of the filter. To this end, primitives have been characterized to evaluate their average power consumption. According to gate level simulations, we assigned a relative weight $W = 30$ to sum, difference and complement.

4   The Evolutionary Algorithm

In order to make filters evolve, a variable population size evolutionary algorithm using an $(n + m)$ strategy and linear ranking selection with elitism has been implemented.

The initial population is seeded with two short random individuals. At every generation, selection determines a set of n surviving individuals, which will be used to produce m offspring by crossover and mutation. Four alternative selection strategies have been considered:

1. an "aging" rule, which assigns a life expectation to every individual at its birth, according to its fitness: life expectation linearly decreases from 100 to 1 generation as the fitness goes from best (f_{best}) to worst (f_{worst});
2. a selection based on normalized fitness and ranking, whereby each individual has a probability $P_s = k\sqrt{f_i' r_i'}$ of surviving, where f_i' is the normalized fitness of the individual of rank i, defined as $f_i' = \frac{f_i - f_{\text{best}}}{f_{\text{best}} - f_{\text{worst}}}$, r_i' is the normalized rank, defined as $r_i' = 1 - \frac{i}{N}$, N is the actual population size, and k is a parameter dynamically calculated to adjust the population size;
3. a sort of linear ranking selection with elitism, whereby the best two individuals survive with probability $P_s = 1$, and the individual of rank i has a probability $P_s = 1 - \frac{i}{2\bar{n}}$ of surviving, where $\bar{n}$ is the average population size;
4. a histogram based selection, whereby the fitness histogram is calculated by dividing the fitness interval $[0, f_{\text{best}}]$ into B bins (with $2 \le B \le 50$, B depending on the population size), and the survival probability of each individual is $P_s = 1$ if the individual lies into a bin less populated than the average, otherwise $P_s < 1$ if it lies into a bin exceeding the average bin population density.

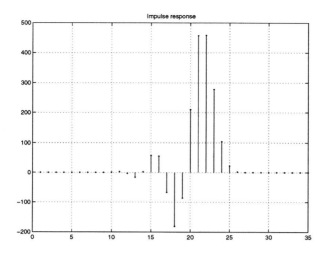

Fig. 5. Impulse response of the best filter generated (pass band: 0 ... 0.25)

The four selection strategies greatly differ in promoting genetic diversity: from experimental evidence, strategy 1 tends to produce a population of individuals identical to the best one, while strategy 4 favours the highest diversity. Strategies 2 and 3 have an intermediate behaviour.

Reproduction is carried out by a multi-point crossover: two parents are randomly divided into the same number of segments, and a new individual is created by catenating segments taken with equal probability from either parent. This reproduction strategy produces individuals with variable length.

Mutation is applied to all new individuals, and consists in randomly modifying, removing or inserting a gene with a small probability p_{mut}.

Fitness is assigned to individuals as follows: the frequency range is sampled at N equally spaced frequencies ω_i, and the filter response $H(\omega_i)$ is calculated for every ω_i in the pass-band and in the stop-band. The partial error ϵ_i is set to zero, if $|H(\omega_i)|$ lies within the specifications; otherwise it is proportional to the overshoot or undershoot with respect to the given tolerance. The total error E_{tot} is simply the sum of all partial errors. Fitness consists of two parts:

1. mask fitness, defined as $f_M = \frac{1}{1+E_{\mathrm{tot}}}$, measures the extent to which the filter complies with frequency specifications; $f_M = 1$ when specifications are completely met;

2. activity fitness, defined as $f_A = 1 + \frac{a}{N_T}$, where N_T is the number of weighted digital transitions per input sample and a is a constant; its contribution is higher for filters with a low transition activity, which is responsible for power consumption.

Table 2. Success of different selection strategies

Selection strategy	% of success	faster result within specifications generation number	faster result within specifications CPU time
1. (aging)	45 %	11109	51 s
2. (norm. fitness and ranking)	50 %	46372	210 s
3. (linear ranking)	33 %	4269	63 s
4. (histogram)	25 %	3646	445 s

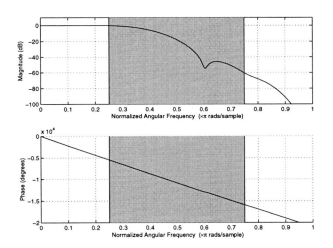

Fig. 6. Frequency response of the best filter generated (pass band: 0 ... 0.25); the gray area represents the "don't care" band

Finally, the global fitness is defined as:

$$f = \begin{cases} f_M & \text{if } E_{\text{tot}} > 0 \\ f_M + f_A & \text{otherwise} \end{cases} \tag{6}$$

Such definition introduces a gap between individuals meeting the specifications and individuals not meeting them. The main function of this gap is just to avoid numerical errors during the ranking for selection or ambiguity during histogram calculation: the gap ensures that the individuals complying with mask specifications are not in the same bin with individuals not meeting them.

5 Experiments and Results

The proposed design method has been applied to the design of a digital filter to be used as a decimation stage in a $\Sigma\Delta$ analog-to-digital converter. The filter specifications are:

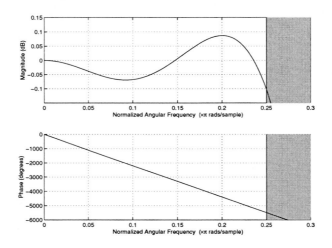

Fig. 7. Detail of the pass-band ripple (pass band: 0 ... 0.25)

- normalized pass-band: 0 ... 0.25
- pass-band maximum ripple: 0.2 dB
- normalized stop-band: 0.75 ... 1
- pass-band minimum attenuation: 60 dB
- normalized "don't care" band: 0.25 ... 0.75

The parameters of the evolutionary algorithm were set as:

- minimum population size: $n_{\min} = 10$
- maximum population size: $n_{\max} = 1000$
- crossover probability: $p_{\mathrm{cross}} = 0.05$
- mutation probability: $p_{\mathrm{mut}} = 0.01$

From these parameters, the average population size is $\bar{n} = 100$ for selection strategies 1, 2, and 3, while selection stategy 4 always maximizes the population size to achieve the maximum genetic diversity.

Several runs have been done with the same parameter set and different selection strategies. Runs are considered successful if they produce a filter design complying with specifications within 100,000 generations (10,000 generations for strategy 4, as the population size is ten times higher). Table 2 summarizes the results, indicating the percentage of successful runs and the number of generations and the CPU time of the first result obtained (which is not necessarily the best one among all the runs. Each line summarizes at least ten different runs.

The successful designs produced by the evolutionary algorithm are automatically encoded in VHDL. In the VHDL description, the algorithm calculates automatically the length of digital words, in order to avoid arithmetic overflow while saving area and power. Filters described in VHDL can be synthesized and simulated according to the conventional digital design methodology.

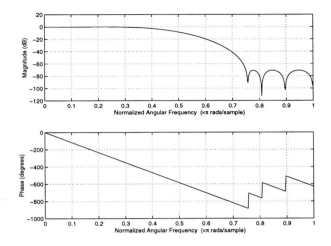

Fig. 8. Frequency response of the filter designed with conventional methodology (pass band: 0 ... 0.25)

Table 3. Filter characteristics (from post-synthesis simulation)

	evolutionary	conventional
No. of coefficients	17	15
No. of primitives	32	60
No. of logic gates	10,000	40,000
Power consumption	14 mW	40 mW

In the following part of this section, we consider two design cases. Both are low-pass filters: the first one with normalized pass band (0, 0.25) and normalized stop band (0.75, 1), and the second one with normalized pass band (0, 0.35) and normalized stop band (0.65, 1).

5.1 Low-Pass Filter with Normalized Pass Band (0, 0.25)

The filter specifications are listed at the beginning of Sect. 5.

The genome of the evolved filter has 46 primitives and corresponds to the impulse response illustrated in Fig. 5. The resulting frequency response is shown in Fig. 6; Fig. 7 contains a detail of the pass-band ripple. It is apparent that the filter meets all design specifications; also the phase is linear within the pass band, although the linear phase requirement was not considered during the evolutionary process.

For comparison, Fig. 8 shows the frequency response of a filter designed using the **remez** function available in Matlab and its Signal Processing Toolbox [15].

```
entity filter is
port(
  y:out std_logic_vector(29 downto 0);
  clk:in std_logic;
  rst:in std_logic;
  x:in std_logic_vector(15 downto 0)
);
end entity;

architecture RTL of filter is
--filter signals
signal y0: std_logic_vector(16 downto 0);
signal y1: std_logic_vector(16 downto 0);
signal y2: std_logic_vector(15 downto 0);
signal y3: std_logic_vector(17 downto 0);
signal y4: std_logic_vector(15 downto 0);
signal y5: std_logic_vector(18 downto 0);
...
signal y45: std_logic_vector(29 downto 0);

begin
y <= y45;
gene0: adder generic map(Bits_x1 => x'length, Bits_x2 => x'length,
        Bits_y => y0'length)
        port map(x1 => x, x2 => x, y => y0, clk => clk, rst => rst);
gene1: adder generic map(Bits_x1 => x'length, Bits_x2 => x'length,
        Bits_y => y1'length)
        port map(x1 => x, x2 => x, y => y1, clk => clk, rst => rst);
gene2: change_s generic map(Bits => y2'length)
        port map(x => x, y => y2, clk => clk, rst => rst);
gene3: adder generic map(Bits_x1 => y1'length, Bits_x2 => y0'length,
        Bits_y => y3'length)
        port map(x1 => y1, x2 => y0, y => y3, clk => clk, rst => rst);
gene4: init generic map(Bits => x'length)
        port map(x => x, y => y4, clk => clk, rst => rst);
gene5: adder generic map(Bits_x1 => y3'length, Bits_x2 => y2'length,
        Bits_y => y5'length)
        port map(x1 => y3, x2 => y2, y => y5, clk => clk, rst => rst);
...
gene45: adder generic map(Bits_x1 => y43'length, Bits_x2 => y42'length,
        Bits_y => y45'length)
        port map(x1 => y43, x2 => y42, y => y45, clk => clk, rst => rst);
end RTL;
```

Fig. 9. Synthesizable VHDL code generated by the algorithm

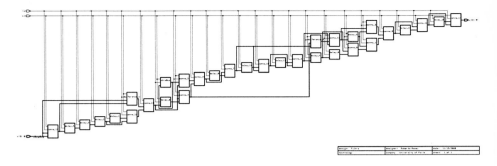

Fig. 10. Schematic diagram of the filter synthesized with Synopsys (pass band: 0 ... 0.25)

Fig. 9 illustrates the VHDL code generated by the algorithm. The RTL architecture is translated by Synopsys into the schematic diagram shown in Fig. 10. The evolved filter is implemented with 10,000 equivalent logic gates; while the conventional filter implementation required about 40,000 gates. By comparing these two figures, we can conclude that the effort of the evolutionary algorithm towards optimisation of transition activity has led also to a dramatic reduction of the required hardware, thus reducing the silicon area (and hence the cost) by a factor of 4. From simulation with pseudorandom input pattern, the evolved filter has a power consumption of 14 mW, while the previously designed filter dissipates 40 mW. Table 3 compares the filter obtained through simulated evolution with the conventional design.

The CPU time required for the evolution was about 300 s.

Fig. 11 illustrates the evolution of the fitness of the best individual, for which the selection strategy 1 (aging) has been used. From the figure, one can observe the typical punctuated equilibria where abrupt changes are interleaved with long periods of stasis.

5.2   Low-Pass Filter with Normalized Pass Band (0, 0.35)

The filter specifications for the second design case are:
- normalized pass-band: 0 ... 0.35
- pass-band maximum ripple: 0.2 dB
- normalized stop-band: 0.65 ... 1
- pass-band minimum attenuation: 60 dB
- normalized "don't care" band: 0.35 ... 0.65

The genome of the evolved filter has 254 primitives and corresponds to the impulse response illustrated in Fig. 12. The resulting frequency response is shown in Fig. 13. It is apparent that also this design example meets all specifications. The phase is linear within the pass band.

The CPU time required for this design was about 3000 s.

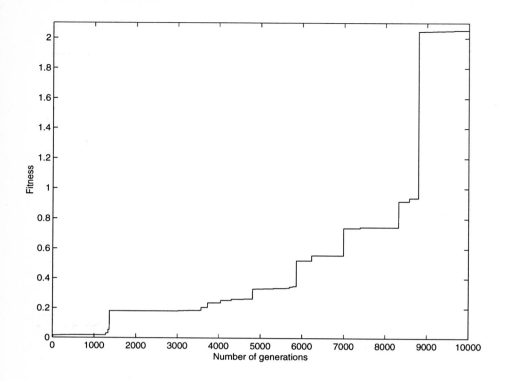

Fig. 11. Evolution of the fitness of the best filter (pass band: 0 ... 0.25)

6   Conclusion

This paper has described an evolutionary approach to the design of digital filters. Genetic encoding of filter primitives has a fine granularity which is exploited by the evolutionary algorithm during its search. From the genetic encoding, the impulse response of the filter can be easily derived, thus allowing a direct evaluation of cost and transition activity of digital blocks. A fitness function has been devised to allow multi-objective evolution. Four selection criteria have been considered: none of them can be considered optimal, since experimental evidence shows that the evolution process may remain stuck for long time into a local maximum, without reaching the design target within a defined number of iterations. Therefore, multiple runs are required to obtain a high probability of success.

The "best" result produced by the algorithm is automatically translated into VHDL code, which can be synthesized into a circuit without any additional operation, according to the standard digital design methodology.

The results obtained with the simulated evolution show that minimisation of transition activity leads to a dramatic reduction of the hardware with re-

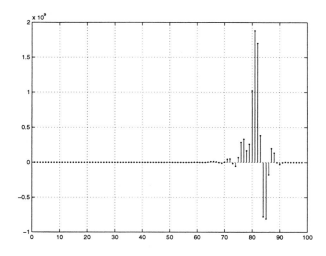

Fig. 12. Impulse response of the best filter generated (pass band: 0 ... 0.35)

spect to the conventional design methodology, while maintaining the same filter performance.

Acknowledgments

This work was supported by ESPRIT Project 29261 – MIXMODEST. The authors wish to thank the anonymous reviewers for their valuable comments.

References

1. Bäck, T.: Evolutionary Algorithms in Theory and Practice. Oxford University Press, Oxford, UK (1996)
2. Darwin, C.: On the Origin of Species by Means of Natural Selection. John Murray, London, UK (1859)
3. Drechsler, R.: Evolutionary Algorithms for VLSI CAD. Kluwer Academic Publishers, Dordrecht, The Netherlands (1998)
4. Sipper, M., Mange, D., Sanchez, E.: Quo vadis evolvable hardware? Communications of the ACM **42** (1999) 50–56
5. Thompson, A., Layzell, P.: Analysis of unconventional evolved electronics. Communications of the ACM **42** (1999) 71–79
6. Liberali, V., Rossi, R., Torelli, G.: Crosstalk effects in mixed-signal ICs in deep submicron digital CMOS technology. Microelectronics Journal **31** (2000) 893–904
7. Pedram, M.: Power minimization in IC design: Principles and applications. ACM Trans. on Design Automation of Electronic Systems **1** (1996) 3–56
8. Jackson, L. B.: Digital Filters and Signal Processing. Kluwer Academic Publishers, Dordrecht, The Netherlands (1986)

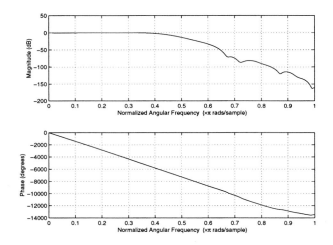

Fig. 13. Frequency response of the best filter generated (pass band: 0 ... 0.35)

9. Jackson, L. B.: Signals, Systems, and Transforms. Addison-Wesley, Reading, MA, USA (1991)
10. Zhao, Q., Tadokoro, Y.: A simple design of FIR filters with power-of-two coefficients. IEEE Trans. Circ. and Syst. **35** (1988) 556–570
11. Pirsch, P.: Architectures for Digital Signal Processing. John Wiley & Sons, Chichester, UK (1998)
12. Koza, J. R.: Genetic Programming: on the Programming of Computers by Means of Natural Selection. The MIT Press, Cambridge, MA, USA (1993)
13. Miller, J. F., Thomson, P.: Cartesian genetic programming. In Poli, R. et al. (Eds.), Genetic Programming European Conference (EuroGP 2000), Springer-Verlag, Berlin, Germany (2000) 121–132
14. Thompson, A., Layzell, P., Zebulum, R. S.: Explorations in design space: Unconventional electronics design through artificial evolution. IEEE Trans. Evolutionary Computation **3** (1999) 167–196
15. The Mathworks, Inc.: , Signal Processing Toolbox. Natick, MA, USA (1983)

Studying the Influence of Communication Topology and Migration on Distributed Genetic Programming

Francisco Fernández[2], Marco Tomassini[1], and Leonardo Vanneschi[1]

[1] Computer Science Institute, University of Lausanne
1015 Lausanne, Switzerland
[2] Dpto. Arquitectura y Tecnología de Computadores
Universidad de Extremadura, Cáceres, Spain

Abstract. In this paper we present a systematic experimental study of some of the parameters influencing parallel and distributed genetic programming (PADGP) by using three benchmark problems. We first present results on the system's communication topology and then we study the parameters governing individual migration between subpopulations: the number of individuals sent and the frequency of exchange. Our results suggest that fitness evolution is more sensitive to the migration factor than the communication topology.

1 Introduction

Evolutionary algorithms (EAs) have traditionally been thought of as sequential algorithms. Although results have been generally encouraging, the time that sequential EAs require to find solutions is sometimes prohibitive. This has led researchers towards searching for ways to accelerate the convergence process in evolving populations. One obvious solution is the application of parallel processing to evolutionary computation. Parallel and distributed versions of evolutionary algorithms not only lead to faster execution but also seem to favor the quality and the robustness of the solutions when structured settings for the population are used. This leads to various spatial approaches such as the *island* model [3] or the *cellular* model [10]. The island model features geographically separated subpopulations among which an exchange of individuals takes place periodically. In the cellular model individuals are placed on a grid, one individual per grid point and all the genetic operators work locally within a small neighborhood of each individual. In the present work we will limit ourselves to the island model, which is by far the most common one in genetic programming (GP). Cantú-Paz and Goldberg [2] and also Whitley *et al.* [15] among others have studied the performance of parallel island genetic algorithms. Andre and Koza [1] in the multipopulation case and Oussaidène *et al.* [12] in the case of parallel fitness evaluation, have been among the first in applying parallel methodologies to GP. But these early studies referred to particular problems with particular settings of the relevant parameters and did not provide general heuristics for guiding the

J. Miller et al. (Eds.): EuroGP 2001, LNCS 2038, pp. 51–63, 2001.
© Springer-Verlag Berlin Heidelberg 2001

choice of researchers as far as those parameters are concerned. Punch [13] was the first in trying to experimentally analyse the dynamics of distributed GP on a few test problems but he did not study the influence of parameters in detail.

Given this state of affairs we decided to start a more systematic study of the relevant issues in Parallel and Distributed Genetic Programming (PADGP). A thorough investigation would require modeling the distributed evolutionary process mathematically but this is very difficult yet, if not impossible, given the present state of GP theory. Therefore, we set out for an empirical study by using simulation. In any event, such a study is a prerequisite for a more principled investigation, the aim being to allow researchers to choose reasonable parameter values in their work.

In previous work [5] we focused on two important parameters in PADGP: the total number of individuals to be used for a given problem and the number of populations. Using a few benchmark problems and a couple of real-life applications, we came to the conclusion that there exists a nearly optimal region for these parameters for each given problem. Other important parameters of PADGP are the communication topology of the populations, the frequency of individual migration and the number of migrating individuals. In [5] these were kept fixed at reasonable values that were determined empirically or taken from the literature. In the present article we complete our observations with an empirical study of the remaining parameters.

The next section 2 describes the parallel model we are using and presents the implementation and the software tools. Section 3 describes the benchmark problems and the statistical measures. Section 4 presents experimental results on the topology comparison and section 5 does the same for the migration parameters. We offer our conclusions in section 6.

2   Parallel and Distributed Genetic Programming (PADGP)

PADGP is based on separated subpopulations that evolve nearly independently of each other. A loose coupling is given by sporadic individual exchange, also called migration. With some specified frequency, a portion of the individuals are allowed to migrate among subpopulations according to different exchange patterns. Two ideas are behind this model: exploring different search areas via different subpopulations, and maintaining diversity within populations thanks to the exchange of individuals. The most common ways for structuring the subpopulations are rings, 2-D and 3-D meshes and hypercubes. The ring and the grid topologies are depicted in figure 1. A *random* communication topology can also be defined in which a given subpopulation sends its emigrants to a randomly chosen subpopulation different from itself.

The most common replacement policy consists in replacing the worst k individuals in the receiving population with k immigrants and is the one used here although other less deterministic schemes have also been used. Several parameters must be taken into account when working with this model: the number of

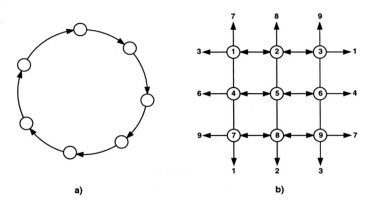

Fig. 1. Two commonly used distributed GP topologies: a) the "ring" topology, b) the "mesh" topology. In the mesh topology processors "wrap around", giving a toroidal structure. The arrows show the direction of the exchange.

subpopulations, the subpopulation size, the frequency of exchange, the number of migrating individuals and the migration topology. As noted in the Introduction, we already studied the influence of the first two in [5]. Here we investigate how the remaining three parameters affect the evolutionary dynamics namely, the communication topology, the number of migrating individuals and the frequency of migration. We must point out that our multipopulation model is *homogeneous*, meaning that each subpopulation has the same individual representation and the same GP parameters. *Heterogeneous* models featuring different parameters or different individual encodings in different populations have also been proposed [9]. In this study we have limited ourselves to homogeneous models which are the most common and easier to investigate. We also remark that sending individuals takes places *synchronously* in our model, while the reception can be asynchronous.

2.1   Implementation and Software Tools

PADGP could be implemented either on a true distributed memory multicomputer or on a network of workstations. The latter is the preferred solution for reasons of cost and availability. Furthermore, if a dedicated cluster is used and a high-speed interconnection network is provided, performances are comparable with those of true parallel computers at a fraction of the cost and with the advantage of the presence of all the standard software tools and state-of-the art off-the-shelf processors on the workstations (see [7]). The implementation of the tool used in this study can be divided into two components: a parallel genetic programming *kernel* implemented in C++ and with MPI message passing, and a graphical user interface (GUI). The parallel system was designed starting from the public domain GPC++ package [14].

The computation can be basically thought of as a collection of processes, each process representing a population for the specific genetic programming problem. The processes/populations can be evolved in parallel and exchange information using the MPI primitives. The messages exchanged by these processes are groups of GP individuals and the communication happens through another process called the *master* that runs in parallel with the others and that implements a given communication topology. The master also sends termination signals to the other processes at the end of the evolution.

Our GUI is written in Java and it was designed so as to be clean and easy to use. Information is displayed on a window featuring the actions that the user can follow. On-line and off-line statistics are easily obtained and automatically displayed. A more detailed description of the software tool, including the graphical interface, can be found in [6].

3   Methodology and Problems Description

In this section we present the methodology used for carrying out the experiments and we describe the test problems studied. The tool we used was the PADGP described in section 2.1.

3.1   Effort of Computation

When using an evolutionary parallel algorithm, one must carefully judge the notion of "improved performance" as improvements could be due to two factors:

- The time saved by a simultaneous execution of code.
- The possible improvement due to the parallel nature of the algorithm.

While the first factor is useful for shortening the time required to find solutions in GP, which is often a slow process, the second might uncover new features of the algorithms compared to the sequential version and our experiments were designed to explore the latter. We have analysed the data by means of the *effort of computation* which has been measured as the total number of nodes GP has evaluated in a population for a given number of generations. To calculate this measure, we must firstly compute the average number of nodes at a generic generation g, taking into account all the populations that are simultaneously working (we will indicate it as avg_length_g) and then compute the partial effort at that generation (that we will indicate as PE_g) defined as:

$$PE_g = i \times p \times avg\_length_g,$$

where p is the number of populations and i is the number of individuals per population. Finally, we calculate the computational effort E_g, at generation g, as

$$E_g = PE_g + PE_{g-1} + PE_{g-2} + ... + PE_0.$$

Thus the computation effort for generation g is the total number of nodes that have been evaluated before generation $g + 1$ takes place. Obviously, this measure is problem-specific but it is useful for comparing different solutions of the same problem.

Since we are working with stochastic processes several executions are required for a given experiment to obtain statistically significant results. The effort is thus computed for each experiment as the average value of 60 runs, each time with a different randomly initialized population. For all experiments we have used a standard GP algorithm on each node, with tournament selection of size 10, maximum crossover depth 17, crossover rate 1, mutation probability 0.01.

3.2   Even Parity 5 Problem

The problem is to decide the parity of a set of 5 bits [8]. The Boolean even-k-parity function of k Boolean arguments returns True if an even number of its Boolean arguments are True, otherwise it returns False. For $k = 5$, 32 different combinations are possible, so 32 fitness cases must be checked to evaluate the accuracy of a particular program in the population. The fitness can be computed as the number of mistakes over the 32 cases. Every problem to be solved by means of GP needs a set of functions and terminals. In the case of the Evenp-5 problem, the set of functions we have employed is the following: $F = \{NAND, NOR\}$ and the terminals are: $T = \{A, B, C, D, E\}$.

3.3   The Artificial Ant Problem on the Santa Fe Trail

This problem aims to identify the path of an artificial ant so as to find all the food pellets lying along the "Santa Fe Trail", on a square toroidal grid in the plane [8]. The problem involves primitive operations enabling the ant to move forward, turn right, turn left and sense food. The function and terminal sets for this problem contains the actions which the ant should execute and are explained in detail in [8]. The natural fitness measure for this problem is the amount of food eaten by the ant during its trail, where a piece of food is eaten whenever the ant steps into the square containing it.

3.4   The Field Programmable Gate Array (FPGA) Problem

This is a real-life problem which consists in programming *Field Programmable Gate Arrays* (FPGAs). FPGAs are arrays of prefabricated logic blocks and wire segments with user-programmable logic and routing resources [11]. The problem when using FPGAs is that circuit descriptions obtained during logic synthesis must be mapped into FPGAs. The well known process of placement and routing must be carried out which is usually a difficult problem to solve. In some previous research [4] we have applied GP for solving this problem. Here we are using the problem to study how PADGP performs in the case of a hard real-life application.

4   Comparing Topologies

We compared the influence of the communication topology on the evolutionary
process on three problems: the even parity, the ant and the FPGA problem. The
topologies used were the ring, the two-dimensional grid and the random topology
(see section 2). The number of populations has been kept fixed to a suitable value
of nine (see section 2), also taking into account that we needed at least nine
islands to implement the grid topology. In all cases we made our measurements
for a few population sizes in order to ascertain whether this parameter has an
influence on the results. In all the following figures "circle" is a synonymous for
ring.

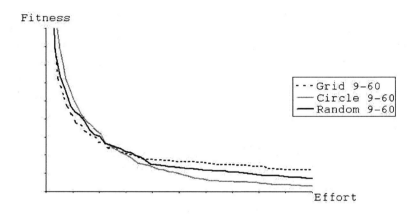

Fig. 2. Fitness as a function of the computational effort. Ant problem. Nine populations
of 50 individuals each.

For the ant problem we found that the ring and the random topology achieve
better results than the mesh for the population sizes tested (see figure 2). The
grid topology gives the best results for the even 5 parity problem when the
subpopulations size is large, as one can see in figure 3. This is in agreement with
the findings of Andre and Koza [1]. On the other hand, when the subpopulation
size is smaller ring and random give slightly better results (figure 4).

In the case of the FPGA problem, for population sizes of 25 and 50 individuals
the random topology gives better results (figure 5). As the population size grows
up to 100 individuals or more the random topology looses its advantage and the
results are almost the same for the three architectures (figure 6).

In conclusion, we observed that the differences among the topologies as far as
the efficiency of solution is concerned are narrow and thus topology does not seem
to be the most important factor in PADGP. On the other hand, the random and

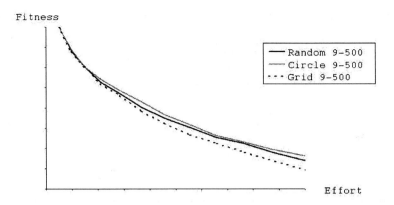

Fig. 3. Fitness as a function of the computational effort. Even 5 parity problem. Nine populations of 500 individuals each.

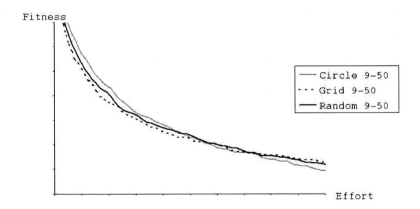

Fig. 4. Fitness as a function of the computational effort. Even 5 parity problem. Nine populations with 50 individuals per population.

the ring topologies possess an advantage in terms of communication efficiency. In fact, a m subpopulations ring or random system only sends m messages at each iteration whereas a $n \times n = m$ grid topology sends $4 \times m$ messages. All considered, using the random topology seems to be advisable in view of the above results given that this topology is the easiest to implement and the more natural one in that it does not prescribe a fixed exchange pattern.

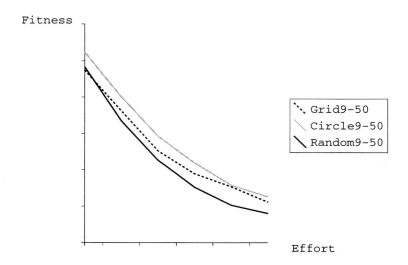

Fig. 5. Fitness as a function of the computational effort. FPGA problem. Nine populations with 50 individuals per population.

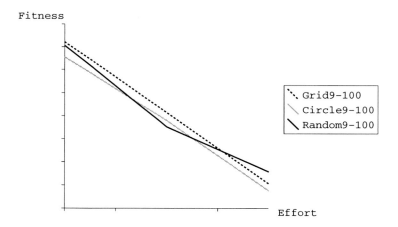

Fig. 6. Fitness as a function of the computational effort. FPGA problem. Nine populations with 100 individuals per population.

5   Studying Migration Parameters

In this section we study the influence of the migration of individuals among subpopulations upon the convergence process. In what follows we call *period* the number of generations elapsed between two successive exchanges of individuals among subpopulations and we call *grain* the number of individuals that are exchanged. In the studies presented in [5] frequency and grain were set to 1. Although this choice is a sensible one and gave a common ground for the investigation of population parameters, now we are interested in varying the frequency and the grain over a wide range in order to assess their influence on the evolutionary process. In the following graphs we monitor what fitness level is reached as the period and the grain are changed, after fixing a maximum computational effort for each problem. All the results reported below are averages over 60 executions. In all the tests the number of individuals, the number of subpopulations and the communication topology were fixed at the outset in order to study the influence of individual migration.

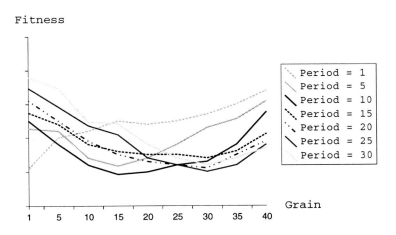

Fig. 7. Even Parity 5 Problem: curves represent fitness as a function of the grain for several values of the period. Five subpopulations with 100 individuals each. The communication topology is random.

Even Parity 5 Problem. For this problem results are shown in figure 7 where fitness curves are given as a function of the grain for a number of period values. This figure shows that the best value of the fitness is reached by the curve representing the period 10 and it is reached for a value of the grain equal to 15. We can also note that for low grain values it is preferable to exchange individuals at each iteration (i.e. period = 1). For values of the grain from 5 to 20 it is better to exchange individuals each 10 iterations, but also a value of the period equal to 5 gives satisfactory results. For values of the grain greater than 25, it is better to exchange individuals less frequently, i.e. each 20 or 25 iterations. This was

expected, since too much mixing of the populations slows down the convergence
process.

The Artificial Ant Problem. The averaged results for the ant problem are depicted in figure 8.

Fitness

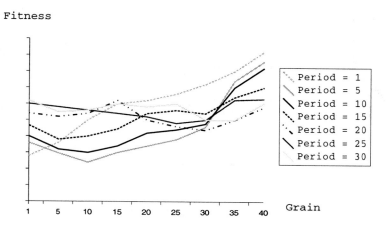

Fig. 8. Ant Problem: curves represent fitness as a function of the grain for several values of the period. Five subpopulations with 100 individuals each. The communication
topology is random.

The figure shows that the best value of the fitness is reached by the curve
representing the period 5 for a value of the grain equal to 10. This means that,
for this problem, a convenient solution consists in exchanging blocks of 10 individuals every 5 iterations. We also remark that for low values of the grain it
is in general better to exchange individuals at each iteration (i.e. period = 1).
For values of the grain from 5 to 25 it is better to exchange individuals with a
period of 5 iterations, but a value of the period equal to 10 gives satisfactory
results too. For values of the grain greater than 30 exchanging individuals less
frequently gives better results due to a smaller mixing effect in the subpopulations. However, for the ant problem large grains always give results that are
worse.

The Field Programmable Gate Array (FPGA) Problem. The average fitness results for this problem are given in figure 9.
 This figure shows that the best value of the fitness is reached by the curve
representing the period 5 for a value of the grain equal to 10. Almost the same
result of fitness value is also reached by the curve representing period 10 for a
value of the grain equal to 5. For low values of the grain it is better to exchange
individuals at each iteration (i.e. period = 1) or with a period up to 5. For

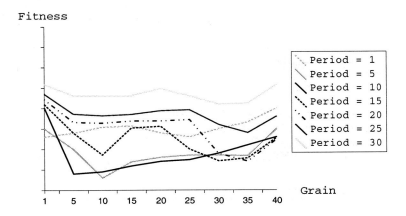

Fig. 9. FPGA Problem: curves represent fitness as a function of the grain for several values of the period. Five subpopulations with 100 individuals each. The communication topology is random.

values of the grain from 3 to 25 it is better to exchange individuals each 5 up to 10 iterations. For values of the grain greater than 30 it is better to exchange individuals less frequently, i.e. each 15 or 20 iterations.

6   Conclusions

In this paper we have studied in detail the influence of the communication topology and of the individual migration parameters on the efficiency of PADGP as a problem solver using two well-known GP benchmarks and a real-life problem. The present study completes our previous investigations which dealt with the effect of the total number of individuals and the number of subpopulations[5] and is, to our knowledge, the first systematic one in the field.

Concerning the topology, the general conclusion is that the communication architecture does not have a marked influence on the results. However, the random topology, which was our choice in previous studies, has been confirmed as being at least as good as the ring and the grid presenting at the same time some implementation advantages.

The results we obtained on the migration issue are reasonable and consistent with those obtained on isolated cases by other researchers. Overall, the numbers that have been empirically chosen by researchers in these last few years have been confirmed: for best results the number of individuals to be sent to another population (i.e. the grain) is about 10% of the population size, and the exchanges should take place every 5 to 10 generations. The results make it also clear that, if few individuals are exchanged, then it is best to do so frequently. On the contrary, a large grain should go hand in hand with a low frequency of exchange, otherwise the genetic material in the populations does not have the time to improve sufficiently from one exchange to the next. But too large a grain slows down the convergence process anyway since this brings about an homogenisation effect that counters the necessary genetic drift of the artificial evolution. All considered, frequent exchanges of a few individuals are to be preferred to infrequent migrations of large blocks. A final important remark is that, contrary to what was the case for population and number of individuals, the period between exchanges and grain results are consistently similar across all the benchmark problems. In other words, these parameter values seem to be robust against problem classes, although to confirm the trend more problems should be studied.

References

1. D. Andre and J. R. Koza. Parallel genetic programming: A scalable implementation using the transputer network architecture. In P. Angeline and K. Kinnear, editors, *Advances in Genetic Programming 2*, pages 317–337, Cambridge, MA, 1996. The MIT Press.
2. E. Cantú-Paz and D. E. Goldberg. Modeling idealized bounding cases of parallel genetic algorithms. In J. R. Koza, K. Deb, M. Dorigo, D. B. Fogel, M. Garzon, H. Iba, and R. L. Riolo, editors, *Genetic Programming 1997: Proceedings of the Second Annual Conference*, pages 456–462. Morgan Kaufmann, San Francisco, CA, 1997.
3. J. P. Cohoon, S. U. Hedge, W. N. Martin, and D. Richards. Punctuated equilibria: A parallel genetic algorithm. In J. J. Grefenstette, editor, *Proceedings of the Second International Conference on Genetic Algorithms*, page 148. Lawrence Erlbaum Associates, 1987.
4. F. Fernández, J. M. Sánchez, and M. Tomassini. Feasibility study of genetic programming for solving the problem of placement and routing on FPGAs. In *Proceedings of the XV Conference on Design of Circuits and Integrated Systems (DCIS 2000)*, pages 24–28. LIRMM, Montpellier University, 2000.
5. F. Fernández, M. Tomassini, W. F. Punch III, and J. M. Sánchez. Experimental study of multipopulation parallel genetic programming. In Riccardo Poli, Wolfgang Banzhaf, William B. Langdon, Julian F. Miller, Peter Nordin, and Terence C. Fogarty, editors, *Genetic Programming, Proceedings of EuroGP'2000*, volume 1802 of *LNCS*, pages 283–293. Springer-Verlag, Heidelberg, 2000.
6. F. Fernández, M. Tomassini, L. Vanneschi, and L. Bucher. A distributed computing environment for genetic programming using MPI. In J. Dongarra, P. Kaksuk, and N. Podhorzsky, editors, *Recent Advances in Parallel Virtual Machine and Message Passing Interface*, volume 1908 of *Lecture Notes in Computer Science*, pages 322–329. Springer-Verlag, Heidelberg, 2000.
7. F. H. Bennet III, J. Koza, J. Shipman, and O. Stiffelman. Building a parallel computer system for $18,000 that performs a half peta-flop per day. In W. Banzhaf, J. Daida, A. E. Eiben, M. Garzon, V. Honavar, M. Jakiela, and R. Smith, editors, *Proceedings of the genetic and evolutionary computation conference GECCO'99*, pages 1484–1490, San Francisco, CA, 1999. Morgan Kaufmann.
8. J. R. Koza. *Genetic Programming*. The MIT Press, Cambridge, Massachusetts, 1992.

9. S. C. Lin, W. F. Punch, and E. D. Goodman. Coarse-grain parallel genetic algorithms: Categorization and a new approach. In *Sixth IEEE SPDP*, pages 28–37, 1994.

10. B. Manderick and P. Spiessens. Fine-grained parallel genetic algorithms. In J. D. Schaffer, editor, *Proceedings of the Third International Conference on Genetic Algorithms*, page 428. Morgan Kaufmann, 1989.

11. D. Mange and M. Tomassini (Eds). *Bio-Inspired Computing Machines: Towards Novel Computational Architectures*. Presses Polytechniques et Universitaires Romandes, Lausanne, 1998.

12. M. Oussaidène, B. Chopard, O. Pictet, and M. Tomassini. Parallel genetic programming and its application to trading model induction. *Parallel Computing*, 23:1183–1198, 1997.

13. W. Punch. How effective are multiple popululations in genetic programming. In J. R. Koza, W. Banzhaf, K. Chellapilla, K. Deb, M. Dorigo, D. B. Fogel, M. Garzon, D. Goldberg, H. Iba, and R. L. Riolo, editors, *Genetic Programming 1998: Proceedings of the Third Annual Conference*, pages 308–313, San Francisco, CA, 1998. Morgan Kaufmann.

14. T. Weinbrenner. Genetic Programming Kernel version 0.5.2 C++ Class Library. *University of Darmstadt*.

15. D. Whitley, S. Rana, and R. B. Heckendorn. Island model genetic algorithms and linearly separable problems. In D. Corne and J. L. Shapiro, editors, *Evolutionary Computing: Proceedings of the AISB Workshop, Lecture notes in computer science, vol. 1305*, pages 109–125. Springer-Verlag, Berlin, 1997.

CAGE: A Tool for Parallel Genetic Programming Applications

Gianluigi Folino, Clara Pizzuti, and Giandomenico Spezzano

ISI-CNR, c/o DEIS, Via P. Bucci Cubo 41C
Univ. della Calabria, 87036 Rende (CS), Italy
{folino,pizzuti,spezzano}@si.deis.unical.it

Abstract. A new parallel implementation of genetic programming based on the cellular model is presented and compared with the island model approach. Although the widespread belief that cellular model is not suitable for parallel genetic programming implementations, experimental results show a better convergence with respect to the island approach, a good scale-up behaviour and a nearly linear speed-up.

1 Introduction

The capability of genetic programming (GP) in solving hard problems coming from different application domains has been largely recognized. Many problems have been succesfully solved by means of GP. It is well known that, in order to find a solution, the evaluation of the fitness is the dominant consuming time task for GP and evolutionary algorithms in general. The success of GP, furthermore, often depends on the use of a population of sufficient size. The choice of the size is determined by the level of complexity of the problem. When applied to large hard problems GP performances may thus drastically degrade because of the computationally intensive task of fitness evaluation of each individual in the population. In the last few years there has been an increasing interest in realizing high performance GP implementations to extend the number of problems GP can cope with. To this end different approaches to parallelize genetic programming have been studied and proposed [3–7, 11, 12, 15]. Extensive surveys on the subject can be found in [2, 18].

In this paper we present a tool for parallel genetic programming applications, called *CAGE (CellulAr GEneting programming tool)*, that realizes a fine-grained parallel implementation of genetic programming on distributed-memory parallel computers. Experimental results on some classical test problems shows that the cellular model outperforms both the sequential canonical implementation of GP and the parallel island model. Furthermore parallel cellular GP has a nearly linear speed-up and a good scale-up behaviour.

The paper is organized as follows. In section 2 a brief overview of the main parallel implementations proposed is given. In section 3 the cellular parallel implementation of GP is presented. In section 4 we show the results of the method on some standard problems.

J. Miller et al. (Eds.): EuroGP 2001, LNCS 2038, pp. 64–73, 2001.

2   Parallel Genetic Programming

Two main approaches to parallel implementations of GP have been proposed :
the *coarse-grained* (*island*) model [10] and the *fine-grained* (*grid*) model [13].

The island model divides the population into smaller subpopulations, called
demes. A standard genetic programming algorithm works on each deme and is
responsible for initializing, evaluating and evolving its own subpopulation. The
standard GP algorithm is augmented with a *migration* operator that periodically exchanges individuals among the subpopulations. How many individuals
migrates and how often migration should occur are parameters of the method
that have to be set [2, 18].

In the grid model (also called cellular [19]) each individual is associated with
a spatial location on a low-dimensional grid. The population is considered as
a system of active individuals that interact only with their direct neighbors.
Different neighborhoods can be defined for the cells. The most common neighborhoods in the two-dimensional case are the 4-neighbor (*von Neumann neighborhood*) consisting of the North, South, East, West neighbors and 8-neighbor
(*Moore neighborhood*) consisting of the same neighbors augmented with the diag-
onal neighbors. Fitness evaluation is done simultaneously for all the individuals
and selection, reproduction and mating take place locally within the neighborhood. Information slowly diffuses across the grid giving rise to the formation of
semi-isolated niches of individuals having similar characteristics.

In [18] it is noted that parallel evolutionary algorithms benefit of the multipopulation approach since the same solution quality can be obtained by using
many populations instead of a single population with the same total number of
individuals. The same results, however, have not been obtained for the coarse
grained parallel implementations of genetic programming. In fact, though Koza
[1, 9] reported a super-linear speedup for the 5-parity problem, in [14], for the
ant and the royal-tree problems, Punch found poorer results of convergence
with respect to the canonical *GP*. In the next section we present a parallel
implementation of *GP* through the cellular model. Afterwards, we show that
such an approach gives better convergence results with respect to both canonical
and island model implementations of *GP*.

3   Parallel Implementation of CAGE

This section describes the implementation of *CAGE* on distributed-memory parallel computers. To parallelize *GP CAGE* uses the cellular model. The cellular
model is fully distributed with no need of any global control structure and is
naturally suited to be implemented on parallel computers. It introduces fundamental changes in the way *GP* works. In this model, the individuals of the
population are located on a specific position in a toroidal two-dimensional grid
and the selection and mating operations are performed, cell by cell, only among
the individual assigned to a cell and its neighbors. This local reproduction has
the effect of introducing an intensive communication among the individuals that

allows to disseminate good solutions across the entire population, but that influences the performance of the parallel implementation of GP. Moreover, unlike genetic algorithms, where the size of individuals is fixed, the genetic programs are individuals of varying sizes and shapes. This requires a large amount of local memory and introduces an unbalanced computational load per grid point. Therefore, an efficient representation of the program trees must be adopted and a load balancing algorithm must be employed to maintain the same computational load among the processing nodes.

The best way to overcome the drawbacks associated with the implementation of the cellular model on a general purpose distributed-memory parallel computer is to use a partitioning technique based upon domain decomposition in conjunction with the *Single-Program-Multiple-Data (SPMD)* programming model. According to this model, an application on N processing elements (PEs) is composed of N similar processes, each of which operates on a different set of data. For an effective implementation, data should be partitioned in such a way that communication takes place locally and the computation load be shared among the PEs in a balanced way. This approach increases the granularity of the cellular model transforming it from a fine-grained model to a coarse-grained model. In fact, instead of assigning only one individual to a processor, the individuals are grouped by *slicing up* the grid and assigning a *slice* of the population to a node.

$CAGE$ implements the cellular GP model using a one-dimensional domain decomposition (in the x direction) of the grid and an explicit message passing to exchange information among the domains. This decomposition is more efficient than a two-dimensional one. In fact in the two-dimensional decomposition the number of messages sent is higher, though the size of the messages is lower. On the other hand, in one-dimensional decomposition, the number of messages sent is lower but their size is higher. Considering that the startup times are much greater than the transfer times, the second approach is more efficient than the former. The concurrent program which implements the architecture of $CAGE$ is composed of a set of identical *slice processes*. No coordinator process is necessary because the computational model is completely decentralized. Each slice process, which contains a strip of elements of the grid, runs on a single processing element of the parallel machine and executes the code, shown in figure 1, on each subgrid point thus updating all the individuals of the sub-population.

Each slice process uses the parameters read from a file (step 1) to configure the genetic programming algorithm that has to be executed on each subgrid point. The parameters concern the population size, the max depth that the trees can have after the crossover, the parsimony factor, the number of iterations, the number of neighbors of each individual, the replacement policy. We have implemented three replacement policies: *direct* (the best of the offspring always replaces the current individual), *greedy* (the replacement occurs only if offspring is fitter), *probabilistic* (the replacement happens according to difference of fitness between parent and offspring (*simulated annealing*)).

1.   Read from a file the configuration parameters
2.   Generate a random sub-population
3.   Evaluate the individuals of the sub-population
4.   **while** not numGenerations **do**
5.   update boundary data
6.   **for** x =1 **to** length
7.   **for** y =1 **to** height
8.   select an individual k (located at position [x',y'])
         neighboring with i (located at position [x,y]);
9.   generate offspring from i and k ;
10.   apply the user-defined replacement policy to update i;
11.   mutate i with probability pmut;
12.   evaluate the individual i;
     end for
     end for
   end while

Fig. 1. Pseudocode of the slice process.

The size of the subpopulation of each slice process is calculated by dividing the population for the number of the processors on which CAGE is executed. Each slice process updates sequentially the individuals belonging to its subgrid. Initially, in each process, a random subpopulation is generated (step 2.) and its fitness is evaluated (step 3.). Then, steps 6-12 are executed for generating the new subpopulation for *numGeneration* iterations. The variables *lenght* and *height* define the boundaries of the 2D subgrid that is contained in a process. It should be noted that two copies of the data are maintained for calculating the new population. In fact, as each element of the current population is used many times, the current population cannot be overwritten.

Because of the data decomposition, physically neighboring strips of data are allocated to different processes. To improve the performances and to reduce the overhead due to the remote communications, we have introduced a local copy of boundary data in each process. This avoids to perform remote communication more than once on the same data. Boundary data are exchanged before applying the selection operator. In our implementation, the processes form a logical ring and each processor determines its right and left neighboring processes. Therefore, the communication between processes is local, only the outermost individuals are to be communicated between the slice processes.

All the communications are performed using the *MPI* (*Message Passing Interface*) portable message passing system so that *CAGE* can be executed across different hardware platforms. Since the processes are connected according to a ring architecture and each process has a limited buffer for storing boundary data, we use asynchronous communication in order to avoid processors to idle.

Each processor has two send buffers (*SRbuf, SLbuf*) and two receive buffers (*RRbuf, RLbuf*). The SRbuf and SLbuf buffers correspond to the outermost (right and left) individuals of the subgrid. The receive buffers are added to the subgrid in order to obtain a bordered grid. The exchange of the boundary data occurs, in each process, by two asynchronous send operations followed by two asynchronous receive operation to the right and left neighboring processes. After this, each process waits until the asynchronous operations are completed.

$CAGE$ uses the standard tool for genetic programming sgpc1.1, a simple GP in the C language, freely available at [16], to apply the GP algorithm to each grid point. However, in order to meet the requirements of the cellular GP algorithm, a number of modifications have been introduced.

We used the same data structure of sgpc1.1 to store a tree in each cell. The structure that stores the population has been transformed from a one-dimensional array to a two-dimensional one and we duplicated this structure in order to store the current and the new generated tree. The selection procedure has been replaced with one that uses only the neighborhood cells and the three replacement policies have been added. Crossover is performed between the current tree and the best tree in the neighborhood. Two procedures to *pack* and *unpack* the trees that must be sent to the other processes have been added. The pack procedure is used to send the trees of the boundary data to the neighbor processes in a linearized form. Data are transmitted as a single message in order to minimize the message startup and transmission time. The unpack procedure rebuilds the data and stores them in the new processor's private address space.

The execution of a parallel program is composed of two phases: *computation* and *communication*. During the computation phase each process of the concurrent program implementing the run-time support executes computations which only manipulate data local to this process. These data can be local variables or boundary data received from neighboring processes. The effective data transmission between processes is done at the end of each local computation. This means that, during the computation phase, no data are exchanged.

In order to equally distribute the computational load among the processing nodes $CAGE$ introduces an intelligent partitioning of the grid. The partitioning strategy is a form of *block-cyclic* decomposition. The idea is to split the grid virtually in a number of folds and assign equal parts of each fold to each of the processes as shown in figure 2. This can lead to load balancing provided that the resulting granules (further referred to as strips) are fine enough to assure that the uneven load distribution across folds is statistically insignificant across processes. It should be noted, that the number of folds and processes should be chosen with caution, since the more strips are used, the bigger is the communication overhead among the processing elements. In the next section the experimental results obtained with our approach are presented.

4   Experimental Results

This section shows the performances of our cellular parallel implementation on three test problems well known in the literature: *discovery of trigonometric identities, even-4-parity* and *artificial ants*. The parallel implementation has been realized on a multicomputer Meiko CS-2. For each problem we present the con-

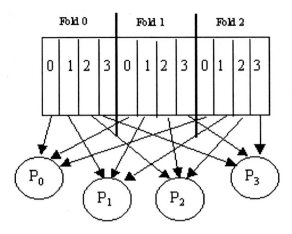

Fig. 2. Load balancing strategy: each fold is divided in four strips.

Table 1. CAGE Parameters

Parameters	Problem Name		
	Regression	Even-4 parity	Ant (Santa Fe)
Terminal symbols	{X,1.0}	$\{d_0, d_1, d_2, d_3\}$	{Forward, Right, Left}
Functions	{+, -, *, %, sin}	{AND, OR NAND, NOR}	{IfFoodAhead Prog2, Prog3}
Population size	3200	3200	3200
Max_depth_for_new_tree	6	6	6
Max_depth_after_crossover	6	17	17
Max_mutant_depth	4	4	2
Grow_method	RAMPED	GROW	RAMPED
Crossover_func_pt_fraction	0.2	0.1	0.8
Crossover_any_pt_fraction	0.2	0.7	0.1
Fitness_prop_repro_fraction	0.1	0.1	0.1
Parsimony_factor	0.0	0.0	0.0

vergence results obtained with *CAGE* and compare them with the sequential canonical *GP* and the island model implementation realized by [11] for the first two problems and the one reported in [14] for the latter problem. We used sgpc1.1 as the canonical sequential implementation of genetic programming. The parameters of the method are shown in table 1. Each problem was run 10 times. For all the experiments we used the *Moore* neighborhood and the *direct* replacement policy.

Experiment 1. ([11]) The *symbolic regression* problem consists in searching for a non trivial mathematical expression that always has the same value of a given mathematical expression. In the experiment our aim was to discover a trigonometric identity for $cos2x$ [8]. 20 values x_i of the independent variable x have been randomly chosen in the interval $[0,2\pi]$ and the corresponding value $y_i = cos2x_i$ computed. The 20 pairs (x_i, y_i) constitute the fitness cases. The fitness is then computed as the sum of the absolute value of the difference between y_i and the value generated by the program on x_i. The maximum number of allowed generations has been set to 100.

Experiment 2. ([11]) The *even-4 parity* problem consists in deciding the parity of a set of 4 bits [8]. A Boolean function receives 4 Boolean variables and it gives true only if an even number of variables is true. Thus the goal function to discover is $f(x_1, x_2, x_3, x_4) = x_1x_2x_3x_4 \lor \overline{x_1}x_2\overline{x_3}x_4 \lor \overline{x_1}x_2x_3\overline{x_4} \lor x_1\overline{x_2}x_3x_4 \lor x_1\overline{x_2}x_3\overline{x_4} \lor x_1x_2\overline{x_3}\overline{x_4} \lor \overline{x_1}\ \overline{x_2}\ \overline{x_3}\ \overline{x_4}$. The fitness cases are the 2^4 combinations of the variables. The fitness is the sum of the Hamming distances between the goal function and the solution found. The maximum number of allowed generations has been set to 100.

Experiment 3. ([14]) The *artificial ant* problem consists in finding the best list of moves that an ant can do on a 32×32 matrix in order to eat all the pieces of food put on the grid [8]. In this experiment we used the *Santa Fe trail* that contains 89 food particles. The fitness function is obtained by diminishing the number of food particles by one every time the ant arrives in a cell containing food. The ant can see the food only if it is in the cell ahead its same direction ($IfFoodAhead$ move) otherwise it can move randomly (*left* or *right*) for two ($Progn2$) or three ($Progn3$) moves. The maximum number of allowed moves has been set to 500.

In figure 3 the convergence results of $CAGE$ with respect to canonical GP are shown for experiment 1 (a) and experiment 2 (b). The figure clearly shows that, after 100 generations, canonical GP is far from the solution whether $CAGE$ after an average of 90 generations is able to discover the trigonometric identity and almost always finds the correct Boolean function for even-4 parity after 100 generations. To compare our method with the island model implementation, in figures 3(c) and 3(d) the results obtained by Niwa and Iba [11] are reported. With regard to cos2x the better implementation they obtain (ring topology) does not always reach a solution after 100 generations, while for the 4-parity they can not find the correct Boolean function neither after 500 generations.

In figure 3(e) the convergence results for the *Ant* problem are shown. The exact solution is almost always found after 100 generations with a population size of 3200 individuals. In figure 3(f) the effect of the population size on the convergence of the method is showed. It can be noticed that the bigger is the size of the population, the lower is the number of generations necessary to find the optimal solution. When the size is 6400, the solution is always found after 70 generations.

In [14] Punch presents the results of his experiments as the number of *Wins* and *Losses*. The wins are denoted as $W : (x, y)$, where x represents the number of optimal solutions found before 500 generations and y the average generation in which the optimal solution was found. The losses are denoted as $L : (q, r, s)$, where q is the number of losses (no optimal solution found before 500 genera-

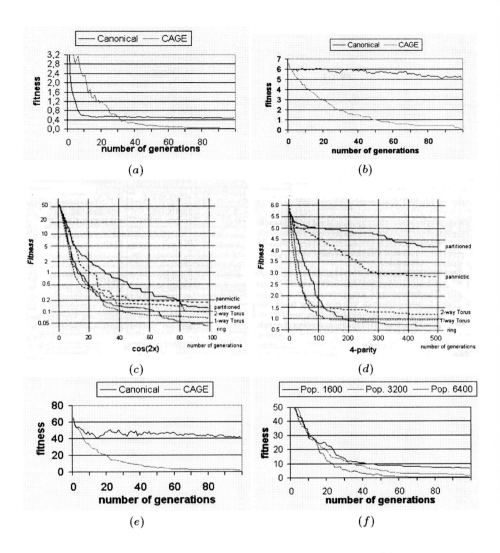

Fig. 3. Experimental results: CAGE for cos2x (a) and 4-parity (b), Niwa and Abi for cos2x (c)and 4-parity (d), CAGE for Ant (e) and Ant convergence for different population sizes.

tions) r is the average best-of-run fitness, and s is the average generation when the best-of-run occurred. To compare our results with those of Punch, we computed the wins and losses by running $CAGE$ the same number of times (16) as Punch reported and the same population size (1000). The best result Punch obtained was W : $(7, 240)$ and L : $(9, 73, 181)$. The result we obtained was W : $(8, 98)$ and L : $(8, 76, 212)$ thus confirming the better performances of the $CAGE$ with respect to the island approach. Finally, in figure 4 the speed-up of the method is showed for experiments 1 and 2.

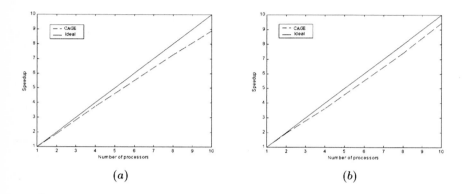

(a) (b)

Fig. 4. Speedup measures for cos2x (a) and even-4 parity (b).

5   Conclusions and Future Work

A tool for parallel genetic programming applications that realizes a fine-grained parallel implementation of genetic programming through cellular model on distributed-memory parallel computers has been presented. Preliminary experimental results shows the good performances of the proposed approach. We are planning an experimental study on a wide number of benchmark problems to substantiate the validity of the cellular implementation.

References

1. Andre D., Koza, J. R. Exploiting the fruits of parallelism: An implementation of parallel genetic programming that achieves super-linear performance. *Information Science Journal*, Elsevier, 1997.
2. Cantú-Paz, E. *A summary of research on parallel genetic algorithms*, Technical Report 950076, Illinois Genetic Algorithm Laboratory, University of Illinois at Urbana Champaign, Urbana, July 1995.

3. Dracopoulos, D. C., Kent, S. Speeding up Genetic Programming: A Parallel BSP implementation. *Genetic Programming 1996, Proceedings of the First Annual Conference*, pp 125-136, MIT Press, Stanford University, July 1996.
4. Fernández, F., Tomassini, M., Punch, W. F., Sánchez, J.M. Experimental Study of Multipopulation Parallel Genetic Programming. *European Conference on Genetic Progamming*, LNCS 1082, Springer, Edinburgh 1999.
5. Fernández, F., Tomassini, M., Vanneschi, L., Bucher, L. A Distributed Computing Environment for Genetic Programming Using MPI. *Recent Advances in Parallel Virtual Machine and Message Passing Interface, 7th European PVM/MPI Users' Group Meeting*, Balatonfured, Hungary, September 2000.
6. Juillé, H., Pollack, J. B. Parallel Genetic Programming on Fine-Grained SIMD Architectures. *Working Notes of the AAAI-95 Fall Symposium on Genetic Programming"*, AAAI Press, 1995.
7. Juillé, H., Pollack, J. B. Massively Parallel Genetic Programming. In P. Angeline and K. Kinnear, editors, *Advances in Genetic Programming: Volume 2*, MIT Press, Cambridge, 1996.
8. Koza, J. R. Genetic Programming: On the Programming of Computers by means of Natural Selection. MIT Press, Cambridge, 1992.
9. J. R. Koza and D.Andre (1995) Parallel genetic programming on a network of transputers. *Technical Report CS-TR-95-1542, Computer Science Department*, Stanford University.
10. W.N. Martin, J. Lienig and J. P. Cohoon (1997), Island (migration) models: evolutionary algorithms based on punctuated equilibria, in T. Bäck, D.B. Fogel, Z. Michalewicz (eds.), *Handbook of evolutionary Computation*. IOP Publishing and Oxford University Press.
11. Niwa, T., Iba, H. Distributed Genetic Programming -Empirical Study and Analisys - *Genetic Programming 1996, Proceedings of the First Annual Conference*, MIT Press, Stanford University, July 1996.
12. Oussaidéne, M., Chopard, B. Pictet, O., Tommasini, M. Parallel Genetic Programming and its Application to Trading Model Induction. *Parallel Computing*, vol. 23, n. 2, September 1997.
13. C. C. Pettey (1997), Diffusion (cellular) models, in T. Bäck, D.B. Fogel, Z. Michalewicz (eds.), *Handbook of evolutionary Computation*. IOP Publishing and Oxford University Press.
14. Punch, W. F. How Effective are Multiple Populations in Genetic Programming. *Genetic Programming 1998, Proceedings of the Third Annual Conference*, MIT Press, University of Winsconsin, July 1998.
15. Salhi, A., Glaser, H., De Roure, D. Parallel Implementation of a Genetic-Programming based Tool for Symbolic Regression. *Technical Report DSSE-TR-97-3*, Dept. Comp. Science, University of Souhampton, 1997.
16. Tackett, W. A., Carmi, A. Simple Genetic Programming in C, *Available through the genetic programmming archive at* ftp://ftp.io.com/pub/genetic-programming/code/sgpc1.tar.Z.
17. T. Toffoli and N. Margolus (1986). *Cellular Automata Machines A New Environment for Modeling.* The MIT Press, Cambridge, Massachusetts.
18. Tomassini M. *Parallel and Distributed Evolutionary Algorithms: A Review*, J. Wiley and Sons, Chichester, K. Miettinen, M. Mkel, P. Neittaanmki and J. Periaux (editors), pp. 113-133, 1999.
19. D.Whitley (1993). Cellular Genetic Algorithms. *Proceedings of the Fifth International Conference on Genetic Algorithms*, Morgan Kaufmann.

Ripple Crossover in Genetic Programming

Maarten Keijzer[1], Conor Ryan[2], Michael O'Neill[3],
Mike Cattolico[4], and Vladan Babovic[5]

[1] DHI Water & Environment, mak@dhi.dk
[2] University of Limerick, conor.ryan@ul.ie
[3] University of Limerick, michael.oneill@ul.ie
[4] Tiger Mountain Scientific Inc., mike@tigerscience.com
[5] DHI Water & Environment, vmb@dhi.dk

Abstract. This paper isolates and identifies the effects of the crossover operator used in Grammatical Evolution. This crossover operator has already been shown to be adept at combining useful building blocks and to outperform engineered crossover operators such as Homologous Crossover. This crossover operator, Ripple Crossover is described in terms of Genetic Programming and applied to two benchmark problems.

Its performance is compared with that of traditional sub-tree crossover on populations employing the standard functions and terminal set, but also against populations of individuals that encode Context Free Grammars. Ripple crossover is more effective in exploring the search space of possible programs than sub-tree crossover. This is shown by examining the rate of premature convergence during the run. Ripple crossover produces populations whose fitness increases gradually over time, slower than, but to an eventual higher level than that of sub-tree crossover.

1 Introduction

An important characteristic that the function and terminal set in any Genetic Programming (GP) experiment should possess is closure [3]. That is, the return type of any node, either function or terminal, can be taken as an argument by any function. An implication of this is that programs produced by GP can only handle a single type, which clearly limits their utility.

Some work on Strongly Typed GP has relieved this by including type information in the system [4, 8, 9, 1]. The most convenient way to describe a representation with multiple types is either through a Context Free Grammar(CFG) where one can specify the parameter and return types of each operator, or through an Attribute Grammar, by virtue of which one can pass very rich information through derivation rules. This information can describe anything from the routine parameter and return types, to the more exotic ones, such as rich type information about data structures created on the fly. An example of this would if one wished to create a grammar that describes the multiplication operator for a structure such a matrix the size of which is not available until derivation time for that particular derivation sequence.

Taking this route, however, one violates the desirable property of closure. Once closure is not guaranteed, one can no longer expect standard GP crossover

J. Miller et al. (Eds.): EuroGP 2001, LNCS 2038, pp. 74–86, 2001.
© Springer-Verlag Berlin Heidelberg 2001

to produce syntactically well formed individuals. This is acknowledged by numerous researchers, all of whom have special, custom-designed constrained crossover operators for their representation scheme [4, 8, 9, 1].

In contrast with these constrained approaches, Grammatical Evolution (GE) [7], [5], a variable length string, GA-based automatic programming method employs a mapping process, where codons (integers) are read from a genome, and used to govern which decisions to make when generating an expression from a CFG. This paper investigates the deceptively simple one-point crossover on variable length strings employed by GE. We term this crossover Ripple Crossover because of its non-local effects on the derivation tree; a single crossover event can remove any number of subtrees to the right of the crossover point.

A number of experiments have been conducted in order to compare the performance of ripple crossover and traditional *sub-tree* crossover with two different representation schemes, i.e. grammars. These experiments show that when using standard GP function and terminal sets, and the closure property they enjoy, ripple crossover appears to be less likely to get trapped in a local optimum than sub-tree crossover.

It is argued that the property of Ripple Crossover to transmit on average half of the genetic material for each parent is the main cause of this. While sub-tree crossover exchanges less and less genetic material when the run progresses, ripple crossover is equally recombinative regardless of the size of the individuals involved.

2   Context Free Grammars and Grammatical Evolution

Context Free Grammars(CFGs) are grammars in which the syntax of a symbol, either a *terminal* which appears in the final output, or a *non-terminal* which is an interim symbol used to help generate the terminals, is the same regardless of what other symbols surround it.

A convenient descriptive notation for CFGs is Backus Naur Form (BNF). BNF grammars consist of **terminals**, which are items that can appear in the language, i.e $+, -$ etc. and **non-terminals**, which can be expanded into one or more terminals and non-terminals. A grammar can be represented by the tuple, $\{N, T, P, S\}$, where N is the set of non-terminals, T the set of terminals, P a set of production rules that maps the elements of N to T, and S is a start symbol which is a member of N. For example, below is a possible BNF for a simple expression, where

$$N = \{expr, op\}$$

$$T = \{+, -, /, *, X, (,)\}$$

$$S = <expr>$$

P can be represented as:

```
(1) <expr> ::= <expr> <op> <expr>      (A)
             | ( <expr> <op> <expr> ) (B)
             | <var>                   (C)

(2) <op> ::= + (A)
           | - (B)
           | / (C)
           | * (D)

(3) <var> ::= X
```

Table 1 summarizes the production rules and the number of choices associated with each of them. When generating a sentence for a particular language, one must choose carefully which productions are to be used, as, depending on the choices made, a sentence may be quite different from the desired one, possibly even of a different length.

Table 1. The number of choices available from each production rule.

Rule no.	Choices
1	3
2	4
3	1

GE exploits this property by maintaining a string of codons (integers) as its genome, which is decoded into a string of choices during the derivation process. In order to select a rule in GE, the next codon value on the genome is examined. As this value typically is larger than the number of available rules for that non-terminal, the modulo of the codon value with the number of rules is taken to decode the choice:

`choice = codonValue MOD numberOfRules`

Consider the selection of a production for rule #1 above. This has three available choices, so the subsequent codon value will have *modulos* 3 applied to it to make the choice.

Substitution of the left-most nonterminal continues until all of them have been replaced by terminals. It is possible for an individual to be over-specified, that is, to have unread codons left over. These codons are simply ignored, but can be subsequently passed on to the offspring. Furthermore, it is also possible for an individual to be under-specified. This happens when all codons have been read, but the individual still contains non-terminals. In this case, several options are available. The individual can be *wrapped*, that is, read through a second time. Wrapping continues until either the individual is completely mapped or a certain upper limit of wrapping events has been reached. The second option is that the individual's genome can be *extended* by making random choices until a complete individual is produced or a depth or size limit is exceeded. If any of these methods fail, the individual is deemed illegal and assigned a suitably punitive fitness value.

Individuals in GE decode into a string of choices that steer the generation of a derivation tree. It is instructive to examine the form these tree take. Quite often the entire genome does not need to be parsed to map an individual to a correct syntactic program. This means that individuals have a *tail* of non-expressed code. The tail is effectively a stack of unexpressed codons. Section 4 describes how crucial the tail is to the system.

3 Closed vs. Context Free Grammars

The term Closed Grammar is used here to denote the type of grammar normally employed by GP practitioners. Although many GP users may be surprised to have it claimed that they have actually being using grammars, rather than simple sets of functions and terminals, this is indeed the case. A function and terminal set implicitly describes a grammar; one indicates the arity of the functions and, as every function can take every terminal as well as the output of every function, it is simply a matter adhering to the arity demands of every function to produce legal programs.

The arity of the functions could easily be described by a CFG. Consider the GP function and terminal set

$$F = \{+, *, -, \%\}$$

$$T = \{x, y\}$$

Where each of the four functions has an arity of two. This can equivalently be expressed in the Context Free Grammar (CFG) :

```
E ::== x | y | (+ E E) | (* E E) | (- E E) | (% E E).
```

where E denotes the start symbol.

This kind of CFG differs from the standard type only in that there is a single non-terminal node. The use of a single non-terminal node implies that the grammar satisfies the closure property, desirable for GP's crossover operator. Notice that use of more than one non-terminal does not preclude a grammar from being closed. In this case, the question of closure can only be resolved by determining if it can be rewritten as an equivalent grammar with a single non-terminal.

If one were to construct a derivation tree for any expression made up from this set, then clearly, any sub-tree from this grammar can replace a non-terminal, regardless of its position in the derivation tree. Standard, untyped, GP exploits this fact, although it uses parse trees rather than derivation trees, an entirely reasonable approach given that there is but a single non-terminal available to the grammar.

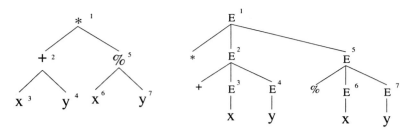

Fig. 1. A parse tree and its derivation tree. Note the numbering of legal crossover points.

Figure 1 shows a parse tree constructed from the above function and terminal set, together with the equivalent derivation tree constructed from the context free grammar also given above. Because this context free grammar uses a prefix notation, the terminals of the derivation tree in Figure 1 form a prefix representation of the parse tree. The prefix ordering can be used as a memory-efficient implementation of a parse tree [2].

The connection between a prefix encoding of a parse tree and a string of rule choices in a context free grammar such as maintained by GE is now obvious. In the prefix encoding, every element is a reference to either a function or terminal. In GE, as this is a closed grammar, every element in the string denotes a choice in the set of rules that are associated with the same symbol. Thus, the prefix string:

* + x y % x y

has a one-to-one correspondence with the string of choices:

3 2 0 1 5 0 1

in the context of the grammar above. However, GE does not maintain a string of choices, but a string of integers, typically bounded above by a number much larger than the maximum number of rules. The decoding from an integer to a choice is usually carried out using the modulo rule. Because of this redundant encoding there is a one to many mapping from a prefix encoding to the integer encoding used by GE.

If one were to introduce more non-terminals into the grammar, sub-tree crossover would have to be constrained to ensure that the result of crossover will be a legal derivation tree. This can be done by employing the type information present in the derivation tree. However, when the number of types in the grammar grows, it can be expected that there will be a limited number of instances of each type in a tree. As sub-tree crossover is usually constrained to swap the same types, it may very well prevent the efficient exploration of the space of possible trees. In grammatical evolution, this is not an issue, as an integer is decoded into a rule at runtime, i.e. decoded in the context of the symbol that is derived at the particular point in the derivation. This property of GE to change its form in the context of a different symbol we refer to as *intrinsic polymorphism*, Figure 2 gives an example of polymorphism in a context free grammar.

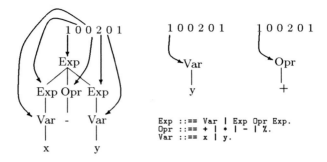

Fig. 2. Intrinsic polymorphism: the same string of numbers can decode to different choices, depending on the symbol that they are being grafted onto.

Notice that, in figure 2, the derivation tree is created in a pre-order fashion, that is, the left-most non-terminal is always the first to be modified by a production rule. This pre-order property has implications for crossover when one views the individuals as trees. We term the crossover employed by GE, and indeed, any tree based system which takes a pre-order view of the trees, *ripple crossover*. The remainder of the paper will focus on *ripple crossover* and its interpretation and utility in a tree based system.

4   Ripple Crossover in GE and GP

The previous section showed that GE individuals can be represented as parse or derivation trees, in a similar way to individuals in GP.

However, ripple crossover does not directly take this kind of tree structure into consideration, as it simply swaps linear structures. Thus, when a crossover event takes place, the nodes to the left of the crossover point are preserved, the nodes to the right are removed. Figure 3 depicts what the effect of ripple crossover has on the underlying derivation tree for a closed grammar: it effectively removes all sub-trees to the right of the crossover point, rendering the derivation tree incomplete, leaving the *spine*, with multiple crossover sites.

Each of the removed sub-trees are then added, intact, to the stack in the individual's tail. Crossover then involves swapping the newly modified tail with that of the mate. Each of the vacated sites on the spine are then filled by a sub-tree from the stack in the tail. If there aren't enough sub-trees removed from the mate, the previously unexpressed genetic material from the stack is used to create new sub-trees.

When a context free grammar with more than a single symbol is used, the picture changes somewhat. The sub-trees that are removed do not have a constant interpretation, that is, there is a possibility that a sub-tree will be grafted

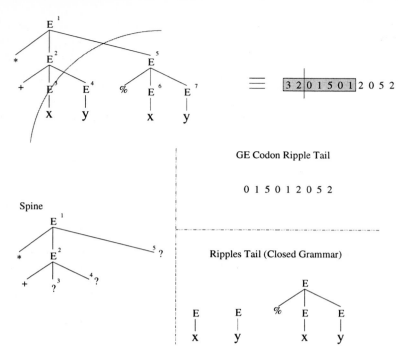

Fig. 3. Selecting crossover point 3 from Figure 1 results in a rippling effect, where points 4,5,6 and 7 will also be removed from the tree. The incomplete tree now needs three subtrees to be complete. The removed sub-trees and the unexpressed tail can be used to fill in crossover points of another tree.

onto a site that is expecting a different symbol. This is where the intrinsic polymorphism of GE takes effect, which can result in a radical re-interpretation of the codons that are used to insert sub-trees.

Because of the more linear nature of ripple crossover, on average half the genetic material of an individual is exchanged during crossover, which is considerably more than for sub-tree crossover, particularly as the average size of individuals increase.

The remainder of the paper will investigate whether the more global nature of ripple crossover indeed succeeds in exploring the search space more effectively than sub-tree crossover.

5   Experiments

In order to compare ripple crossover with sub-tree crossover, a number of experiments were performed on two common benchmark problems: the simple symbolic regression problem and the Santa Fe trail problem. To isolate the effects of crossover within these experiments, all experiments are performed using only crossover, and employ the same initialization procedure. All results have been obtained on 100 independent runs.

The runs using subtree crossover were performed using the derivation tree and associated type information, ripple crossover was performed using a codon based implementation.

The initialization procedure consists of a random walk through the grammar, i.e. making random choices at each choice point. The individuals are initialized by extracting either the constructed derivation tree (for sub-tree crossover) or the sequence of choices (for ripple crossover). This is analagous to GP and GE, respectively. Because such a random walk has a strong tendency to produce short individuals multiple times, a simple occurence check is implemented that re-creates an individual when it is already present in the population.

The sub-tree crossover used in the experiments was implemented in its purest form: no bias was set to select terminals less frequently than non-terminals [3], or, in the case of crossover on context free grammars, no a-priori probabilities were specified to select certain symbols more often than others [8].

The ripple crossover used was also simple. If, during the decoding process the generative string runs out of of genetic material, the individual is killed (i.e. gets worst fitness). No attempt was made to initialize the tail of the individual, no wrapping was used.

For the symbolic regression problem, two grammars are used, the closed grammar:

```
E ::== x | (+ E E) | (* E E) | (- E E) | (/ E E).
```

And the context free grammar:

```
Exp ::== Var | Exp Op Exp.
Var ::== x.
Op  ::== + | * | - | /.
```

Note that the division operator is not protected, division by zero results in a runtime error and the individual will get the worst fitness available [1]. Further details of are provided in Table 2.

The Santa Fe trail problem used the following closed grammar:

```
E ::== move() | left() | right() | iffoodahead(E E) | prog2(E, E).
```

And the context free grammar:

```
Code      ::== Line | prog2(Line, Code).
Line      ::== Condition | Action.
Action    ::== move() | right() | left().
Condition ::== iffoodahead(Code, Code).
```

---

[1] Strictly speaking the closure property is violated by not protecting the division operator, but on the other hand, in realistic applications, default return values in the case of an arithmatic error are usually less desireable than the occasional faulty individual.

Table 2. Setup of the experiments.

Algorithm	Steady state replacement
Tournament size	5
Population Size	500
No. of Generations	50
Crossover prob.	1.0
Significance Testing	two-tailed t-test + resampling test
Significance Level	5%
Simple Symbolic Regression:	
Objective	find $x^4 + x^3 + x^2 + x$
Success Predicate	Root Mean Squared Error < 0.001
Values for x	twenty equally spaced points between [-1,1]
Grammars	See text
Santafe Trail:	
Objective	Navigate the Santa Fe trail
Success Predicate	find 89 pieces of food within 600 steps
Grammars	See text

Where the function *prog2* executes the commands in sequence, *iffoodahead* checks whether there is food in front of the artificial ant and executes either the first or the second argument depending on the result. The *move* function moves the ant forward and *left* and *right* rotate the ant 90 degrees in the specified direction.

6   Results

Figure 4 shows the success rates for the four different configurations on the symbolic regression problem. Although the setups employing ripple crossover both obtain a 100% success rate, it can not be concluded that for this problem ripple crossover performs significantly better than sub-tree crossover on the closed grammar. These three do however perform significantly better than sub-tree crossover on the context free grammar [2]. Failure rates of the ripple crossover on the closed grammar were on average 12% at the end of the run (against 0% on the context free grammar). This did not seem to impede the performance.

For the three top-contenders the symbolic regression problem is easy to solve, so the question remains why the sub-tree crossover on the context free grammar performs so poorly. It may be explained by the fact that the *Var* type in this grammar makes up a large part of any tree. Unlike with the closed grammar, the sub-tree crossover on the context free grammar is constrained to swap like with like, thus always swapping a variable with a variable. However, the fact that

---

[2] Both the t-test and the re-sampling test indicated that the difference was highly significant (probability of a type 1 error was 0%).

there is only one variable in the problem definition results with a large number of crossovers producing identical trees. Although this can be circumvented by avoiding crossing over on the *Var* type, it does beg the question how much the user of such a system must know about the intricate relationship between the grammar, the derivation trees and the genetic operators to be able to set up this system in order to get good results reliably.

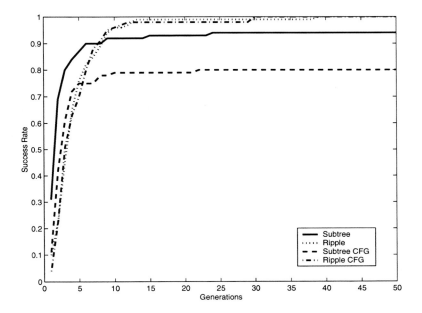

Fig. 4. Success rates on the symbolic regression problem, averaged over 100 runs.

For the Santa Fe trail problem, the success rates are depicted in Figure 5. Here the runs on the context free grammars perform significantly better than their counterparts on the closed grammar. The success rates between ripple crossover and sub-tree crossover on the context free grammar are however not significantly different [3]. Similarly as before, the failure rate was on average 12% on the closed grammar and 0% on the context free grammar.

It is important to note that while the sub-tree crossover seems to converge before generation 20, the ripple crossover runs keep on improving. To investigate whether ripple crossover does indeed help the search to continue to improve, a new set of 100 runs was executed, however this time for 200 generations. Figure 6 clearly depicts the capability of ripple crossover to keep on improving over time. An extended run up to 500 generations (not depicted here) showed that ripple crossover approaches a success rate of 70%, which is almost twice the success rate achieved by sub-tree xover.

---

[3] This was tested on an independent set of 100 runs, not depicted here.

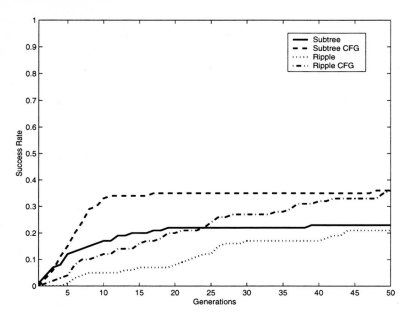

Fig. 5. Success rates on the Santa Fe trail problem, averaged over 100 runs.

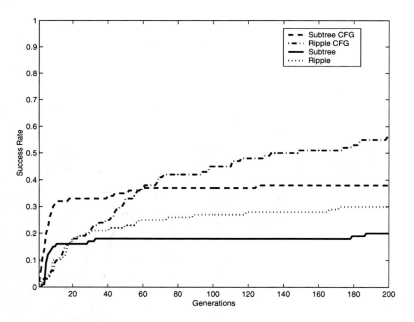

Fig. 6. Success rates on the Santa Fe trail problem, averaged over 100 runs, each running for 200 generations.

7   Discussion

The results bring up some important issues. While it is difficult to identify clearly which crossover method is best, each appears to have its own particular strength. As suggested by an initially steep curve, sub-tree crossover is particularly adept at obtaining solutions very early in a run. However, in all experiments, performance soon plateaus, with only the occasional increase in performance. This finding is in keeping with [6] in which is was suggested that GP performs a global search early on in a run, before gradually changing to a more local search as the run progresses and the population becomes characterised by large and often bloated individuals of similar if not identical fitness.

Ripple crossover, on the other hand, performs a more global search throughout a run, and is far less likely to become trapped at a local minimum. Indeed, for the Symbolic Regression problem, it never got trapped, while in the case of the Santa Fe trail experiments, fitness kept improving. This is because, regardless of how large individuals get, on average half the genetic material is exchanged during each crossover. It is this disruptive behaviour of the crossover operator that drives the population on to continually higher areas in the fitness landscape, but, ironically, it is also the cause of the relatively slow performance at the start of run.

This suggests that the use of ripple crossover will permit longer runs, with less chance of premature convergence. Such a property could be extremely valuable when one tackles more difficult problems that require more time to produce an optimal solution.

8   Conclusions

In this paper we have shown the isomorphism between a simple one-point crossover on variable length strings of integers and ripple crossover on derivation trees. This ripple crossover removes and inserts subtrees to the right of the crossover point, and has the desireable property of exchanging on average half of the genetic material.

Our experiments clearly indicate that experiments which use ripple crossover have an altogether more graceful evolution than their sub-tree employing counterparts. Although the rate of increase is slower at the start relative to sub-tree crossover, it keeps steady for more generations, hence it ends up at a higher level of fitness. This was taken to be an indication that the global nature of ripple crossover makes it less susceptible to get trapped in a local optimum.

In the writing of this paper, the value of linear chromosomes in general, and the GE system in particular, became quite clear to us. Ripple crossover occurs effectively for free in a linear system, because of the pre-order nature of tree construction. Furthermore, the phenomenon of *intrinsic polymorphism* identified by this paper demonstrates the utility of context sensitive genes (groups of codons), that is, genes that can change their behaviour depending on the manner in which they are used. Rather elegantly, although the genes are polymorphic, they will always return to their initial state if used in the same manner again.

Acknowledgements

The first and last author would like to acknowledge the Danish Technical Research Council (STVF) for partly funding Talent Project 9800463 entitled "Data to Knowledge – D2K" http://www.d2k.dk

References

1. Frederic Gruau, *On using syntactic constraints with genetic programming*, Advances in Genetic Programming 2 (Peter J. Angeline and K. E. Kinnear, Jr., eds.), MIT Press, Cambridge, MA, USA, 1996, pp. 377–394.
2. Mike J. Keith and Martin C. Martin, *Genetic programming in C++: Implementation issues*, Advances in Genetic Programming (Kenneth E. Kinnear, Jr., ed.), MIT Press, 1994, pp. 285–310.
3. John R. Koza, *Genetic programming: On the programming of computers by means of natural selection*, MIT Press, Cambridge, MA, USA, 1992.
4. David J. Montana, *Strongly typed genetic programming*, Evolutionary Computation **3** (1995), no. 2, 199–230.
5. Michael O'Neill and Conor Ryan, *Grammatical evolution*, IEEE Trans. Evolutionary Computation (2001).
6. Riccardo Poli, *Is crossover a local search operator?*, Position paper at the Workshop on Evolutionary Computation with Variable Size Representation at ICGA-97, 20 July 1997.
7. Conor Ryan, J. J. Collins, and Michael O Neill, *Grammatical evolution: Evolving programs for an arbitrary language*, Proceedings of the First European Workshop on Genetic Programming (Paris) (Wolfgang Banzhaf, Riccardo Poli, Marc Schoenauer, and Terence C. Fogarty, eds.), LNCS, vol. 1391, Springer-Verlag, 14-15 April 1998, pp. 83–95.
8. Peter Alexander Whigham, *Grammatical bias for evolutionary learning*, Ph.D. thesis, School of Computer Science, University College, University of New South Wales, Australian Defence Force Academy, 14 October 1996.
9. Man Leung Wong and Kwong Sak Leung, *Data mining using grammar based genetic programming and applications*, Genetic Programming, vol. 3, Kluwer Academic Publishers, January 2000.

Evolving Receiver Operating Characteristics for Data Fusion

William B. Langdon and Bernard F. Buxton

Computer Science, University College
Gower Street, London, WC1E 6BT, UK
{W.Langdon,B.Buxton}@cs.ucl.ac.uk
http://www.cs.ucl.ac.uk/staff/W.Langdon
http://www.cs.ucl.ac.uk/staff/B.Buxton
Tel: +44 (0) 20 7679 4436,   Fax: +44 (0) 20 7387 1397

Abstract. It has been suggested that the "Maximum Realisable Receiver Operating Characteristics" for a combination of classifiers is the convex hull of their individual ROCs [Scott *et al.*, 1998]. As expected in at least some cases better ROCs can be produced. We show genetic programming (GP) can automatically produce a combination of classifiers whose ROC is better than the convex hull of the supplied classifier's ROCs.

1   Introduction

There is considerable interest in automatic means of making large volumes of data intelligible to people. The terms Data Mining and Knowledge Discovery are commonly used for this. There are two common aims: 1) to produce a summary of all or an interesting part of the available data 2) to find interesting subsets of the data buried within it. Of course these may overlap. A large range of "intelligent" or "soft computing" techniques, such as artificial neural networks, decision tables, fuzzy logic, radial basis functions, inductive logic programming, support vector machines, are being increasingly used. Many of these techniques have been used in connection with evolutionary computation techniques such as genetic algorithms and genetic programming [Freitas, 1999]. Of particular interest is their use to perform drug discovery for the pharmaceutical industry. To this end we have investigated four techniques and compared the accuracy of the classifiers produced and the computer time needed to train them [Burbidge *et al.*, 2001].

We investigate ways of combining these and other classifiers with a view to producing one classifier which is better than each. Firstly we need to decide how we will measure the performance of a classifier. In practise when using any classifier a balance has to be chosen between missing positive examples and generating too many spurious alarms. Such a balancing act is not easy. Especially in the medical field where failing to detect a disease, such as cancer, has obvious consequences but raising false alarms also has implications for patient well being. Receiver Operating Characteristics (ROC) curves allow us to graph the trade

J. Miller et al. (Eds.): EuroGP 2001, LNCS 2038, pp. 87–96, 2001.

off each classifier makes between "false positive rate" (false alarms) and "true positive rate" [Swets *et al.*, 2000]. An example ROC curve is shown in Fig. 2. We can treat each classifier as though it has a sensitivity parameter (e.g a threshold) which allows the classifier to be tuned. At the lowest sensitivity level the classifier produces no false alarms but detects no positive cases, i.e. the origin of the ROC. As the sensitivity is increased, the classifier detects more positive examples but may also start generating false alarms (false positives). Eventually the sensitivity may become so high that the classifier always claims each case is positive. This corresponds to both true positive and false positive rates being unity, i.e. the top right hand corner of the ROC. Naturally we want our classifiers to have ROC curves that come as close to a true positive rate of one and simultaneously a false positive rate of zero. We score our each classifier by the area under its ROC curve. An ideal classifier has an area of one. We will also require our initial classifiers not only to indicate which class they think a data point belongs to but also how confident they are of this. Values near zero indicate the classifier is not sure, possibly because the data point lies near the classifier's decision boundary.

Arguably the well known "boosting" techniques combine classifiers to get a better one. However boosting is normally applied to only one classifier and produces improvements by iteratively retraining it. Here we will assume the classifiers we have are fixed, i.e. we do not wish to retrain them. Similarly boosting is normally applied by assuming the classifier is operated at a single sensitivity (e.g a single threshold value). This means on each retraining it produces a single pair of false positive and true positive rates. Which is a single point on the ROC rather than the curve we require.

In the next section we discuss Scott's "Maximum Realisable" ROC then (Sect. 3) we present a simple example and show we can easily do better than the "Maximum Realisable ROC". Section 4 shows genetic programming can automatically do better. The discussion of our results (Sect. 5) is followed by our conclusions (Sect. 6) and plans (Sect. 7).

2   "Maximum Realisable" ROC

[Scott *et al.*, 1998] say the "best" way of combining two (or more) classifiers is by taking the convex hull on the ROC curve. I.e. a random linear combination of them both. Scott proves it is always possible to form a classifier with true positive v. false positive rates lying between those of two existing classifiers (A and B) by combing the classifiers. The combination is done by randomly choosing between the answers between given by A and B. E.g. if a ROC point on a line half way between the ROC points of A and of B is needed, then the composite classifier will randomly give the answer given by A half the time and that given by B the other half. (Of course it may not be straightforward to persuade patients to accept such a random diagnose).

3 An Example

Figure 1 shows an example of a deterministic classification problem. Given the features (inputs) the data lie in one of two classes, called positive and negative. The response of two classifiers X and Y are plotted in Fig. 1.

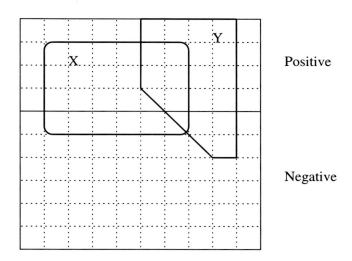

Fig. 1. Data points above horizontal line are in the class, while those below it are not. The deterministic classifiers X and Y return true if the input lies within them and otherwise false.

The performance of the classifiers X and Y in terms of the fraction of positive examples correctly classified as positive (true positives) etc. are calculated in Table 1 and shown graphically in Fig. 2. Also calculated are the performance of two classifier created by taking the union of X and Y and from the intersection of X and Y. Note the performance of both of the combined classifiers is superior to that indicated by the convex hull of X and Y.

Table 1. Classifier Accuracies

Classifier	True Positive	True Negative	False Positive	False Negative
X	18.0/40 = 0.45	54.0/60	6.0/60 = 0.1	22.0/40
Y	15.5/40 = 0.3875	56.0/60	4.0/60 = 0.066666	24.5/40
X ∪ Y	28.0/40 = 0.7	50.5/60	9.5/60 = 0.158333	12.0/40
X ∩ Y	5.5/40 = 0.1375	59.5/60	0.5/60 = 0.008333	34.5/40
1	40.0/40 = 1	.0/60	60.0/60 = 1	.0/40
0	.0/40 = 0	60.0/60	.0/60 = 0	40.0/40

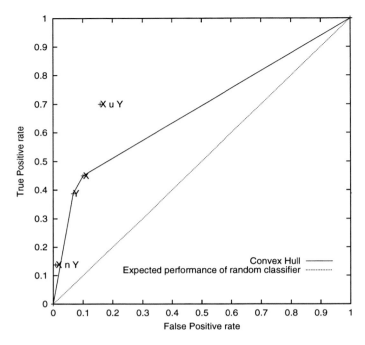

Fig. 2. Receiver Operating Characteristics (ROC) of: the two classifiers shown in Fig. 1, their union $(X \cup Y)$ and their intersection $(X \cap Y)$. The convex hull of X and Y is also plotted. Note, in this example, both the classifier formed by taking the union of X and Y and that formed by taking their intersection lie outside the convex hull.

4 Evolving a Combined Classifier

4.1 Function and Terminal Sets

The function set [Langdon, 1998] included the four floating arithmetic operators $(+, \times, -$ and protected division) and Maximum and Minimum (both takes two arguments) and IFLTE. See Table 2. IFLTE takes four arguments. If the first is less than or equal to the second, IFLTE returns the value of its third argument. Otherwise it returns the value of its fourth argument.

The fixed threshold classifiers shown in Fig. 1 are both extended to include a threshold. When this is zero, the area both classifiers say is positive shrinks to a single point. See Figs. 3 and 4. As the threshold is increased, their positive areas increase. X's positive area is always rectangular (until it expands into the boundary of the unit square). Y's lozenge shape grows from $(0.9, 1.0)$. Only at the largest threshold values does Y suggest the area right of $i = 0.9$ is positive. Eventually it, like X, expands its positive area to cover the whole space.

The two classifier X and Y are represented as floating point functions. Their threshold is supplied as their single argument. If the current fitness test point lies within the decision boundary the function returns a positive value and if it

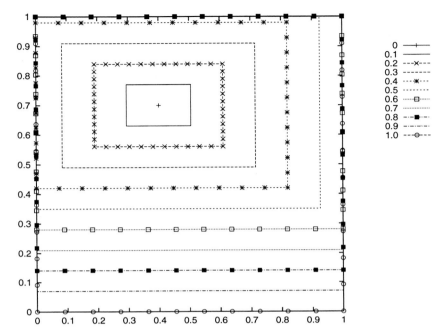

Fig. 3. Decision boundary for classifier X at 11 thresholds.

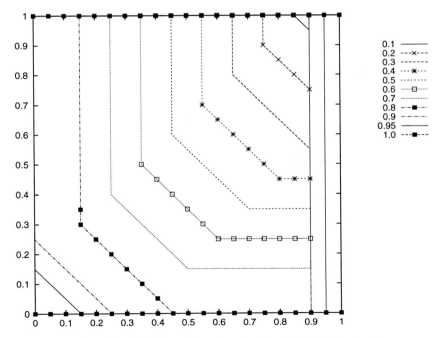

Fig. 4. Decision boundary for classifier Y at 11 thresholds.

is outside a negative value. The magnitude of the result is related to the distance between the test point and the boundary (with the given threshold setting).

There is one terminal. This is the current value of the threshold being applied to the classifier being evolved by GP. Finally the GP population was initially constructed from 200 randomly chosen floating point values between -1 and +1. These constants do not change as the population evolves.

4.2   Fitness Function

For each new invidual, 1024 test points were uniformly randomly chosen in the unit square (cf. Fig. 1). Each new individual is tested on each with the threshold parameter (T) taking values from 0 to 1 every 0.1 (i.e. 11 values). So it is run 11,264 times. For each threshold value the number of correct positive cases it gets right divided by the total number of positive cases, i.e. the true positive rate, is calculated. Similarly its false positive rate is given by the number of negative cases it gets wrong divided by the total number of negative cases.

The eleven true positive and false positive rates are plotted and the area under their convex hull is calculated. Since a classifier can always achieve both a zero success rate and 100% false positive rate, the points (0,0) and (1,1) are always included when constructing the convex hull. The area under the convex hull is the fitness of the individual GP program. Note the GP is not only rewarded for getting answers right but also (using the threshold parameter) to get a range of high scores.

Table 2. GP Parameters

Objective:	Evolve a function of X and Y classifiers with Maximum Convex Hull Area
Functions set:	XC YC Max Min MUL ADD DIV SUB IFLTE
Terminal set:	T, 200 constants randomly chosen in $-1 \ldots +1$
Fitness:	Area under convex hull of 11 ROC points 1024 randomly chosen points
Selection:	generational (non elitist), tournament size 7
Wrapper:	$\geq 0 \Rightarrow$ positive, negative otherwise
Pop Size:	500
Max Program Size:	200
Initial pop:	ramped half-and-half (randomly half terminals are T, the other half are constants)
Parameters:	90% crossover 10% mutation (point mutation 2.5%, Constant change 2.5%, Shrink mutation 2.5% subtree mutation 2.5%)
Termination:	by generation 50

An Adaptive Mapping for Developmental Genetic Programming

Steve Margetts and Antonia J. Jones

Department of Computer Science, Cardiff University,
Queen's Buildings, Newport Road, PO Box 916
Cardiff CF24 3XF, U.K.
S.Margetts@cs.cf.ac.uk
Phone: +44 (0)29 2087 4812

Abstract. In this article we introduce a general framework for constructing an adaptive genotype-to-phenotype mapping, and apply it to developmental genetic programming. In this preliminary investigation, we run a series of comparative experiments on a simple test problem. Our results show that the adaptive algorithm is able to outperform its non-adaptive counterpart.

1 Introduction

Genetic programming can be thought of as the construction of programs guided by evolutionary search. The fitness of a program is measured by executing it, and the aim of the system is to find a program with some desired functionality. In the case of traditional genetic programming, programs are represented by LISP S-expressions [5]. New programs are created from old by the application of various genetic operators acting directly on the LISP expressions themselves. There is therefore no distinction between the structures that undergo evolutionary modification (the genotypes) and the structures that are used to calculate fitness (the phenotypes).

This does not have to be the case: we could use binary strings [1], or even executable graphs [13] as our genotypes. The study of genetic programming with alternative genotype structures is known as *developmental genetic programming* [3] [11].

One of the advantages of separating the genotype $\mathbb{G}$ from the phenotype $\mathbb{P}$ is that the genetic operators used by the system can be simpler, and better suited to the structures on which they act. The general scheme is given in figure 1, where the mapping from genotype to phenotype is represented by the function **grow**. The dotted circle represents the genotypes in the current population.

One way to do this is to specify a *fixed* mapping from the genotype to the phenotype. But as each problem is different and requires a different problem-specific function set, we must find a new mapping for each. Unfortunately, there are often many different ways to convert a particular type of genotype into a program, and not all of these are equal [4]. Given that we want to obtain the

J. Miller et al. (Eds.): EuroGP 2001, LNCS 2038, pp. 97–107, 2001.

Fig. 1. An illustration of a genotype to phenotype mapping. The symbols $\mathbb{G}$, $\mathbb{P}$ and $\mathbb{F}$ denote the set of genotypes, phenotypes and fitness values respectively (we usually take $\mathbb{F}$ to be the positive real numbers). The function `grow` converts a given genotype into its corresponding phenotype, which can then be assessed using the fitness function `fitness`.

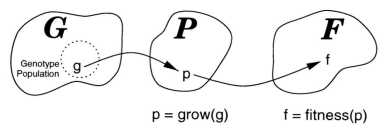

$$p = \mathrm{grow}(g) \qquad\qquad f = \mathrm{fitness}(p)$$

best possible performance from our genetic programming systems, selecting the best genotype-to-phenotype mapping is a critical but difficult task.

In this article we present an *adaptive* genotype-to-phenotype mapping for genetic programming. This mapping is able to adjust itself in response to feedback on its progress, and thus side-steps many of the problems of a fixed mapping. We will start by outlining the nature of the genetic programming system we are interested in. After describing our adaptive mapping, we will then compare it with a fixed mapping on a simple test problem.

2   Stack-Based Genetic Programming

One of the simplest abstract computing devices is a stack machine. The field of genetic programming with such a machines is termed *stack-based genetic programming*, and has been shown to be at least as effective as traditional genetic programming [8] [12]. A program for a stack-machine is simply a list of instructions, each of which alters the state of the machine. In this respect, a program can be thought of as a type of "machine-code". If we regard each machine instruction as an element of a function set $\mathbb{F}$, then the phenotype for our system is $\mathbb{F}^*$, the set of all possible strings drawn from $\mathbb{F}$.

The machine we will use here consists of a general-purpose stack combined with an output register, and a schematic is shown in figure 2. We can broadly classify the instruction set for this machine into the following: constants, variables, problem-specific functions, and general-purpose functions that affect the stack directly.

Given a program in the form of a list of instructions, we process each one in turn. If we encounter a constant or a variable we push its associated value onto the stack. If we encounter a function, we take the required number of arguments from the stack, present them to the function, and push any return value back onto the stack. (If there are insufficient arguments on the stack, then the function simply does nothing.)

Fig. 2. A schematic of the virtual stack machine used in our developmental genetic programming system. The value in the register at the end of the run is used as the program's output.

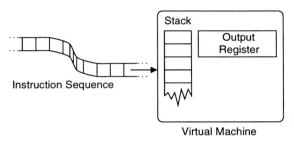

To evaluate the fitness of a program, the genetic programming system sets the values of any variables, sets the output register to zero, and submits the program to the stack-machine. The output of the program is taken to be the value in the register at the end of the program. Coupled with the fact that functions with insufficient arguments are ignored, this means that *any* sequence of instructions forms a valid program.

Stack-based genetic programming provides a natural distinction between genotype and phenotype. Having specified the computational engine and the phenotype we hope to use, we must now turn our attention to the genotype. Following the work of [1], we will choose fixed-length binary strings. This means that we can use a standard genetic algorithm [2] as our genetic programming system.

3   An Adaptive Genotype to Phenotype Mapping

We now need some way to generate an instruction sequence (the phenotype) from a fixed-length binary string (the genotype). One possible way to do this is to associate each instruction in the function set $\mathbb{F}$ with a unique binary sequence. We would like the number of binary digits representing each instruction to be as small as possible, as this will ensure that the system can make the best use it can from the fixed-length binary string. However, if $\mathbb{F}$ has n elements, we will need at least $\lceil \log_2 n \rceil$ digits to represent each instruction.

If the number of instructions is an exact power of two, then there is no problem: we can easily assign one sequence to each symbol. If not, then we will have some "spare" sequences, and we must decide how to deal with these. We believe that what we do with these spare sequences in the decoding process is critical to the performance of the algorithm as a whole. If we encounter an unrecognised binary sequence when decoding a particular binary string, our options are:

- Ignore it, i.e. skip over a entire block of bits
- Skip single bits until we come to a sequence we recognise
- Encode one or more functions multiple times

All of these options have disadvantages. Skipping over unassigned blocks or enough bits until we reach a valid code is wasteful in that we are not using the binary string to its fullest. And encoding one or more functions multiple times necessarily biases the system towards these functions as multiply-encoded symbols are more likely to appear in a binary string drawn at random.

In effect, encoding a symbol multiple times increases its relative importance, and imposes a ranking upon the function set. This is not necessarily a bad thing: if we could arrange the ranking in such a way as to emphasis those functions that are "important" for a given problem, we may be able to improve the performance of our algorithm. Of course, the difficulty here is in choosing an appropriate ranking. The "best" ranking of the functions in the function set is likely to be problem dependent, and may even change during the execution of the algorithm.

The function set could also contain elements that are of little or no use for the problem being tackled. This situation is particularly relevant to symbolic regression problems, as we often do not know which inputs are important in terms of accurately modelling the training data. Each "useless" function makes the problem harder, as not only must the algorithm learn to solve the problem, it must also learn to avoid using these functions.

3.1 Using a Huffman-Decoding Mapping

The solution is to allow the algorithm to choose its own assignment of binary sequences to function symbols. One way we can do this is by *Huffman encoding* (e.g. [10]), which works in the following manner. Imagine for a moment that we have a message consisting of a sequence of symbols that we wish to send over an error-free communication channel. Suppose also that the channel can only send binary signals, and that we require the transmission time to be minimised. The problem is then to represent the message efficiently as a binary string.

The simplest solution is to assign each symbol in the message a unique binary sequence. To create the message we simply convert each symbol into its binary sequence and transmit it. Provided the receiver has a copy of the encoding table used, it is easy to decode the message. However, this message is unlikely to be the shortest possible.

A better solution is to take account of the composition of the message. One approach is to note that the frequencies of symbols in any "typical" message are likely to be non-uniform. That is, we expect certain symbols to occur more often than others (for example, the most common letter in a typical piece of English prose is 'e'). If we can arrange for these frequently-used symbols to be transmitted using a small number of bits, we will reduce the overall message length. The idea of Huffman encoding is a simple extension of this: we aim to transmit each symbol with a number of bits that is proportional to its frequency in the message. Again, once we have decided on an encoding, the message can easily be converted into a binary string and transmitted.

Using this scheme, each symbol may now be represented using a different number of bits. To decode a symbol we can use a *decoding tree*, which has as its branches the values '0' and '1', and symbols at its leaves. To decode a binary

Fig. 3. An illustration of an adaptive genotype to phenotype mapping. The symbols $\mathbb{G}$, $\mathbb{M}$, $\mathbb{G}^*$, $\mathbb{P}$ and $\mathbb{F}$ denote the set of genotypes, mappings, intermediate genotypes, phenotypes and fitness values respectively. An intermediate genotype is constructed by combining an element of $\mathbb{G}$ (a "solution") with an element of $\mathbb{M}$ (a mapping). This is then converted into a phenotype by the function grow, and can then be assessed by the fitness function fitness.

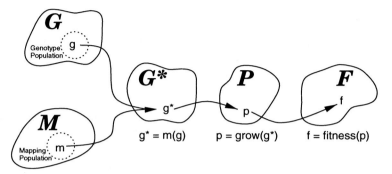

sequence we follow the path through the tree until we reach a leaf node, where we return the associated symbol. Provided the receiver has the encoding we used to create the transmission, it is a simple matter to recover the original message.

The shape of the decoding tree, and thus the binary sequence for each symbol, is controlled entirely by the frequency information used to construct it. Hence we can adjust the encoding simply by adjusting these frequencies. However, we are not actually interested in *encoding* a sequence of symbols, but in *decoding* the binary string, so the frequencies here refer to the average number of occurrences of a symbol in a program generated from a random binary string, rather than the frequency of a symbol in a message.

To recap, what we have here is a way of representing the encoding of a set of function symbols into binary strings as a real-valued vector. Our overall aim is to let the algorithm control this vector, so that it can choose which mapping it should use on a per-problem basis. To do this, we turn to the idea of an *adaptive mapping*.

3.2 A Coevolutionary Model for Adaptive Mappings

Our basic idea is very simple: we use coevolution (in the sense of [9]) to search for a useful mapping at the same time as searching for a solution to the problem. To do this , we therefore establish *two* populations: one to represent the possible solutions (i.e. what would be the set of genotypes in a standard genetic programming system), and the other to represent the possible mappings.

A general framework for this scheme is given in figure 3. Here, the sets of possible solutions and mappings are denoted by $\mathbb{G}$ and $\mathbb{M}$ respectively, and the dotted circles within each set represent the individuals of the current population.

To evaluate the fitness of a candidate genotype g, we must first select a member of the mapping population m. In our implementation, we have chosen to select the m with the current highest fitness, although other schemes are possible. However we choose m, the result is g^*, a member of the "intermediate" genotype space, to which we can apply the (fixed) mapping function grow. This yields the phenotype p, to which the fitness measure is applied.

The intermediate genotype space $\mathbb{G}^*$ is intended to separate the actual genotype from the phenotype. The reason for this is that in many cases, the set of valid phenotypes is a subset of all possible phenotypes. In such cases it would be rather difficult to constrain each possible mapping the algorithm might generate to produce only valid phenotypes. We can then implement any restrictions on the allowable phenotypes in grow, the mapping between $\mathbb{G}^*$ and $\mathbb{P}$. Note that in most cases, we can take $\mathbb{G} = \mathbb{G}^*$.

While we can see how to find the fitness of a member of $\mathbb{G}$, it is less clear how we can evaluate the fitness of a candidate mapping m. Perhaps the best method is to evaluate the fitnesses of the entire population of solutions in the context of m, and take the average fitness of these as the fitness of m. Unfortunately, this is too computationally expensive to be practical.

Instead, we will evaluate the fitness of the member of $\mathbb{G}^*$ created by applying the current best member of the solution population to m. Although this does not return as much information about the mapping as an exhaustive evaluation of the entire population of solutions, it does mean that the best mapping will match itself to the best solution and vice-versa. The resulting algorithm is also pleasantly symmetric.

In summary, the use of coevolution in this scheme naturally breaks the problem into two symbiotic parts: one being the search for a mapping and the other being the search for the solution.

4   Experimental Setup

To evaluate this idea, we will use the *maximum output* problem (e.g. [6]). The task here is to produce a program that takes no arguments but which outputs a numeric value that is as large as possible, using just simple arithmetic operators and constants. The function set for our version of this problem is listed in table 1.

We ran a set of comparative experiments between a non-adaptive algorithm and our adaptive algorithm on this domain. For the non-adaptive algorithm, we generated a random encoding of binary strings to the function set, as given in table 1. The adaptive algorithm was free to evolve its own encoding in the manner outlined above.

In using *fixed-length* binary strings as genotypes we are effectively constraining the maximum size of the programs the system can produce. To investigate the effects of this we ran experiments using genotypes with 50, 100, 150, 200 and 250 bits. The binary strings used for the population of adaptive mappings were fixed at 70 bits, using 10 bits for each of the 7 frequencies in the mapping. All

Table 1. The function set and default encoding used by the non-adaptive algorithm on the maximum output problem.

FUNCTION SYMBOL	ENCODING	DESCRIPTION
plus	011	Addition: pop two items from stack, add and push result onto stack
times	00	Multiplication: pop two items from stack, multiply and push result onto stack
const	110	Constant: interpret next N bits as number and push value onto stack
dup	100	Duplicate item at top of stack
pop	111	Remove item at top of stack
s2r	101	Copy item at top of stack into output register (does not affect stack)
r2s	010	Push output register onto stack

Table 2. The results of the non-adaptive algorithm on the maximum output problem. The mean and best outputs were calculated over the 10 independent runs for each genotype size, each run being 5000 function evaluations. The mean number of instructions used were calculated from best programs produced at the end of each run.

No. BITS	MEAN VALUE	BEST VALUE	MEAN NUMBER OF INSTRUCTIONS
50	19797	65536	13.4
100	515367	2.0×10^6	25.7
150	2.0×10^7	8.4×10^7	40.9
200	3.3×10^7	1.9×10^8	56.3
250	6.5×10^7	3.4×10^8	67.9

real values were generated in the interval $[0, 1]$, using the counting-ones mapping described in [7].

To ensure a fair comparison all experiments used a population of 200 individuals in total (i.e. the adaptive algorithm used two populations of 100 individuals). We ran each experiment for a total of 5000 function evaluations, repeating each one 10 times. The best and average value of the output at the end of each experiment was recorded.

5 Results

The results for the non-adaptive algorithm are shown in table 2. This table gives the mean and best output values achieved, along with the mean number of instructions used by the best programs in each case.

Table 3. The results of the adaptive algorithm on the maximum output problem. The mean and best outputs were calculated over the 10 independent runs for each genotype size, each run being 5000 function evaluations. The mean number of instructions and the mean function frequencies were both calculated from the best programs produced at the end of each run.

No. Bits	Mean Value	Best Value	Mean Inst.	const	pop	dup	s2r	r2s	plus	times
50	5953	59049	12.9	0.48	0.37	0.50	0.50	0.40	0.44	0.35
100	2.5×10^6	8.0×10^6	29.5	0.39	0.29	0.51	0.54	0.30	0.43	0.34
150	1.7×10^7	7.2×10^7	43.2	0.30	0.23	0.52	0.46	0.38	0.42	0.26
200	2.2×10^8	1.1×10^9	59.3	0.39	0.42	0.56	0.66	0.54	0.68	0.45
250	6.8×10^9	4.3×10^{10}	85.1	0.34	0.28	0.39	0.51	0.38	0.56	0.38

The results for the adaptive algorithm are shown in table 3. This table gives the mean and best output values achieved, and the mean number of instructions used by the best programs as before. It also gives the mean frequency of each symbol in the mappings used by the best programs at the end of the run.

It is clear from these tables that increasing the string length allows the programs to output larger values. We can also see that in all but the first case, the adaptive algorithm tends to produce longer programs than its non-adaptive counterpart, particularly when using longer genotypes. Perhaps because of this, the adaptive algorithm tends to produce greater output values for most of these cases.

It is worth taking a quick look at the case where the adaptive algorithm was outperformed by the standard one in more detail. The best result for the 50-bit string is shown below. (Instructions in italic type do not contribute to the final value returned by the program.)

```
const(1) dup dup plus dup plus s2r dup times dup times dup
times s2r
```

Note particularly the repeated "dup times" sequence, which squares the value at the top of the stack. This short sequence is a good way to produce a large number, and similar expressions were found in all the best programs. The number of wasted instructions here is small: only the central s2r function does not contribute to the overall value. By using only 50 bits to represent a program, we appear to be forcing the system to be economical in its usage of functions. With such short bit-strings, it is likely that any individuals which do not maximise their use of their genotype will be out-evolved.

The corresponding program for the adaptive algorithm is given next, along with the encoding used to construct this solution. It is clear that this program is longer than the one above, even though it produces a smaller output.

dup const(1) dup dup dup plus plus dup times dup dup times dup
times times s2r

Encoding

const	pop	dup	s2r	r2s	plus	times
111	011	00	10	–	010	110

This program is longer because the mapping ignores the **r2s** function. As this instruction pushes the contents of the output register onto the stack, it is of little direct use in this problem. By ignoring this function, two of the remaining symbols can be represented using only two bits. As one of these is the useful **dup** function, this represents a substantial saving.

As a comparison, we can look at the best program generated by the non-adaptive algorithm on a 250-bit genotype (below). We can see that this program has a higher proportion of "useless code"; in one place it even calls the **pop** function, which removes the item at the top of the stack.

times plus const(0.6) *times plus* const(1) *times* const(0.9)
plus *times plus* s2r r2s times r2s plus s2r dup r2s times dup
dup pop s2r dup times plus r2s times dup s2r times dup dup
s2r r2s times times dup plus r2s plus plus const(0.9) s2r *s2r*
plus dup s2r plus plus *times* r2s plus dup plus r2s plus *times*
times times s2r r2s plus dup plus s2r *times times* dup plus
r2s plus s2r *r2s*

To complete the set we have the best program and mapping found by the adaptive algorithm when using 250 bits.

dup dup dup plus pop const(0.8) s2r *plus* dup *plus* dup plus
r2s plus s2r r2s times dup times dup times s2r *s2r* r2s times
dup times *plus* dup r2s plus plus dup s2r plus *plus* r2s r2s
plus s2r r2s dup plus plus dup dup plus plus dup plus s2r dup
plus r2s plus dup dup plus s2r *s2r* r2s dup plus plus dup plus
dup plus plus dup plus dup plus dup plus s2r *r2s s2r r2s*

Encoding

const	pop	dup	s2r	r2s	plus	times
0000	0001	111	01	001	10	110

The mapping found here is slightly different to that found for the 50-bit program above: instead of removing a symbol entirely, the mapping represents both the **const** and the **pop** instructions using four bits. As the **const** symbol is used only once in the program, and the **pop** symbol is not used at all, the program does not need to worry too much about using four bits to represent this symbol. However, doing so allows the remaining symbols to be represented with only two or three bits. The resulting program is longer, and so returns a larger value than its fixed-mapping counterpart.

6   Conclusions

The adaptive algorithm is able to outperform the non-adaptive algorithm as it is able to maximise the length of the program that it can extract from a fixed-length binary string. In addition, it is able to bias the function set to those instructions that are best suited to the problem at hand.

7   Future Work

This work is perhaps best regarded as a preliminary study – it has always been our intention to apply this idea to other genetic programming problems, for example that of symbolic regression. The ability to remove functions from the function set in this domain provides a form of feature-selection. This is because we have instructions that represent the inputs from the dataset. It may be that inputs that are not "important" in predicting the output will be dropped from the function set.

In investigating this simple problem, we have noticed that the simple iterative mapping from binary strings to instruction sequences is inherently brittle. By this, we mean that making a small change near the beginning of the string can cause a huge change in the functionality of the program, simply because each instruction can affects all those that follow it. One idea that we are currently considering is a way to use the idea of an adaptive mapping to evolve a more robust encoding.

References

1. Wolfgang Banzhaf. Genotype-phenotype-mapping and neutral variation – a case study in genetic programming. In Y. Davidor, H.-P. Schwefel, and R. Männer, editors, *Proceedings of Parallel Problem Solving from Nature III*, pages 322–332, Berlin, 1994. Springer.
2. David E. Goldberg. *Genetic Algorithms in Search Optimization and Machine Learning*. Addison-Wesley Publishing Company Inc., 1989.
3. Robert E Keller and Wolfgang Banzhaf. Genetic programming using genotype-phenotype mappings from linear genomes to linear phenotypes. In John R Koza, David E Goldberg, David B Fogel, and Rick L Riolo, editors, *Genetic Programming 1996: Proceedings of the First Annual Conference*, Cambridge, USA, 1996. MIT Press.
4. Robert E Keller and Wolfgang Banzhaf. The evolution of genetic code in genetic programming. In Wolfgang Banzhaf, Jason Daida, Agoston E Eiben, Max H Garzon, Mark Jakiela, and Robert E Smith, editors, *Proceedings of the Genetic and Evolutionary Computation Conference*, volume 2, pages 1077–1082, San Francisco, California, 1999. Morgan Kaufmann. ISBN 1-55860-611-4.
5. John R. Koza. *Genetic Programming - On the Programming of Computers by Means of Natural Selection*. The MIT Press, Massachusetts, Cambridge, 1992. ISBN 0-262-11170-5.

6. William B. Langdon and Ricardo Poli. An analysis of the MAX problem in genetic programming. In John R. Koza, K. Deb, Marco Darigo, David B. Fogel, Max Garzon, Hitoshi Iba, and Rick L. Riolo, editors, *GP97: Proceedings of the Second Annual Conference on Genetic Programming*, pages 222–230, Stanford University, USA, July 1997. Morgan-Kaufmann.
7. Steve Margetts and Antonia J. Jones. Phlegmatic mappings for function optimisation with genetic algorithms. In Darrell Whitley, David Goldberg, Erick Cantu-Paz, Lee Spector, Ian Parmee, and Hans-Georg Beyer, editors, *Proceedings of the Genetic and Evolutionary Computation Conference (GECCO-2000)*, pages 82–89, Las Vegas, Nevada, USA, 10-12 July 2000. Morgan Kaufmann.
8. Timothy Perkis. Stack-based genetic programming. In *Proceedings of the 1994 IEEE World Congress on Computational Intelligence*, pages 148–153. IEEE Press, 1994.
9. Mitchell A. Potter. *The Design and Analysis of a Computational Model of Cooperative Coevolution*. Phd thesis, George Mason University, Fairfax, Virginia, Spring 1997. Supervised by Kenneth A. De Jong.
10. Robert Sedgewick. *Algorithms in C++*. Addison-Wesley Publishing Company Inc., 1992. ISBN 0-201-51059-6.
11. Lee Spector and Kilian Stoffel. Ontogenetic programming. In John R Koza, David E Goldberg, David B Fogel, and Rick L Riolo, editors, *Genetic Programming 1996: Proceedings of the First Annual Conference*, Cambridge MA, 1996. MIT Press.
12. Kilian Stoffel and Lee Spector. High-performance, parallel, stack-based genetic programming. In John R Koza, David E Goldberg, David B Fogel, and Rick L Riolo, editors, *Genetic Programming 1996: Proceedings of the First Annual Conference*, pages 224–229, Cambridge MA, 1996. The MIT Press.
13. Astro Teller. *Advances in Genetic Programming II*, chapter 3: Evolving Programmers: The Co-evolution of Intelligent Recombination Operators. MIT Press, 1996.

A Schema Theory Analysis of the Evolution of Size in Genetic Programming with Linear Representations

Nicholas Freitag McPhee[1] and Riccardo Poli[2]

[1] Division of Science and Mathematics, University of Minnesota
Morris; Morris, MN, USA
mcphee@mrs.umn.edu, http://www.mrs.umn.edu/~mcphee
[2] School of Computer Science, The University of Birmingham
Birmingham, B15 2TT, UK
R.Poli@cs.bham.ac.uk, http://www.cs.bham.ac.uk/~rmp/

Abstract. In this paper we use the schema theory presented in [20] to better understand the changes in size distribution when using GP with standard crossover and linear structures. Applications of the theory to problems both with and without fitness suggest that standard crossover induces specific biases in the distributions of sizes, with a strong tendency to over sample small structures, and indicate the existence of strong redistribution effects that may be a major force in the early stages of a GP run. We also present two important theoretical results: An exact theory of bloat, and a general theory of how average size changes on flat landscapes with glitches. The latter implies the surprising result that a single program glitch in an otherwise flat fitness landscape is sufficient to drive the average program size of an infinite population, which may have important implications for the control of code growth.

1 Introduction

The phenomenon of bloat, or code growth, has been observed in genetic programming (GP) from the very beginning [5], and over the years the study of bloat has probably been one of the most active areas of foundational GP research [3, 13, 15, 24, 21, 11, 6, 8, 7]. Numerous theories have been proposed to explain bloat, but these have typically been qualitative rather than quantitative in nature. It is likely that none of these proposed mechanisms is the complete story, and that they in fact interact in complex ways that vary over the course of a GP run. Their qualitative nature, however, makes it difficult to perform the kinds of quantitative study that would allow one to begin to tease out these complex relationships. In this paper we show how recent results in GP schema theory can be used to take what may be the first steps towards providing a unified theoretical framework for understanding code growth in GP.

In recent work [20, in this proceedings] we present an exact schema theory for Genetic Programming (GP) using standard crossover on linear representations. We also show how that theory can be used to understand the significant biases standard crossover introduces on the distribution and sampling of programs of different lengths even when the fitness landscape is flat. In this paper we apply that schema theory to the problem of better understanding changes in the distribution of lengths under standard crossover. We find that in problems both with and without fitness, standard crossover induces very

J. Miller et al. (Eds.): EuroGP 2001, LNCS 2038, pp. 108–125, 2001.

specific biases in the distribution of sizes, with a strong tendency to over sample the smaller structures. There also appear to be significant redistribution effects that may be a major force in the early stages of a GP run. We then generalize these results, yielding two important theoretical results. The first is an exact theory of bloat which gives a formula for the change in average program size for infinite populations of linear structures when using standard crossover without mutation. The second is a general theory of how average sizes change on a flat landscape with "glitches" (sets of strings with above or below average fitness), which implies the surprising result that a single program glitch is sufficient to drive the average program size of an infinite population.

While the work reported here is all on GP with linear structures, the schema theorem used is a special case of a more general GP schema theorem [17, in this proceedings]. We have chosen in these early applications to focus on linear structures because the theoretical analysis is more manageable and the computations are more tractable. This has yielded a number of important results for the linear case, and preliminary results further suggest that many of the key ideas here are also applicable (at least in broad terms) to the non-linear tree structures typically used in GP.

In the remainder of this section we will briefly survey three key theories of bloat, and discuss why theoretical tools are crucial in our attempts to understand foundational phenomena like bloat. In Sec. 2 we will present the schema theorem for GP using linear structures and standard crossover. In Sec. 3 we will summarize *theoretical* results from [20] showing that bloat does not happen on flat fitness landscapes when using standard GP crossover (for related empirical results see, e.g., [9]), and in fact standard crossover heavily over samples the shorter programs; we also present the exact schema theorem there. We then apply the theory in Sec. 4 to a problem that does bloat and use the theory to both predict and better understand the changes in the distribution of sizes. In Sec. 5 we show how the schema theory can be used to derive some general results relating variations in the fitness landscape to changes in the average program size, and then finish with some conclusions and ideas for future research (Sec. 6).

1.1   Three Theories of Bloat

As mentioned earlier, bloat in GP is an old problem that has received quite a lot of attention over the years. Many techniques have been proposed to combat bloat but, as noted in [11], these are mostly *ad hoc*, preceding rather than following from knowledge of the causes of bloat. To date there are three major theories that propose to at least partially explain bloat:

1. Replication accuracy, or protection against bad crossover
2. Removal bias
3. Nature of program search spaces

It is not generally claimed that any one of these is sufficient, or even that this set is complete, but each of these does appear to explain some interesting facet of the problem, and in combination they provide a valuable set of tools for understanding code growth. They are, however, primarily qualitative rather than quantitative in nature, which ultimately limits their predictive power.

The replication accuracy theory [13, 3, 15] is based on the idea (common in evolutionary biology) that an important component of the success of an organism (in our case a GP individual) is its ability to reproduce accurately, i.e., have offspring that are functionally similar to the parent (see, e.g., [4, 1]). This would suggest that if an evolutionary computation system could evolve towards representations (including specific sizes and shapes) that increased replication accuracy then, all other things being equal, it would do so. One way this can happen in GP is through the evolution of large blocks of code that do not contribute to the semantics of the individual. The larger these blocks, the greater the chance that crossover points will be chosen there, ensuring that the offspring are semantically equivalent to the root parent.

One drawback of the replication accuracy hypothesis is that it is presented solely in terms of individuals avoiding disruption, and does not consider creation effects. Creation effects, however, are crucial, because without them one cannot have the evolution of new structures. Replication accuracy is typically assumed to be most important later in the run, when there's little or no change in the best fitness and creation effects may indeed be minimal. It tells us little, however, about the changes in program size we observe in the early stages of runs. The replication accuracy hypothesis also provides no way of judging the relative importance of potentially competing forces. If, for example, there is a fitness induced bias favoring smaller trees, and replication accuracy favors larger trees, how will these biases interact? In many cases these interactions may change over the course of a run, and this hypothesis currently provides little help in understanding these phase transitions.

The removal bias theory [22, 11] is based on the observation that the semantically irrelevant nodes of a GP tree tend to be in the lower parts of the tree and are therefore the root of subtrees that are smaller than the average subtree for that individual. If it is indeed the case that successful crossovers will tend to replace semantically irrelevant nodes, then the removed subtree will tend to be a smaller than average subtree. There is no size bias with respect to the inserted subtree, however, since that subtree will have no semantic impact. This means that fitness neutral crossover events will tend to replace smaller subtrees with larger subtrees, which will lead to bloat.

The removal bias hypothesis is closely related to the replication accuracy hypothesis, and not surprisingly it suffers essentially the same drawbacks: Failure to consider creation effects, no way of predicting the interactions of competing forces, and a primary applicability to the later stages of a run. It further hinges, though, on important assumptions about the structure of program trees, such as the assumption that the semantically important nodes tend to be clustered near the root of the tree. While there is evidence that this is true in many cases, it is unclear how well this generalizes, e.g., to problems with side-effecting primitives.

The nature of program search spaces theory [11] is based on the experimental observation that, for a variety of test problems (e.g., [10, 6]), above a certain problem dependent size, the distribution of fitnesses does not vary a great deal with the size of the programs. Since there are more (syntactically) different long programs, the number of long programs of a given fitness is greater than the number of short programs of the same fitness. Thus, all other things being equal, over time one is more likely to sample the long programs simply because there are more of them.

This theory has the advantage of being quite general. Since it talks about the search space rather than the search mechanism, it potentially applies to a whole variety of variable length search techniques (see [11] for examples). It relies, however, on two crucial assumptions. First it requires that the distribution of fitnesses is roughly independent of length. As mentioned above, this has been observed experimentally on a variety of problems, and [6] provides a theoretical analysis which shows that certain general classes of problems will always have this property. It is, however, easy to construct (artificial) problems where this assumption does not hold, yet bloat still occurs (e.g., the one-then-zeros problem in Sec. 4). Second, this hypothesis assumes that the search operators sample the space in a manner that is neutral with regard to size. Recent schema theory results on flat fitness landscapes and linear structures [20] raise serious doubts about the veracity of that assumption when one is using standard crossover. While there are GP crossover operators that are neutral with regard to size (e.g., one-point GP crossover [18]), standard crossover clearly is not, being instead heavily biased (on flat fitness landscapes over linear structures) towards an over sampling of the smaller structures.

1.2   Why Theory Matters

Before proceeding to the presentation of the schema theory and its applications to bloat, it is worth looking at an example of why theoretical tools are so important.

Six years ago McPhee and Miller [13] examined bloat in the INC-IGNORE problem, an artificial problem designed specifically to help isolate the causes of bloat. In this problem there is a single terminal, 0, and two unary functions, INC and IGNORE, defined by $INC(x) = x + 1$ and $IGNORE(x) = 0$. Thus INC adds one to its argument, and IGNORE returns a constant 0 regardless of its argument. The goal is to generate a string having value 100; the fitness is the absolute value of the difference between the string's value and the target of 100, with low values being better. Thus a correct individual would be a string of 100 INCs followed by either the terminal 0, or an IGNORE which could then be followed by any number of nodes of any type (since their value would be ignored).

We re-implemented this problem and did new runs, getting very similar behavior to that reported in [13].[1] Fig. 1(a) shows the changes in the average fitness and the average size over time in a representative run, and one can see a clear relationship between the abrupt discovery of a solution and the onset of bloat.

Due to practical limitations, the runs reported in [13] were only taken out 100 generations. What effect did this limitation have? Fig. 1(b) shows the development of the average size in a new run taken out to 3000 generations. In this extended run bloat appears to continue steadily for several hundred generations, but with an increasing amount of noise. After that initial steady rise, though, the behavior becomes very erratic. By showing more generations, Fig. 1(b) shows a much more complex picture than that in Fig. 1(a). This raises questions about whether or how long the code growth would continue if we ran more generations. The overall trends are a little easier to read in Fig. 2, where we show the average of 20 runs of INC-IGNORE out to 2000 generations. While there is clearly a change in the rate of growth after several hundred generations, the average size past that point is still remarkably noisy despite the averaging, and it's unclear whether, for example, the long term behavior will be asymptotic.

The point here is not to criticize the methodology in [13]; all empirical papers are subject to practical limits, and any such paper might yield new ideas and information

---

[1] To get the fairly flat fitness one sees in the early generations in Fig. 1(a) it is necessary to bias the initial population so there are many more IGNORE nodes than INC nodes; a ratio of 20 : 1 was used both here and in [13].

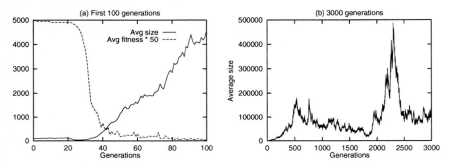

Fig. 1. Graphs of the average size over time of a representative run of the INC-IGNORE problem. Graph (a) (based on [13]) also includes the average fitness (multiplied by 50 so the ranges coincide). The population size is 200.

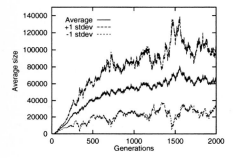

Fig. 2. Graph of the average size over time in the INC-IGNORE problem averaged over 20 runs. Also plotted are the average ± one standard deviation. The population size is 200.

if one were able to extend the experiments. The point is that any empirical study is unavoidably limited, and can perforce only provide a small window on the large and complex picture of GP behavior. How do we get around those limitations? In this paper we propose to use schema theory.

2   Schema Theory for GP on Linear Structures

In recent work the GA schema theory in [23] has been extended to GP [16, 17]. Unlike most previous schema theory work, which provides lower bounds on the number of instances of a schema, this new work provides exact formulas for the transmission of schemata from one generation to the next.

GP is a highly complex process and, as might be expected, the schema theory to describe its behavior is also relatively complex. To make matters more tractable in this paper, we will only consider applications of the theory to a specific simplified domain, namely that of linear structures; thus we will restrict our attention to problems with only unary operators. See [17] for a more general treatment.

2.1   Schema Theory Definitions

In this section we will present a series of crucial definitions that allow us to represent schemata, and count and build instances of schemata.

In a linear-structure GP where $\mathcal{F}$ is the set of non-terminal nodes and $\mathcal{T}$ is the set of terminal nodes, individuals can be seen as sequences of symbols $c_0 c_1 \ldots c_{N-1}$ where $c_i \in \mathcal{F}$ for $i < N - 1$ and $c_{N-1} \in \mathcal{T}$. We will then define a linear GP *schema* as the same kind of sequence $c_0 c_1 \ldots c_{N-1}$ except that a new "don't care" symbol '=' is added to both $\mathcal{F}$ and $\mathcal{T}$.[2] Thus schemata represent sets of linear structures, where the positions labelled '=' can be filled in by any element of $\mathcal{F}$ (or $\mathcal{T}$ if it is the terminal position). A few examples of schema are:[3]

- $(=)^N$: The set of all sequences of length N.
- $1(=)^a$: The set of all sequences of length $a + 1$ starting with a 1.
- $1(0)^a$: The singleton set containing the string 1 followed by a 0's.

Now that we can represent schemata, we present a series of definitions that allow us to count instances of schemata.

Definition 1 (Proportion in Population). *$\phi(H, t)$ is the proportion of strings in the population at time t matching schema H. For finite populations of size M, $\phi(H, t) = m(H, t)/M$, where $m(H, t)$ is the number of instances of H at time t.*

Definition 2 (Selection Probability). *$p(H, t)$ is the probability of selecting an instance of schema H from the population at time t. This is typically a function of $\phi(H, t)$, the fitness distribution in the population, and the details of the selection operators. With fitness proportionate selection, for example, $p(H, t) = \phi(H, t) \times f(H, t)/\overline{f}(t)$, where $f(H, t)$ is the average fitness of all the instances of H in the population at time t and $\overline{f}(t)$ is the average fitness in the population at time t.*

Definition 3 (Transmission Probability). *$\alpha(H, t)$ is the probability that the schema H will be constructed in the process of creating the population for time $t + 1$ out of the population at time t. This will typically be a function of $p(K, t)$, for the various schemata K that could play a role in constructing H, and of the details of the various recombination and mutation operators being used.*

Given these definitions, we can model the standard evolutionary algorithm as the repeated application of the cycle

$$\phi(H, t) \xrightarrow{\text{selection}} p(H, t) \xrightarrow[\text{crossover}]{\text{mutation}} \alpha(H, t) .$$

For an *infinite* population $\phi(H, t + 1) = \alpha(H, t)$ for $t \geq 0$, which means we can iterate these equations to *exactly* model the behavior of an infinite population over time.

---

[2] This new '=' symbol plays a role similar to that of the '#' "don't care" symbol in GA schema theory. For historical reasons, however, '#' has been assigned another meaning in the more general version of the GP schema theory [17].

[3] We will use the superscript notation from theory of computation, where x^n indicates a sequence of n x's.

To formalize the creation of instances of a linear schema we define

$$u(H, i, k) = c_0 c_1 \ldots c_{i-1} (=)^{k-i}$$
$$l(H, i, n) = (=)^{n-N+i} c_i c_{i+1} \ldots c_{N-1}$$

Here $u(H, i, k)$ is the schema of length k matching the leftmost i symbols of H, and $l(H, i, n)$ is the schema of length n matching the rightmost $N - i$ symbols of H.[4] The important thing about u and l is that if you use standard crossover to crossover *any* instance of $u(H, i, k)$ at position i with *any* instance of $l(H, i, n)$ at position $n - N + i$, the result will be an instance of H, provided[5] $k + n > N$, and $0 \uparrow (N-n) \leq i < N \downarrow k$. Further, these are the *only* ways to use standard crossover to construct instances of H, so these definitions fully characterize the mechanism for constructing instances of H.

2.2   The Schema Theorem

Given these definitions, we now present the exact schema theorem for linear structures from [20] in a more compact form:

Theorem 1 (Schema Theorem for Linear Structures and Standard Crossover). *For GP on linear structures using standard crossover with probability p_{xo} and no mutation we have*

$$\alpha(H, t) = (1 - p_{xo}) \times p(H, t) + p_{xo} \times \alpha_{xo}(H, t)$$

where

$$\alpha_{xo}(H, t) = \sum_{\substack{k > 0 \\ n > 0 \\ k+n > N}} \left(\frac{1}{k \times n} \times \sum_{0 \uparrow (N-n) \leq i < N \downarrow k} p(u(H, i, k), t) \times p(l(H, i, n), t) \right).$$

To simplify the calculations in the remainder of the paper we will assume $p_{xo} = 1$ throughout.

2.3   An Exact Theory of Bloat

One way to calculate the average length of the population at time t, which we shall write as $\mu(t)$, is

$$\mu(t) = \sum_N (N \times \phi((=)^N, t)) . \tag{1}$$

For an infinite population (where $\phi(H, t+1) = \alpha(H, t)$), we can rewrite Eq. (1) as $\mu(t+1) = \sum_N (N \times \alpha((=)^N, t))$. A surprising result from [20], though, shows that you can replace α by p to get the average size for the next generation:

---

[4] u and l are based on operators U and L (see, e.g., [17]) which match the *upper* and *lower* parts of general, non-linear, GP schemata.

[5] We will use $\uparrow$ as a binary infix *max* operator, and $\downarrow$ as a binary infix *min* operator.

Theorem 2. *For GP using infinite populations, linear structures, standard crossover, and no mutation we have*

$$\mu(t+1) = \sum_N (N \times p((=)^N, t)) \ . \tag{2}$$

Implicit it these results, but clarified here for the first time, is:

Theorem 3 (Exact Theory of Length Change for Infinite Populations). *For GP using infinite populations, linear structures, standard crossover, and no mutation we have*

$$\mu(t+1) - \mu(t) = \sum_N (N \times \alpha((=)^N, t)) - \sum_N (N \times \phi((=)^N, t)) \tag{3}$$

or equivalently

$$\mu(t+1) - \mu(t) = \sum_N (N \times p((=)^N, t)) - \sum_N (N \times \phi((=)^N, t)) \ . \tag{4}$$

For infinite populations Theorem 3 gives an exact quantitative theory of the changes in the average size of a population over time.[6] Previous theories of bloat are then in some sense approximations of this result, usually based on some simplifying assumptions (e.g., that a run has "plateaued"). This result also makes it clear that it would be rather surprising if there wasn't some sort of change in the average size, since this would require an unlikely balance between the selection probability and the length distribution.

3 Flat Fitness Landscapes

In [20, in this proceedings] we applied the Schema Theorem from the previous section to the case of a flat fitness landscape; due to space limitations we won't repeat those results here. A key result in this context, however, was that standard crossover on a flat landscape heavily over samples the shorter programs. This sampling bias in favor of shorter programs raises serious questions about the "all other things being equal" assumption in the "Nature of program search spaces" theory of bloat (Sec. 1.1). That theory depends crucially on at least an approximately uniform sampling of the search space by the operators, and here, at least, we clearly do *not* have uniform sampling by standard crossover. So while that theory may well be valuable in helping explain behaviors in other contexts, it is not clear how it can be applied in this setting.

4 The One-then-Zeros Problem

We will now apply the Schema Theorem in a setting where there is bloat, namely the *one-then-zeros problem*. We will start by defining and motivating the problem, and we will then use the Schema Theorem to derive length distribution results similar to those reported in [20] for the flat fitness landscape case. In contrast to the flat fitness case, in the one-then-zeros problem we do observe bloat, as well as some important length redistribution effects in the early generations.

---

[6] We can, in fact, extend this to the finite population case, but to do so we need to replace the exact value on the left hand side with an expectation, namely, $E[\mu(t+1) - \mu(t)]$.

4.1   One-then-Zeros Problem Definition

In this problem we have $\mathcal{F} = \{0+, 1+\}$ and $\mathcal{T} = \{0\}$. Both $0+$ and $1+$ are unary operators that add 0 and 1 respectively to their argument. This gives us a problem that is essentially equivalent to studying variable length strings of 0's and 1's, with the constraint that the strings always end in a 0. Note that $1+$ is INC, and $0+$ can be seen as DON'T-INC, so this problem is structurally quite similar to the earlier INC-IGNORE problem. Fitness in this problem will be 1 if the string starts with a 1 and has zeros elsewhere, i.e., the string has the form $1(0)^a$ where $a > 0$; fitness will be 0 otherwise.

Both the replication accuracy and the removal bias hypotheses (Sec. 1.1) suggest that this problem might exhibit bloat. For replication accuracy, increasingly long tails of 0's could act as a mechanism for increasing the probability of constructing "correct" offspring (avoiding bad crossover). Similarly there is a slight removal bias since the one "bad" crossover involves removing the entire root parent and replacing it with a substring consisting of all 0's, which would on average be shorter than the removed string. Note, however, that the nature of program search spaces hypothesis does not appear to apply here, as the proportion of fit individuals is not constant with respect to length. There is in fact just a single "correct" string for any given length, so the density of solutions drops dramatically as length increases. In this case the program search space hypothesis would not appear to suggest bloat, and might instead be seen as suggesting the opposite, since the odds of finding a correct short individual would seem to be much higher than the odds of finding a correct long individual.

4.2   Calculating $\alpha_{xo}((=)^N, t)$ and $\alpha_{xo}(1(0)^a, t)$

We will start[7] by deriving schema equations for $\alpha((=)^N, t)$ so we can study the evolution of length.

Theorem 4 (Length Distribution for One-then-Zeros). *Using the Schema Theorem (Theorem 1) we can show that for GP on the one-then-zeros problem using standard crossover and no mutation, the distribution of lengths is characterized (for $N > 0$) by*

$$\alpha_{xo}((=)^N, t) = \sum_{\substack{k > 0 \\ n > 0 \\ k+n > N}} \left(\frac{N \downarrow k - 0 \uparrow (N-n)}{k \times n} \times p(1(0)^{k-1}, t) \times p(1(0)^{n-1}, t) \right).$$

In the flat fitness case, the formula for $\alpha((=)^N, t)$ depended only on probabilities of the form $p((=)^a, t)$, so if we wanted to iterate the equation we only needed to keep track of $\phi((=)^a, t)$ for all the legal a at each generation. In this case, though, $\alpha((=)^N, t)$ depends on probabilities of the form $p(1(0)^a, t)$, so we also need to know $\phi(1(0)^a, t)$ at each generation. Thus we need to use the Schema Theorem a second time to compute $\alpha(1(0)^a, t)$ for $a > 0$.

---

[7] The derivation of the results in this section are more lengthy than illuminating and will be omitted as a result. See [12] for the details.

Theorem 5 $(1(0)^a$ **Distribution for One-then-Zeros**). *Using the Schema Theorem (Theorem 1) we can also show that for $a > 0$*

$$\alpha_{xo}(1(0)^a, t) = \sum_{k>0} \left[\frac{p(1(0)^{k-1}, t) \times p(1(0)^a, t)}{k \times (a+1)} \right.$$

$$+ \sum_{\substack{n>0 \\ n+k>a+1}} \frac{(a+1) \downarrow k - 1 \uparrow (a+2-n)}{k \times n} \times p(1(0)^{k-1}, t) \times p(1(0)^{n-1}, t) \Bigg] .$$

Fortunately we find here that $\alpha(1(0)^a, t)$ only depends on probabilities of the form $p(1(0)^d, t)$, so no further calculations are needed. Unfortunately most problems are not so restricted, and it is possible for this process to quickly balloon until one is forced to track the proportion of every different string. This is essentially intractable, though, since the number of different strings grows doubly exponentially with the generation t. As a result it is, at this point in the development of the theory, still a rare problem where one can do this level of exact analysis.

4.3   One-then-Zeros Results

We can numerically iterate the equations in Theorems 4 and 5 to better understand the behavior of an infinite GP population on this problem. Note, however, that tracking these distributions over time becomes expensive in terms of computational effort. In this case, for example, generating both $\alpha((=)^N, t)$ and $\alpha(1(0)^a, t)$ are $O(2^{3t})$ where t is the generation.[8] A crucial point, though, is that these equations only need to be run once, and have no stochastic effects. They are *exact* calculations of the relevant quantities (up to the limitations of the floating point representation), and once computed need never be computed again. This is in contrast to typical empirical results in evolutionary computation, where combinations of large populations and multiple runs are necessary to smooth out the stochastic effects, and even then there is no guarantee that any two sets of runs will have similar behavior.

Here we calculated $\alpha((=)^N, t)$ and $\alpha(1(0)^a, t)$ for 75 generations, with an initial population consisting entirely of the only fit individual of length 3, namely "100" (so $p(100, 0) = 1$). The key results are summarized in Figures 3 and 4. Fig. 3(a) shows that after a few generations, the average length begins to grow quite steadily, at least for those 75 generations. As we saw in Sec. 1.2, though, there are significant risks in over generalizing from a small view like this, so it is by no means clear that this growth will continue. Our eventual goal is to develop something like a closed form for the average size at time t to better understand the long term behavior.

Both Figures 3 and 4 show interesting behavior in the first few generations that deserves attention. In Fig. 3(a) we see a flat section at the beginning, which then changes to steady growth. In Fig. 3(b) we see a *very* high proportion of short individuals at the beginning, which then drops quite steeply. In Fig. 4 we see a surprising dip in the proportion of fit individuals in the first few generations, which is then followed by the

---

[8] We have found, though, that ignoring values of α below some small threshold (we have used 10^{-10}) seems to have little impact on the numeric results and can greatly speed up the calculations since it significantly slows the growth of the number of strings that need to be tracked.

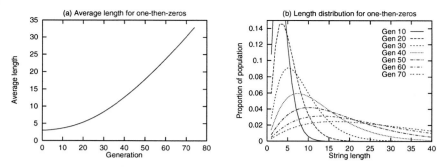

Fig. 3. Graph (a), on the left, shows the growth in the average length of the (infinite) population in the one-then-zeros problem. Graph (b), on the right, shows the distribution of lengths plotted for every 10 generations. The general shapes resemble the gamma distributions for the flat landscape in [20], but here the height of the distributions clearly drops and the peak moves to the right over time, reflecting the increase in average size shown in (a).

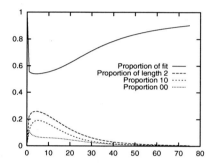

Fig. 4. The proportion of fit individuals (or, equivalently for this problem, the average fitness) in the one-then-zeros problem as a function of time, plotted alongside the proportion of individuals of length 2 and the proportion of both "10" and "00". (Note that *every* individual in the initial population is fit.)

expected rise. While we have no definitive explanation for these behaviors, we can suggest some possibilities. It seems likely, for example, that the rise in the proportion of strings of length 2 is simply a move in the early generations towards a gamma-like distribution with a mean length near 3 (the mean length of the initial distribution). This may, in turn, be the indirect cause of both the lack of initial bloat and the initial drop in the proportion of fit individuals.

In Fig. 4 the initial dip in the proportion of fit individuals corresponds closely to very high proportions of individuals of length 2. As the average size grows, however, the proportion of strings of length 2 in the (still gamma-like) distributions soon drops. Note also the significant proportion of the unfit string "00", which contributes to the initial dip in the proportion of fit individuals. After a sharp drop in the proportion of "00" in the first few generations, its proportion drops quite slowly thereafter (especially given that it has fitness 0). In contrast, the proportion of "10" (which has fitness 1) rises for several generations, but then drops *much* more quickly than that of "00", soon being almost equal to it. Since "00" has fitness 0, it can never be selected as a parent, so neither replication accuracy nor removal bias can tell us anything about why a non-trivial proportion of the population's resources are devoted to sampling this string. It exists strictly as a creation effect, an effect frequently dismissed in other theories.[9]

These observations suggest that it may be common for runs to have an initial period that is heavily influenced (and in some cases dominated) by a redistribution of lengths towards a gamma-like distribution. This redistribution may have little to do with fitness, being instead driven by the size bias of standard crossover. There is, for example, considerable anecdotal evidence that many GP runs are initially dominated by short, moderately fit trees, and that the heavy sampling of these short trees can interfere with the progress of the run. The results presented here suggest this might be especially true if the initial average size is small (as in this case), as the gamma distribution with a small mean has a *very* strong bias towards over sampling small trees. It is possible that further exploration of these ideas could lead to important new understanding in the area of population initialization.

5   Landscape Levels and Program Size

In the previous sections we saw how the schema theory could be used to better understand the evolution of length distributions over time both in cases where there was no bloat and in cases where there was bloat. In this section we will show how the theory can be used to predict some important behaviors in cases where the fitness can be seen as essentially two-valued.[10] What we find is that in the infinite population case the average length of the population moves away from the *average* length of the strings having the lower fitness. Thus the particulars of the fitness landscape are not important; what is important is simply the average length of the strings having the lower fitness and the average length of the population. Quite surprising, perhaps, is the fact that this holds even if one of the two levels is sampled by just a *single* string,[11] which means that even a single string with fitness different from that in an otherwise flat landscape is sufficient to drive the average size of the entire population. We will call small parts of the search space having the lower fitness "holes", and small parts of the search space having the higher fitness "spikes"; we will use the term "glitch" to describe both holes and spikes.

These results are based on the assumption of an infinite population, which ensures that the average size of the strings in the two fitness levels is accurately sampled. In the finite population case stochastic effects make it possible for one of the levels to not be sampled accurately (especially if that level only represents a small proportion of the search space). As an example, consider an a fitness landscape where the fitness

---

[9] It is also a small example of the possible use of bloat as a repository for genetic material, as suggested in [2]. In this case the material in question never directly contributes positively to the fitness of individuals it's inserted into, but it does suggest that specific structures could be preserved in bloat and recovered later.

[10] The requirement that the fitness function has only two values might, at first, seem quite restrictive. There are settings, however, where this may not be such a unrealistic model. In a highly converged run of a discrete problem, for example, the selection process may well only turn up a limited number of fitness values (see, e.g., [7]).

[11] Here we mean a single string in the search space and *not* a single individual in the population.

of every string is 1 except for the string "00", which has fitness 0. If the population contains many short strings, then the hole is likely to be heavily sampled and, as we shall see shortly, bloat will likely occur. If, however, the population consists of very long strings, then it is much less likely that the hole will ever be sampled, and if it isn't then the system will presumably behave (at least temporarily) as if it's acting on a flat fitness landscape. It is possible that this is at least part of the explanation for the increasingly noisy behavior of the size curves in the INC-IGNORE problem (Fig. 1(b)). As the average size in the small population grows, the sampling of the unfit strings may become increasingly erratic, causing (in part) this highly noisy behavior.

5.1   Computing the Mean Size

Since one of our key goals is tracking the changes in the mean population size over time, it would be nice if we could find an equation that relates the average size at time $t+1$ in terms of the average size at time t. In this section we will derive such an equation under the assumption that the fitness function has only two values, and the assumption of an infinite population.

Theorem 2 gave us the following formula for the average size of an infinite population at time t:

$$\mu(t+1) = \sum_N (N \times p((=)^N, t)) \ . \tag{5}$$

We will start by extending this result to include schemata other than those of the form $(=)^N$. Assume that the set of possible strings is partitioned into a set S of disjoint, fixed length schemata. We will write $S = \{S_i\}$ where the S_i are the schemata in question, and denote the length of the strings in S_i by $|S_i|$. Further assume that the fitness function is constant within each of these schemata; we will write $f(S_i)$ for the fitness shared by all instances of S_i. Note that the assumptions here are not restrictive since for any fitness function we can always decompose the space into singleton schemata, one for each different string, and those singleton schemata would trivially satisfy these conditions.

Given these new assumptions one can rewrite Eq. (5) as

$$\mu(t+1) = \sum_i (|S_i| \times p(S_i, t)) \tag{6}$$

and Eq. (1) (from Sec. 2.3) as

$$\mu(t) = \sum_i (|S_i| \times \phi(S_i, t)) \ . \tag{7}$$

It is useful in what follows to generalize μ so that we can compute the mean length of strings matching a particular subset Q of the schemata (i.e., $Q \subset S$):

$$\mu(Q, t) = \frac{\sum_i (|Q_i| \times \phi(Q_i, t))}{\sum_i \phi(Q_i, t)} \ . \tag{8}$$

Eq. (7) is now a special instance of Eq. (8) where $Q = S$, in which case the denominator is 1.

For fitness proportionate selection we know that

$$p(S_i, t) = \phi(S_i, t) \times f(S_i)/\overline{f}(t) = \frac{\phi(S_i, t) \times f(S_i)}{\sum_k (\phi(S_k, t) \times f(S_k))} \ . \tag{9}$$

Putting Eq. (9) into Eq. (6), we then get

Theorem 6 ($\mu(t+1)$ **in Terms of** $\phi(t)$). *If the set of possible strings is partitioned into a set of disjoint, fixed length schemata* $\{S_i\}$ *of uniform fitness, we have, for an infinite population, standard crossover, no mutation, and fitness proportionate selection, that*

$$\mu(t+1) = \frac{\sum_i (|S_i| \times \phi(S_i, t) \times f(S_i))}{\overline{f}(t)} = \frac{\sum_i (|S_i| \times \phi(S_i, t) \times f(S_i))}{\sum_k (\phi(S_k, t) \times f(S_k))} \ . \tag{10}$$

Note that in Eq. (10), the numerator is nearly Eq. (7) for $\mu(t)$ except for the presence of the $f(S_i)$ term. This suggests that if we make some simplifying assumptions about the fitness, we might be able to write this in terms of $\mu(t)$. Assume, then, that the fitness function only has two values, 1 and $1 + \hat{f}$. Then we can split the set $\{S_i\}$ of schemata into a disjoint union $\{S_i\} = \{A_x\} \cup \{B_y\}$ where $\{A_x\} = \{S_i \mid f(S_i) = 1\}$, and $\{B_y\} = \{S_i \mid f(S_i) = 1 + \hat{f}\}$. This allows us to further rewrite Eq. (10):

$\mu(t+1)$

$= \quad \langle$ Eq. (10); definition of $\{A_x\}, \{B_y\}.\ \rangle$

$\dfrac{\sum_x(|A_x| \times \phi(A_x, t) \times f(A_x)) + \sum_y(|B_y| \times \phi(B_y, t) \times f(B_y))}{\sum_x(\phi(A_x, t) \times f(A_x)) + \sum_y(\phi(B_y, t) \times f(B_y))}$

$= \quad \langle\ f(A_x) = 1, f(B_y) = 1 + \hat{f}\ \rangle$

$\dfrac{\sum_x(|A_x| \times \phi(A_x, t)) + \sum_y(|B_y| \times \phi(B_y, t) \times (1 + \hat{f}))}{\sum_x \phi(A_x, t) + \sum_y(\phi(B_y, t) \times (1 + \hat{f}))}$

$= \quad \langle$ Distributing across $(1 + \hat{f}); \{S_i\} = \{A_x\} \cup \{B_y\}\ \rangle$

$\dfrac{\sum_i(|S_i| \times \phi(S_i, t)) + \hat{f} \times \sum_y(|B_y| \times \phi(B_y, t))}{\sum_i \phi(S_i, t) + \hat{f} \times \sum_y \phi(B_y, t)}$

$= \quad \langle$ Equations (7) and (8).$\ \rangle$

$\dfrac{\mu(t) + \hat{f} \times \mu(\{B_y\}, t) \times \sum_y \phi(B_y, t)}{1 + \hat{f} \times \sum_y \phi(B_y, t)}$

$= \quad \langle$ Factor out $\mu(t).\ \rangle$

$\mu(t) \times \dfrac{1 + \frac{\mu(\{B_y\}, t)}{\mu(t)} \times \hat{f} \times \sum_y \phi(B_y, t)}{1 + \hat{f} \times \sum_y \phi(B_y, t)}$

.

This, then, gives us the following:

Theorem 7 (Size Evolution Equation). *If* $\{B_y\}$ *is a set of disjoint, fixed length schemata of uniform fitness* $1 + \hat{f}$, *and the rest of the search space has fitness 1, then,* for an infinite population, standard crossover, no mutation, and fitness proportionate selection, we have

$$\mu(t+1) = \mu(t) \times \frac{1 + \frac{\mu(\{B_y\},t)}{\mu(t)} \times \hat{f} \times \sum_y \phi(B_y,t)}{1 + \hat{f} \times \sum_y \phi(B_y,t)}. \qquad (11)$$

The numerator and denominator in Eq. (11) differ only by $\mu(\{B_y\},t)/\mu(t)$. This allows us to fully characterize the change in the (infinite) population's average size from time t to $t+1$ solely in terms of the sign of $\hat{f}$ and whether $\mu(\{B_y\},t)/\mu(t)$ is greater or less than 1. For "spikes", i.e., when $\hat{f} > 0$, we have

$$\mu(\{B_y\},t)/\mu(t) > 1 \iff \mu(t+1) > \mu(t)$$
$$\mu(\{B_y\},t)/\mu(t) < 1 \iff \mu(t+1) < \mu(t).$$

For "holes", i.e., $\hat{f} < 0$, the converse is true:

$$\mu(\{B_y\},t)/\mu(t) > 1 \iff \mu(t+1) < \mu(t)$$
$$\mu(\{B_y\},t)/\mu(t) < 1 \iff \mu(t+1) > \mu(t).$$

Thus if the fitness of the B_i is better than the fitness of the A_i, the average size of the population will move *towards* the average size of the B_i. If, on the other hand, the fitness of the B_i is worse than the fitness of the A_i, then the average size of the population will move *away from* the average size of the B_i.

It is important to note that this latter case could lead to either bloat *or* a shrinking average size depending on whether $\mu(t)$ is above or below $\mu(\{B_y\},t)$. Thus we see that the same forces that can lead to bloat in one setting can lead to the opposite effect in another setting. It is also important to note that while this tells us that (in these conditions) bloat will continue forever, it does *not* tell us that the magnitude of the bloat is unbounded; it is possible, for example, that the average size will continue to grow towards some asymptotic limit.

One of the most remarkable implications of this is that a *single* string with higher or lower fitness than an otherwise flat landscape is sufficient (in the infinite population case) to drive the average size of the entire population. Preliminary experiments with finite populations indicate that small holes are also capable of affecting change in the average length for a time, although sampling effects eventually take over. It's possible, therefore, that one might be able to use these ideas to develop new methods for managing the size of individuals during a run.

6   Conclusions and Future Work

In this paper we have shown how the schema theory for linear-structure GP from [20] can be productively applied to the important challenge of better understanding the changes in size distributions during a GP run. We have seen (Sec. 1.2) that, while experimental work is crucial, one must be very careful in interpreting the data that comes from unavoidably small views on a large and complex process. Applications of the schema theory to problems both with (Sec. 4) and without fitness (Sec. 3) suggest that standard crossover induces some very specific biases in the distributions of sizes, with a very strong tendency to over sample the smaller structures. There also appear to be significant redistribution effects that may be a major force in the early stages of a GP run. We have also generalized these specific results, yielding two important theoretical results. The first is an exact theory of bloat (Sec. 2.3) which gives a formula for the change in average program size for infinite populations of linear structures when using standard crossover without mutation. The second is a general theory of how average sizes change on flat landscapes with glitches (Sec. 5), including the surprising result that a single string glitch is sufficient to drive the average program size of an infinite population.

These ideas open up numerous possible avenues for future research, both theoretical and applied. While this paper has concentrated on standard GP crossover without mutation, we have extended this elsewhere to include headless chicken crossover and two different types of subtree mutation [19, 14]. The theory could then be extended to combinations of operators, complete with different likelihood of application. Also, since the length distribution for the one-then-zeros problem (Fig. 3(b)) doesn't appear to reach a limit distribution as it did in the flat fitness landscape, finding a closed form for that distribution over time would be of real value. The two-level fitness theory tells us that under certain conditions bloat will happen, and will in fact continue forever, but at the moment it's not clear whether the average size rises towards some asymptotic value, or instead continues without bound.

One of the most intriguing possible applications of these ideas is the possibility of using artificially created "holes" to control code growth. The two-level fitness theory suggests that one might be able to slow or stop bloat either by lowering the fitness of a (possibly small) set of large individuals, or by raising the fitness of a set of small individuals. There are important issues, such as sampling errors, that would also need to be studied, but one might eventually be able to develop a method that would allow us to control code growth in a way which limits the changes made to the fitness landscape, thereby limiting the introduced bias.

Another key application is to the question of population initialization. Most of the existing initialization techniques are fairly ad hoc, and may in fact interact badly with the sampling bias induced by standard crossover. Our theoretical results could be used as the basis for new initialization techniques that minimize the potentially distributive effects of both length redistribution and over sampling of small structures.

In sum, we have seen that the schema theory can be successfully applied to a variety of linear problems, and that the results help answer important questions and suggest interesting new lines of inquiry. It is our expectation that further development will continue to yield valuable results.

Acknowledgements

The authors would like to thank Jonathan Rowe and other members of the EEBIC (Evolutionary and Emergent Behaviour Intelligence and Computation) group at Birmingham for helpful comments and discussion. We are also grateful for the valuable feedback provided by Bill Langdon and the anonymous reviewers.

The first author would like to extend special thanks to The University of Birmingham School of Computer Science for graciously hosting him during his sabbatical, and various offices and individuals at the University of Minnesota, Morris, for making that sabbatical possible.

References

[1] L. Altenberg. The evolution of evolvability in genetic programming. In K. E. Kinnear, Jr., editor, *Advances in Genetic Programming*, chapter 3, pages 47–74. MIT Press, 1994.

[2] P. J. Angeline. Genetic programming and emergent intelligence. In K. E. Kinnear, Jr., editor, *Advances in Genetic Programming*, chapter 4, pages 75–98. MIT Press, 1994.

[3] T. Blickle and L. Thiele. Genetic programming and redundancy. In J. Hopf, editor, *Genetic Algorithms within the Framework of Evolutionary Computation (Workshop at KI-94, Saarbrücken)*, pages 33–38, Im Stadtwald, Building 44, D-66123 Saarbrücken, Germany, 1994. Max-Planck-Institut für Informatik (MPI-I-94-241).

[4] R. Dawkins. *The selfish gene*. Oxford University Press, Oxford, 1976.

[5] J. R. Koza. *Genetic Programming: On the Programming of Computers by Means of Natural Selection*. MIT Press, Cambridge, MA, USA, 1992.

[6] W. B. Langdon. Scaling of program tree fitness spaces. *Evolutionary Computation*, 7(4):399–428, Winter 1999.

[7] W. B. Langdon. Quadratic bloat in genetic programming. In D. Whitley, D. Goldberg, E. Cantu-Paz, L. Spector, I. Parmee, and H.-G. Beyer, editors, *Proceedings of the Genetic and Evolutionary Computation Conference (GECCO-2000)*, pages 451–458, Las Vegas, Nevada, USA, 10-12 July 2000. Morgan Kaufmann.

[8] W. B. Langdon and W. Banzhaf. Genetic programming bloat without semantics. In M. Schoenauer, K. Deb, G. Rudolph, X. Yao, E. Lutton, J. J. Merelo, and H.-P. Schwefel, editors, *Parallel Problem Solving from Nature - PPSN VI 6th International Conference*, volume 1917 of *LNCS*, pages 201–210, Paris, France, Sept. 16-20 2000. Springer Verlag.

[9] W. B. Langdon and R. Poli. Fitness causes bloat. In P. K. Chawdhry, R. Roy, and R. K. Pant, editors, *Soft Computing in Engineering Design and Manufacturing*, pages 13–22. Springer-Verlag London, 23-27 June 1997.

[10] W. B. Langdon and R. Poli. Why ants are hard. In J. R. Koza, W. Banzhaf, K. Chellapilla, K. Deb, M. Dorigo, D. B. Fogel, M. H. Garzon, D. E. Goldberg, H. Iba, and R. Riolo, editors, *Genetic Programming 1998: Proceedings of the Third Annual Conference*, pages 193–201, University of Wisconsin, Madison, Wisconsin, USA, 22-25 July 1998. Morgan Kaufmann.

[11] W. B. Langdon, T. Soule, R. Poli, and J. A. Foster. The evolution of size and shape. In L. Spector, W. B. Langdon, U.-M. O'Reilly, and P. J. Angeline, editors, *Advances in Genetic Programming 3*, chapter 8, pages 163–190. MIT Press, Cambridge, MA, USA, June 1999.

[12] N. F. McPhee. A note on the derivation of transmission probabilities for a flat fitness landscape and for the one-then-zeros problem. 2000. Unpublished; contact the author at mcphee@mrs.umn.edu for a copy.

[13] N. F. McPhee and J. D. Miller. Accurate replication in genetic programming. In L. Eshelman, editor, *Genetic Algorithms: Proceedings of the Sixth International Conference (ICGA95)*, pages 303–309, Pittsburgh, PA, USA, 15-19 July 1995. Morgan Kaufmann.

[14] N. F. McPhee, R. Poli, and J. E. Rowe. A schema theory analysis of mutation size biases in genetic programming with linear representations. Technical Report CSRP-00-24, University of Birmingham, School of Computer Science, December 2000.

[15] P. Nordin and W. Banzhaf. Complexity compression and evolution. In L. Eshelman, editor, *Genetic Algorithms: Proceedings of the Sixth International Conference (ICGA95)*, pages 310–317, Pittsburgh, PA, USA, 15-19 July 1995. Morgan Kaufmann.

[16] R. Poli. Exact schema theorem and effective fitness for GP with one-point crossover. In D. Whitley, D. Goldberg, E. Cantu-Paz, L. Spector, I. Parmee, and H.-G. Beyer, editors, *Proceedings of the Genetic and Evolutionary Computation Conference (GECCO-2000)*, pages 469–476, Las Vegas, Nevada, USA, 10-12 July 2000. Morgan Kaufmann.

[17] R. Poli. General schema theory for genetic programming with subtree-swapping crossover. In *Genetic Programming, Proceedings of EuroGP 2001*, LNCS, Milan, 18-20 Apr. 2001. Springer-Verlag.

[18] R. Poli and W. B. Langdon. A new schema theory for genetic programming with one-point crossover and point mutation. In J. R. Koza, K. Deb, M. Dorigo, D. B. Fogel, M. Garzon, H. Iba, and R. L. Riolo, editors, *Genetic Programming 1997: Proceedings of the Second Annual Conference*, pages 278–285, Stanford University, CA, USA, 13-16 July 1997. Morgan Kaufmann.

[19] R. Poli and N. F. McPhee. Exact GP schema theory for headless chicken crossover and subtree mutation. Technical Report CSRP-00-23, University of Birmingham, School of Computer Science, December 2000.

[20] R. Poli and N. F. McPhee. Exact schema theorems for GP with one-point and standard crossover operating on linear structures and their application to the study of the evolution of size. In *Genetic Programming, Proceedings of EuroGP 2001*, LNCS, Milan, 18-20 Apr. 2001. Springer-Verlag.

[21] T. Soule. *Code Growth in Genetic Programming*. PhD thesis, University of Idaho, Moscow, Idaho, USA, 15 May 1998.

[22] T. Soule and J. A. Foster. Removal bias: a new cause of code growth in tree based evolutionary programming. In *1998 IEEE International Conference on Evolutionary Computation*, pages 781–186, Anchorage, Alaska, USA, 5-9 May 1998. IEEE Press.

[23] C. R. Stephens and H. Waelbroeck. Schemata evolution and building blocks. *Evolutionary Computation*, 7(2):109–124, 1999.

[24] B.-T. Zhang and H. Mühlenbein. Balancing accuracy and parsimony in genetic programming. *Evolutionary Computation*, 3(1):17–38, 1995.

Exact Schema Theorems for GP with One-Point and Standard Crossover Operating on Linear Structures and Their Application to the Study of the Evolution of Size

Riccardo Poli[1] and Nicholas Freitag McPhee[2]

[1] School of Computer Science, The University of Birmingham
Birmingham, B15 2TT, UK
R.Poli@cs.bham.ac.uk, http://www.cs.bham.ac.uk/~rmp/
[2] Division of Science and Mathematics, University of Minnesota, Morris
Morris, MN, USA
mcphee@mrs.umn.edu, http://www.mrs.umn.edu/~mcphee

Abstract. In this paper, firstly we specialise the exact GP schema theorem for one-point crossover to the case of linear structures of variable length, for example binary strings or programs with arity-1 primitives only. Secondly, we extend this to an exact schema theorem for GP with standard crossover applicable to the case of linear structures. Then we study, both mathematically and numerically, the schema equations and their fixed points for infinite populations for both a constant and a length-related fitness function. This allows us to characterise the bias induced by standard crossover. This is very peculiar. In the case of a constant fitness function, at the fixed-point, structures of any length are present with non-zero probability. However, shorter structures are sampled exponentially much more frequently than longer ones.

1 Introduction

In recent work [6] an exact schema theorem for GP with one-point crossover has been introduced. This gives an exact expression for the expected number of instances of a schema H at generation $t + 1$, $E[m(H, t + 1)]$, in terms of macroscopic quantities (i.e. properties of schemata, like their fitness or number of instances, as opposed to microscopic properties of the individuals in the population, like their selection probability) measured at generation t.

The theorem has the form $E[m(H, t + 1)] = M\alpha(H, t)$, where M is the number of individuals in the population and $\alpha(H, t)$, which we term the *total transmission probability* of H, is the probability that an individual created through the selection/crossover/mutation process samples H [12]. [6] provides an exact value of $\alpha(H, t)$ for a GP system with *one-point crossover* [9, 11]. This operator works by selecting a common crossover point in the parent programs and then swapping the corresponding subtrees, like standard crossover. To account for the possible structural diversity of the two parents, one-point crossover selects the crossover point only in the part of the two trees which have the same topology. This is called the *common region*.

The theory is based on the definition of GP schema proposed in [9] in which a *schema* is a tree composed of functions from the set $\mathcal{F} \cup \{=\}$ and terminals from the

J. Miller et al. (Eds.): EuroGP 2001, LNCS 2038, pp. 126–142, 2001.

set $\mathcal{T} \cup \{=\}$, where $\mathcal{F}$ and $\mathcal{T}$ are the function set and the terminal set used in a GP run. The symbol $=$ is a "don't care" symbol which stands for a *single* terminal or function. A schema H represents programs having the same shape as H and the same labels for the non-$=$ nodes. In order to be able to represent programs of different sizes and shapes the theory requires also the definition of the concept of hyperschema [7]. A *GP hyperschema* is a rooted tree composed of functions from the set $\mathcal{F} \cup \{=\}$ and terminals from the set $\mathcal{T} \cup \{=, \#\}$. The symbol $=$ is as above, while the symbol $\#$ stands for any valid subtree. The notion of hyperschema is a generalisation of both the GP schemata defined above (which are hyperschemata without $\#$ symbols) and Rosca's schemata [13] (which are hyperschemata without $=$ symbols).

With these definitions one can prove [6] that the total transmission probability for a GP schema H under one-point crossover and no mutation is:

$$\alpha(H,t) = (1 - p_{xo})p(H,t) + p_{xo}\sum_j\sum_k \frac{1}{\mathbf{NC}(G_j, G_k)}$$
$$\cdot \sum_{i \in C(G_j, G_k)} p(L(H,i) \cap G_j, t)p(U(H,i) \cap G_k, t) \qquad (1)$$

where: p_{xo} is the probability of crossover; $p(H,t)$ is the probability of selecting an individual matching the schema H; $G_1, G_2, \cdots$ are all the different schemata that can be built from $=$ nodes only;[1] the indices j and k range over all the different G_i; $C(G_j, G_k)$ is the set of crossover points in the common region between schema G_j and schema G_k; $\mathbf{NC}(G_j, G_k) = |C(G_j, G_k)|$ is the number of nodes in the common region; the index i ranges over all the crossover points in $C(G_j, G_k)$; $L(H,i)$ is the hyperschema obtained by replacing all the nodes on the path between crossover point i and the root node with $=$ nodes, and all the subtrees connected to these nodes with $\#$ nodes; $U(H,i)$ is the hyperschema obtained by replacing the subtree below crossover point i with a $\#$ node (more details on these definitions can be found in [6, 7]). In fitness proportionate selection, $p(H,t) = \frac{m(H,t)f(H,t)}{M\bar{f}(t)}$ where $m(H,t)$ is the number of programs matching the schema H at generation t, $f(H,t)$ is the mean fitness of the programs matching H, and $\bar{f}(t)$ is the mean fitness of the programs in the population. The hyperschemata $L(H,i)$ and $U(H,i)$ are important because they allow the identification of parents that may lead to the creation of offspring in H: if one crosses over at point i *any* individual in $L(H,i)$ with *any* individual in $U(H,i)$, the resulting offspring is always an instance of H.

In [6] an example was presented which used only unary functions. With this function set only linear trees can be created and, therefore, GP becomes a sort of variable-length GA. In that example, the new schema theorem was applied to a specific schema and a specific population. In this paper we study in much greater depth what happens in a GP system handling linear structures. We start by specialising the schema theorem for one-point crossover to such a case, but without focusing on any particular schema (as was the case in the example in [6]), and by then extending this to an exact schema theorem for GP with standard crossover applicable to the case of linear structures.

---

[1] Thus the G_i can be seen as cataloguing all the different program shapes.

2   Exact Schema Theory for Linear Structures

When only unary functions are used in GP, schemata (and programs) can only take the form $(h_1(h_2(h_3....(h_{N-1}h_N)....)))$ where $N > 0$, $h_i \in \mathcal{F} \cup \{=\}$ for $1 \leq i < N$, and $h_N \in \mathcal{T} \cup \{=\}$. Therefore, they can be written unambiguously as strings of symbols of the form $h_1h_2h_3....h_{N-1}h_N$.

In order to make the specialisation of Equation 1 to the linear case easier we represent repeated symbols in a string using the power notation where x^y means x repeated y times. For example, the schema 11100000===1 can be written as $1^3 0^5 (=)^3 1$. Since in this case all trees are linear, the space of program shapes can be enumerated by $\{G_n\}$ where G_n is $(=)^n$ for $n > 0$. Given this, the common region between shapes G_j and G_k is simply the shorter of the two schemata, and the size of the common region, $\mathbf{NC}(G_j, G_k)$, is simply $\min(j, k)$. Therefore, the set of crossover points in the common region, $C(G_j, G_k)$, can be identified with the set of indices $\{0, 1, ..., \min(j, k) - 1\}$ where the index 0 represent a crossover point before the first symbol in a string (the root node). In this linear representation the hyperschemata $L(H, i)$ and $U(H, i)$ are particularly simple: $U(H, i)$ is $h_1...h_i\#$ and $L(H, i)$ is $(=)^i h_{i+1}...h_N$, where $0 \leq i < N$ (with the convention that for $i = 0$ the hyperschema $h_1...h_i\#$ is simply $\#$). So,

$$U(H, i) \cap G_k \equiv \begin{cases} h_1...h_i(=)^{k-i} & \text{if } i < k, \\ \emptyset & \text{otherwise,} \end{cases}$$

and

$$L(H, i) \cap G_j \equiv \begin{cases} (=)^i h_{i+1}...h_N & \text{if } j = N, \\ \emptyset & \text{otherwise,} \end{cases}$$

where $\emptyset$ is the empty set. Therefore, the summation in j in Equation 1 disappears because $p(L(H, i) \cap G_j, t) = 0$ for all $j \neq N$. As a result of these simplifications, one can transform Equation 1 into:

Theorem 1. *The total transmission probability for a linear GP schema of the form* $h_1...h_N$ *under one-point crossover and no mutation is*

$$\alpha(h_1...h_N, t) = (1 - p_{xo})p(h_1...h_N, t) + p_{xo} \cdot \tag{2}$$

$$\sum_k \frac{1}{\min(N, k)} \cdot \sum_{i=0}^{\min(N,k)-1} p(h_1...h_i(=)^{k-i}, t)p((=)^i h_{i+1}...h_N, t).$$

This result can then be extended to obtain the following:

Theorem 2. *The total transmission probability for a linear GP schema of the form* $h_1...h_N$ *under standard crossover with uniform selection of the crossover points and no mutation is*

$$\alpha(h_1...h_N, t) = (1 - p_{xo})p(h_1...h_N, t) + \tag{3}$$

$$p_{xo} \sum_k \frac{1}{k} \sum_{i=0}^{\min(N,k)-1} p(h_1...h_i(=)^{k-i}, t) \sum_{n=N-i}^{\infty} \frac{p((=)^{n-N+i} h_{i+1}...h_N, t)}{n}.$$

Proof. The theorem can be derived as a special case of the more general result reported in [8]. However, here we provide an direct proof which shows how this result can be derived by modifying Equation 2.

Equation 2 clearly indicates that one-point crossover with a given crossover point i can create new instances of the schema $h_1...h_N$ only if selection picks up a first parent whose first i nodes match $h_1...h_i$ and a second parent whose last $N - i$ nodes match $h_{i+1}...h_N$. Given that one-point crossover forces the selection of a common crossover point, this means that the second parent must be always of length N. However, if one used standard crossover, one could create instances of $h_1...h_N$ even if the length of the second parent is different from N, provided that the last $N - i$ nodes of the second parent match $h_{i+1}...h_N$ and the second crossover point excised such nodes. If the second crossover point is at position l, this can happen if selection picks up a second parent matching $(=)^l h_{i+1}...h_N$ for any value of $l \geq 0$. Thus, an extra summation needs to be added to Equation 2 to deal with standard crossover. The probability of choosing crossover point l in a second parent matching $(=)^l h_{i+1}...h_N$ is $1/(l + N - i)$. Therefore, after the change of variable $n = l + N - j$ one obtains that the probability of obtaining the subschema $h_{i+1}...h_N$ from the second parent is $\sum_{n=N-i}^{\infty} \frac{p((=)^{n-N+i} h_{i+1}...h_N, t)}{n}$. This should replace the term $p((=)^i h_{i+1}...h_N, t)$ in Equation 2. Since standard crossover does not limit the crossover point in the first parent to belong to the common region, the probability of selecting crossover point i needs to change from $1/\min(N, k)$ to $1/k$. This completes the proof of the theorem. $\square$

Equation 3 is in a form which makes it easy to see the similarities with Equation 2. However, the reader might find it easier to understand the same result rewritten as in the following:

Corollary 1. *The total transmission probability for a linear GP schema of the form $h_1...h_N$ under standard crossover with uniform selection of the crossover points and no mutation can be written in the following equivalent forms:*

$$\alpha(h_1...h_N, t) = (1 - p_{xo})p(h_1...h_N, t)+ \tag{4}$$
$$p_{xo} \sum_{i=0}^{N-1} \sum_{k>i} \sum_{n \geq N-i} \frac{1}{kn} p(h_1...h_i(=)^{k-i}, t)p((=)^{n-N+i} h_{i+1}...h_N, t),$$

$$\alpha(h_1...h_N, t) = (1 - p_{xo})p(h_1...h_N, t)+ \tag{5}$$
$$p_{xo} \sum_{i=0}^{N-1} \sum_{k>0} \sum_{n \geq 0} \frac{1}{(k+i)(n-i+N)} p(h_1...h_i(=)^k, t)p((=)^n h_{i+1}...h_N, t).$$

Equation 4 makes the idea of summing over the set of possible crossover points clearer. Equation 5 makes the idea of summing over varying lengths of "don't care" symbols clearer.

3   Evolution of Size in Linear Systems

Equations 2 and 3 can be used to study, among other things, the evolution of size in linear GP/GA systems. This is because they can be specialised to describe the transmission probability of schemata of the form $(=)^N$. For one-point crossover (Equation 2) one obtains:

$$\alpha((=)^N, t) = (1 - p_{xo})p((=)^N, t) + p_{xo} \sum_k \sum_{i=0}^{\min(N,k)-1} \frac{p((=)^k, t)p((=)^N, t)}{\min(N, k)}$$

$$= (1 - p_{xo})p((=)^N, t) + p_{xo}p((=)^N, t) \sum_k p((=)^k, t)$$

$$= p((=)^N, t), \tag{6}$$

where we exploited the fact that $\sum_k p((=)^k, t) = 1$ since $\bigcup_k (=)^k$ represents the entire search space and $(=)^k \cap (=)^j$ is the empty set for any $k \neq j$. This result indicates that length evolves under one-point crossover as if selection only was acting (p_{xo}, for example, has no effect). So, one-point crossover is totally unbiased with respect to program length. This is made particularly clear if one assumes a flat fitness landscape in which $f(H, t) = \bar{f}(t)$ for all H. In these conditions all the dynamics in the system must be caused by crossover or by sampling effects. For a flat landscape under fitness proportionate selection Equation 6 becomes $\alpha((=)^N, t) = m((=)^N, t)/M$ for finite populations, and $\alpha((=)^N, t) = \alpha((=)^N, t - 1)$ in the infinite population limit. This is because, in the infinite population case, the quantity $\alpha(H, t)$ can be interpreted in two entirely equivalent ways: as the total transmission probability of the schema H at generation t or as the proportion of individuals in the population in H at generation $t + 1$. In this second interpretation, we conventionally define $\alpha(H, -1)$ as the proportion of programs in H at generation 0. Clearly, $\alpha(H, -1)$ is entirely determined by the initialisation procedure adopted.

The equation $\alpha((=)^N, t) = \alpha((=)^N, t - 1)$ obtained for the infinite population case is particularly important because it shows that when one-point crossover alone is acting, any initial distribution of lengths, $\alpha((=)^N, -1)$, is a fixed point for the system.

For standard crossover (Equation 3) one obtains:

$$\alpha((=)^N, t) = (1 - p_{xo})p((=)^N, t) + \tag{7}$$

$$p_{xo} \sum_k \sum_{i=0}^{\min(N,k)-1} \frac{p((=)^k, t)}{k} \sum_{n=N-i}^{\infty} \frac{p((=)^n, t)}{n},$$

which can be transformed into

$$\alpha((=)^N, t) = (1 - p_{xo})p((=)^N, t) + p_{xo} \sum_k \frac{p((=)^k, t)}{k}. \tag{8}$$

$$\sum_{n=\max(1,N-k+1)}^{\infty} \frac{p((=)^n, t)}{n} \min(N, k, n, k + n - N).$$

Alternative formulations for this equation can be obtained specialising Corollary 1. For example, from Equation 4 one obtains:

$$\alpha((=)^N, t) = (1 - p_{xo})p((=)^N, t) + p_{xo} \sum_{i=0}^{N-1} \sum_{k>i} \frac{p((=)^k, t)}{k} \sum_{n \geq N-i} \frac{p((=)^n, t)}{n}.$$

An alternative way of expressing $\alpha((=)^N, t)$ for standard crossover in terms of *microscopic* quantities is the following:

$$\alpha((=)^N, t) = (1 - p_{xo})p((=)^N, t \tag{9}$$

$$+p_{xo} \sum_{z_1 \in P} \sum_{z_2 \in P} \sum_{x_1=0}^{N(z_1)-1} \sum_{x_2=0}^{N(z_2)-1} \frac{p(z_1,t)p(z_2,t)}{N(z_1)N(z_2)} \delta(x_1 + N(z_2) - x_2 = N)$$

in which P is the population at generation t, z_1 and z_2 vary over all the possible parents (i.e. the members of P) while x_1 and x_2 vary over all the possible crossover points in z_1 and z_2, respectively. This equation explicitly includes one term for each of the possible ways in which offspring can be created from the parents in the population for all possible crossover points. In the equation, the term $\frac{p(z_1,t)p(z_2,t)}{N(z_1)N(z_2)}$ represents the probability that each of such event be the case, while the term $\delta(x_1 + N(z_2) - x_2 = N)$ makes sure that only the probabilities of the events that lead to the creation of an offspring of length N are included in the sum.

These equations show that for standard crossover not every initial distribution of program lengths is a fixed point (for an infinite population) even if one considers the case of a flat landscape. For example, if one started at generation 0 with only programs of length X, i.e. $\alpha((=)^x, -1) = \delta(x = X)$, assuming $p_{xo} = 1$ one would obtain the following distribution of lengths at generation 1:

$$\alpha((=)^N, 0) = \max\left(\frac{X - |X - N|}{X^2}, 0\right). \tag{10}$$

This implies that $\alpha((=)^X, 0) = 1/X$ which is in general different from $\alpha((=)^X, -1) = 1$ (except for the trivial case in which $X = 1$).[2] So, standard crossover imposes its own specific bias on the distribution of lengths, although we expect that such a bias will have no influence on the average length of programs, since on average the subtrees/substrings swapped by crossover are of the same size. This conjecture can actually be proven mathematically obtaining the following:

Theorem 3. *The mean size of the programs at generation* $t+1$, $\mu(t+1)$, *in a linear GP system with standard crossover, uniform selection of the crossover points, no mutation and an infinite population is*

$$\mu(t + 1) = \sum_N Np((=)^N, t) \tag{11}$$

with the same meaning of the symbols as in previous theorems.

Proof. By definition of mean $\mu(t+1) = \sum_N N\alpha((=)^N, t)$. By substituting Equation 9 into this equation one obtains:

$$\mu(t + 1) = (1 - p_{xo}) \sum_N Np((=)^N, t) + p_{xo} \sum_N N \times$$

---

[2] If all programs include only one node (a terminal), standard crossover, like one-point crossover, cannot produce programs with more than one node.

$$\sum_{z_1 \in P} \sum_{z_2 \in P} \sum_{x_1=0}^{N(z_1)-1} \sum_{x_2=0}^{N(z_2)-1} \frac{p(z_1,t)p(z_2,t)}{N(z_1)N(z_2)} \delta(x_1 + N(z_2) - x_2 = N)$$

$$= (1 - p_{xo}) \sum_N Np((=)^N, t) + p_{xo} \sum_{z_1 \in P} \sum_{z_2 \in P} \frac{p(z_1,t)p(z_2,t)}{N(z_1)N(z_2)} \times$$

$$\sum_{x_1=0}^{N(z_1)-1} \sum_{x_2=0}^{N(z_2)-1} \sum_N N\delta(x_1 + N(z_2) - x_2 = N).$$

With a few calculations it is possible to show that

$$\sum_{x_1=0}^{N(z_1)-1} \sum_{x_2=0}^{N(z_2)-1} \sum_N N\delta(x_1 + N(z_2) - x_2 = N) = N(z_1)N(z_2)\frac{N(z_1) + N(z_2)}{2}$$

whereby

$$\mu(t+1) = (1 - p_{xo}) \sum_N Np((=)^N, t)$$

$$+ p_{xo} \sum_{z_1 \in P} \sum_{z_2 \in P} p(z_1,t)p(z_2,t)\frac{N(z_1) + N(z_2)}{2}$$

$$= (1 - p_{xo}) \sum_N Np((=)^N, t) + p_{xo} \sum_{z_1 \in P} p(z_1,t)\frac{N(z_1)}{2} \sum_{z_2 \in P} p(z_2,t)$$

$$+ p_{xo} \sum_{z_2 \in P} p(z_2,t)\frac{N(z_2)}{2} \sum_{z_1 \in P} p(z_1,t)$$

$$= (1 - p_{xo}) \sum_N Np((=)^N, t) + p_{xo} \sum_{z \in P} p(z,t)N(z)$$

$$= (1 - p_{xo}) \sum_N Np((=)^N, t) + p_{xo} \sum_k N((=)^k) \cdot \sum_{z \in P \cap (=)^k} p(z,t)$$

$$= (1 - p_{xo}) \sum_N Np((=)^N, t) + p_{xo} \sum_k kp((=)^k, t)$$

$$= \sum_N Np((=)^N, t).$$

$\square$

Corollary 2. *On a flat landscape,*

$$\mu(t+1) = \mu(t). \tag{12}$$

It is very difficult to find the fixed points (or to prove that there are none) for a GP system using standard crossover even on the hypothesis of infinite populations and flat landscapes. However, it is possible to find such fixed points numerically by implementing the schema equations and iterating them as described in the next section. We will show in Section 5 how the information provided by such simulations, along with a substantial amount of luck, has allowed us to identify a mathematical function which is provably a fixed point for the size distribution in a linear GP system with standard crossover operating on a flat landscape.

4   Experimental Results

In our experiments we were interested in studying the evolution of program size and the bias imposed by different crossovers. Since the effects of selection on its own have been already studied in great depth in various studies, we concentrated on the effects produced by crossover, i.e. by setting $p_{xo} = 1$. In the experiments we iterated the schema equations provided in the previous section on the assumption of infinite populations. This corresponds to studying either the exact behaviour of a GP system with an infinite population or the average behaviour of the GP system with a finite population over an infinite number of runs.

In the simulations we kept track of $\alpha((=)^N, t)$ for $N > 0$ such that $\alpha((=)^N, t) > 0$. Since in an infinite population standard crossover nearly doubles the length of the longest program in each generation, the number of N that need to be tracked grows exponentially as a function of t. As a result we restricted our attention to $t \leq 4$. Fortunately, this small number of generations was still sufficient to show the system convergence.

In the experiments we used three different initial conditions: the *one peak* distribution,

$$\alpha((=)^N, -1) = \delta(N = 20)$$

where only programs of length 20 are present, the *two peak* distribution

$$\alpha((=)^N, -1) = \begin{cases} 0.5 & \text{if } N = 14 \text{ or } N = 26, \\ 0 & \text{otherwise,} \end{cases}$$

and the *uniform* distribution

$$\alpha((=)^N, -1) = \begin{cases} 1/39 & \text{if } 0 < N < 40, \\ 0 & \text{otherwise.} \end{cases} \tag{13}$$

These three distributions are all characterised by the same average lengths of 20.

In addition to a flat fitness landscape, realised by a fitness function which always returned the value 10, we used the following *size-related* fitness function

$$f(h_1...h_N) = (20 - |20 - N|)\delta(0 < N < 40) \tag{14}$$

which returns 20 minus the distance between the program length, N, and a target length of 20 for $0 < N < 40$, and 0 for $N \geq 40$.

On the flat fitness landscape one-point crossover behaved as expected. All initial distributions $\alpha((=)^N, -1)$ we tried were fixed points.

The situation was very different for standard crossover. As shown in Figure 1, with the *one-peak* initialisation, after one iteration (i.e. at $t = 1$) we obtained the triangular profile calculated in the previous section.[3] As hypothesised, in later generations the average program size remained constant. However, the distribution of sizes does not remain symmetric. In fact, it quickly approaches a limit distribution, where most of the programs were quite short. Exactly the same fixed point distribution was approached when initialising the system using the two-peak and the uniform distributions as shown in Figures 2 and 3. This fixed point distribution closely resembles a gamma distribution, a fact that is explored in more detail in the next section.

As a sanity check to make sure that these results were not an artifact of our numerical simulations, we performed real GP runs with a population of 10,000 individuals initialised with the uniform distribution of lengths in Equation 13. The fitness function was flat. The runs were continued for 250 generations. No depth limit was imposed on the offspring produced by crossover. The distribution of lengths in the last 50 generations was recorded. Figure 4 shows the average proportion of programs of each length in the last 50 generations of one run (middle line) along with the 2-standard-deviation wide confidence intervals. It is easy to see how close the average distribution of lengths is to the fixed point distribution obtained by iterating the schema equations (Figure 3, thick line).

In the schema-equation experiments we obtained different fixed point distributions only when we used initial conditions with a different average size, suggesting that the fixed point distribution for standard crossover is only a function of the average size, and independent of the actual shape of the initial distribution. This family of fix-point distributions characterises the search bias imposed by standard crossover when acting on linear structures: in the absence of other biases standard crossover will tend to more heavily sample the space of smaller-than-average programs and will be unable to focus its search on programs of a particular size. This means that if selection prefers longer-than-average programs or programs of a certain length, standard crossover may negatively bias the search. This does not happen with one-point crossover, provided that the initial population includes sufficient variety of shapes.

This effect becomes evident when the size-related fitness function in Equation 14 is used. With this fitness function programs of length 20 are maximally fit. However, due to the biases of standard crossover, the fixed point distribution obtained with different initial conditions (see Figures 5, 6 and 7) all share the same features: inability to focus on the maximally fit length and bias towards short programs.

For comparison, Figure 8 shows the behaviour of one-point crossover on the same function with uniform initial conditions. This corroborates the theoretical results in Section 3 which indicated that one-point crossover is a transparent (i.e. unbiased) operator as far as program lengths are concerned.

---

[3] In this and the following figures, the plots for generation 0 and 1 are shown with thin lines. The lines become progressively thicker as the number of generations increase. Because of the quick convergence to a fixed point, the plots for $t = 3$ and $t = 4$ are often indistinguishable.

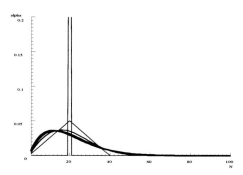

Fig. 1. Total transmission probability for standard crossover on a flat landscape with one-peak initial conditions. The first four generations are shown.

Fig. 2. Total transmission probability for standard crossover on a flat landscape with two-peak initial conditions. The first four generations are shown.

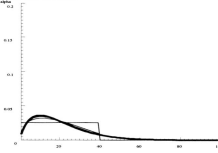
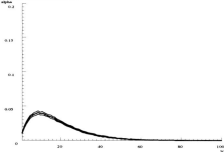

Fig. 3. Total transmission probability for standard crossover on a flat landscape with uniform initial conditions. The first four generations are shown.

Fig. 4. Proportion of programs of each length in a real GP run for standard crossover on a flat landscape with uniform initial conditions.

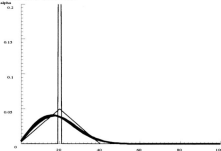
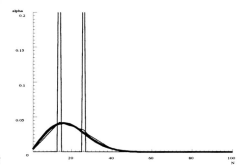

Fig. 5. Total transmission probability for standard crossover on a size-related landscape (Equation 14) with one-point initial conditions. The first four generations are shown.

Fig. 6. Total transmission probability for standard crossover on a size-related landscape with two-point initial conditions. The first four generations are shown.

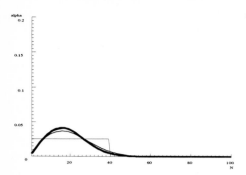

Fig. 7. Total transmission probability for standard crossover on a size-related landscape with uniform initial conditions. The first four generations are shown.

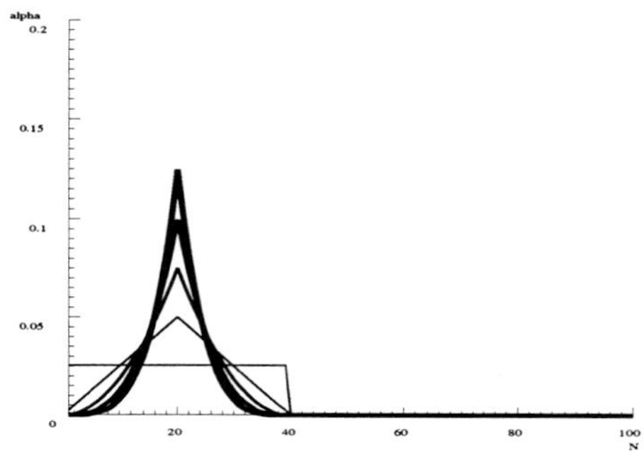

Fig. 8. Total transmission probability for one-point crossover on a size-related landscape with uniform initial conditions. The first four generations are shown.

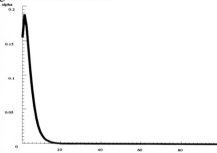

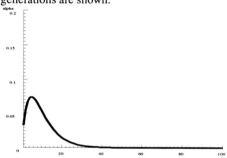

Fig. 9. Total transmission probability for standard crossover on a flat landscape with initial conditions $g_d(2, N)$.

Fig. 10. Total transmission probability for standard crossover on a flat landscape with initial conditions $g_d(5, N)$.

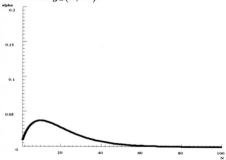

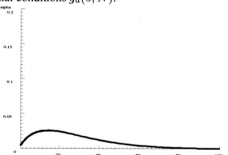

Fig. 11. Total transmission probability for standard crossover on a flat landscape with initial conditions $g_d(10, N)$.

Fig. 12. Total transmission probability for standard crossover on a flat landscape with initial conditions $g_d(15, N)$.

5   Fixed-Point Size Distribution for Standard Crossover on a Flat Landscape

As noted in the previous section, the fixed-point distribution of lengths approached in the experiments with a flat landscape under standard crossover strongly resembles a gamma distribution. This observation prompted us to try to verify mathematically whether this is indeed the case.

A gamma distribution has the following form:

$$g(a, b, x) = \frac{x^{a-1} e^{-x/b}}{\Gamma(a) b^a} \tag{15}$$

where $\Gamma(a)$ is a generalisation of the factorial function[4] defined by

$$\Gamma(a) = \int_0^\infty e^{-t} t^{a-1} dt.$$

The gamma distribution has two parameters a and b that change its shape. For values of $a > 1$, $g(a, b, 0) = 0$. Also $\lim_{x \to \infty} g(a, b, x) = 0$ and the distribution has its maximum when $x = b(a - 1)$. The mean of a gamma distribution is $\mu = ab$. So, the maximum of the distribution is shifted with respect to the mean by a distance b (i.e. the maximum is when $x = \mu - b$).

In order to verify if $g(a, b, x)$ is a fixed-point distribution for standard crossover on a flat landscape, firstly one has to specialise Equation 8 by setting $p(H, t) = \alpha(H, t - 1)$. This produces

$$\alpha((=)^N, t) = (1 - p_{xo})\alpha((=)^N, t - 1) + p_{xo} \sum_k \frac{\alpha((=)^k, t - 1)}{k}. \tag{16}$$

$$\sum_{n=\max(1, N-k+1)}^{\infty} \frac{\alpha((=)^n, t - 1)}{n} \min(N, k, n, k + n - N).$$

Then one assumes that the system is in the hypothesised fixed point and substitutes $\alpha((=)^x, t - 1) = g(a, b, x)$ in this equation. If $\alpha((=)^x, t - 1) = g(a, b, x)$ is indeed a fixed-point for the system, then the r.h.s. resulting from this substitution must be equivalent to $g(a, b, N)$.

If one uses the general form for $\alpha((=)^x, t - 1) = g(a, b, x)$, it is actually very difficult to check whether this is a fixed point for Equation 16. However, the experiments in the previous section suggested that a good value for the parameter a would be $a = 2$, which gives

$$g(2, b, x) = \frac{x e^{-x/b}}{b^2}.$$

This function is intuitively very appealing as a potential fixed point because it transforms terms of the form $\frac{\alpha((=)^x, t-1)}{x}$ in Equation 16 into exponentials of the form $\frac{e^{-x/b}}{b^2}$.

---

[4] For integer $a > 0$, $\Gamma(a) = (a - 1)!$.

Indeed, assuming $\alpha((=)^x, t - 1) = g(2, b, x)$ allows one to simplify the r.h.s. of Equation 16 dramatically, obtaining:

$$\alpha((=)^N, t) = \left(\frac{Ne^{-N/b}}{b^2}\right)\left(\frac{1}{b^2(1 - e^{-\frac{1}{b}})(e^{\frac{1}{b}} - 1)}\right). \qquad (17)$$

So,

$$\alpha((=)^N, t) = \alpha((=)^N, t - 1)\left(\frac{1}{b^2(1 - e^{-\frac{1}{b}})(e^{\frac{1}{b}} - 1)}\right). \qquad (18)$$

Since, in general, $b^2(1 - e^{-\frac{1}{b}})(e^{\frac{1}{b}} - 1) \neq 1$, we can conclude from this result that the assumed gamma distribution is not a fixed point for the system.[5] This had to be expected because the gamma distribution is a continuous probability distribution. While $\int_{x \geq 0} g(a, b, x)dx = 1$, it is not true that $\sum_{x \geq 0} g(a, b, x) = 1$. So, sampling $g(a, b, x)$ does not produce a discrete probability distribution. This is why $\alpha((=)^k) = g(2, a, k)$ cannot be a fixed point. However, the distribution obtained by sampling $g(2, b, x)$ can be transformed into a probability distribution by simply normalising each sample, obtaining:

$$g_d(b, x) = xe^{-x/b}(1 - e^{-\frac{1}{b}})(e^{\frac{1}{b}} - 1). \qquad (19)$$

Naturally, $g_d(b, 0) = 0$ and $\lim_{x \to \infty} g_d(b, x) = 0$ and the distribution has a maximum for $x = b$, like $g(2, b, x)$. The mean of the discrete gamma distribution is $\mu = (1 + e^{-\frac{1}{b}})/(1 - e^{-\frac{1}{b}})$, which is only slightly different from (and quickly converges to) $2b$. So, the maximum of the distribution is shifted with respect to the mean by a distance $x = \mu - b \approx b$.

This discrete gamma distribution can be shown mathematically to be a fixed point. So, if

$$\alpha((=)^N, t - 1) = Ne^{-N/b}(1 - e^{-\frac{1}{b}})(e^{\frac{1}{b}} - 1), \qquad (20)$$

then $\alpha((=)^N, t + T) = \alpha((=)^N, t - 1)$ for any positive value of b and T. This can be reformulated in terms of the mean μ of $g_d(b, N)$ by setting $b = -1/\ln((\mu-1)/(\mu+1))$ in $g_d(b, N)$, obtaining

$$\alpha((=)^N, t - 1) = Ne^{N\ln(\frac{\mu-1}{\mu+1})}\left(\frac{\mu + 1}{\mu - 1} - 1\right)\left(1 - \frac{\mu - 1}{\mu + 1}\right), \qquad (21)$$

which can be written more simply

$$\alpha((=)^N, t - 1) = Nr^{N-1}(r - 1)^2, \qquad (22)$$

---

[5] The relative difference between $\alpha((=)^N, t)$ and $\alpha((=)^N, t - 1)$, $\Delta(b) = \frac{b^2(1-e^{-\frac{1}{b}})(e^{\frac{1}{b}}-1)-1}{b^2(1-e^{-\frac{1}{b}})(e^{\frac{1}{b}}-1)}$, is always very small and decreases very quickly as b increases. For example, $\Delta(1) \approx 0.08$, $\Delta(2) \approx 0.02$, $\Delta(5) \approx 0.003$, $\Delta(10) \approx 0.0008$, $\Delta(20) \approx 0.0002$ and $\Delta(100) \approx 8 \times 10^{-6}$. So, for most practical purposes a gamma distribution can be considered to be a fixed point for the evolution of size under standard crossover on a flat landscape.

where $r = (\mu - 1)/(\mu + 1)$. (For an alternative derivation of this and related results see [14].)

This result was also corroborated numerically by initialising the system at $\alpha((=)^N, -1) = g_d(b, N)$ for different values of b and iterating the schema equations for a few generations, as shown in Figures 9–12 where the plots for the first four generations coincide perfectly.

As noted before, on average standard crossover inserts and removes the same amount of genetic material. Therefore, on a flat landscape and with an infinite population no change in mean length can occur. So, given any initial distribution of lengths $\alpha((=)^N, -1)$, if one assumes that there are no fixed points other than the family of discrete gamma functions $g_d(b, x)$, then, by setting $\mu = \sum_N N\alpha((=)^N, -1)$ (the mean length of the programs in the initial generation), Equation 21 gives the fixed point to which GP will converge.

At this stage we are unable to prove that there are no other fixed points in the system. So, we cannot guarantee that the length distribution in GP with standard crossover on a flat landscape will always converge towards a discrete gamma distribution or converge at all. The experiments described in the previous section always seemed to do so, which suggests that other fixed points might be unlikely. Also, even if there are other fixed point distributions, it seems likely that they will share important characteristics with $g_d(b, x)$. This is because GP with standard crossover will always be able to produce programs which are much longer than average. So, the only way in which the average length can remain constant is to have more shorter-than-average programs than longer-than-average ones.

6   Search Space Sampling under Standard Crossover

It is important to understand the consequences of the bias described in the previous section. Let us imagine that our linear GP system operating on a flat landscape is at the fixed point $g_d(b, x)$ for some value of b. Since, there are $n(x) = |\mathcal{F}|^{x-1}|\mathcal{T}|$ different programs of length x in the search space, it is possible to compute the average probability $p_{\text{sample}}(x)$ that each of these will be sampled by standard crossover, namely

$$p_{\text{sample}}(x) = g_d(b, x)/n(x). \tag{23}$$

It is easy to study this function and to conclude that, for a flat landscape, standard GP will sample a particular short program much more often than it will sample a particular long one. Figures 13 and 14 show the average sampling probability for programs of a given length for standard crossover on a flat landscape at the fixed points $g_d(b, x)$ for $b = 2, 5, 10, 20, 50, 100, 1000, 100000, 1000000$ assuming $|\mathcal{F}| = |\mathcal{T}| = 2$. In general, an increase in length of one order of magnitude corresponds to a drop in sampling probability of many orders of magnitude and this trend is largely independent of the particular value of b. For example, when $b = 10$ (i.e. when the average program length is about 20), on average (and approximately) GP will resample the same program of length 5 every 1054 crossovers, while it will resample the same program of length 50 every 3.33×10^{17} crossovers with a difference of 13 orders of magnitude! This difference does not change significantly even for much larger values of b.

Indeed $\lim_{b\to\infty} p_{\text{sample}}(5)/p_{\text{sample}}(50) = \lim_{b\to\infty} \frac{2^{45}}{10}e^{\frac{45}{b}} = \frac{2^{45}}{10} \approx 3.5 \times 10^{12}$ which is still a huge number. An alternative way of looking at this is to calculate the ratio $\frac{p_{\text{sample}}(x)}{p_{\text{sample}}(x+1)} = \frac{2x}{x+1}e^{\frac{1}{b}} > \frac{2x}{x+1}$, which for large values of x is approximately 2.

Preliminary work suggests that similar results hold for GP with standard crossover operating on trees. If these results are confirmed the widely reported tendency to bloat is particularly remarkable.

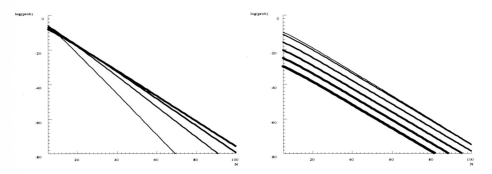

Fig. 13. Plot of the average sampling probability $p_{\text{sample}}(N)$ vs. program length N for standard crossover on a flat landscape at the fixed points $g_d(b, N)$ for $b = 2, 5, 10, 20$ for $|\mathcal{F}| = |\mathcal{T}| = 2$. Thicker plots represent higher values of b. Note the use of a logarithmic scale.

Fig. 14. Plot of the average sampling probability $p_{\text{sample}}(N)$ vs. program length N for standard crossover on a flat landscape at the fixed points $g_d(b, N)$ for $b = 50, 100, 1000, 100000, 1000000$ for $|\mathcal{F}| = |\mathcal{T}| = 2$. Thicker plots represent higher values of b. Note the use of a logarithmic scale.

7   Conclusions

In this paper, an exact schema theorem for genetic programming operating on linear structures using standard crossover has been provided. Using this theorem and the corresponding version for one-point crossover, which is also reported, we have been able to study the evolution of size and the biases introduced by the operators both mathematically and in simulations.

This research establishes a link between important areas of theoretical research in GP: the study of the evolution of shape and size [1], the biases imposed by different operators [10] and the theory of schemata [9, 7, 6]. In recent research we have started using these results to study bloat in linear representations [3]. In the future we hope to be able to use this theory to model mathematically and better understand the operator bias as well as the reasons for bloat, intron proliferation and code compression [2, 4, 5] in non-linear structures.

Acknowledgements

The authors would like to thank Bill Langdon, Jonathan Rowe and other members of the EEBIC (Evolutionary and Emergent Behaviour Intelligence and Computation) group at Birmingham for helpful comments and discussion.

The second author would like to extend special thanks to The University of Birmingham School of Computer Science for graciously hosting him during his sabbatical, and various offices and individuals at the University of Minnesota, Morris, for making that sabbatical possible.

References

[1] W. B. Langdon, T. Soule, R. Poli, and J. A. Foster. The evolution of size and shape. In L. Spector, W. B. Langdon, U.-M. O'Reilly, and P. J. Angeline, editors, *Advances in Genetic Programming 3*, chapter 8, pages 163–190. MIT Press, Cambridge, MA, USA, June 1999.

[2] N. F. McPhee and J. D. Miller. Accurate replication in genetic programming. In L. Eshelman, editor, *Genetic Algorithms: Proceedings of the Sixth International Conference (ICGA95)*, pages 303–309, Pittsburgh, PA, USA, 15-19 July 1995. Morgan Kaufmann.

[3] N. F. McPhee and R. Poli. A schema theory analysis of the evolution of size in genetic programming with linear representations. In *Genetic Programming, Proceedings of EuroGP 2001*, LNCS, Milan, 18-20 Apr. 2001. Springer-Verlag.

[4] P. Nordin and W. Banzhaf. Complexity compression and evolution. In L. Eshelman, editor, *Genetic Algorithms: Proceedings of the Sixth International Conference (ICGA95)*, pages 310–317, Pittsburgh, PA, USA, 15-19 July 1995. Morgan Kaufmann.

[5] P. Nordin, F. Francone, and W. Banzhaf. Explicitly defined introns and destructive crossover in genetic programming. In J. P. Rosca, editor, *Proceedings of the Workshop on Genetic Programming: From Theory to Real-World Applications*, pages 6–22, Tahoe City, California, USA, 9 July 1995.

[6] R. Poli. Exact schema theorem and effective fitness for GP with one-point crossover. In D. Whitley, D. Goldberg, E. Cantu-Paz, L. Spector, I. Parmee, and H.-G. Beyer, editors, *Proceedings of the Genetic and Evolutionary Computation Conference*, pages 469–476, Las Vegas, July 2000. Morgan Kaufmann.

[7] R. Poli. Hyperschema theory for GP with one-point crossover, building blocks, and some new results in GA theory. In R. Poli, W. Banzhaf, and *et al.*, editors, *Genetic Programming, Proceedings of EuroGP 2000*. Springer-Verlag, 15-16 Apr. 2000.

[8] R. Poli. General schema theory for genetic programming with subtree-swapping crossover. In *Genetic Programming, Proceedings of EuroGP 2001*, LNCS, Milan, 18-20 Apr. 2001. Springer-Verlag.

[9] R. Poli and W. B. Langdon. A new schema theory for genetic programming with one-point crossover and point mutation. In J. R. Koza, K. Deb, M. Dorigo, D. B. Fogel, M. Garzon, H. Iba, and R. L. Riolo, editors, *Genetic Programming 1997: Proceedings of the Second Annual Conference*, pages 278–285, Stanford University, CA, USA, 13-16 July 1997. Morgan Kaufmann.

[10] R. Poli and W. B. Langdon. On the search properties of different crossover operators in genetic programming. In J. R. Koza, W. Banzhaf, K. Chellapilla, K. Deb, M. Dorigo, D. B. Fogel, M. H. Garzon, D. E. Goldberg, H. Iba, and R. Riolo, editors, *Genetic Programming 1998: Proceedings of the Third Annual Conference*, pages 293–301, University of Wisconsin, Madison, Wisconsin, USA, 22-25 July 1998. Morgan Kaufmann.

[11] R. Poli and W. B. Langdon. Schema theory for genetic programming with one-point crossover and point mutation. *Evolutionary Computation*, 6(3):231–252, 1998.

[12] R. Poli, W. B. Langdon, and U.-M. O'Reilly. Analysis of schema variance and short term extinction likelihoods. In J. R. Koza, W. Banzhaf, K. Chellapilla, K. Deb, M. Dorigo, D. B. Fogel, M. H. Garzon, D. E. Goldberg, H. Iba, and R. Riolo, editors, *Genetic Programming 1998: Proceedings of the Third Annual Conference*, pages 284–292, University of Wisconsin, Madison, Wisconsin, USA, 22-25 July 1998. Morgan Kaufmann.

[13] J. P. Rosca. Analysis of complexity drift in genetic programming. In J. R. Koza, K. Deb, M. Dorigo, D. B. Fogel, M. Garzon, H. Iba, and R. L. Riolo, editors, *Genetic Programming 1997: Proceedings of the Second Annual Conference*, pages 286–294, Stanford University, CA, USA, 13-16 July 1997. Morgan Kaufmann.

[14] J. E. Rowe and N. F. McPhee. The effects of crossover and mutation operators on variable length linear structures. Technical Report CSRP-01-7, University of Birmingham, School of Computer Science, January 2001.

General Schema Theory for Genetic Programming with Subtree-Swapping Crossover

Riccardo Poli

School of Computer Science, The University of Birmingham
Birmingham, B15 2TT, UK
R.Poli@cs.bham.ac.uk, http://www.cs.bham.ac.uk/~rmp/

Abstract. In this paper a new, general and exact schema theory for genetic programming is presented. The theory includes a microscopic schema theorem applicable to crossover operators which replace a subtree in one parent with a subtree from the other parent to produce the offspring. A more macroscopic schema theorem is also provided which is valid for crossover operators in which the probability of selecting any two crossover points in the parents depends only on their size and shape. The theory is based on the notions of Cartesian node reference systems and variable-arity hyperschemata both introduced here for the first time. In the paper we provide examples which show how the theory can be specialised to specific crossover operators and how it can be used to derive an exact definition of effective fitness and a size-evolution equation for GP.

1 Introduction

Schema theories often provide information about a property of a subset of the population (a schema) at the next generation in terms of macroscopic quantities, like schema fitnesses, population fitness, or number of individuals in a schema, measured at the current generation. Some schema theories express the same macroscopic property using only microscopic quantities, such as the fitnesses of all the individuals in the population, or a mixture of microscopic and macroscopic quantities. We will refer to these as *microscopic schema theories* to differentiate them from the purely macroscopic ones. This distinction is important because the latter are simpler and easier to analyse than the former.

The theory of schemata in genetic programming has had a difficult childhood. After some excellent early efforts leading to different worst-case-scenario schema theorems [6, 1, 11, 24, 17, 21], only very recently exact schema theories have become available [14, 12] which give exact formulations (rather than lower bounds) for the expected number of instances of a schema at the next generation. These exact theories are applicable to GP with one-point crossover [16, 17, 18]. No exact macroscopic schema theory for standard crossover (or any other GP crossover) has ever been proposed.

This paper fills this theoretical gap and presents a new exact general schema theory for genetic programming which is applicable to standard crossover as well as many other crossover operators. The theory includes two main results describing the propagation of GP schemata: a microscopic schema theorem and a macroscopic one. The microscopic version is applicable to crossover operators which replace a subtree in one parent

J. Miller et al. (Eds.): EuroGP 2001, LNCS 2038, pp. 143–159, 2001.

with a subtree from the other parent to produce the offspring. So, the theorem covers standard GP crossover [6] with and without uniform selection of the crossover points, one-point crossover [17, 18], size-fair crossover [7], strongly-typed GP crossover [9], context-preserving crossover [3] and many others. The macroscopic version is valid for a large class of crossover operators in which the probability of selecting any two crossover points in the parents depends only on their size and shape. So, for example, it holds for all the above-mentioned crossover operators except strongly typed GP crossover.

The paper is organised as follows. Firstly, we provide a review of earlier relevant work on schemata in Sec. 2. Then, in Sec. 3, we introduce the notion of node reference systems and we use it in Sec. 4 to define the concept of functions over them. Then, in Sec. 5 we show how these ideas can be used to build probabilistic models of different crossover operators. We use these to derive a general microscopic schema theorem for GP with subtree-swapping crossover in Sec. 6. We transform this into a macroscopic schema theorem in Sec. 7. In Sec. 8 we give an example that shows how the theory can be specialised to obtain schema theorems for specific types of crossover operators, and we illustrate how it can be used to obtain other general results, such as a size-evolution equation and an exact definition of effective fitness for GP. Some conclusions are drawn in Sec. 9.

2   Background

Schemata are sets of points of the search space sharing some syntactic feature. For example, in the context of GAs operating on binary strings, syntactically a schema is a string of symbols from the alphabet $\{0,1,*\}$, where the character * is interpreted as a "don't care" symbol. Typically schema theorems are descriptions of how the number of members of the population belonging to a schema vary over time. If we denote with $\alpha(H,t)$ the probability that a newly created individual samples the schema H, which we term the *total transmission probability* of H, an exact schema theorem is simply [19]

$$E[m(H,t+1)] = M\alpha(H,t), \tag{1}$$

where M is the population size, $m(H,t+1)$ is the number of individuals in H at generation $t+1$ and $E[\cdot]$ is the expectation operator. Holland's [5] and other worst-case-scenario schema theories normally provide a lower bound for $\alpha(H,t)$ or, equivalently, for $E[m(H,t+1)]$.

Obtaining theoretical results for GP using the idea of schema is much less straightforward than for GAs. A few alternative definitions of schema have been proposed in the literature [6, 1, 11, 24, 17, 21], but for brevity here we will describe only the definition introduced in [17, 18]. This is used in the rest of this paper. We will refer to this kind of schemata as fixed-size-and-shape schemata.

Syntactically a GP *fixed-size-and-shape schema* is a tree composed of functions from the set $\mathcal{F} \cup \{=\}$ and terminals from the set $\mathcal{T} \cup \{=\}$, where $\mathcal{F}$ and $\mathcal{T}$ are the function and terminal sets used in a GP run. The primitive $=$ is a "don't care" symbol which stands for a *single* terminal or function. A schema H represents programs having the same shape as H and the same labels for the non-$=$ nodes. For example, if $\mathcal{F}=\{+, *\}$ and $\mathcal{T}=\{x, y\}$ the schema (+ x (= y =)) represents the four programs (+ x (+ y x)),   (+ x (+ y y)),   (+ x (* y x))   and (+ x (* y y)).

In [17, 18] a worst-case-scenario schema theorem was derived for GP with point mutation and one-point crossover. One-point crossover works by selecting a common crossover point in the parent programs and then swapping the corresponding subtrees, like standard crossover. To account for the possible structural diversity of the two parents, one-point crossover analyses the two trees from the root nodes and considers for the selection of the crossover point only the parts of the two trees, called the *common region*, which have the same topology.[1] As discussed in [15], the theorem in [17, 18] is a generalisation of Holland's schema theorem to variable size structures. This result was improved in [14, 12] where an exact schema theory for GP with one-point crossover was derived which was based on the notion of hyperschema. A *GP hyperschema* is a rooted tree composed of internal nodes from $\mathcal{F} \cup \{=\}$ and leaves from $\mathcal{T} \cup \{=, \#\}$. Again, = is a "don't care" symbols which stands for exactly one node, while # stands for any valid subtree. For example, the hyperschema (* # (= x =)) represents all the programs with the following characteristics: a) the root node is a product, b) the first argument of the root node is any valid subtree, c) the second argument of the root node is any function of arity two, d) the first argument of this function is the variable x, e) the second argument of the function is any valid node in the terminal set. One of the results obtained in [12] is the following macroscopic model

$$\alpha(H,t) = (1 - p_{xo})p(H,t) + \tag{2}$$
$$p_{xo} \sum_k \sum_k \frac{1}{\mathbf{NC}(G_k, G_l)} \sum_{i \in C(G_k, G_l)} p(U(H,i) \cap G_k, t)p(L(H,i) \cap G_l, t)$$

where: p_{xo} is the crossover probability; $p(H, t)$ is the selection probability of the schema H;[2] $G_1, G_2, \cdots$ are all the possible program shapes, i.e. all the possible fixed-size-and-shape schemata containing = signs only; $\mathbf{NC}(G_k, G_l)$ is the number of nodes in the common region between shape G_k and shape G_l; $C(G_k, G_l)$ is the set of indices of the crossover points in such a common region; $L(H, i)$ is the hyperschema obtained by replacing all the nodes on the path between crossover point i and the root node with = nodes, and all the subtrees connected to those nodes with # nodes; $U(H, i)$ is the hyperschema obtained by replacing the subtree below crossover point i with a # node.[3] The steps involved in the construction of $L(H, i)$ and $U(H, i)$ for the schema $H = (* = (+ x =))$ are illustrated in Fig. 1. If a crossover point i is in the common region between two programs but it is outside the schema H, then $L(H, i)$ and $U(H, i)$ are empty sets. The hyperschemata $L(H, i)$ and $U(H, i)$ are important because, if one crosses over at point i *any* individual in $L(H, i)$ with *any* individual in $U(H, i)$, the resulting offspring is always an instance of H.

---

[1] The common region is defined formally in Sec. 4, Eq. 3.

[2] In fitness proportionate selection $p(H, t) = m(H, t)f(H, t)/(M\bar{f}(t))$, where $m(H, t)$ is the number of strings matching the schema H at generation t, $f(H, t)$ is their mean fitness, and $\bar{f}(t)$ is the mean fitness of the strings in the population.

[3] Eq. 2 is in a slightly different form than the result in [12]. However, the two results are equivalent since $C(G_k, G_l) = C(G_l, G_k)$ and $\mathbf{NC}(G_k, G_l) = \mathbf{NC}(G_l, G_k)$.

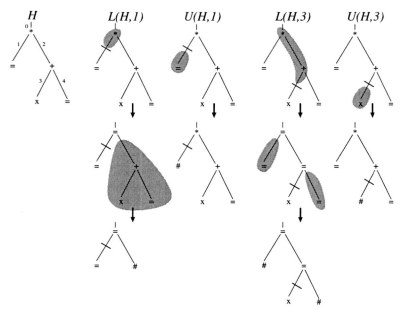

Fig. 1. Example of schema and some of its potential hyperschema building blocks. The crossover points in H are numbered as shown in the top left.

As discussed in [15], it is possible to show that, in the absence of mutation, Eq. 2 generalises and refines not only the GP schema theorem in [17, 18] but also Holland's [5] and more modern GA schema theory [22, 23].

3   Node Reference Systems

Given a syntax tree like, for example, the one in Fig. 2 which represents the S-expression (A (B C D) (E F (G H))), there can be different methods to indicate unambiguously the position of one particular node in the tree. One method is to use the path from the root node [3]. The path can be specified indicating which branch to select to find the target node for every node encountered starting from the root of the tree. This reference system presents the disadvantage of not corresponding to our typical notion of a Cartesian reference system, because the number of coordinates necessary to locate a node grows with the depth of the node in the tree.

A better alternative from this point of view is to organise the nodes in the tree into layers of increasing depth (see Fig. 3), to align them to the left and and then to assign an index to each node in a layer. The layer number d and the index i can then be used to define a Cartesian coordinate system. So, for example, node G in Fig. 2 would be at coordinates (2,3). This reference system presents the problem that it is not possible to infer the structure of a tree from the coordinates of its nodes.

A coordinate system similar to this one but without this problem can be defined by assuming that the trees to represent have nodes with arities not bigger than a predefined maximum value a_{max}. Then one could define a node-reference system like the previous

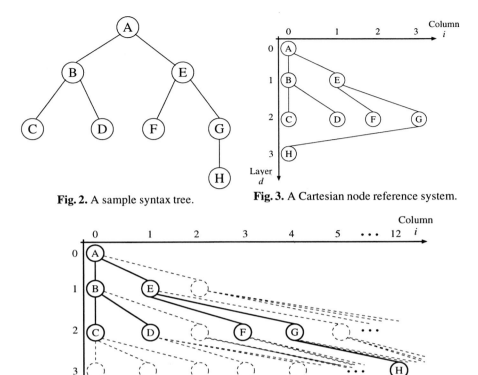

Fig. 2. A sample syntax tree.   **Fig. 3.** A Cartesian node reference system.

Fig. 4. Tree-independent Cartesian node reference system. The syntax tree for the program (A (B C D) (E F (G H))) is drawn with solid lines. Nodes and links of the maximal tree are drawn with dashed lines.

one for the largest possible tree that can be created with nodes of arity $a_{\max}$. This maximal tree would include 1 node of arity $a_{\max}$ at depth 0, $a_{\max}$ nodes of arity $a_{\max}$ at depth 1, $a_{\max}^2$ nodes of arity $a_{\max}$ at depth 2, etc.. Finally one could use the maximal system also to locate the nodes of non-maximal trees. This is possible because a non-maximal tree can always be described using a subset of the nodes and links in the maximal tree. This is illustrated in Fig. 4 assuming $a_{\max} = 3$. So, for example, node G in Fig. 2 would have coordinates (2,4) while node H would have coordinates (3,12). In this reference system it is always possible to find the route to the root node from any given valid pair of coordinates. Also, if one chooses a_{max} to be the maximum arity of the functions in the function set, it is possible to use this reference system to represent the structure of any program in any population. Because of these properties, we will use this reference system in the rest of this paper.

As clarified in the following section, it is sometimes necessary to be able to express the location of nodes in different trees at the same time. In this case we can extend the node-reference systems just introduced by concatenating the coordinates of the nodes in each reference system into a single multi-dimensional coordinate vector. For example, we can indicate two nodes, (d_1, i_1) in one tree and (d_2, i_2) in another tree, at the same time using the point (d_1, i_1, d_2, i_2) in a four-dimensional coordinate system.

Finally, it should be noted that in the Cartesian reference system in Fig. 4 it is possible to transform pairs of coordinates into integers by counting the nodes in the reference system in breadth-first order. Conversely, it is also possible to map integers into node coordinates unambiguously. We will use this property to simplify the notation in some of the following sections.

4   Functions over Node Reference Systems

Given a node reference system it is possible to define functions over it. An example of such functions is a function which represents a particular computer program. If one considers the program h one could define it as the function $h(d, i)$ which returns the node in h stored at position (d, i) if (d, i) is a valid pair of coordinates. If (d, i) is not in h then a conventional default value, $\emptyset$, is returned to represent the absence of a node. For example, for the program $h=$(A (B C D) (E F (G H))) represented in Fig. 4, this function would return the following values: $h(0, 0) =$ A, $h(1, 0) =$ B, $h(1, 1) =$ E, $h(1, 2) = \emptyset$, $h(2, 0) =$ C, $h(2, 1) =$ D, $h(2, 2) = \emptyset$, $h(2, 3) =$ F, $h(2, 4) =$ G, $h(2, 5) = \emptyset$, etc.. So, programs can be seen as functions over the space $\mathbb{N}^2$. Below we will refer to $h(d, j)$ as the *name function* for h and we will denote it with $N(d, i, h)$.

Other examples of node functions include:

- The *size function* $S(d, i, h)$ which represents the number of nodes present in the subtree rooted at coordinates (d, i) in tree h, with the convention that $S(d, i, h) = 0$ if (d, i) indicates an inexistent node. The size function can be defined using the name function (see [13]).
- The *arity function* $A(d, i, h)$ which returns the arity of the node at coordinates (d, i) in h. For example, for the tree in Fig. 4, $A(0, 0, h) = 2$, $A(1, 0, h) = 2$, $A(2, 1, h) = 0$ and $A(2, 4, h) = 1$.
- The *type function* $T(d, i, h)$ which returns the *data type* of the node at coordinates (d, i) in h.
- The *function-node function* $F(d, i, h)$ which returns 1 if the node at coordinates (d, i) is in h and it is a function, 0 otherwise. The number of internal nodes in h is therefore given by $\sum_d \sum_i F(d, i, h)$.

Similarly, it is possible to define functions on multi-dimensional node-coordinate systems. Useful functions of this kind include:

- The *position match function*

$$\mathrm{PM}(d_1, i_1, d_2, i_2, h_1, h_2) = \begin{cases} 1 & \text{if } (d_1, i_1) = (d_2, i_2),\ N(d_1, i_1, h_1) \neq \emptyset \text{ and} \\ & N(d_2, i_2, h_2) \neq \emptyset, \\ 0 & \text{otherwise.} \end{cases}$$

- The *type match function*

$$\mathrm{TM}(d_1, i_1, d_2, i_2, h_1, h_2) = \begin{cases} 1 & \text{if } T(d_1, i_1, h_1) = T(d_2, i_2, h_2), \\ 0 & \text{otherwise.} \end{cases}$$

– The *common region membership function*:

$$\mathcal{A}(d_1, i_1, d_2, i_2, h_1, h_2) =$$
$$\begin{cases} 1 & \text{if } (d_1, i_1) = (d_2, i_2) = (0, 0), \\ 1 & \text{if } (d_1, i_1) = (d_2, i_2), \\ & A\left(d_1 - 1, \lfloor i_1/a_{\max} \rfloor, h_1\right) = A\left(d_2 - 1, \lfloor i_2/a_{\max} \rfloor, h_2\right) \text{ and} \\ & \mathcal{A}\left(d_1 - 1, \lfloor i_1/a_{\max} \rfloor, d_2 - 1, \lfloor i_2/a_{\max} \rfloor, h_1, h_2\right) = 1, \\ 0 & \text{otherwise}, \end{cases}$$

where $\lfloor \cdot \rfloor$ is the integer-part function. The notion of common region membership function allows us to formalise the notion of *common region*:

$$C(h_1, h_2) = \{(d, i) \mid \mathcal{A}(d, i, d, i, h_1, h_2) = 1\}. \tag{3}$$

5 Modelling Subtree-Swapping Crossovers

Most genetic operators used in GP require the selection of a node where to perform a transformation (e.g. the insertion of a random subtree, or of a subtree taken from another parent) which leads to the creation of an offspring. In most cases the selection of the node is performed with a stochastic process of some sort. It is possible to model this process by assuming that a probability distribution is defined over the nodes of each individual. If we use the node-reference system introduced in the previous section, this can be expressed as the function:

$$p(d, i|h) = \Pr\{\text{A node at depth } d \text{ and column } i \text{ is selected in program } h\}, \tag{4}$$

where we assume that $p(d, i|h)$ is zero for all the coordinates (d, i) which represent inexistent nodes in h.[4] For example, if we consider the tree in Fig. 4 and we select nodes with uniform probability, then $p(d, i|h) = \frac{1}{8}$ if (d, i) is a node, $p(d, i|h) = 0$ otherwise. If instead we select functions with a probability 0.9 and any node with a probability 0.1, like in standard GP crossover [6], then $p(0, 0|h) = p(1, 0|h) = p(1, 1|h) = p(2, 4|h) = 0.2375$, $p(2, 0|h) = p(2, 1|h) = p(2, 3|h) = p(3, 12|h) = 0.0125$, and $p(d, i|h) = 0$ for all other coordinate pairs.

There are many possible uses for $p(d, i|h)$ and other probability distributions over node reference systems (see [13]). However, here we will concentrate on their use in modelling crossover operators.

In general in order to model crossover operators we need to use the following conditional probability distribution function over the space $\mathbb{N}^4$:

$$p(d_1, i_1, d_2, i_2|h_1, h_2) = \Pr \begin{cases} \text{A node at depth } d_1 \text{ and column } i_1 \text{ is selected in parent } h_1 \text{ and} \\ \text{a node at depth } d_2 \text{ and column } i_2 \text{ is selected in parent } h_2 \end{cases},$$

---

[4] For this probability distribution we use the notation $p(d, i|h)$ rather than $p(d, i, h)$ to emphasise the fact that $p(d, i|h)$ can be seen as the conditional probability of selecting node (d, i) if (or given that) the program being considered is h. In the rest of the paper, we will do the same for other probabilities distributions.

with the convention $p(d_1, i_1, d_2, i_2|h_1, h_2) = 0$ if $N(d_1, i_1, h_1) = \emptyset$ or $N(d_2, i_2, h_2) = \emptyset$, where $N(d, i, h)$ is the name function defined in Sec. 4. If the selection of the crossover points is performed independently in the two parents, then

$$p(d_1, i_1, d_2, i_2|h_1, h_2) = p(d_1, i_1|h_1) \cdot p(d_2, i_2|h_2),$$

where $p(d, i|h)$ is defined in Eq. 4. We will call *separable* crossover operators for which this relation is true.

Standard crossover is a separable operator. Indeed, assuming uniform selection of the crossover points,

$$p_{\text{StdUnif}}(d_1, i_1, d_2, i_2|h_1, h_2) = \frac{\delta(N(d_1, i_1, h_1) \neq \emptyset)\delta(N(d_2, i_2, h_2) \neq \emptyset)}{N(h_1)N(h_2)}, \quad (5)$$

where $N(h) = S(0, 0, h)$ is the number of nodes in h.

For standard crossover with a 90%-function/10%-any-node selection policy, it is easy to show that

$$p_{\text{Std}90/10}(d_1, i_1, d_2, i_2|h_1, h_2) = \quad (6)$$
$$\left(0.9\frac{F(d_1, i_1, h_1)}{\sum_d \sum_i F(d, i, h_1)} + 0.1\frac{\delta(N(d_1, i_1, h_1) \neq \emptyset)}{N(h_1)}\right) \times$$
$$\left(0.9\frac{F(d_2, i_2, h_2)}{\sum_d \sum_i F(d, i, h_2)} + 0.1\frac{\delta(N(d_2, i_2, h_2) \neq \emptyset)}{N(h_2)}\right),$$

where $F(d, i, h)$ is the function-node function defined in Sec. 4.

In some crossover operators the selection of the crossover points in the two parents is not performed independently. For example in one-point crossover, the first and second crossover points must have the same coordinates. In this case, if we assume to use a uniform probability of node selection, then

$$p_{1\text{pt}}(d_1, i_1, d_2, i_2|h_1, h_2) = \begin{cases} 1/\mathbf{NC}(h_1, h_2) & \text{if } (d_1, i_1) = (d_2, i_2) \text{ and} \\ & (d_1, i_1) \in C(h_1, h_2), \\ 0 & \text{otherwise,} \end{cases} \quad (7)$$

where $\mathbf{NC}(h_1, h_2)$ is the number of nodes in the common region $C(h_1, h_2)$ between program h_1 and program h_2. This can also be expressed using the common region membership function $\mathcal{A}(d_1, i_1, d_2, i_2, h_1, h_2)$ defined in Sec. 4 (see [13]):

$$p_{1\text{pt}}(d_1, i_1, d_2, i_2|h_1, h_2) = \frac{\mathcal{A}(d_1, i_1, d_2, i_2, h_1, h_2)}{\mathbf{NC}(h_1, h_2)}.$$

Similarly, it is possible to model strongly typed GP crossover [9] and context-preserving crossover [3] using the functions defined in Sec. 4 obtaining:

$$p_{\text{stgp}}(d_1, i_1, d_2, i_2|h_1, h_2) = \frac{\text{TM}(d_1, i_1, d_2, i_2, h_1, h_2)}{\sum_{d_1} \sum_{i_1} \sum_{d_2} \sum_{i_2} \text{TM}(d_1, i_1, d_2, i_2, h_1, h_2)},$$

$$p_{\text{context}}(d_1, i_1, d_2, i_2|h_1, h_2) = \frac{\text{PM}(d_1, i_1, d_2, i_2, h_1, h_2)}{\sum_{d_1} \sum_{i_1} \text{PM}(d_1, i_1, d_1, i_1, h_1, h_2)}.$$

Most other subtree-swapping crossover operators can be modelled using probability distribution functions over node reference systems (see [13] for other examples).

Thanks to these probabilistic models of crossover, it is possible to develop a general schema theory for GP as described in the following sections.

6   Microscopic Exact GP Schema Theorem for Subtree-Swapping Crossovers

For simplicity in this and the following sections we will use a single index to identify nodes unless otherwise stated. We can do this because, as indicated in Sec. 3, there is a one-to-one mapping between pairs of coordinates and natural numbers.

In order to obtain a schema theory valid for subtree-swapping crossovers, we need to extend the notion of hyperschema summarised in Sec. 2. We will call this new form of hyperschema a *Variable Arity Hyperschema* or *VA hyperschema* for brevity.

Definition 1. *A* Variable Arity hyperschema *is a rooted tree composed of internal nodes from the set $\mathcal{F} \cup \{=, \#\}$ and leaves from $\mathcal{T} \cup \{=, \#\}$, where $\mathcal{F}$ and $\mathcal{T}$ are the function and terminal sets. The operator $=$ is a "don't care" symbols which stands for exactly one node, the terminal # stands for any valid subtree, while the function # stands for exactly one function of arity not smaller than the number of subtrees connected to it.*

For example, the VA hyperschema (# x (+ = #)) represents all the programs with the following characteristics: a) the root node is any function in the function set with arity 2 or higher, b) the first argument of the root node is the variable x, c) the second argument of the root node is +, d) the first argument of the + is any terminal, e) the second argument of the + is any valid subtree. If the root node is matched by a function of arity greater than 2, the third, fourth, etc. arguments of such a function are left unspecified, i.e. they can be any valid subtree. VA hyperschemata generalise most previous definitions of schema in GP (see [13]).

Thanks to VA hyperschemata and to the notion of probability distributions over node reference systems, it is possible to obtain the following general result:

Theorem 1. *The total transmission probability for a fixed-size-and-shape GP schema H under a subtree-swapping crossover operator and no mutation is*

$$\alpha(H,t) = (1 - p_{xo})p(H,t)+ \tag{8}$$

$$p_{xo} \sum_{h_1} \sum_{h_2} p(h_1,t)p(h_2,t) \sum_{i \in H} \sum_j p(i,j|h_1,h_2)\delta(h_1 \in U(H,i))\delta(h_2 \in L(H,i,j))$$

where: p_{xo} is the crossover probability; $p(H,t)$ is the selection probability of the schema H; the first two summations are over all the individuals in the population; $p(h_1,t)$ and $p(h_2,t)$ are the selection probabilities of parents h_1 and h_2, respectively; the third summation is over all the crossover points (nodes) in the schema H; the fourth summation is over all the crossover points in the node reference system; $p(i,j|h_1,h_2)$ is the probability of selecting crossover point i in parent h_1 and crossover point j in parent h_2; $\delta(x)$ is a function which returns 1 if x is true, 0 otherwise; $L(H,i,j)$ is the hyperschema *obtained by rooting at coordinate j in an empty reference system the subschema of H below crossover point i, then by labelling all the nodes on the path between node j and the root node with # function nodes, and labelling the arguments of those nodes which are to the left of such a path with # terminal nodes; U(H, i) is the hyperschema obtained by replacing the subtree below crossover point i with a # node.*

The hyperschema $L(H, i, j)$ represents the set of all programs whose subtree rooted at crossover point j matches the subtree of H rooted in node i. The idea behind its definition is that, if one crosses over at point j *any* individual matching $L(H, i, j)$ and at point i *any* individual matching $U(H, i)$, the resulting offspring is always an instance of H. Before we proceed with the proof of the theorem, let us try to understand with examples how $L(H, i, j)$ is built (refer to Sec. 2 and Fig. 1 to see how $U(H, i)$ is built). In the examples, we will use 2–D coordinates to designate the nodes i and j. Let us consider the schema $H = (* = (+ x =))$. As indicated in Fig. 5(a), $L(H, (1, 0), (1, 1))$ is obtained through the following steps: a) we root the subschema below crossover point $(1, 0)$, i.e. the symbol =, at coordinates $(1, 1)$ in an empty reference system, b) we label the node at coordinates $(0, 0)$ with a # function node (in this case this is the only node on the path between node $(1, 1)$ and the root), and c) we label node (1,0) with a # terminal (this is because the node is to the left of the path between $(1, 1)$ and the root, and it is an argument of one of the nodes replaced with #). Another example is provided in Fig. 5(b), where $L(H, (1, 1), (2, 2))$ is obtained through the following steps. Firstly, we root the subschema below crossover point $(1, 1)$, i.e. the tree $(+ x =)$, at coordinates $(2, 2)$ in an empty reference system. Note that this is not just a rigid translation: while the + is translated to position $(2, 2)$, its arguments need to be translated more, i.e. to positions $(3, 4)$ and $(3, 5)$, because of the nature of the reference system used. Then, we label the nodes at coordinates $(0, 0)$ and $(1, 1)$ with # functions (these two nodes are on the path between node $(2, 2)$ and the root). Finally, we label node (1,0) with a # terminal (this node is the only argument of one of the nodes replaced with # to be to the left of the path between $(2, 2)$ and the root node).

Once the concept of $L(H, i, j)$ is available, the theorem can easily be proven.

Proof. Let $p(h_1, h_2, i, j, t)$ be the probability that, at generation t, the selection/crossover process will choose parents h_1 and h_2 and crossover points i and j. Then, let us consider the function

$$g(h_1, h_2, i, j, H) = \delta(h_1 \in U(H, i))\delta(h_2 \in L(H, i, j)).$$

Given two parent programs, h_1 and h_2, and a schema of interest H, this function returns the value 1 if crossing over h_1 at position i and h_2 at position j yields an offspring in H. It returns 0 otherwise. This function can be considered as a measurement function (see [2]) that we want to apply to the probability distribution of parents and crossover points at time t, $p(h_1, h_2, i, j, t)$. If h_1, h_2, i and j are stochastic variables with joint probability distribution $p(h_1, h_2, i, j, t)$, the function $g(h_1, h_2, i, j, H)$ can be used to define a stochastic variable $\gamma = g(h_1, h_2, i, j, H)$. The expected value of γ is:

$$E[\gamma] = \sum_{h_1} \sum_{h_2} \sum_i \sum_j g(h_1, h_2, i, j, H) p(h_1, h_2, i, j, t). \tag{9}$$

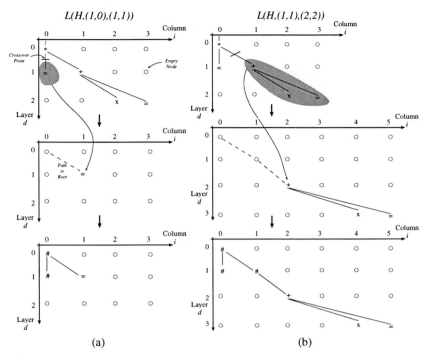

Fig. 5. Phases in the constructions of the VA hyperschema building block $L(H, (d_1, i_1), (d_2, i_2))$ of the schema $H = (\ast \; = \; (+ \; x \; =))$ within a node coordinate system with $a_{max} = 2$ for: (a) $(d_1, i_1) = (1, 0)$ and $(d_2, i_2) = (1, 1)$ and (b) $(d_1, i_1) = (1, 1)$ and $(d_2, i_2) = (2, 2)$.

Since γ is a binary stochastic variable, its expected value also represent the proportion of times it takes the value 1. This corresponds to the proportion of times the offspring of h_1 and h_2 are in H.

We can write

$$p(h_1, h_2, i, j, t) = p(i, j | h_1, h_2)p(h_1, t)p(h_2, t), \tag{10}$$

where $p(i, j | h_1, h_2)$ is the conditional probability that crossover points i and j will be selected when the parents are h_1 and h_2, while $p(h_1, t)$ and $p(h_2, t)$ are the selection probabilities for the parents. Substituting Eq. 10 into Eq. 9 and noting that if crossover point i is outside the schema H, then $L(H, i, j)$ and $U(H, i)$ are empty sets, lead to

$$E[\gamma] = \sum_{h_1} \sum_{h_2} p(h_1, t)p(h_2, t) \sum_{i \in H} \sum_{j} g(h_1, h_2, i, j, H)p(i, j | h_1, h_2). \tag{11}$$

The contribution to $\alpha(H, t)$ due to selection followed by crossover is $E[\gamma]$. By multiplying this by p_{xo} (the probability of doing selection followed by crossover) and adding the term $(1 - p_{xo})p(H, t)$ due to selection followed by cloning one obtains the r.h.s. of Eq. 8. □

7 Macroscopic Exact GP Schema Theorem

In order to transform Eq. 8 into an exact macroscopic description of schema propagation we will need to make one additional assumption on the nature of the subtree-swapping crossovers used: that the choice of the crossover points in any two parents, h_1 and h_2, depends only on their shapes, $G(h_1)$ and $G(h_2)$, not on the actual labels of their nodes, i.e. that $p(i, j|h_1, h_2) = p(i, j|G(h_1), G(h_2))$. We will term such operators *node-invariant* crossovers.

Theorem 2. *The total transmission probability for a fixed-size-and-shape GP schema H under a node-invariant subtree-swapping crossover operator and no mutation is*

$$\alpha(H, t) = (1 - p_{xo})p(H, t) + \tag{12}$$

$$p_{xo} \sum_{k,l} \sum_{i \in H} \sum_{j} p(i, j|G_k, G_l)p(U(H, i) \cap G_k, t)p(L(H, i, j) \cap G_l, t),$$

where the schemata G_1, G_2, $\cdots$ are all the possible fixed-size-and-shape schemata of order 0 (program shapes) and the other symbols have the same meaning as in Theorem 1.

Proof. The schemata $G_1, G_2, \cdots$ represent disjoint sets of programs. Their union represents the whole search space. So, $\sum_k \delta(h_1 \in G_k) = 1$. Likewise, $\sum_l \delta(h_2 \in G_l) = 1$. If we append the l.h.s. of these equations at the end of the triple summation in Eq. 8 and reorder the terms, we obtain:

$$\sum_{k,l} \sum_{h_1,h_2} p(h_1, t)p(h_2, t) \sum_{i \in H} \sum_{j} p(i, j|h_1, h_2) \times$$

$$\delta(h_1 \in U(H, i))\delta(h_1 \in G_k)\delta(h_2 \in L(H, i, j))\delta(h_2 \in G_l)$$

$$= \sum_{k,l} \sum_{h_1 \in G_k, h_2 \in G_l} p(h_1, t)p(h_2, t) \times$$

$$\sum_{i \in H} \sum_{j} p(i, j|h_1, h_2)\delta(h_1 \in U(H, i))\delta(h_2 \in L(H, i, j)).$$

For node-invariant crossover operators $p(i, j|h_1, h_2) = p(i, j|G(h_1), G(h_2))$, which substituted into the previous equation gives:

$$\sum_{k,l} \sum_{h_1 \in G_k, h_2 \in G_l} p(h_1, t)p(h_2, t) \times$$

$$\sum_{i \in H} \sum_{j} p(i, j|G(h_1), G(h_2))\delta(h_1 \in U(H, i))\delta(h_2 \in L(H, i, j))$$

$$= \sum_{k,l} \sum_{h_1 \in G_k, h_2 \in G_l} p(h_1, t)p(h_2, t) \times$$

$$\sum_{i \in H} \sum_{j} p(i, j|G_k, G_l)\delta(h_1 \in U(H, i))\delta(h_2 \in L(H, i, j))$$

$$= \sum_{k,l} \sum_{i \in H} \sum_{j} p(i,j|G_k,G_l) \underbrace{\sum_{h_1 \in G_k} p(h_1,t)\delta(h_1 \in U(H,i))}_{p(U(H,i)\cap G_k,t)} \times$$

$$\underbrace{\sum_{h_2 \in G_l} p(h_2,t)\delta(h_2 \in L(H,i,j))}_{p(L(H,i,j)\cap G_l,t)},$$

which completes the proof of the theorem.   □

The sets $U(H,i) \cap G_k$ and $L(H,i,j) \cap G_l$ either are (or can be represented by) fixed-size-and-shape schemata or are the empty set $\emptyset$. So, the theorem expresses the total transmission probability of H only using the selection probabilities of a set of lower- (or same-) order schemata.

8 Applications and Specialisations

In this section we give examples that show how the theory can be specialised to obtain schema theorems for specific crossover operators, and we illustrate how it can be used to obtain other general theoretical results, such as an exact definition of effective fitness and a size-evolution equation for GP.

8.1 Macroscopic Exact Schema Theorem for GP with Standard Crossover

Let us apply Theorem 2 to standard crossover. It is easy to show that standard crossover is node invariant (see [13]). So, we can substitute the expression of $p(i,j|G_k,G_l)$ in Eq. 12 with the expression

$$p(i,j|G_k,G_l) = \frac{\delta(N(i,G_k) \neq \emptyset)\delta(N(j,G_l) \neq \emptyset)}{N(G_k)N(G_l)},$$

obtained from Eq. 5. This yields

$$\alpha(H,t) = (1-p_{xo})p(H,t) + p_{xo}\sum_{k,l}\sum_{i \in H}\sum_{j}\frac{\delta(N(i,G_k) \neq \emptyset)}{N(G_k)} \times$$

$$\frac{\delta(N(j,G_l) \neq \emptyset)}{N(G_l)}p(U(H,i)\cap G_k,t)p(L(H,i,j)\cap G_l,t).$$

From this we obtain

Theorem 3. *The total transmission probability for a fixed-size-and-shape GP schema H under standard crossover with uniform selection of crossover points is*

$$\alpha(H,t) = (1-p_{xo})p(H,t)+ \qquad (13)$$
$$p_{xo}\sum_{k,l}\frac{1}{N(G_k)N(G_l)}\sum_{i \in H\cap G_k}\sum_{j \in G_l}p(U(H,i)\cap G_k,t)p(L(H,i,j)\cap G_l,t).$$

If one further specialises this result to the case of linear structures (see [13]), the schema theorem for linear structures reported in [20] is obtained.

8.2 Size-Evolution Equation for GP with Subtree-Swapping Crossover

Let us call *symmetric* any crossover operator for which $p(i, j|h_1, h_2) = p(j, i|h_2, h_1)$. Then, by using the microscopic schema theorem in Eq. 8 it is possible to prove (see [13]) the following

Theorem 4. *The expected mean size of the programs at generation $t + 1$, $E[\mu(t + 1)]$, in a GP system with a symmetric subtree-swapping crossover operator in the absence of mutation can equivalently be expressed in microscopic form as*

$$E[\mu(t + 1)] = \sum_{h \in \mathcal{P}} N(h)p(h, t), \tag{14}$$

where $\mathcal{P}$ denotes the population, or in macroscopic form as

$$E[\mu(t + 1)] = \sum_l N(G_l)p(G_l, t). \tag{15}$$

The theorem is important because it indicates that for symmetric subtree-swapping crossover operators the mean program size evolves as if selection only was acting on the population. This means that if there is a variation in mean size, like for example in the presence of bloat, that can only be attributed to some form of positive or negative selective pressure on some or all the shapes G_l.

From this theorem it follows that on a flat landscape

$$E[\mu(t + 1)] = \sum_l N(G_l)p(G_l, t) = \sum_l N(G_l)\frac{m(G_l, t)}{M}$$

(or $E[\mu(t + 1)] = \sum_l N(G_l)\alpha(G_l, t - 1)$ for infinite populations), whereby

Corollary 1. *On a flat landscape,*

$$E[\mu(t + 1)] = \mu(t). \tag{16}$$

For infinite populations, the expectation operator can be removed from the previous theorem and corollary. In [20] we obtained more specific versions of these results for one-point crossover and standard crossover acting on linear structures.

8.3 Effective Fitness for GP with Subtree-Swapping Crossovers

Once an exact schema theorem is available, it is easy to extend to GP with subtree-swapping crossovers the notion of effective fitness provided in [22, 23]:

$$f_{\text{eff}}(H, t) = \frac{\alpha(H, t)}{p(H, t)}f(H, t). \tag{17}$$

By using this definition and the value of $\alpha(H, t)$ in Eq. 12, we obtain the following

Theorem 5. *The effective fitness of a fixed-size-and-shape GP schema H under a node-invariant subtree-swapping crossover operator and no mutation is*

$$f_{\text{eff}}(H,t) = f(H,t)\Big[1 - p_{xo} \times \tag{18}$$

$$\Big(1 - \sum_{k,l} \sum_{i \in H,j} p(i,j|G_k,G_l)\frac{p(U(H,i) \cap G_k,t)p(L(H,i,j) \cap G_l,t)}{p(H,t)}\Big)\Big].$$

This result gives the *true effective fitness for a GP schema* under subtree swapping crossover: it is not an approximation or a lower bound.

It is possible to specialise this definition to standard crossover:

Corollary 2. *The effective fitness of a fixed-size-and-shape GP schema H under standard crossover with uniform selection of crossover points is*

$$f_{\text{eff}}(H,t) = f(H,t)\Big[1 - p_{xo} \times \tag{19}$$

$$\Big(1 - \sum_{k,l} \sum_{i \in H \cap G_k} \sum_{j \in G_l} \frac{p(U(H,i) \cap G_k,t)p(L(H,i,j) \cap G_l,t)}{N(G_k)N(G_l)p(H,t)}\Big)\Big].$$

In future work we intend to compare this definition with the approximate notions of effective fitness and operator-adjusted fitness introduced in [10] and [4], respectively.

9   Conclusions

In this paper a new general schema theory for genetic programming is presented. The theory includes two main results describing the propagation of GP schemata: a microscopic schema theorem and a macroscopic one. The microscopic version is applicable to crossover operators which replace a subtree in one parent with a subtree from the other parent to produce the offspring. The macroscopic version is valid for subtree-swapping crossover operators in which the probability of selecting any two crossover points in the parents depends only on their size and shape. Therefore, these theorems are very general and can be applied to model most GP systems used in practice.

Like other recent schema theory results [22, 23, 14, 12], our theory gives an exact formulation (rather than a lower bound) for the expected number of instances of a schema at the next generation. One special case of this theory is the exact schema theorem for standard crossover: a result that has been awaited for many years.

As shown by some recent explorations reported in [20, 8], exact schema theories can be used, for example, to study the exact schema evolution in infinite populations over multiple generations, to make comparisons between different operators and identify their biases, to study the evolution of size, and investigate bloat. Also, as discussed in [15] for one-point crossover, exact macroscopic theories open the way to future work on GP convergence, population sizing, and deception, only to mention some possibilities. In the future we hope to use the general schema theory reported in this paper to obtain new general results in at least some of these exciting directions.

Acknowledgements

The author would like to thank the members of the EEBIC (Evolutionary and Emergent Behaviour Intelligence and Computation) group at Birmingham, Nic McPhee, Jon Rowe, Julian Miller, Xin Yao, and Bill Langdon for useful discussions and comments.

References

[1] L. Altenberg. Emergent phenomena in genetic programming. In A. V. Sebald and L. J. Fogel, editors, *Evolutionary Programming — Proceedings of the Third Annual Conference*, pages 233–241. World Scientific Publishing, 1994.

[2] L. Altenberg. The Schema Theorem and Price's Theorem. In L. D. Whitley and M. D. Vose, editors, *Foundations of Genetic Algorithms 3*, pages 23–49, Estes Park, Colorado, USA. 1995. Morgan Kaufmann.

[3] P. D'haeseleer. Context preserving crossover in genetic programming. In *Proceedings of the 1994 IEEE World Congress on Computational Intelligence*, volume 1, pages 256–261, Orlando, Florida, USA, 27-29 June 1994. IEEE Press.

[4] D. E. Goldberg. Genetic algorithms and Walsh functions: II. Deception and its analysis. *Complex Systems*, 3(2):153–171, Apr. 1989.

[5] J. Holland. *Adaptation in Natural and Artificial Systems*. University of Michigan Press, Ann Arbor, USA, 1975.

[6] J. R. Koza. *Genetic Programming: On the Programming of Computers by Means of Natural Selection*. MIT Press, Cambridge, MA, USA, 1992.

[7] W. B. Langdon. Size fair and homologous tree genetic programming crossovers. *Genetic Programming And Evolvable Machines*, 1(1/2):95–119, Apr. 2000.

[8] N. F. McPhee and R. Poli. A schema theory analysis of the evolution of size in genetic programming with linear representations. In *Genetic Programming, Proceedings of EuroGP 2001*, LNCS, Milan, 18-20 Apr. 2001. Springer-Verlag.

[9] D. J. Montana. Strongly typed genetic programming. *Evolutionary Computation*, 3(2):199–230, 1995.

[10] P. Nordin and W. Banzhaf. Complexity compression and evolution. In L. Eshelman, editor, *Genetic Algorithms: Proceedings of the Sixth International Conference (ICGA95)*, pages 310–317, Pittsburgh, PA, USA, 15-19 July 1995. Morgan Kaufmann.

[11] U.-M. O'Reilly and F. Oppacher. The troubling aspects of a building block hypothesis for genetic programming. In L. D. Whitley and M. D. Vose, editors, *Foundations of Genetic Algorithms 3*, pages 73–88, Estes Park, Colorado, USA, 31 July–2 Aug. 1994 1995. Morgan Kaufmann.

[12] R. Poli. Exact schema theorem and effective fitness for GP with one-point crossover. In D. Whitley, *et al.*, editors, *Proceedings of the Genetic and Evolutionary Computation Conference*, pages 469–476, Las Vegas, July 2000. Morgan Kaufmann.

[13] R. Poli. General schema theory for genetic programming with subtree-swapping crossover. Technical Report CSRP-00-16, University of Birmingham, School of Computer Science, November 2000.

[14] R. Poli. Hyperschema theory for GP with one-point crossover, building blocks, and some new results in GA theory. In R. Poli, W. Banzhaf, and *et al.*, editors, *Genetic Programming, Proceedings of EuroGP 2000*. Springer-Verlag, 15-16 Apr. 2000.

[15] R. Poli. Exact schema theory for genetic programming and variable-length genetic algorithms with one-point crossover. *Genetic Programming and Evolvable Machines*, 2(2), 2001. Forthcoming.

[16] R. Poli and W. B. Langdon. Genetic programming with one-point crossover. In P. K. Chawdhry, R. Roy, and R. K. Pant, editors, *Soft Computing in Engineering Design and Manufacturing*, pages 180–189. Springer-Verlag London, 1997.

[17] R. Poli and W. B. Langdon. A new schema theory for genetic programming with one-point crossover and point mutation. In J. R. Koza, *et al.*, editors, *Genetic Programming 1997: Proceedings of the Second Annual Conference*, pages 278–285, Stanford University, CA, USA, 13-16 July 1997. Morgan Kaufmann.

[18] R. Poli and W. B. Langdon. Schema theory for genetic programming with one-point crossover and point mutation. *Evolutionary Computation*, 6(3):231–252, 1998.

[19] R. Poli, W. B. Langdon, and U.-M. O'Reilly. Analysis of schema variance and short term extinction likelihoods. In J. R. Koza, *et al.*, editors, *Genetic Programming 1998: Proceedings of the Third Annual Conference*, pages 284–292, University of Wisconsin, Madison, Wisconsin, USA, 22-25 July 1998. Morgan Kaufmann.

[20] R. Poli and N. F. McPhee. Exact schema theorems for GP with one-point and standard crossover operating on linear structures and their application to the study of the evolution of size. In *Genetic Programming, Proceedings of EuroGP 2001*, LNCS, Milan, 18-20 Apr. 2001. Springer-Verlag.

[21] J. P. Rosca. Analysis of complexity drift in genetic programming. In J. R. Koza, *et al.*, editors, *Genetic Programming 1997: Proceedings of the Second Annual Conference*, pages 286–294, Stanford University, CA, USA, 13-16 July 1997. Morgan Kaufmann.

[22] C. R. Stephens and H. Waelbroeck. Effective degrees of freedom in genetic algorithms and the block hypothesis. In T. Bäck, editor, *Proceedings of the Seventh International Conference on Genetic Algorithms (ICGA97)*, pages 34–40, East Lansing, 1997. Morgan Kaufmann.

[23] C. R. Stephens and H. Waelbroeck. Schemata evolution and building blocks. *Evolutionary Computation*, 7(2):109–124, 1999.

[24] P. A. Whigham. A schema theorem for context-free grammars. In *1995 IEEE Conference on Evolutionary Computation*, volume 1, pages 178–181, Perth, Australia, 29 Nov. - 1 Dec. 1995. IEEE Press.

Evolving Modules in Genetic Programming by Subtree Encapsulation

Simon C. Roberts[1], Daniel Howard[1], and John R. Koza[2]

[1] Software Evolution Centre
Systems & Software Engineering Centre
Defence Evaluation and Research Agency (DERA)
Malvern, Worcestershire WR14 3PS, UK
dhoward@dera.gov.uk
[2] Stanford University, Los Altos, CA 94023
koza@stanford.edu

Abstract. In tree-based genetic programming (GP), the most frequent subtrees on later generations are likely to constitute useful partial solutions. This paper investigates the effect of encapsulating such subtrees by representing them as atoms in the terminal set, so that the subtree evaluations can be exploited as terminal data. The encapsulation scheme is compared against a second scheme which depends on random subtree selection. Empirical results show that both schemes improve upon standard GP.

1   Introduction

A number of researchers have investigated modularisation in GP. The first approach was subtree encapsulation which was introduced by Koza [9]. This method randomly selected a subtree in a relatively fit chromosome and added a terminal type to the primitive set in order to reference the subtree. This encapsulation protected the subtree from the potential disruption of recombination, and it facilitated reuse by allowing the reference node to diffuse throughout the population via mutation. However, a brief empirical study showed that implementing this encapsulation procedure as a genetic operator with a low probability gave "no substantial difference in performance".

The current most common approach to modularisation is the use of automatically defined functions (ADFs) [9, 10]. Different primitive sets can be used to evolve each ADF, whereas all other approaches develop modules built from the same primitives as the main program. Koza has shown that ADFs lead to an improved performance for a wide variety of problems, and he concluded that the improvements were due to the discovery of problem decomposability and the exploitation of regularities in the problem environment. These key issues gave rise to other advantages including less required computational effort, smaller evolved solutions and improved scalability. It has been shown that GP can simultaneously solve a problem and evolve the architecture of an overall program including ADFs [10, 11].

J. Miller et al. (Eds.): EuroGP 2001, LNCS 2038, pp. 160–175, 2001.

Another modularisation approach for GP is known as the module acquisition (MA) technique which uses a *genetic library builder* [3]. MA created modules by randomly selecting subtrees for atomisation and then truncating nodes below the subtree's root to specify formal arguments. MA employed an expansion operator to overcome problems due to a lack of genetic diversity. The *evolution defined function* approach [1] is a hybrid method which uses the mutation operators of MA to govern ADFs.

All of the above approaches depend on *random* selection, but the *adaptive representation through learning* (ARL) algorithm [16] overcame this dependence by attempting to discover *building blocks* during evolution [2,5]. ARL did this by extending the primitive set with subroutines drawn from offspring which gave the best improvement on their parents' fitness. ARL was shown to perform well against standard GP and GP using 2 ADFs. However, ARL requires many control parameters and relies on random selection to specify formal arguments. The ARL framework has been used to compare various heuristics for module selection and extensions to ARL were proposed [4].

This paper introduces a simple two-stage modularisation scheme using subtree encapsulation, where module selection is based on subtree survival and frequency.

2 Subtree Encapsulation Scheme

2.1 Selecting Subtrees for Modularisation

Module selection heuristics are more difficult to specify than chromosome selection heuristics because *components* of chromosomes have no associated fitness. However, the schema theorem for genetic algorithms (GAs) [5,6] can be interpreted to suggest the following heuristic for GP [3]. *A module that gives a sufficient selection advantage to the chromosomes that contain it, will tend to appear in additional chromosomes in the next generation.* Hence subtrees which frequently occur in the population are likely to occur in relatively fit chromosomes, thus such subtrees should have a selection advantage themselves with regard to module acquisition.

Therefore, the modularisation scheme detailed in the following sections encapsulates the most frequent subtrees in the population. However, the current implementation does *not* perform subtree encapsulation during an evolution run, but instead it employs a *subtree database* to monitor the *usage* of each subtree during the run. After the run has evolved for a preset number of generations, the most frequent subtrees are encapsulated by representing them as atoms in the terminal set, thus allowing further runs to exploit the subtree evaluations as terminal data.

Subtrees which do not give their associated chromosomes any selection advantage would tend to be driven to extinction. Hence, performing the encapsulation after a number of generations have elapsed, should capture subtrees which are more *evolutionarily viable* [3] than those randomly selected during evolution in the original encapsulation scheme [9].

2.2   Subtree Database

A database was designed to store the subtrees generated during evolution in order to allow the usage of each subtree to be monitored. The database contained the following information for each subtree: depth, total size, the frequency in the entire population, the body of nodes and the evaluation over all fitness cases. Subtree evaluations were stored to enable equivalence grouping (described below). However, the storage could also reduce evolution run-time by recalling subtree evaluations in order to ascertain chromosome fitness, as opposed to repeatedly re-evaluating each required subtree.

The subtree database was initialised when the population was created and it was updated after each offspring was generated. All created subtrees were added to the database, regardless of subtree depth or size. An extinct subtree was retained in the database because it was possible for it to be regenerated, and the pre-calculated subtree output could thus be retrieved for chromosome evaluation. However, the database had a limited capacity (limited by RAM) and so the database was refreshed when the maximum capacity was reached. The refresh procedure identified all the extinct subtrees so that they could later be replaced as the need arose.

An *alphabetisation* procedure was devised to minimise the demands on the database capacity. The procedure simply swapped the arguments to a commutative function node if the arguments contravened the ordering prescribed by an arbitrary alphabet. This procedure was applied to each chromosome during the population initialisation and then to each offspring at birth. The alphabetisation thus minimised the number of operationally identical subtrees which could be added to the database, but as it swapped only the nodes at the level immediately below a commutative function, it did not significantly change chromosome topology.

It was still possible for subtrees which were operationally equivalent yet structurally distinct to be stored in the database, partly because of the issue of *introns* [12]. Such subtrees were identified by grouping all subtrees which gave the same output over all fitness cases. This allowed module selection to be based on the frequency of subtree *operation* as opposed to the frequency of structural representation. The frequency of a particular subtree operation was calculated by summing the frequency of the subtrees in the associated equivalents group.

It should be stressed that the subtrees were *not* encapsulated in the population during evolution, and so crossover and mutation were free to manipulate the chromosomes as if the database did not exist. This approach overcomes the loss of genetic diversity which was found in MA [3]. However, each function node in the population indicated the index of its associated subtree in the database in order to assist database management.

2.3   Encapsulation Procedure

Figure 1 displays the procedure for subtree encapsulation. A first evolution stage involved multiple independent GP runs which processed an initial terminal set for N_{gen} generations. The subtree database for the best run was then analysed to group subtrees which were operationally equivalent. The evaluations for the subtree operations were then exported, and the terminal set was augmented to include a terminal for each of the N_{st} most frequent subtree operations. Subtree evaluations were then imported as terminal data to perform multiple GP runs in a second evolution stage, where each run began with an initialised population.

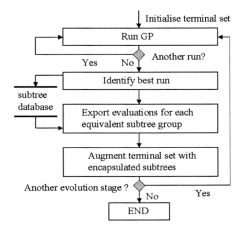

Fig. 1. Subtree encapsulation procedure

Encapsulating subtrees from the best of a series of runs has an advantage arising from the following issues. Firstly, fitness improvement becomes increasingly more difficult during the course of evolution. Secondly, there is a strong inverse correlation between the depth of recombination point and its effect on fitness [8]. Consequently, standard GP tends to converge on a particular root structure in early generations [13]. Furthermore, recombination near the root becomes less likely as trees *bloat* [12]. Thus multiple runs were needed to explore different root structures and to discover modules which apply in the context of the best root structure.

The following issues should be considered when setting N_{gen}. In early generations, recombined subtrees must substantially improve chromosome fitness in order to survive, but in later generations recombined subtrees are more likely to represent *nearly neutral code* as it becomes increasingly more difficult to improve fitness. Furthermore, recombined subtrees in later generations may simply be acting as padding to preserve the active subtrees against disruption from the genetic operators [2]. Therefore, useful subtrees are more likely to be identified from earlier generations, but there is then a greater risk of encapsulating subtrees which become obsolete as the evolution matures.

The value of N_{gen} would ideally be set to coincide with a convergence to a local optimum, as this would reduce wasted effort on embellishing sub-optimal solutions. Moreover, the encapsulation would still enrich the terminal set with modules beneficial to solving the problem, but the multiple second-stage runs would be free to exploit these modules in different regions of the fitness space. The convergence to a local optimum can be identified by a plateau in the best-of-generation fitness [16], and so preliminary first-stage runs could be observed in order to set N_{gen} to coincide with such a plateau.

Figure 1 shows that the encapsulation procedure can be iterated for multiple evolution stages where each stage augments the terminal set with new encapsulated subtrees. However, this iteration remains an area for further work.

3   Subtree Encapsulation for Target Detection

This section outlines an empirical study of subtree encapsulation by evolving detectors to identify cars in infra-red line-scan (IRLS) images. Note that the emphasis of the study was on the investigation of encapsulation as opposed to evolving an optimum detector. Experiments focused on the detection problem with more realistic training data are presented in [7, 15].

3.1   Training Data

The IRLS images were obtained by low-flying aircraft and they pertained to industrial, suburban and rural environments. The training points were based on results from previously evolved lower-level detectors which were applied to three images having a total coverage of approximately 60 million pixels. The detectors identified 596 points positioned on the 121 cars in the images and 3787 points that were false alarms.

Figure 2 illustrates the training data taken from the imagery. Four concentric pixel rings were centred on each training point and statistics were calculated for each ring. Statistics were also calculated over an area of approximately five car-lengths square and were used for training points positioned towards the centre of this area.

The target detection problem depended on many variables including the diversity of the environments captured in the images, the flight altitudes, the ground perspective, the atmospheric conditions, the thermal signature variation across the cars and the context in which the cars appeared (e.g. parked next to buildings, other cars or in isolation). Examples of the cars are shown in Figure 3. The lower-level detectors had drastically filtered the images and the remaining false alarms were consequently very difficult to discriminate from the cars. The training data was considered to be insufficient to yield satisfactory detection rates for this challenging generalisation task, but the data was adequate for the purpose of this study to investigate subtree encapsulation.

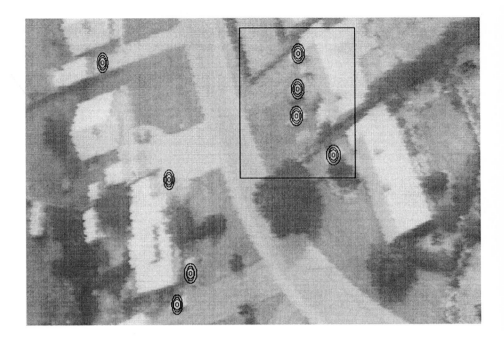

Fig. 2. IRLS imagery showing the form of the training data. Note that the rings and the rectangular area were scaled according to ground perspective.

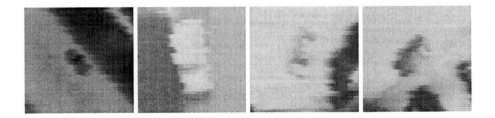

Fig. 3. Examples of cars from the IRLS images. The cars vary in size due to different flight altitudes.

3.2   GP Specifications

The experiments used steady-state GP where each chromosome was represented as a tree comprising function and terminal nodes. The population was initialised using the ramped-half-and-half technique [9] with a maximum initial tree depth of 4 levels. The GP parameters are given in Table 1 where the terminal set consisted of 11 types including pixel averages and standard deviations. 50 independent runs were conducted for each GP scheme investigated.

Table 1. GP parameters

parameter	setting
functions	$+$, $-$, $*$, $/$ $(x/0 = 1)$, $\min(A, B)$, $\max(A, B)$, if $(A < B)$ then C else D,
terminals	altitude in feet av. and s.d. over: (a) 4 concentric rings (b) wider square area
population	2000
mate radius	2000
kill tournament	size 2
breed tournament	size 4
regeneration	90% crossover (single child), 10% truncation mutation
internal crossover	60%
max generations	60
max tree size	1000 nodes

The truncation mutation involved randomly selecting a node in the parent chromosome and replacing the subtree rooted at that node with a randomly selected terminal. This mutation operator was essential because of the large number of terminals, O(100), which resulted from augmenting the terminal set with encapsulated subtrees. Without this operator, GP could manipulate only the terminal contexts that were captured by chance in the initial population.

Each chromosome was trained to give an output greater or equal to zero to denote a *hit* (i.e. a vehicle detection) according to the following fitness measure,

$$\text{fitness} = \frac{v}{121 + (f/256)} \tag{1}$$

where v was the number of vehicles hit out of the total 121 vehicles and f was the number of false alarms, i.e. the number of non-vehicle training points hit.

3.3   Target Detection Performance

Table 2 gives the best-of-generation results from 50 runs of standard GP (SGP), i.e. without subtree encapsulation. Each of the corresponding detectors hit all the vehicles and so only the false alarm rate f is shown. This was the case for all detectors pertaining to the results in this section. The table gives the minimum, average and standard deviation in f at various generations across all runs.

Table 2. Summary of target detection performance from 50 runs without subtree encapsulation

gen	min f	av. f	s.d. f
15	1821	2256	250
30	1313	1816	315
45	1056	1589	324
60	832	1410	305

Analysis of the SGP runs revealed that a plateau in the best-of-generation fitness tended to occur around generation 15. The subtree database from the best run at this generation was analysed to give the encapsulated subtrees for a second evolution stage. The database stored 25000 subtrees, 10098 of which occurred more than once in the population. As subtree frequency was the issue under consideration, these subtrees only were analysed to yield 3731 equivalents groups. The most common subtree existed in the form of 749 structural variants which was an unusually high number. The average number of equivalent subtrees in a group was three and many subtrees were operationally unique.

Figure 4 shows the frequency of the most common subtrees after equivalence grouping. The highest frequency was 22063 but this dropped by an order of magnitude by the 19th most common subtree. The 7 most common subtrees were represented by a structural variant with the smallest possible size of 3 nodes. Even though smaller subtrees had a greater likelihood of being created by chance, the extremely high frequency of these subtrees suggested that they represented useful partial solutions. The operation of the most common subtree is interpreted in Section 3.6.

Table 3a shows the performance of the second evolution stage when using the 100 most frequent encapsulated subtrees, i.e. $N_{st} = 100$. For comparison, further runs were conducted which each used 100 subtrees selected randomly from the 3731 possible subtrees, i.e. different runs used different terminal sets. Hence, this gave two second evolution stage strategies using different module selection schemes: one with usage-biased subtree selection and one with random subtree selection. The results for the random selection scheme are given in Table 3b.

An interesting issue arises regarding which generations should be compared in order to assess the influence of encapsulation. For example, are the results at generation 60 with and without encapsulation comparable? This question arises because the setting of N_{st} controls a balance between restarting a run afresh (i.e. $N_{st} = 0$) and continuing a run by exploiting a large quantity of pre-evolved components (i.e. setting N_{st} much larger than the size of the initial terminal set). However, using a large N_{st} was distinct from continuing a run by evolving

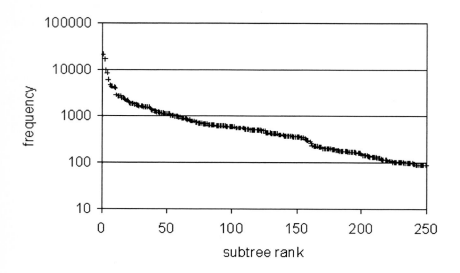

Fig. 4. The frequency of the most common subtrees after equivalence grouping

a population for further generations, because the population was fully initialised at the start of each second-stage run.

A worse case comparison would correspond to the run continuation extreme. Subtrees were encapsulated after the first stage had evolved for 15 generations. (Although the runs were terminated after 60 generations to allow a comparative study.) Hence, the worst case is to compare the runs without encapsulation at generation 60 against the runs with encapsulation at generation 45. The best case is to compare the different schemes at the same generation.

The worst case comparison of the two subtree selection schemes against SGP are shown in Figure 5 and the best case comparisons are shown in Figure 6. *Freq*

Table 3. Summary of target detection performance from 50 runs using (a) the 100 most frequent encapsulated subtrees and (b) 100 randomly selected encapsulated subtrees

(a)					(b)			
gen	min f	av. f	s.d. f		gen	min f	av. f	s.d. f
15	1498	1930	184		15	1224	1594	149
30	1116	1490	213		30	942	1258	168
45	829	1264	256		45	761	1071	157
60	737	1099	266		60	652	942	150

denotes encapsulation using the 100 most frequent subtrees and *Rand* denotes encapsulation using 100 randomly selected subtrees. The figures show that subtree encapsulation improved the target detection performance by reducing the false alarms whilst retaining the maximum number of vehicle detections.

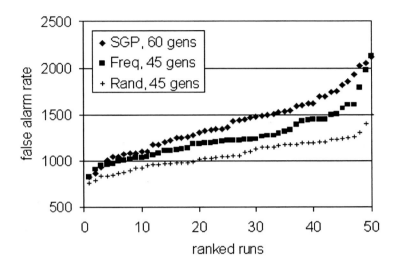

Fig. 5. Best-of-run false alarm rate for 50 runs using different subtree selection schemes at generations corresponding to the worst case comparison

It can be seen by comparing Tables 2 and 3 that the percentage to which encapsulation reduced the average false alarm rate for the worst case comparison was 90% for *Freq* and 76% for *Rand*, and these reduced to 78% and 67% respectively when considering the best case comparison. Significance tests using the t-test showed that the null hypothesis was rejected at 1% chance for the worst case comparisons. Improvements in performance gained by using encapsulation can also be observed by comparing Tables 2 and 3 for other generations.

The results show that encapsulation with random subtree selection performed better than encapsulation with usage-biased selection. It is important to note that all encapsulated subtrees had survived the first evolution stage to exist in multiple instances after 15 generations. Hence, all encapsulated subtrees could be deemed as evolutionarily viable, regardless of how they were selected for the second stage. Therefore, the random subtree selection was distinct from that used in the original encapsulation scheme [9].

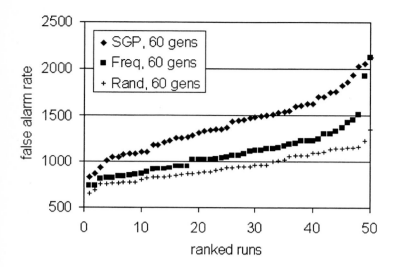

Fig. 6. Best-of-run false alarm rate for 50 runs using different subtree selection schemes at generations corresponding to the best case comparison

The developers of MA assumed, with regard to the schema theorem [6], that "a significant portion of the population will rely on a beneficial module and its number of calls per generation will be high" [3]. (Note that this statement does not impact on the selection of modules in MA but instead refers to observations on the invocation of randomly selected modules.) The fact that the above results show that random subtree selection out-performed usage-biased selection suggests that it is an over-simplification to interpret this statement, for GP, to mean that subtree frequency is a good indicator of potential module usefulness. This is consistent with the results reported in [4] which show that although subtree frequency was one of the better selection heuristics, it had no advantage over the random selection used in the original subtree encapsulation scheme [9].

The most likely downfall of the frequency indicator was the probable accumulation of introns [12], where many instances of a subtree may actually be redundant. This notion was supported by the observation that some equivalents groups contained many subtree variants, and it implies that caution should be used when considering the GA schema theorem for GP (see also [14]). However, attempts to eradicate introns from module selection have lead to disappointing results [4], thus suggesting that introns play a role in modularisation.

Comparison of Tables 2 and 3 shows that the encapsulation lead to a lower standard deviation across the 50 runs than was the case for SGP. This was despite the fact that encapsulation substantially increased the size of the terminal set and thus intuitively complicated the search space. However, encapsulated subtrees formed a higher-level abstraction relative to the initial terminals, and thus they did not introduce new raw information about the problem environment. Instead, the results suggest that encapsulation reduced the dimensionality of the search space, perhaps by fixing partial solutions which addressed various dimensions of the problem, as was proposed in [3].

Furthermore, the lower deviation may be partly due to changing the bias in the position of recombination points. Section 2.3 explained that the root structure of an evolved solution tends to become fixed in early generations. Subtree encapsulation counteracts this bias by fixing structures from the leaf-nodes upwards, and it effectively manipulates nodes further from the leaves by exploring the use of subtrees in different contexts.

3.4   Varying the Number of Encapsulated Subtrees

Tables 4 and 5 show that target detection performance generally improved when more encapsulated subtrees were included in the terminal set, i.e. when N_{st} was increased. The data corresponds to the best detectors from 50 independent GP runs at generation 45, each of which hit all vehicles and thus the tables measure performance using the minimum, average and standard deviation in false alarm rate f.

Table 4. Variation of N_{st} at generation 45 for encapsulation using the most frequent subtrees

N_{st}	min f	av. f	s.d. f	t-test (%)
25	924	1487 (105%)	235	2e-3
50	1006	1388 (98%)	306	3
100	829	1264 (90%)	256	-
200	895	1177 (83%)	166	5
400	757	1049 (74%)	157	3e-4
800	741	1081 (77%)	164	6e-3

Table 5. Variation of N_{st} at generation 45 for encapsulation using randomly selected subtrees

N_{st}	min f	av. f	s.d. f	t-test (%)
25	897	1229 (87%)	209	5e-3
50	771	1194 (85%)	176	4e-2
100	761	1071 (76%)	157	-
200	753	1064 (75%)	153	81
400	686	1069 (76%)	148	95
800	754	1058 (75%)	133	65

The percentage to which encapsulation reduced the average f relative to SGP at generation 60 is given in brackets, i.e. the worst case comparison as defined in Section 3.3. These percentages support the notion that N_{st} controlled a balance between run restart and run continuation. For example, the use of the lowest N_{st} in Table 4 was more akin to restarting runs and then comparing results from generation 45 to those from generation 60, thus revealing a poorer average performance.

The last column in the tables gives the significance of the results relative to using $N_{st} = 100$ for that encapsulation scheme. As expected, increasing N_{st} had a more significant impact when encapsulating the most frequent subtrees, where the null hypothesis was rejected at 5% chance. Conversely, Table 5 shows no significant improvement for $N_{st} > 100$ when encapsulating randomly selected subtrees. Comparing the tables shows that the encapsulation of $N_{st} \geq 400$ of the most frequent subtrees gave a similar performance to using $N_{st} \geq 100$ randomly selected subtrees.

The poorer performance gains obtained from encapsulating the most frequent subtrees may be partly due to a saturation of genetic material in addition to the issues discussed in Section 3.3. This is because the most common subtrees at the end of the first evolution stage were necessarily the smallest possible subtrees (i.e. 2 levels deep), because the database stored all used subtrees and a nested subtree must be at least as common as its parent subtree. Furthermore, it was likely that these small subtrees were recreated in the second evolution stage, although this likelihood decreased as N_{st} increased. Therefore, the encapsulation of the most frequent subtrees promoted the proliferation of code which may easily become widespread from normal recombination. Moreover, this code may rapidly saturate the population and hinder the evolutionary drive, especially if the code was redundant in the first instance. Increasing N_{st} counteracts this by encouraging genetic diversity.

3.5   Computation Time

Table 6 gives the average computation time to evolve for 5 generations at various stages of evolution, measured from 50 runs on a 450MHz Pentium II MMX PC. The average cumulative time, t_c, is also given. The table shows that the computation time increased sharply during the first 30 generations and increased more gradually thereafter (by less than 5% for each subsequent 5 generation step). This was due to rapid tree growth during the earlier generations.

Table 6 indicates that a two-stage evolution strategy involving 15 generations without encapsulated subtrees followed by 45 generations with encapsulated subtrees would gain a computational saving of approximately 5300s (nearly 1.5 hours) per run, compared to evolving for 60 generations without encapsulated subtrees. This was because 5941s were saved by not continuing beyond generation 45 but an extra 652s were needed for the additional first stage.

The overhead incurred from using subtree encapsulation was the exporting of additional terminal data from the best first stage run, which currently required manual intervention. However, the importing of additional terminal data at the

Table 6. Average computation time to evolve at various generations

gen	$t(s)$	$t_c(s)$	gen	$t(s)$	$t_c(s)$
5	35	35	35	1718	6216
10	162	198	40	1793	8009
15	454	652	45	1865	9874
20	909	1561	50	1927	11801
25	1338	2900	55	1983	13784
30	1598	4498	60	2030	15815

start of a second stage run had negligible duration. A comparative study of computation time using an optimised subtree database is an area for further work. In the light of the above results, such work should consider multi-stage encapsulation where the terminal set is augmented after every N_{gen} generations (see Section 2.3).

3.6   Interpretation of Subtree Operation

Table 7 displays examples of subtrees giving their identification index in the database, their frequency rank and their body which can invoke other subtrees. Note that these subtrees are taken from the first evolution stage and so a nested invocation was represented in the population by the presence of the *full* nested subtree, whereas the subtree database used an atom to reference the nested sub-tree. For clarity the table denotes the output of nested subtrees by an SID node. PS1, PS4 and AS were nodes in the initial terminal set, representing standard deviations in pixel value over the inner concentric ring, the outer concentric ring and the wider area of approximately five car-lengths square.

Table 7. Examples of subtrees from the database used for encapsulation

ID	rank	expression
537	0	(- PS4 PS1)
8724	27	(min S537 AS)
6235	34	(min S537 PS1)
546	38	(+ AS PS1)
21497	40	(min S537 S546)

The most common subtree, 537, represented the difference between pixel deviations at the central locality and the immediate surrounding of a given point. When a point was centrally positioned on a car, it was likely that the outer ring intercepted the car's boundary whereas the inner ring was contained within the car, thus S537 would probably be relatively high. Conversely, S537 would probably be relatively low (negative) if the point lay on a small object.

S537 would be close to zero in locally uniform areas. This subtree therefore gives a very basic indication for the presence of car-sized objects.

Subtrees 8724 and 6235 gave S537 a more contextual meaning based on the widest area and the narrowest area respectively. Subtree 21497 behaved similarly, but its reference value was the sum of the deviations over the widest and narrowest areas provided by subtree 546.

The above interpretation highlights low-level code reuse, and it suggests how the encapsulation of these subtrees for a second evolution stage can facilitate the development of a hierarchical abstraction which can be exploited to evolve an overall solution. This section also illustrates how the subtree database aids interpretation via its explicit representation of code reuse.

4   Conclusions

This paper investigates a simple modularisation scheme for GP which uses sub-tree encapsulation without a maximum depth restriction, and is characterised by the following novel features. The creation of modules was based on monitoring the survival and frequency of subtrees in the population as opposed to random selection during evolution. Modules were created from the best run from a *first evolution stage*. Module deletion was effectively discovered by a *second evolution stage* which could drive encapsulated subtrees to extinction. Structural varia-tion (including the notion of introns) was discarded during module selection by considering operational equivalence.

Subtree encapsulation evolves better solutions faster than standard GP, typi-cally reducing the false alarm rate to 75% in a target detection task. The observed performance gains can be explained by the following issues which are introduced by encapsulation: code protection through atomisation, code reuse facilitating the exploitation of regularities inherent in the task, and problem decomposition through an emergent hierarchical abstraction. Explicit code reuse also aids pro-gram interpretation and phenotypic implementation, where reused components need only be processed the once for each application of the phenotype.

The random selection of surviving subtrees out-performed usage-biased selec-tion thus proving that subtree frequency was *not* the best indicator of potential module usefulness. Probable reasons for this relate to introns and code satu-ration. This conclusion supports the finding reported in [4] that near-random module selection was difficult to improve upon.

Further work could attempt to discover the best indicator of potentially useful modules by analysing which randomly selected surviving subtrees proved most beneficial. The best indicator may be correlated to the genetic operators used, e.g. subtree frequency may be a better indicator if mutation were used with a higher probability.

An iterative application of the subtree encapsulation procedure shown in Figure 1 is an area for further work. This would strengthen hierarchical ab-straction via the explicit nesting of subtrees. An alternative approach would be to perform encapsulation during evolution, but this would preclude the current encapsulation from the best of a series of GP runs.

References

1. Ahluwalia M. and Bull L.: Coevolving functions in genetic programming: Classification using K-nearest-neighbour. Proceedings of the Genetic and Evolutionary Computation Conference, Orlando, Florida (1999) 947–953 Morgan Kaufmann
2. Altenberg L.: The evolution of evolvability in genetic programming. Advances in Genetic Programming, Kinnear K. E. Jr. (ed.) (1994) 47–74 MIT Press
3. Angeline P. J. and Pollack J. B.: Coevolving high-level representations. Artificial Life III, Langton C. G. (ed.) (1994) 55–71 Addison-Wesley
4. Dessi A., Giani A. and Starita A.: An analysis of automatic subroutine discovery in genetic programming. Proceedings of the Genetic and Evolutionary Computation Conference, Orlando, Florida (1999) 996–1001 Morgan Kaufmann
5. Goldberg D. E.: Genetic Algorithms in Search, Optimization and Machine Learning (1989) Addison-Wesley
6. Holland J. H.:
   Adaptation in Natural and Artificial Systems, An Introductory Analysis with Applications to Biology, Control and Artificial Intelligence (1992) Second edition (First edition 1975) MIT Press
7. Howard D. and Roberts S. C.: A staged genetic programming strategy for image analysis. Proceedings of the Genetic and Evolutionary Computation Conference, Orlando, Florida (1999) 1047–1052 Morgan Kaufmann
8. Igel C. and Chellapilla K.: Investigating the influence of depth and degree of genotypic change on fitness in genetic programming. Proceedings of the Genetic and Evolutionary Computation Conference, Orlando, Florida (1999) 1061–1068 Morgan Kaufmann
9. Koza J. R.: Genetic Programming: On the Programming of Computers by Means of Natural Selection (1992) MIT Press
10. Koza J. R.: Genetic Programming II: Automatic Discovery of Reusable Programs (1994) MIT Press
11. Koza J. R., Bennett F. H. III, Andre D. and Keane M. A.: Genetic Programming III: Darwinian Invention and Problem Solving (1999) Morgan Kaufmann
12. Luke S.: Code growth is not caused by introns. Late Breaking Papers at the Genetic and Evolutionary Computation Conference, Las Vegas, Nevada (2000) 228–235
13. McPhee N. F. and Hopper N. J.: Analysis of genetic diversity through population history. Proceedings of the Genetic and Evolutionary Computation Conference, Orlando, Florida (1999) 1112–1120 Morgan Kaufmann
14. O'Reilly U. M. and Oppacher F.: The troubling aspects of a building block hypothesis for genetic programming. Foundations of Genetic Algorithms 3, Whitley L. D. and Vose M. D. (eds.) (1995) 73–88 San Mateo, CA, Morgan Kaufmann
15. Roberts S. C. and Howard D.: Evolution of vehicle detectors for infrared line scan imagery. Joint Proceedings of the European Workshop on Evolutionary Image Analysis, Signal Processing and Telecommunications, Göteborg, Sweden (1999) 111–125 Springer LNCS
16. Rosca J. P. and Ballard D. H.: Discovery of subroutines in genetic programming. Advances in Genetic Programming 2, Angeline P. J. and Kinnear K. E. Jr. (eds.) Chapter 9 (1996) MIT Press

Evolution of Affine Transformations and Iterated Function Systems Using Hierarchical Evolution Strategy

Anargyros Sarafopoulos

Media School
National Centre for Computer Animation, Bournemouth University
Talbot Campus Fern Barrow, Poole, Dorset BH12 5BB, UK
asarafop@bournemouth.ac.uk

Abstract. Often optimization problems involve the discovery of many scalar coefficients. Although genetic programming (GP) has been applied to the optimization and discovery of functions with an arbitrary number of scalar coefficients, recent results indicate that a method for fine-tuning GP scalar terminals can assist the discovery of solutions. In this paper we demonstrate an approach where genetic programming and evolution strategies (ES) are seamlessly combined. We apply our GP/ES hybrid, which we name Hierarchical Evolution Strategy, to the problem of evolving affine transformations and iterated function systems (IFS). We compare the results of our approach with GP and notice an improvement in performance in terms of discovering bsetter solutions and speed.

1 Introduction

Discovery of scalar coefficients is an important problem in evolutionary computation especially in the case of optimization problems. Evolution strategies (ES) [1,19] and evolutionary programming (EP) [1] provide techniques that are focused towards the evolution of real valued vectors. In the case of GP many problems involve the fine-tuning of scalar terminals [4,5,8,9,15,16,17,18]. Several methods have been used in the GP literature in order to mutate constants systematically [9,17,18]. These methods include simulated annealing [9] and numerical partial gradient ascent [18] to update constant values. Sometimes mutation using normal distribution is applied to update GP scalar terminals [17,4,5]. Work has also been carried out using GP/ES hybrid for the reconstruction of CAD surfaces [8] where constants representing position, size or orientations are randomly modified using normal distribution in order "to tune the evolved geometric surface with many smaller and few bigger changes" [8]. Also a two-stage strategy where GP results are feed into an ES run is reported to produce better results than GP [15]. In this paper we demonstrate a method that combines GP and ES in order to allow the evolution of variable length programs and the fine-tuning of scalar parameters of these programs. This approach was devised in order to allow the evolution of affine transformation and iterated function systems. However a similar approach can be applied in other problems where variable length encoding in conjunction with fine-tuning of real valued vectors is required.

J. Miller et al. (Eds.) : EuroGP 2001, LNCS 2038, pp. 176-191, 2001.
© Springer-Verlag Berlin Heidelberg 2001

1.1 Evolution of Affine Transformations and Iterated Function Systems

Affine transformations have many applications in several fields. They are typically used in graphics applications that involve image processing, animation, and real time 3D graphics [6,20]. Affine transformations are also used in IFS theory (see Section 4) and fractal image compression applications [2,3,12]. We have previously demonstrated evolution of affine transformations using GP [16], however the problem of evolving affine transformations invariably requires the fine-tuning of a large number of scalar coefficients.

We compare GP and Hierarchical Evolution Strategy using the *inverse problem for affine transformations*, and the *inverse problem for IFS*. The inverse problem for affine transformations is described in Section 3, and the inverse IFS problem in Section 4. The Hierarchical Evolution Strategy is described in Section 2.

2 Hierarchical Evolution Strategy

Evolution Strategies (ES) as described by Back [1] and Schwefel [19] operate on real valued vectors. The elements of these real valued vectors that correspond to the coding of a (optimization) problem are referred to as *object variables* [1]. In ES an individual is defined as vector *a*, such as:

$$\vec{a} = (\vec{v}, \vec{s}, \vec{r}) \in I = R^n \times R_+^{n_\sigma} \times [-\pi, \pi]^{n_\alpha}, \qquad (1)$$

$$n_\sigma \in \{1, \ldots, n\}$$

$$n_\alpha \in \{0, (2n - n_\sigma)(n_\sigma - 1)/2\}.$$

Where vector *v* represents *object variables*. Each individual also incorporates the *standard deviation* vector *s*, as well as the *correlation coefficient* vector *r*. One of the most important features of ES is variation of *object variables* using normally distributed mutations (other distributions may also be used for the mutation of object variables). Equally important is the self-adaptation of the *standard deviations* and *correlation coefficients* of normally distributed mutations [1,19]. For a detailed description of ES see Back [1].

We combine GP and ES by using a method that allows encoding an ES individual as a Lisp symbolic expression (S-expression). In the light of this one could implement ES within a GP system by simply allowing ES individuals to be coded (as symbolic expressions) out of GP functions and terminals. The structure of an ES program can be seen as a hierarchical (tree) graph as illustrated in Figure 1. A tree graph representation allows incorporating ES individuals into GP seamlessly. We call this tree graph an *evolution strategies individual* (ES individual). We allow for ES style mutation as described by Back [1] to operate on ES individuals.

We implemented ES individuals, using a strongly typed genetic programming (STGP) [13] (see Section 3.2). STGP recombination can also be applied to ES individuals.

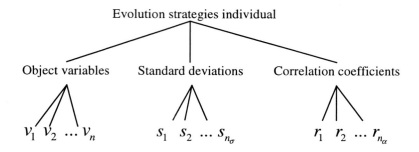

Fig. 1. Tree graph that defines an ES individual, corresponds to vector a of Equation 1.

A Hierarchical Evolution Strategy (HES) is defined as an S-expression that contains ES individuals. According to this definition ES itself is a subset of the hierarchical evolution strategy, defined by a single ES individual. Such structure (as in ES) will be of fixed size. GP architectures that contain scalar terminals could code these terminals as ES individuals. The potential benefit of this is that each ES individual can be fine-tuned separately using ES style mutation operations.

The hierarchical evolution strategy has two major potential benefits: a) it provides a GP architecture that contains a self adapting mechanism, in terms of mutating scalar terminals, b) it provides a modified ES that is variable length. Variable length coding has been reported in early work using ES [19]. Nevertheless the architecture has to be described in terms of ES individuals, which have to remain of constant length within the evolutionary simulation cycle.

2.1 Strongly Typed Genetic Programming

In GP as described by Koza [10] individuals are S-expressions composed of two types of functions. Functions that accept arguments called *non-terminal functions*, and functions that accept no arguments called *terminal functions*. For brevity we use the term *function* to mean *non-terminal function*. One important constraint of GP is the property of *closure*. That is, all functions have to accept arguments and return values of the same data type. Koza [10] has proposed a method to relax *closure* using *constrained syntactical structures*. We use strongly typed GP [13] to allow S-expressions that are made of functions that accept arguments and return values of different data types. The hierarchical evolution strategy, as well as all other experiments, is implemented using a STGP system. In STGP we need three sets to describe S-expressions: a set of *data types D*, a set of *functions F*, and a set of *terminals T*. In GP as described by Koza [10] only two sets are needed (*functions* and *terminals*). The notation

$$r \leftarrow f(a_1,\dots,a_n), where \qquad (2)$$

$$r \in D,$$

$$a_i \in D, i \in \{1,\dots,n\}.$$

describes a function f *that* accepts n arguments and returns a value of data type r, where D is the set of data types. If the number of arguments n is equal to zero, the above notation describes a terminal returning data type r. We use this notation in order to simplify the description of STGP functions and terminals (see Section 3).

3   Evolution of Affine Transformations

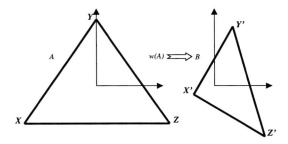

Fig. 2. Affine transform w that takes equilateral triangle A on the left, centered at the origin with side of length 2/3, to triangle B on the right. Where w = {a, b, c, d, e, f}={0.5, 0.04, -0.340, 0.85, 0.02, 0.07045}.

Before proceeding with the inference problem for IFS (see section 4), we test GP and HES against a problem of lesser degree of difficulty, where a general solution is known. This problem was selected because of its relevance to the more complex inference problem for IFS. The problem was set in order to compare the accuracy of GP against HES in terms of discovering scalar coefficients. We compare GP and HES using the *inverse problem for affine transformations*. The *inverse problem for affine transformations* is defined as follows: We want to find an affine transformation w that takes triangle A with vertices at $(x_1, x_2), (y_1, y_2),$ and (z_1, z_2) to a given triangle B with corresponding vertices at $(\tilde{x}_1, \tilde{x}_2), (\tilde{y}_1, \tilde{y}_2),$ and $(\tilde{z}_1, \tilde{z}_2),$ see Figure 2. Here we use two dimensional (2D) affine transformations. A 2D affine transformation w is defined as linear transformation L followed by a translation T:

$$w(x) = L(x) + T = \begin{bmatrix} a & b \\ c & d \end{bmatrix}\begin{bmatrix} x_1 \\ x_2 \end{bmatrix} + \begin{bmatrix} e \\ f \end{bmatrix}. \tag{3}$$

An affine transformation that takes triangle A to triangle B will have to minimize

$$g(w) = d(w(x), \tilde{x}) + d(w(y), \tilde{y}) + d(w(z), \tilde{z}). \tag{4}$$

Where $d(x, y)$ is the Euclidean distance between points x and y. One can always find an affine transformation that takes triangle A to a given triangle B and therefore minimize Equation 2 by solving a set of linear equations, see Equation 5.

$$
\begin{aligned}
x_1 a + x_2 b + e &= \tilde{x}_1, \\
y_1 a + y_2 b + e &= \tilde{y}_1, \\
z_1 a + z_2 b + e &= \tilde{z}_1, \\
x_1 c + x_2 d + f &= \tilde{x}_2, \\
y_1 c + y_2 d + f &= \tilde{y}_2, \\
z_1 c + z_2 d + f &= \tilde{z}_2.
\end{aligned}
\tag{5}
$$

3.1 STGP Architecture

An affine transformation is a linear transformation followed by a translation (see Equation 3). It is well known that any non-singular linear transformation can be constructed by composition of a scale, skew and rotate linear transformations. We use this property to provide a STGP coding of the inverse problem. We have previously demonstrated evolution of affine transformations using similar architecture [16]. The set of data types D for this problem consists of

$$D = \{map, linear, trans, ephScale, ephSkew, ephAngle, ephTrans\}. \tag{6}$$

map is the data type that stores an affine transformation, i.e. the floating point coefficients {a, b ,c, d, e, f} of Equation 3. *map* is the output or return type of S-expressions. *linear* is the data type that stores a linear transformation, i.e. four coefficients {a, b, c , d}. *trans* is the data type that stores a translation, i.e. two coefficients {e, f}. *ephScale, ephSkew, ephAngle,* and *ephTrans* store an ephemeral floating point variable, each representing scaling ratios, skew ratios, rotation angles, and translation constants respectively.

The function set F for this problem consists of

$$F = \{map \leftarrow affine(linear, translation), \qquad (7)$$
$$trans \leftarrow translation(ephTrans, ephTrans),$$
$$trans \leftarrow trans\_composition(trans, trans)$$
$$linear \leftarrow composition2(linear, linear),$$
$$linear \leftarrow composition3(linear, linear, linear),$$
$$linear \leftarrow scale(ephScale, ephScale),$$
$$linear \leftarrow skew(ephSkew),$$
$$linear \leftarrow rotate(ephAngle)\}.$$

The set of terminals T for this problem consists of

$$T = \{ephScale \leftarrow tScale(\ ), \qquad (8)$$
$$ephSkew \leftarrow tSkew(\ ),$$
$$ephAngle \leftarrow tAngle(\ ),$$
$$ephTrans \leftarrow tTrans(\ )\}.$$

The composition functions concatenate linear transformations by post multiplying their corresponding matrixes. Translations are combined by addition of their corresponding coefficients. Allowing for different types of constants disables crossover between types which are not related such as the combination of rotation angles with scaling rations, skew ratios, or translation constants.

3.2 Architecture Using the Hierarchical Evolution Strategy

Encoding is based on S-expressions that contain a single ES individual. The technique outlined in section 2 was adopted in order to code ES individuals in terms of *data types*, *functions*, and *terminals*. This resulted in a coding where syntactically correct individuals are of fixed size. The set of data types D for this problem consists of

$$D = \{map, obj, dev, rot, ephObj_i, ephDev_i, ephRot_j\}, \qquad (9)$$
$$i \in \{1, \ldots 6\}, j \in \{1, \ldots 15\}.$$

map is the data type that stores an ES individual (i.e. vector a of Equation 1). *map* is the output or return type of S-expressions for this problem. The data type *obj* stores the *object variables* (see Section 2) of an ES individual. The *object variables* in this case correspond to floating-point coefficients *{a, b, c, d, e, f}* of an affine transformation (see Equation 3). *dev* is the data type that stores the *standard deviations* of an the ES individual. *rot* is the data type that stores rotations that stand for *linearly correlated mutation coefficients* of an ES individual (see Section 2). We have six *object variable* coefficients, and six *standard deviation* coefficients. Finally we have *n(n-1)/2 correlation coefficients*, where n is the number of object variables (see Back [1] and Schwefel [19]). *ephObj* data types, *ephDev* data types, and *ephRot* data types store an ephemeral floating point variable each, that corresponds to an object variable, a standard deviation, or a correlation coefficient respectively. Each coefficient of an ES individual is given a different data type so it could be recombined only with the same coefficient of a different individual. The function set *F* for this problem consists of

$$F = \{map \leftarrow f\_map(obj, dev, rot), \tag{10}$$
$$obj \leftarrow f\_obj(ephObj_1, ephObj_2, \cdots, ephObj_6),$$
$$dev \leftarrow f\_dev(ephDev_1, ephDev_2, \cdots, ephDev_6),$$
$$rot \leftarrow f\_rot(ephRot_1, ephRot_2, \cdots, ephRot_{15})\}.$$

The terminal set *T* for this problem consists of

$$T = \{ephObj_i \leftarrow t\_objv_i(\,), \tag{11}$$
$$ephDev_i \leftarrow t\_dev_i(\,),$$
$$ephRot_j \leftarrow t\_rot_j(\,)\},$$
$$i \in \{1,\ldots 6\}, j \in \{1,\ldots 15\}.$$

Functions, terminals, and data types are designed to construct S-expressions that mirror the graph in Figure 1.

3.3 Mutation for ES Individuals, Fitness Function, and Control Parameters

We tested STGP and HES against the inverse problem using a population number of 500 individuals, for 200 generations, and 5 runs. The fitness function was defined to be the sum of the distances of the transformed vertices of triangle *A* from the vertices of the target triangle *B* (see Figure 2), i.e. Equation 4. We used several triangle pairs to test HES and STGP against the inverse problem and obtained very similar results from each test case. The results for the case outlined in Table 1 are shown in Figure 3.

In the case of STGP coding the selection method was tournament selection with tournament size 6. The mutation probability was set to 0.2, and maximum tree depth to 8. The generation method for the initial population was ramped half-and-half.

In the case of coding using the hierarchical-ES, ES mutation operation [1,19] was introduced to the STGP system as a special mutation operation for ES individuals. The mutation frequency of ES individuals was set to 100% (as in ES). Three selection methods were tested in the case of the hierarchical-ES. The results using proportional selection were poor but the results improved dramatically when using tournament and even more when using (μ,λ)-ES style elitist selection [1]. The generation of the initial population was implemented by ES style mutation of an individual with object variable coefficients *{a, b, c, d, e, f}* = {1.0, 0.0, 0.0, 1.0, 0.0, 0.0} (i.e. the identity matrix), standard deviation coefficients equal to 0.3, and correlation coefficients set to 0.

Table 1. Table for the infence problem for affine maps.

Objective	Find the affine transform w that takes an equilateral triangle, centered at the origin with side of length 2/3, A to a target triangle B. Where $w = \{a, b, c, d, e, f\}=\{0.50, 0.040, -0.340, 0.850, 0.020, 0.07045\}$ see Figure 2.
Fitness Cases	3 (the vertices of target triangle B)
Standardized Fitness	The sum of the distances of transformed vertices of triangle A to the vertices of the target triangle B (see Figure 2). This is the result of Equation 4.
Mutation frequency for ES individuals in HES	100%
Mutation frequency in STGP	2%
Crossover probability	100%
Selection Scheme for HES	(μ,λ)-ES style elitist selection. μ=1 and λ=500.
Selection Scheme for STGP	Tournament selection with tournament size 6 and population size of 500
Hits	Number of fitness cases for which the value of the transformed vertex of triangle A comes within 1e-05 distance of the target vertex of triangle B (see Figure 2).
Success predicate	An expression scores 3 hits

3.4   Results for the Inverse Problem for Affine Transformations

None of the STGP runs managed to satisfy the success predicate as defined in Table 1. All of the HES runs succeeded in solving the problem before reaching generation 100. Results shows (see Figure 3) that HES performs much better that STGP for the inverse problem for affine transformations. Although many variations of the STGP architecture described in Section 3.1 were also tested, none provided significant improvement on the results presented in this paper (and therefore compared more favorably with HES). The results suggest that HES is better at fine-tuning scalar coefficients than STGP. The results also suggest that the problem is easier to solve by direct modifications of the coefficients of the affine transformation, rather than composition of scale, skew, rotate, and translate operations.

4   Evolution of Iterated Function Systems

IFS offer a method of generating fractal shapes. J. Hutchinson originally developed the idea of IFS [7]. An affine IFS is a finite set of contractive affine transformations

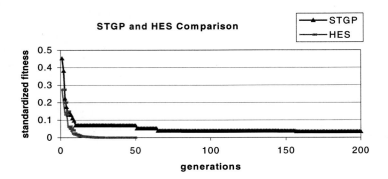

Fig. 3. Best of generation fitness curves for the inference problem for affine transformations using STGP and HES. The graph shows the results of the best run for STGP and HES.

[2,3]. Points in space affected by contractive transformations are placed always closer together. It has been shown that a shape can be represented using IFS, by discovering a set of contractive transformations that take that shape onto itself [2,3]. That is, in order to represent a shape A using an IFS, the union (*collage*) of the shapes of A under the transformations has to generate A. This is known as the *collage theorem*. The notation for an IFS is $\{w_n, n=1,2,...,n\}$. Applying an IFS to finite shape A is defined as a transformation W:

$$W(A) = \bigcup_{i=1}^{n} w_n(A). \tag{12}$$

A fractal shape can be constructed by calculating the *attractor* of an IFS. The attractor of an IFS is defined by:

$$Lim_{n \to \infty} W^{\circ n}(A). \tag{13}$$

There are two well-known methods of constructing IFS fractals the *photocopy algorithm*, and the *chaos game algorithm* [2,3]. For a detailed description of IFS see Barnsley [2,3]. A challenging problem when constructing IFS fractals is the inverse or inference problem.

We compare STGP and hierarchical ES using the inverse problem for IFS. According to the inverse or inference problem for IFS we are asked to find an unspecified number of contractive affine transformations whose attractor is a given image. Here we attempt solve the inference problem for the Barnsley Fern [2,3]. The Barnsley Fern was chosen because of its complex self-similar shape. The fern shape was also chosen because it has a well-known solution that contains four transformations, each different from the others, one of which is singular (i.e. non-invertible). This singularity, as well as the complexity of the shape of the fern makes the problem difficult [16].

4.1 Architecture Using the Hierarchical Evolution Strategy

An IFS does not contain a predefined number of contractive affine transformations. Therefore we use a coding that allows the representation of a variable length list of affine transformations. The coding is based on S-expressions that contain a *list* of ES individuals.

The set of data types *D* for this problem consists of

$$D = \{ifs, map, obj, dev, rot, ephObj_i, ephDev_i, ephRot_j\}, \qquad (14)$$

$$i \in \{1,\ldots 6\}, \, j \in \{1,\ldots 15\}.$$

and is almost identical to the set represented in Equation 9 (Section 3.2). The only addition here is the data type *ifs*. *ifs* stores a list of two or more transformations. *ifs* is the return data type of S-expressions for this problem. The data type *map* stores a list of one or more ES individuals (see Section 3.2).

The function set *F* for this problem consists of

$$F = \{ifs \leftarrow f\_ifs(map, map), \qquad (15)$$

$$map \leftarrow f\_list(map, map),$$

$$map \leftarrow f\_map(obj, dev, rot),$$

$$obj \leftarrow f\_obj(ephObj_1, ephObj_2, \cdots, ephObj_6),$$

$$dev \leftarrow f\_dev(ephDev_1, ephDev_2, \cdots, ephDev_6),$$

$$rot \leftarrow f\_rot(ephRot_1, ephRot_2, \cdots, ephRot_{15})\}.$$

Set *F* is very similar to the set represented in Equation 10, in Section 3.2. The only additions are function *f_ifs*, and *f_list*. The function *f_ifs* is used to ensure that IFS have two or more affine transformations. Function *f_list* is used to connect affine transformations in a list. The terminal set for this problem is same as in Equation 11.

4.2 Architecture Using STGP

Here as in section 3.1 we use an architecture that is based on decomposition of an affine transformation, into scale, skew, rotate, and translate primitives. S-expressions are made out of functions that combine these primitives. The architecture is the same as the one described in [16].

4.3 Fitness Function

Two fitness functions were tested, the *Nettleton* fitness, and the *overlap* fitness. The *Nettleton fitness* was also used in [16], and was originally proposed by Nettleton, and Garigliano [14]. The *overlap fitness* combines the Nettleton fitness with a calculation of the pixel overlap of affine transformations of an IFS.

Here we deal with (fractal) *shapes* that are black-on-white drawings. Strictly speaking fractal shapes are defined as compact subsets of 2D Euclidean space [2]. However, in terms of the fitness function the universal set U is the set of pixels of a 128x128 bitmap. A *shape* is defined as a subset of the set pixels of a 128x128 bitmap. We are searching though the set H of all subsets of U. The *target shape* or *target* for this experiment is the *shape* of the Barnsley Fern. Let $N(a)$ be the number of pixels of *shape a*. Let *collage*, for a given IFS w_n, be the *shape* created by applying transformation W (see Equation 12) to the *target shape*.

We calculate the standardized fitness of individuals, in the Nettleton case by:

$$error = N(target) + N(collage \cap target^{-1}) - N(collage \cap target) \qquad (16)$$

where a^{-1} is the complement of set a. That is, each individual in the population strives to produce a collage that covers pixels of the target shape. The more pixels of the *target* an individual covers and less of the rest of the image, the greater the reward. Nettleton fitness can lead to the evolution of "opportunistic" transformations. That is transformations that cover a large portion of the target will tend to spread fast among the population. However, such transformations are not necessarily optimal, nor do they necessarily lead to a solution. One way to reduce this effect is to introduce a term in the fitness function, which punishes individuals that contain transformations that overlap. Thus reducing the spread of a transformation that happen to cover many pixels of the target. Therefore encouraging transformations that cover a small number of pixels.

We calculate the standardized fitness in the *overlap* case as *error + sharing*, where *error* is defined in Equation 16, and *sharing* is defined by:

$$sharing = \sum_{j=1}^{n} \sum_{\substack{i=1 \\ i \neq j}}^{n} N(w_j(target) \cap w_i(tagret)) \qquad (17)$$

where n is the number of affine transformations of a given IFS.

In order to avoid non-contractive IFS individuals, any IFS individual with contractivity greater than 0.85 was not selected for reproduction.

4.4 Control Parameters

In the case of the HES coding, the selection scheme was (μ,λ)-ES type elitist selection $\mu=9$, and $\lambda=16000$. Affine transformations for individuals in the initial population were generated by ES mutation of an affine transformation with $\{a, b, c, d, f\} = \{0.2, 0.0, 0.0, 0.2, 0.0, 0.0\}$. Standard deviations were initialized to 0.4. The initial values for correlation coefficients were set to 0. ES style mutation operation was allowed to help fine-tune the parameters of transformations within given IFS. The ES mutation operation was applied to a randomly selected ES individual of an S-expression. The affine transformations were not directly constrained, and therefore were not made contractive after mutation.

However, in order to reduce mutations that produce non-contractive maps we repeated the mutation operation until a contractive individual was found or a maximum number of iterations were reached. In the case of STGP the initial population was initialized using the ramped half and half method. Mutation frequency was set to 2%. The selection method was tournament selection with tournament size 7. In both cases (STGP and HES) the population number was set to 16000, the generation number was set to 30, and the number of runs to 6. The results are shown in Figure 4, and Figure 5.

4.5 Results for the Inverse Problem for IFS

Hierarchical ES performs better in the case of *Nettleton* fitness (see Section 4.3). The attractors of the best of generation individuals using the HES are shown in Figure 6. The results suggest that hierarchical ES performs better (see Figure 4) because it can discover transformations which are more precise than those discovered by STGP. This is also shown, when using *overlap* fitness (see Section 4.3). In the case of *overlap* fitness, hierarchical ES performs, as well as STGP (see Figure 5). However HES achieves its performance by finding fewer affine transformations, but with much greater precision (see Figures 7 and 8). STGP finds a solution, which contains more affine transformations, which are positioned roughly in the right place, and achieve a much more coarse fit to the target shape (see Figure 8). In the case of the *overlap* fitness, HES is disadvantaged because the initial population is generated through mutation of a single individual, which leads to an initial population where transformations of individuals tend to overlap. Most of the six runs using overlap fitness, in the case of HES, produced individuals with no more than 2 affine transformations.

5 Conclusions

Our results suggest that Hierarchical Evolution Strategy can be used to help improve results in problems were a large number of scalar constants need to be evolved. The hierarchical ES provides improvements in results in terms of evolving affine transformations, in both inverse problems (for affine transformations, and iterated function systems). However the solution of the inverse problem for IFS, does not only depend on discovering affine transformations. It is the interaction between affine transformations that is very important, and although hierarchical ES can help fine-tune coefficients it cannot help GP solve that problem.

References

1.   Back, T.: Evolutionary Algorithms in Theory and Practice. Oxford University Press 1996
2.   Barnsley, M. F.: Fractals Everywhere. Academic Press, (1993)
3.   Barnsley, M. F., and Hurd, L. P.: Fractal Image Compression. AK Peters, (1993)

4. Collet, P., Lutton, E., Raynal, F., and Schoenauer, M.: Individual GP: an alternative viewpoint for the resolution of complex problems. Proceedings of the Genetic and Evolutionary Computation Conference, volume 2, Morgan Kaufmann, (1999) 974-981
5. Cretin, G., Lutton, E., Levy-Vehel, J., Glevarec, P. and Roll, C.: Mixed IFS: Resolution of the inverse problem using genetic programming. Artificial Evolution, volume 1063 of LNCS Springer Verlag, (1996) 247-258
6. Foley, J. D., van Dam, A., Feiner, S. K., Huges, J.F.: Computer Graphics Principle and Practice. Addison-Wesley, (1990)
7. Hutchinson, J.E.: Fractals and Self Similarity. Indiana University Journal, Vol. 35, No. 5, (1981)
8. Keller, R.E., Banzhaf, W., Mehnen, J., and Weinert, K.: CAD surface reconstruction from digitized 3D point data with a genetic programming/evolution strategy hybrid. Advances in Genetic Programming 3, MIT Press, (1999) 41-65
9. Sharman, K. C., Esparcia Alcazar, A. I., and Li, Y.: Evolving signal processing algorithms by genetic programming. First International Conference on Genetic Algorithms in Engineering Systems: Innovations and Applications, GALESIA, IEE, volume 414, (1995) 473-480
10. Koza, J.R.: Genetic Programming: On the Programming of Computers by Means of Natural Selection. MIT Press (1992)
11. Langdon, W. B.: Genetic Programming and Data Structures, Kluwer Academic Publishers, (1998)
12. Lu, N.: Fractal Imaging. Academic Press, (1997)
13. Montana, J. D.: Strongly Typed Genetic Programming, Evolutionary Computation, 3(2), (1995) 199-230
14. Nettleton, D. J. and Garigliano, R.: Evolutionary algorithms and the construction of fractals: solution of the inverse problem. Biosystems (33), Elsevier Science (1994) 221-231
15. Racine, A., Hamida, S.B., and Schoenauer, M.: Parametric coding vs genetic programming: A case study. In W. B. Langdon, Riccardo Poli, Peter Nordin, and Terry Fogarty, editors,Late-Breaking Papers of EuroGP-99, Goteborg, Sweeden, (1999) 13-22
16. .Sarafopoulos, A.: Automatic generation of affine IFS and strongly typed genetic programming. Springer-Verlag, Genetic Programming, Proceedings of EuroGP'99, volume 1598 of LNCS, (1999) 149-160
17. Schoenauer, M., Lamy, B., and Jouve F.: Identification of mechanical behaviour by genetic programming part II: Energy formulation. Technical report, Ecole Polytechnique, 91128 Palaiseau, France, (1995)
18. Schoenauer, M., Sebag, M., Jouve, F., Lamy, B., and Maitournam, H.: Evolutionary identification of macro-mechanical models. Advances in Genetic Programming 2, MIT Press, (1996) 467-488
19. Schwefel, P. H.: Evolution and Optimum Seeking. John Wiley & Sons, (1995)
20. Watt, A., and Watt, M.: Advanced Animation and Rendering Techniques Theory and Practice. Addison-Wesley, (1992)

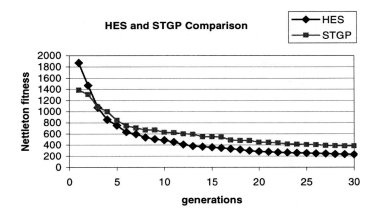

Fig. 4. Best of generation fitness curves for the inference problem for IFS using *Nettleton* fitness. The graph shows the results of the best run for STGP and HES.

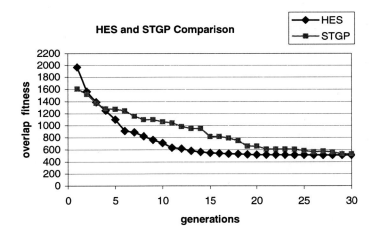

Fig. 5. Best of generation fitness curves for the inference problem for IFS using *overlap* fitness. The graph shows the results of the best run for STGP and HES.

Fig. 6. Attractors of the best of generations 1, 2, 3, 5, 8, 9, 10, 12, 16, 23, and 30, using the Nettleton fitness, and hierarchical ES. The hierarchical ES converges very quickly to a shape that is close to the target and then spends a great deal of time trying to fine-tune/improve that overall shape. The top left image is the image of the target shape, the Barnsley Fern. The attractor of the best individual in the population is shown at the bottom left of the image. The best individual was made out of 9 transformations.

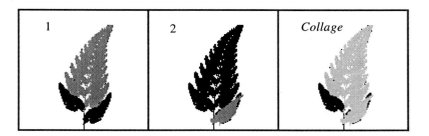

Fig. 7. Best individual using hierarchical ES with the overlap fitness. The target shape is drawn with black. The shapes that are dark gray and cover the target show the target shape under a transformation. The light gray shape is the *collage* of the target under the transformations (see Section 4.3). In this case the individual is made out of two transformations. Transformation 1 on the left of the figure scales and translates the target so it covers the top of the fern. The second transformation scales and rotates the shape onto a leaf on the bottom left of the fern. The image on the right shows the collage superimposed onto the target. The individual succeeds in finding transformations that do not overlap, and cover some parts of the fern tightly, but misses other important parts of the fern.

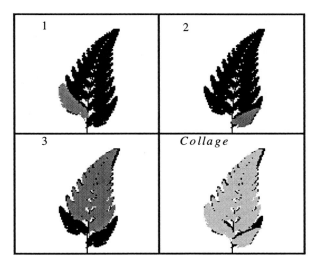

Fig. 8. Best individual using STGP with overlap fitness. The individual is made out of three transformations. Transformation 1 takes the target to a leaf on bottom left side of the fern. The second transformation takes the target to leaf on the lower right part of the fern. The third transformation scales the target to cover the upper part of the fern. Finally the collage on the bottom right side of the figure, shows that the individual succeeds, in finding transformations that cover most parts of the fern, except the stem. However, each transformation, is not as precise in covering the parts of the fern as the transformations, in Figure 7.

Evolving Turing Machines for Biosequence Recognition and Analysis

Edgar E. Vallejo[1] and Fernando Ramos[2]

[1] Computer Science Department, ITESM Campus Estado de México
Apdo. Postal 50, Módulo de Servicio Postal Campus Estado de México del ITESM
52926 Atizapán, Edo. México, México
evallejo@campus.cem.itesm.mx
[2] Computer Science Department, ITESM Campus Morelos
Ave. Paseo de la Reforma 182 Col. Lomas de Cuernavaca, 62589
Cuernavaca, Morelos, México
framos@campus.mor.itesm.mx

Abstract. This article presents a genetic programming system for biosequence recognition and analysis. In our model, a population of Turing machines evolves the capability of biosequence recognition using genetic algorithms. We use HIV biosequences as the working example. Experimental results indicate that evolved Turing machines are capable of recognizing HIV biosequences in a collection of training sets. In addition, we demostrate that the evolved Turing machines can be used to approximate the multiple sequence alignment problem.

1 Introduction

The area of bioinformatics is concerned with the analysis of biosequences to determine the structure and function of biological molecules [3]. The ultimate goal of bioinformatics is the understanding of life at the molecular level. Increasing interests in these studies arise as a consequence of the discovery of the human genome. Medicine and pharmacology are areas that will be beneficially affected by bioinformatics developments.

A central question of evolutionary biology is: What are the properties that characterize particular species at the molecular level? The identification of such properties provides the necessary information attributes to discriminate genetically unrelated species, as well as to construct phylogenetic trees that organize genetically related species.

Automata theory provides a formal framework for the analysis of biosequences. For instance, the problem of discrimination of species at the molecular level reduces to the problem of language recognition in the context of automata theory. In particular, the solution of this problem involves the construction of a finite state machine that recognizes a collection of biosequences corresponding to the same species.

From a finite collection of biosequences, constructing a non-deterministic finite automaton that accepts every sequence in the set and rejects anything else

J. Miller et al. (Eds.): EuroGP 2001, LNCS 2038, pp. 192–203, 2001.

is a trivial task. From the closure property of regular languages under union, we know that every finite language is a regular language. Therefore, it is possible to construct a non-deterministic finite automaton that recognizes the set of biosequences using the closure construction under union for regular languages [11].

The non-determinist finite automaton described above is capable of recognizing a finite collection of related biosequences. However, this machine has not generalization capabilities. In addition, the inherent memory limitations of the finite automata model restricts the recognition process to the discovery of repetitive, contiguous patterns present in biosequences.

Are there more complex patterns in biosequences that can not be described using regular languages? In this work, we assume that biosequences are part of recursively enumerable languages, which are the less restricted class of languages that can be recognized by an effective procedure. This hypothesis implies that there exists a Turing machine that recognize any collection of biosequences. So the problem of biosequence recognition can be reformulated as the design of a Turing machine that accepts every sequences in the set. However, the design of Turing machines to perform language recognition can be extremely difficult to accomplish.

Tanomaru [12] has demostrated that an artificial evolutionary process can be used to evolve Turing machines that compute simple fuctions. Using a genetic algorithm to evolve state transition tables, he showed the evolution of machines that are capable of computing sorting and unary arithmetic.

In addition, Hu [7] has demonstrated that genetic programming can be applied to the discovery of consensus patterns in a collection of biosequences. In his work, the consensus patterns are represented with ambiguous symbols and flexible gaps. The patterns are matched against a collection of positive and negative examples. He demonstrated the effectiveness of his approach on several protein families in PROSITE database.

Similarly, Koza and his colleagues [8] have applied genetic programming to the evolution of motifs for recognizing the D-E-A-D box family of proteins and for recognizing the manganese superoxide dismutase family of proteins. They employed automatically define functions to detect the repetition of common patterns. The genetic programming system was able to perform better than the human-written motifs found in the PROSITE database.

In this work, we present a genetic programming model for the recognition and analysis of biosequences. In our model, a population of Turing machines evolves recognition capabilities. We use a collection of African and American HIV sequences as the working example. The identification of regularities in retrovirus biosequences can be very important, given the accelerated mutation rates that characterize these species.

Experimental results indicate that our model can be used to automatically evolve programs that decide membership to formal languages defined by HIV biosequences. In addition, we show that evolved machines can be used to approximate the multiple sequence alignment problem.

2   Turing Machines as the Model of Computation of GP

Genetic programming is the direct evolution of programs for the purpose of inductive learning [4]. Under this definition the concept of program is very general and comprises several different alternative definitions of a program, such as sequences of statements, composition of functions or Horn clauses.

Traditionally, genetic programming systems are designed to evolve LISP S-expressions using functional programming; recently there have been many additions to this approach such as the incorporation of side effects through mechanism for manipulation of indexed memory, data structures and control structures[4]. Also, several programming languages have been used to represent the executable structures in genetic programming such as machine code, C, C++ and Prolog [4]. It is evident that genetic programming is not tied to pure functional programming style and now there are many systems that use alternative programming methodologies.

Informally, a program is specification of a computation; there are several alternative formal definitions of computation based on different theoretical abstractions (Turing machines, lambda calculus, SLD-resolution) all of which have previously proved to be equivalent. Programming languages are notations to write programs. Underlying each programming language there is a particular definition of computation or model of computation which determines the way we think about programs.

Using Turing machines as the model of computation of a genetic programming system provides the sufficient conditions to prove a general and important property of genetic programming. In general, *genetic programming is undecidable*. This follows from the undecidability of the Halting problem of Turing machines.

Genetic programming reduces to the Halting problem. This reduction is trivial when genetic programming system evolves Turing machines. In effect, this genetic programming system simulates Turing machines along with its input to evaluate fitness. In general, this problem can not be solved by effective procedures. In fact, this is a limitation of any computational system that manipulates programs.

In general, we think that Turing machines provides a better framework for studying the theoretical capabilities and limitations of genetic programming than high level programming languages. Moreover, we firmly advocate the use of Turing machines for language recognition problems.

3   Experiments

3.1   Experiment 1: Turing Machines

In this experiment we applied a genetic algorithm to a population of Turing machines. The population evolves the ability of discriminating a collection of HIV sequences from a collection of positive examples and counterexamples with similar statistical properties.

A Turing machine has an infinite read-write input tape with the input string at the leftmost squares of the tape. The input-output tape head can read one symbol at a time, write one symbol on the tape in that position, and in one move the input-output tape head can shift one square to the left or shift one square to the right. We introduce a restricted Turing machine model for practical reasons.

Formally, a *restricted Turing machine* is a 9-tuple $(Q, \Sigma, \Gamma, \delta, q_0, q_{accept}, q_{reject}, t_{size}, s_{max})$, where

1. Q is a finite set of states,
2. Σ is the input alphabet not containing the special *blank* symbol ⊔,
3. Γ is the tape alphabet where ⊔ $\in \Gamma$ and $\Sigma \subseteq \Gamma$,
4. $\delta : Q \times \Gamma \to Q \times \Gamma \times \{L, R\}$ is the transition function
5. $q_0 \in Q$ is the start state,
6. $q_{accept} \in Q$ is the accept state,
7. $q_{reject} \in Q$ is the reject state, where $q_{reject} \neq q_{accept}$
8. t_{size} is the tape size, and
9. s_{max} is the maximum number of computation steps.

The head starts at the leftmost square of the tape. Once the machine starts, the computation proceeds according to the rules described by the transition function. If the machine ever tries to move its head to the left of the left-hand end of the tape, the head stays in the same place for that move, even though the transition function indicates L. Similarly, if the machine ever tries to move its head to the right of the right-end of the tape, the head stays in the same place for that move, even though the transition function indicates R. The computation continues until it enters either the accept or reject states at which point it halts. If neither occurs, the machine goes until the maximum number of computation steps is reached.

The restriction of the tape size allows an efficient implementation of the genetic programming system. The restriction of the maximum number of computation steps will guarantee that the Turing machine will never reach an infinite loop. However, both restrictions negatively affect the computation capabilities of Turing machines.

We use a generational genetic algorithm with tournament selection and elitism [10] to evolve the population of Turing machines. In general, the design of a genetic algorithm involves the determination of the genome representation, genetic operators, fitness function, and parameters for the runs.

Genome Representation. An immediate question that arises when designing the genome representation is: What is the appropiate size of the Turing machine to perform HIV biosequence recognition? The existence of an universal Turing machine indicates that there exists a certain minimum level of complexity in any model of computation that is sufficient to perform any computation. It has been shown that the essential requeriments of any effective procedure can be achieved by very simple formal systems, including a Turing machine with seven states and an alphabet containing four symbols [9]. We use this fact to determine the size of the Turing machines to evolve in our experiments.

The representation of the genome consists of the concatenation of values of the state transition function of the Turing machine using the order imposed by the state transition table. For example, consider the transition function shown in figure 1.

δ	a	b
q_1	(q_1, a, R)	(q_2, b, L)
q_2	(q_3, a, L)	(q_2, b, R)
q_3	(q_2, b, R)	(q_2, a, R)

Fig. 1. State transition function

The values of the state transition function are codified in the genome using the order imposed by the table. In this way, values are indexed in the genome and can be accessed directly. Concatenating the values for all entries in the table yields the following genome:

$$(q_1, a, R)(q_2, b, L)(q_3, a, L)(q_2, b, R)(q_2, b, R)(q_2, a, R)$$

In general, a restricted Turing machine is represented as follows:

$$q_{0,0}a_{0,0}m_{0,0}q_{0,1}a_{0,1}m_{0,1}\cdots q_{1,0}a_{1,0}m_{1,0}q_{1,1}a_{1,1}m_{1,1}\cdots q_{|Q|,|\Sigma|}a_{|Q|,|\Sigma|}m_{|Q|,|\Sigma|}$$

where $q_{i,j}a_{i,j}m_{i,j}$ indicates the table entry at row i and column j. $|Q|$ and $|\Sigma|$ are the cardinalities of the set of states and the alphabet, respectively.

Genetic Operators. Because we are using a non binary representation of the genome, genetic operators are properly designed to preserve the sintactic structure in order to avoid the generation of points that fall outside the solution space.

Fitness Function. Fitness can be defined as the number of HIV biosequences accepted. We use seven African type HIV sequences and seven American type HIV sequences taken from the GENEBANK. However, by using only positive examples, an over generalization problem might arise. That is, a Turing machine that not only accepts the positive examples, but any other sequence as well is not useful for our purposes.

In other to avoid over generalization, we construct a training set consisting of positive examples and a collection of counterexamples that are randomly generated. These negative examples have similar frequencies of nucleotide bases with respect to positive examples. The training set is shown in figure 2.

Thenceforth, fitness is defined as the number of sequences correctly classified.

Positive examples	Counterexamples 1	Counterexamples 2
HIV2BEN	HIV2BENX	HIV2BENY
HIV2D194	HIV2D194X	HIV2D194Y
HIV2GH1	HIV2GH1X	HIV2GH1Y
HIV2ISY	HIV2ISYX	HIV2ISYY
HIV2NIHZ	HIV2NIHZX	HIV2NIHZY
HIV2ROD	HIV2RODX	HIV2RODY
HIV2ST	HIV2STX	HIV2STY
HIVBRU	HIVBRUX	HIVBRUY
HIVELI	HIVELIX	HIVELI
HIVHAN	HIVHANX	HIVHANY
HIVMAL	HIVMALX	HIVMALY
HIVMN	HIVMNX	HIVMNY
HIVNDK	HIVNDKX	HIVNDKY
HIVRF	HIVRFX	HIVRFY

Fig. 2. Training set

Parameters of the Runs. The experiments use a machine with 32 states and an tape alphabet containing 8 symbols (4 nucleotide bases, 3 marking symbols and the blank symbol). A Turing machine with this characteristics has the sufficient conditions for universal computation as explained before. However, it is important to point out that the restrictions of bounded tape and computation steps are not present in the universal machine.

We use a population of 1024 individuals, and a maximum of 1000 generations. We set the crossover and mutation probabilities to $p_c = 0.6$ and $p_m = 0.001$, respectively. These values are commonly used in practice [5]. Also, we set the maximum number of computation steps to 64000.

Results. We performed several runs with this model. In preliminary runs, the evolutionary process yielded a Turing machine capable of classifying all but one sequence. This false negative sequence was HIV2BEN. Later, we found that this problem was caused by the inclusion of a *long terminal repeat* which is a sequence that flanks the structural genes of a retrovirus. This sequence was removed from the HIV2BEN sequence. Thenceforth, the genetic algorithm found a Turing machine that correctly classifies all sequences in the training set. The state transition table of the evolved Turing machine is shown in figure 3. For this Turing machine we have $q_0 = q_{start}$, $q_{30} = q_{accept}$, $q_{31} = q_{reject}$, ·

Figure 4 shows several configurations of the Turing machine with input HIV2BEN.

In this experiment we also explore the generalization capabilities of the Turing machines found in our experiments. The evolved Turing machines were capable of accepting several HIV biosequences not included in the training set.

δ	a	c	g	t	x	y	z	$\sqcup$
q_0	(q_3,a,L)	(q_{27},g,L)	$(q_{30},\sqcup,R)$	(q_4,z,L)	(q_{10},x,L)	(q_{20},y,L)	(q_6,y,L)	(q_9,c,L)
q_1	(q_1,t,R)	(q_{27},a,R)	(q_3,z,L)	(q_{20},z,L)	(q_{22},c,L)	(q_{20},a,R)	(q_{11},x,R)	(q_5,a,L)
q_2	(q_{16},y,R)	(q_{27},y,L)	$(q_{21},\sqcup,R)$	(q_5,a,R)	$(q_1,\sqcup,R)$	(q_{19},a,R)	$(q_{14},\sqcup,L)$	(q_6,z,L)
q_3	(q_{26},x,L)	(q_9,x,L)	(q_4,t,L)	(q_{12},t,L)	$(q_{21},\sqcup,L)$	(q_{14},a,L)	(q_{12},z,R)	$(q_{27},\sqcup,R)$
q_4	(q_{18},a,R)	(q_{11},a,L)	$(q_{12},\sqcup,L)$	(q_2,z,R)	(q_3,z,L)	(q_{21},y,L)	(q_{24},y,R)	(q_{30},c,L)
q_5	(q_{13},x,R)	(q_{12},y,L)	$(q_0,\sqcup,R)$	(q_9,a,R)	(q_3,x,L)	(q_{18},c,R)	(q_{16},x,L)	(q_{19},t,R)
q_6	(q_{19},t,R)	(q_{12},x,R)	$(q_6,\sqcup,L)$	$(q_{11},\sqcup,L)$	(q_2,x,L)	$(q_{15},\sqcup,R)$	(q_{10},a,R)	(q_{30},y,L)
q_7	(q_{13},g,R)	(q_{10},c,R)	(q_{20},a,L)	(q_{24},t,L)	$(q_{26},\sqcup,L)$	$(q_{13},\sqcup,L)$	(q_{13},a,L)	(q_0,x,R)
q_8	(q_{25},c,L)	(q_{16},t,R)	$(q_{11},\sqcup,L)$	$(q_{17},\sqcup,R)$	(q_3,t,R)	(q_4,y,L)	(q_{27},g,R)	$(q_{23},\sqcup,R)$
q_9	$(q_2,\sqcup,L)$	(q_7,y,R)	(q_2,z,L)	$(q_{25},\sqcup,R)$	(q_{15},t,R)	(q_{27},a,L)	$(q_3,\sqcup,R)$	$(q_{21},\sqcup,L)$
q_{10}	$(q_{29},\sqcup,L)$	(q_{21},a,R)	(q_0,g,L)	(q_{30},g,L)	(q_{25},t,R)	(q_{21},c,R)	(q_0,y,L)	(q_8,g,R)
q_{11}	(q_{13},c,R)	(q_{25},a,R)	$(q_{20},\sqcup,L)$	(q_{16},g,L)	$(q_9,\sqcup,L)$	(q_{16},g,L)	(q_2,c,R)	(q_{26},g,L)
q_{12}	(q_0,c,L)	(q_{16},y,L)	(q_{29},x,L)	$(q_{18},\sqcup,L)$	(q_{19},c,R)	(q_7,a,R)	(q_1,t,L)	(q_{15},g,L)
q_{13}	$(q_{16},\sqcup,R)$	(q_{19},x,L)	(q_3,g,L)	(q_9,x,L)	$(q_{24},\sqcup,R)$	$(q_{17},\sqcup,R)$	(q_{24},g,L)	(q_{11},x,R)
q_{14}	(q_3,z,L)	(q_{22},t,R)	(q_{27},a,R)	(q_6,c,L)	(q_3,t,L)	(q_0,g,L)	(q_9,x,L)	(q_9,y,R)
q_{15}	(q_{11},y,L)	(q_{10},a,R)	(q_5,c,R)	(q_{19},a,R)	(q_{13},c,R)	(q_3,z,L)	$(q_{14},\sqcup,L)$	$(q_4,\sqcup,L)$
q_{16}	(q_6,c,L)	(q_{28},g,L)	(q_{20},x,R)	(q_{24},a,L)	(q_{27},x,L)	(q_4,a,L)	(q_{30},y,L)	(q_{18},z,L)
q_{17}	(q_{31},c,L)	(q_{21},z,R)	(q_2,t,L)	(q_{25},x,L)	(q_{27},g,R)	(q_{11},g,L)	(q_{22},c,L)	(q_4,x,R)
q_{18}	(q_{12},a,R)	(q_{24},x,R)	(q_0,z,L)	(q_{21},y,L)	(q_{10},t,L)	(q_{25},t,R)	(q_{12},c,L)	(q_8,z,R)
q_{19}	$(q_{14},\sqcup,L)$	(q_7,a,L)	(q_{22},y,L)	(q_9,x,R)	(q_{17},z,L)	(q_{14},x,L)	(q_7,t,L)	(q_8,x,R)
q_{20}	(q_{20},a,R)	(q_{30},g,L)	(q_{25},c,R)	(q_{11},c,R)	(q_2,x,L)	(q_3,t,L)	$(q_{26},\sqcup,L)$	(q_8,y,L)
q_{21}	(q_{24},x,L)	(q_{22},y,L)	(q_{18},t,L)	$(q_{16},\sqcup,L)$	(q_0,g,L)	(q_{16},t,L)	(q_5,g,L)	(q_{11},a,L)
q_{22}	(q_0,z,L)	(q_3,t,R)	(q_{23},t,R)	(q_7,y,L)	(q_{21},x,L)	(q_8,g,L)	(q_{18},x,R)	(q_{14},x,R)
q_{23}	(q_{30},z,L)	(q_{23},a,R)	(q_8,t,L)	$(q_{27},\sqcup,L)$	(q_{26},y,L)	(q_{24},g,R)	(q_{25},z,R)	(q_{11},c,R)
q_{24}	$(q_{16},\sqcup,R)$	(q_{29},t,L)	(q_{20},c,L)	(q_{20},t,L)	(q_{19},a,R)	(q_{12},c,R)	(q_{29},t,L)	(q_{24},y,L)
q_{25}	(q_1,c,L)	(q_{30},a,R)	(q_{18},c,L)	(q_{22},x,R)	(q_{15},g,L)	(q_{10},g,L)	(q_{12},z,L)	(q_5,a,L)
q_{26}	(q_7,a,R)	(q_{31},c,R)	(q_8,a,L)	(q_1,g,L)	(q_{12},y,L)	(q_{21},c,L)	(q_3,t,L)	(q_2,a,L)
q_{27}	(q_3,g,R)	(q_1,a,L)	(q_7,g,L)	(q_{16},a,R)	(q_{17},z,R)	(q_{11},g,R)	(q_8,g,R)	(q_{23},y,L)
q_{28}	(q_4,y,R)	(q_0,z,R)	(q_{12},z,L)	(q_{26},y,R)	(q_{19},a,R)	(q_7,t,L)	(q_{14},g,L)	(q_{10},z,L)
q_{29}	$(q_4,\sqcup,L)$	(q_{21},a,L)	(q_1,x,R)	(q_{20},x,R)	$(q_{17},\sqcup,L)$	(q_0,y,L)	(q_{20},y,L)	(q_{29},t,L)
q_{30}	(q_9,x,R)	(q_{20},x,R)	(q_{26},z,L)	(q_{13},x,L)	(q_{24},z,L)	$(q_8,\sqcup,L)$	$(q_{17},\sqcup,L)$	(q_{12},c,R)
q_{31}	(q_5,x,R)	(q_{15},a,L)	(q_{25},x,R)	(q_{17},c,L)	(q_{31},g,L)	(q_{14},t,L)	(q_{27},z,L)	(q_{19},g,L)

Fig. 3. Evolved Turing machine

Input: HIV2BEN

$\vdash q_0\,tgcaagggat\ldots$

$\vdash q_4\,zgcaagggatg\ldots$

$\vdash yq_{24}\,gcaagggat\ldots$

$\vdash q_{20}\,yccaagggatg\ldots$

$\vdash q_2\,xccaagggatgt\ldots$

$\vdash \sqcup q_1\,ccaagggatgtt\ldots$

$\vdash caq_{27}\,caagggatgttt\ldots$

$\vdash cq_1\,aaaagggatgtt\ldots$

$\vdash cttq_1\,aagggatgt\ldots$

$\vdash ctttq_1\,agggatgt\ldots$

$\vdash cttttq_1\,gggatgt\ldots$

$\vdots$

Fig. 4. Configurations with input HIV2BEN

3.2   Experiment 2: Two-Way Deterministic Finite Automata

In this experiment we applied a genetic algorithm to a population of two-way deterministic finite automata. The population evolves the ability of discriminating HIV sequences without modifying the contents of the input tape.

Two-way deterministic finite automaton is a special type of Turing machine that recognizes a language. It has a read-only input tape. The input tape head can read one symbol at a time, and in one move the input tape head can shift one square to the left or shift one square to the right. We introduce a restricted two-way deterministic finite automaton model for practical reasons.

Formally, a *restricted two-way deterministic finite automaton* is a 8-tuple $(Q, \Sigma, \delta, q_0, q_{accept}, q_{reject}, t_{size}, s_{max})$, where

1. Q is a finite set of states,
2. Σ is the input alphabet,
3. $\delta : Q \times \Sigma \to Q \times \{L, R\}$ is the transition function
4. $q_0 \in Q$ is the start state,
5. $q_{accept} \in Q$ is the accept state,
6. $q_{reject} \in Q$ is the reject state, where $q_{reject} \neq q_{accept}$,
7. t_{size} is the tape size, and
8. s_{max} is the maximum number of computation steps.

The class of languages that two-way deterministic finite automata can recognize is the class of regular languages [6]. Therefore, these machines can recognize only repetitive, contiguous patterns in biosequence. However, it can be useful to aproximate the multiple sequence problem as we demostrate in experiment 3.

In addition, automata theory provides a formal description of regularities in biosequences. For instance, we can reduce the two-way deterministic finite automaton to an equivalent deterministic finite automaton with minimum number of states. From this machine, we can obtain an regular expression that describes the languages of the machine [11]. Regular expressions provides a compact description based on the specification of contiguous, repetitive patterns found in biosequences.

Genome Representation. As before, the representation of the genome consists of the values of the state transition function of the Turing machine using the order imposed by the state transition table. For example, consider the transition function shown in figure 5.

δ	a	b
q_1	(q_1, R)	(q_2, L)
q_2	(q_3, L)	(q_2, R)
q_3	(q_2, R)	(q_2, R)

Fig. 5. State transition function

Similarly, concatenating the values for all entries in the table yields the following genome:

$$(q_1, R)(q_2, L)(q_3, L)(q_2, R)(q_2, R)(q_2, R)$$

In general, a restricted two-way deterministic finite automaton is represented as follows:

$$q_{0,0}m_{0,0}q_{0,1}m_{0,1} \cdots q_{1,0}m_{1,0}q_{1,1}m_{1,1} \cdots q_{|Q|,|\Sigma|}m_{|Q|,|\Sigma|}$$

where $q_{i,j}m_{i,j}$ indicates the table entry at row i and column j. $|Q|$ and $|\Sigma|$ are the cardinalities of the set of states and the alphabet, respectively.

Genetic Operators. As before, because we are using a non binary representation of the genome, genetic operators are properly designed to preserve the syntactic structure of the genome in order to avoid the generation of points that fall outside the solution space.

Fitness Function. Fitness is defined as the number of sequences correctly classified. We use the same training set of experiment 1.

Parameters of the Runs. The experiments use a machine with 32 states and an tape alphabet containing 8 symbols (4 nucleotide bases, and the blank symbol).

As before, we use a population of 1024 individuals, and a maximum of 1000 generations. We set the crossover and mutation probabilities to $p_c = 0.6$ and $p_m = 0.001$, respectively. We set the maximum number of computation steps to 64000.

Results. We performed several runs with this model. In each run, the evolutionary process yielded a deterministic two-way finite automaton that correctly classifies all sequences in the training set without modifying the input tape.

3.3   Experiment 3: Multiple Sequence Alignment

In this experiment we used the evolved two-way deterministic finite automata in experiment 2 in order to approximate the multiple sequence aligment problem.

A *multiple alignment* of a set of biosequences is a rectangular arrangement, where each row consists of one sequence padded by gaps, such that the columns indicate similarity/conservation between positions.

It is possible to generalize the Knuth-Morris-Pratt algorithm [2] to solve the multiple alignment problem. However, it has been shown that the multiple sequence alignment is a NP-complete problem. Therefore, a procedure that approximates the problem would increment the viability of multiple sequence analysis.

In this experiment, the two way finite automaton computes each sequence multiple times by starting at every position in the sequence. This procedure is repeated for every positive example. The machine explores the input tape back and forth and eventually accepts or rejects the sequence. If two sequences have a common pattern, the machine will exhibit identical behavior on both sequences.

Multiple aligment can be achieved by registering the starting position, the sequence length, the leftmost and the rightmost positions of the tape that the machine visited before either accepting or rejecting. If sequence length do match for both sequences, it is very probable that the sequence explored by the machine is a consensus pattern.

Results. The machines evolved in previous experiments were capable of discovering many consensus patterns in multiple biosequences. For example, figure 6 shows several consensus patterns found in the collection of all HIV biosequences.

4   Conclusions and Future Work

Turing machines are simple, general models of computation. In this work, we propose the evolution of Turing machines to perform biosequence recognition and analysis. Depending on the research goals, Turing machines can be very useful to represent the executable structures of genetic programming systems. Additionally, Turing machines can be coded in a simple, parsimonious form. These studies will provide a framework for understanding the structural and functional properties of species at the molecular level.

We use a collection of African and American HIV biosequences to perform recognition. Experimental results indicate that the proposed genetic programming model is capable of evolving Turing machines with general biosequence recognition capabilities. Also, we present an efficient method to approximate sequence alignment problem using two-way deterministic finite automata.

The focus of this study has been the recognition and multiple sequence alignment of biosequences. An immediate extension of this work is the consideration of other bioinformatics problems such as the pairwise aligment, structurally verified alignment, and edit operations. Other extensions include the varible length representation of the genome to evolve Turing machines of unbounded size. A more detailed analysis of the Turing machine computation by exploring the output tape could elucidate properties present in biosequences.

Additionally, a genetic programming based on the evolution of Turing machines using genetic algorithms provides a convenient framework for understanding the fundamental theoretical capabilities and limitations of genetic programming.

Start position	Output	Sequence length	Leftmost position	Rightmost position
1	*rejected*	4	0	3

Consensus pattern:
tgca

Start position	Output	Sequence length	Leftmost position	Rightmost position
2	*accepted*	36	2	37

Consensus pattern:
caagggatgtttacagtaggaggagacatagaatc

Start position	Output	Sequence length	Leftmost position	Rightmost position
5	*accepted*	75	4	79

Consensus pattern:
gggatgttttacagtaggaggagacatagaatcctagacatatacctagaaaaagaggaagggataataccagat

Start position	Output	Sequence length	Leftmost position	Rightmost position
32	*accepted*	80	31	110

Consensus pattern:
tagaatcctagacatatacctagaaaaagaggaagggataataccagattggcagaattatactcatgggccaggagtaa

Start position	Output	Sequence length	Leftmost position	Rightmost position
93	*accepted*	154	92	245

Consensus pattern:
*actcatgggccaggagtaaggtacccaatgtacttcgggtggctgtggaagctagtatcagtagaactctcacaagaggca
gaggaagatgaggccaactgcttagtacacccagcacaaacaagcagacatgatgatgagcatggggagacat*

Start position	Output	Sequence length	Leftmost position	Rightmost position
186	*accepted*	212	184	395

Consensus pattern:
*ggccaactgcttagtacacccagcacaaacaagcagacatgatgatgagcatggggagacattagtgtggcagtttgactcc
atgctggcctataactacaaggccttcactctgtacccagaagagtttgggcacaagtcaggattgccagagaaagaatgga
aggcaaaactgaaagcaagagggataccatatagtgaataacaggaac*

Start position	Output	Sequence length	Leftmost position	Rightmost position
381	*accepted*	275	378	652

Consensus pattern:
*atagtgaataacaggaacaaccatacttggtcaaggcaggaagtagctactaagaaacagctgaggctgcagggactttcc
agaaggggctgtaaccaagggagggacatgggaggagctggtggggaacgccctcatacttactgtataaatgtacccgct
tcttgcattgtattcagtcgctctgcggagaggctggcagatcgagccctgagaggttctctccagcactagcaggtagag
cctgggtgttccctgctggactctcaccagta*

Fig. 6. Multiple sequence alignment

References

1. Aho, A. V., Hopcroft, J. E., Ullman, J. D. 1974. *The Design and Analysis of Computer Algorithms. Third Edition.* Addison Wesley Publishing Company.
2. Baase, S., Van Gelder, A. 2000. *Computer Algorithms Introduction to Design and Analysis.* Addison Wesley Publishing Company.
3. Baldi, P., Brunak, S. 1998. *Bioinformatics The Machine Learning Approach.* The MIT Press.

4. Banzhaf, W., Nordin, P., Keller, R. E., Francone, F. D. 1998. *Genetic Programming An Introduction.* Morgan Kaufmann Publishers, Inc..
5. Goldberg, D. E. 1989. *Genetic Algorithms in Search, Optimization and Machine Learning.* Addison Wesley Publishing Company.
6. Hopcroft, J. E., Ullman, J. D. 1979. *Introduction to Automata Theory, Languages and Computation* Addison Wesley Publishing Company.
7. Hu, Y. J. 1998. Biopattern Discovery by Genetic Programming. In J. Koza, W. Banzhaf, K. Chellapilla, K. Deb, M. Dorigo, D. Fogel, M. Garzon, D. Goldberg, H. Iba, R. Riolo (eds.) *Genetic Programming 1998. Proceedings of the Third Annual Conference.* pp 152-157, Morgan Kaufmann Publishers, Inc.
8. Koza, J. R., Bennett III, F. H., Andre, D., Keane, M. A. 1999. *Genetic Programming III Darwinian Invention and Problem Solving* Morgan Kaufmann Publishers, Inc.
9. Minsky, M. 1967. *Computation: Finite and Infinite Machines* Prentice Hall.
10. Mitchell, M. 1996. *An Introduction to Genetic Algorithms* The MIT Press.
11. Sipser, M. 1997. *Introduction to the Theory of Computation.* PWS Publishing Company.
12. Tanomaru, J. 1998. *Evolving Turing Machines from Examples* In J.-K. Hao, E. Lutton, E. Ronald, M. Schoenauer, D. Snyers(eds.) *Artificial Evolution Third European Conference, AE'97* LNCS 1363. Springer-Verlag.

Neutrality and the Evolvability
of Boolean Function Landscape

Tina Yu[1] and Julian Miller[2]

[1]Chevron Information Technology Company, San Ramon CA 94583, U.S.A.
`tiyu@chevron.com`, `http://www.addr.com/~tinayu`

[2]School of Computer Science, University of Birmingham
Birmingham B15 2TT, U.K.
`j.miller@cs.bham.ac.uk`, `http://www.cs.bham.ac.uk/~jfm`

Abstract. This work is a study of neutrality in the context of Evolutionary Computation systems. In particular, we introduce the use of explicit neutrality with an integer string coding scheme to allow neutrality to be measured during evolution. We tested this method on a Boolean benchmark problem. The experimental results indicate that there is a positive relationship between neutrality and evolvability: *neutrality improves evolvability*. We also identify four characteristics of adaptive/neutral mutations that are associated with high evolvability. They may be the ingredients in designing effective Evolutionary Computation systems for the Boolean class problem.

1   Introduction

The Darwinian theory of evolution is based on two principles: *selection* and *mutation*. It states that through the process of natural selection, organisms become progressively adapted to their environments by accumulating beneficial mutations. During the study of population genetics, Sewall Wright observed that "genetic drift" (the random change in the frequency of alleles in a population that are not related to selection) plays an important role in the process of evolution [18]. Although it did not deny the role of selection in evolution, Motoo Kimura's neutral theory argued that the majority of evolutionary changes at the molecular level are the results of random fixation of selectively neutral mutations rather than the results of Darwinian selection acting on advantageous mutations. In other words, the mutations involved are neither advantageous nor disadvantageous to the survival and reproduction of individuals. Such random genetic drift, as the theory claims, should be considered as an important explanatory factor of evolution [7][8][9]. This radical view has led to a controversy (often called "neutralist-selectionist controversy") which still is a matter for strong debate in Evolutionary Biology. Nevertheless, new data supporting neutral theory continues to be reported [10].

Evolutionary Computation (EC) systems model the process of natural evolution for problem solving. With strong Darwinian influences, most EC systems adopt a selectionist's point of view to model evolution process, i.e. no explicit neutral mutations are coded in the evolved entities. One interesting EC paradigm is Genetic Pro-

J. Miller et al. (Eds.): EuroGP 2001, LNCS 2038, pp. 204–217, 2001.

gramming (GP) [11] where neutral mutations are implicitly embedded in its evolved computer programs through *functional redundancy* and *introns* (see Section 2). There have been studies reported on these implicit neutral mutations [1]. In this work, we study neutrality in general through *explicit* neutral mutations. Moreover, the relationship between neutrality and evolvability of a GP system is analyzed.

The concept of evolvability has interested many researchers who want to understand the characteristics of evolvable systems so that they can incorporate these ingredients in their EC systems to evolve complex problem solutions. According to Altenberg, evolvability is the ability of a population to produce variants fitter than any yet existing. He believes that to achieve high evolvability, "conservation of fitness score" during evolution is very important. This "conservativeness", however, is difficult to obtain when the population has become fit and mutation is disruptive in transmitting the fitness of an individual to its offspring. The implicit neutral mutations in the GP program representation provide a buffer against disruptive mutations; this enables more fitter offspring to be generated [1]. The work of Hinton and Nowlan showed that lifetime learning of individuals can increase evolvability. To solve a "needle in a haystack" problem (Only the genotype with the correct combinations is rewarded with the perfect fitness. Any other genotypes are rewarded with fitness value 0), they added a new allele "?" in the genotype representation. The experimental results show that evolutionary search was able to learn to use the new representation and to generate fitter solution [5].

The goal of this paper is to elucidate quantitatively how neutrality improves the evolutionary search process for a Boolean benchmark problem (even-3-parity). The work extends earlier findings on the advantages of neutrality for digital circuit evolution [20]. Evolving Boolean functions is a challenging endeavor and is likely to be important in the Evolvable Hardware research community. Moreover, we believe that understanding the advantages and role of neutrality on this class of problem will be of interest to the wider research community.

The paper is organized as the following: Section 2 explains neutrality in the context of EC systems. Section 3 describes the Cartesian GP system that we used to conduct our experiments. In Section 4, we describe the implementations of our experiments. The results are presented in Section 5. In Section 6, the interaction between neutrality and evolvability in the fitness landscape is analyzed. Section 7 summaries related work and Section 8 gives our conclusions and future work.

2   Neutrality: Implicit Versus Explicit

The standard GP program representation provides two forms of implicit neutral mutations: functional redundancy and introns. Functional redundancy refers to many different programs (genotypes) representing the same function (phenotype). For example, the following 3 genotypes represent the same function xor:

```
G1: nor (and x₁ x₂) (nor x₁ x₂)
G2: nor (nand (nand x₁ x₂) (or x₁ x₂)) (nor x₁ x₂)
G3: nor (and x₁ x₂) (nor (nor x₁ x₂) (nand x₁ x₂))
```

Genetic transformation from one genotype to another, e.g. G1 to G2, has a neutral effect on the program's behavior. Functional redundancy therefore provides neutrality during programs evolution process.

Introns refer to the code that are part of a program but are semantically redundant to the program's behavior. For example, the function or with input False are introns in the following genotype:

G4: or False (nor (and x_1 x_2) (nor x_1 x_2))

Genetic transformation by removing introns from a genotype, e.g. G4 to G1, has neutral effect on the program's behavior. Introns therefore also provide neutrality in the programs evolution process.

Functional redundancy and introns can emerge within an evolving genetic program. They are not easy to identify or control during the program evolution process. We therefore propose including extra code in the genotype to provide *explicit neutrality*. In this approach, a genotype can have part of its genes active and the others inactive. For example, the following 2 genotypes have extra code that is not active (in gray), yet still represent the xor function:

G5: nor (and x_1 x_2) (nor x_1 x_2) (nor x_1 x_2)
G6: nor (and x_1 x_2) (and x_1 x_2) (nor x_1 x_2)

Genetic changes on inactive genes that transform one genotype to another, e.g. G5 to G6, have a neutral effect on the program's behavior. Genotypes with inactive genes, therefore provide neutrality during the program evolution process.

The advantage of explicitly encoding neutral mutations in the genotypes is that it provides a way to measure neutrality in the evolutionary process. Using an integer string graph representation (see Section 3), neutrality between two genotypes with the same fitness can be measured by their hamming distance (see Section 4.3). Moreover, functional redundancy and introns can be measured using the same method (see Section 4.3). By studying explicit neutral mutations, we hope to understand neutrality in general and to be able to evaluate its impact on the evolvability of a GP system.

2.1   Neutral Versus Adaptive Mutation

Mutation on a genotype that has part of its genes active and others inactive produces different effects. Mutation on active genes is adaptive because it exploits the accumulated beneficial mutations. In contrast, mutation on inactive genes has neutral effect on a genotype's fitness, yet it provides an exploratory power by maintaining genetic diversity. Under the dynamics of the evolutionary process, active genes may become inactive while inactive genes may become active. Consequently, mutations on such kind of genotype representation provide two roles in the evolutionary search: exploitation and exploration. Yet, what is the best balance between neutral and adaptive mutation that would enable evolution to generate fitter offspring? We investigate this question using the Cartesian GP system on a Boolean function problem.

3   Cartesian Genetic Programming

Cartesian Genetic Programming (CGP) was originally formulated as an effective method for evolving digital electronic circuits, particularly Field Programmable Gate Arrays (FPGA) [12][13][14]. In CGP, a program is represented as an indexed, directed, acyclic graph, which can be mapped to the physical structure of a FPGA. For example, a one-bit adder with carry is represented in Figure 1. This gate array consists of 4 logic gates (2 xor, 1 and and 1 mux). A and B and C_{in} represent the primary inputs. C_{out} and Sum are the output bits of the adder. The upper right xor gate (output link 5) has input connections 3,2,1. This means that the first input is connected to the output of the upper left xor gate. The second input is connected to the primary input C_{in}, and the third input is connected to primary input B. The output C_{out} is connected to the output of the mux gate (lower right). This gate array is represented as a graph using an integer string in Figure 1(b). A gate array can have any number of rows and columns. Moreover, each gate can be connected to any other gates. The indexed, directed, acyclic graph is therefore a more natural representation than parse tree for digital electronic circuits

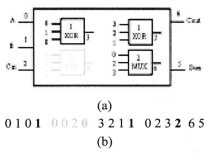

(a)

0 1 0 1 0 0 2 0 **3 2 1 1** 0 2 3 **2** 6 5

(b)

Figure 1   A one-bit adder with carry: (a) gate array representation
(b) graph representation.

Unlike the parse tree representation, a graph allows its nodes to be unconnected to any other nodes. Those nodes that are not connected to the graph that links to the gate array's input and output nodes are inactive and have no effect on the behavior of the program. For example, Figure 2 (b) is an even-3 parity function (described in Section 4.1) represented as a graph with 3 inactive nodes:

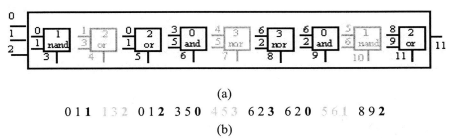

(a)

0 1 **1** 1 3 2 0 1 **2** 3 5 **0** 4 5 3 6 2 **3** 6 2 **0** 5 6 1 8 9 **2**

(b)

Figure 2   An even-3-parity function: (a) gate array representation
(b) graph representation.

The alleles in bold take value from the set {0, 1, 2, 3}, which represent the two-arity Boolean functions and, nand, or, nor respectively. The program inputs are denoted by labels 0, 1, 2. The gate outputs are labeled from 3 to 11. There are 3 inactive nodes in this genotype, grayed in the graph representation.

4   Experiments

4.1   Even-3-Parity Problem

The problem studied in this paper is the even-3-parity Boolean function. This function takes 3 Boolean inputs and returns `True` only if an even number of inputs are `True`. The function set chosen was {and, nand, or, nor} and the terminal set was {x_0, x_1, x_2} which represent the three inputs to the program. There are 2^3 different possible inputs combination, hence 8 test cases. The fitness of a program is the number of the correct outputs for the 8 test cases, i.e. a program can have fitness between 0 and 8.

4.2   Evolutionary Algorithm

The experiments were conducted using a simplified (1+4) Evolution Strategy [19], i.e. one parent with 4 offspring (population size 5). The algorithm is described as follows:

1. Generate initial population of 5 programs randomly;
2. Evaluate fitness of the population;
3. Select the best of the 5 in the population as the winner;
4. Carry out point-wise mutation on the winning parent to generate 4 offspring;
5. Construct a new generation with the winner and its 4 offspring;
6. Select a winner from the current population using the following rules:
   - If any of the offspring has better fitness than the parent, it becomes the winner.
   - Otherwise, an offspring with the same fitness as the parent is randomly selected. If the parent-offspring genotype pair has hamming distances within the permitted range (see Section 4.3), the offspring becomes the winner.
   - Otherwise, the current parent remains as the winner.
7. Go to step 4 unless the maximum number of generations has reached.

For even-3-parity, each node has 3 genes (two inputs link values and one Boolean function value). To obtain statistically meaningful results, we made 100 runs on different mutation rate with different neutrality size (explained in the following section). Moreover, each run continues until the maximum number of generation is reached. Table 1 summarizes the parameters used to conduct the experiments.

Table 1: Summary of Parameters

Genotype Length	Mutation Rate (%) on Genotype	Max Generation
100 nodes (300 genes)	1,2,4,6,8,10,12,14,16,18,20	10,000

4.3   Neutrality Measured with Hamming Distance

When a mutation operation generates a different genotype with the same fitness during step 4 in Section 4.2, it involves a number of neutral mutations. Neutral mutations on active genes are the results of functional redundancy or introns, hence represent implicit neutrality. In contrast, neutral mutations on inactive genes represent explicit neutrality. Regardless the source of neutrality (implicit or explicit), the overall amount of neutral mutations between the parent-offspring genotypes pair can be measured according to their hamming distance. For example, the following two genotypes have hamming distances 9. The number of active genes changes between the two genotypes is 8 (the node with output link number 6 contributes 3 active genes changes because it was inactive in Genotype 1 but becomes active in Genotype 2). The number of inactive genes changes is 2 (corresponding to the node with output link number 4).

```
Output link      3       4       5       6         7
Genotype 1     2 1 3   0 1 2   1 3 0   4 3 2   1 5 9
Genotype 2     2 0 2   0 3 3   1 3 2   5 0 2   6 5 2
```

If neutrality is not permitted, evolution has to constantly provide fitness improvement, i.e. only a *better* offspring is accepted to replace current parent as winner. Hamming distance 0 indicates that neither implicit nor explicit neutrality is allowed to be present during evolution.

When the hamming distance range is a non-0 value, neutrality is allowed to be present, i.e. evolution can proceed in the presence of genetic drift where no fitness improvement occurs. The larger the permitted hamming distance range is, the larger the amount of neutral mutations is allowed during evolution. When the range of hamming distance permitted is the same as the length of the genotype (300 in this study), evolution can freely undergo unrestricted genetic drift until an improved offspring is obtained. In this work, we study the interaction between neutrality and evolution by experimenting with 6 different hamming distance thresholds (0, 50, 150, 200, 250, 300). The results are reported in the next section.

5   Results

The experimental results show that a larger amount of neutrality is better on this problem, regardless of the mutation rates. Figure 3 summarizes the average population fitness of 4 different mutation rates under the 6 different hamming distance implementations. These runs have initial average fitness between 3.96 and 3.99. However, for the purpose of contrasting the performance under different hamming distances implementation, only the fitness range that distinguishes their performance is plotted. As shown, hamming distance 250 and 300 implementations have very similar performance and generate better average fitness than the others. In other words, by supporting more freedom of genetic drift, evolution can generate fitter offspring, i.e. *neutrality improves evolvability.* We will analyze this interesting result in the following section.

6   Analysis and Discussion

There are 256 Boolean functions with 3 Boolean inputs and 1 Boolean output (see [11] page 216 for the listing). The 256 functions can handle the 8 test cases differently and are assigned different fitness accordingly. Figure 4 shows the fitness distribution of the 256 functions in the search space. Since there are many more functions with fitness 4, random search is more likely to generate a function with fitness 4. This explains why the average fitness of initial population is between 3.96 and 3.99 in the experiments.

The elitism selection mechanism used in our experiments keeps the best-so-far individual as the current winner. Moreover, the current winner can only be replaced by another genotype with *equal* or *better* fitness. When a genotype is replaced by a different genotype with the same fitness, evolutionary search is undergoing neutral walk in the search space. When a genotype with improved fitness is found, the search jumps into another partition of the search space and continues the process of neutral walk and the search of fitness improvement. In other words, evolutionary search is a progressive process that travels from one subspace with lower fitness functions to another subspace with higher fitness functions. We therefore analyze the evolutionary search within each of the subspaces, i.e. subspace of genotypes with fitness 5 and 6, 6 and 7, 7 and 8. We skip the subspace of genotypes with fitness 4 and 5 because it is very easy for evolutionary search to find a genotype with fitness 5. Also, we only use data of runs that have sequential fitness improvement, e.g. 4 to 5 to 6. This is because runs that had winning genotypes whose fitness are improved in a non-sequential manner (e.g. 4 to 6 to 7 to 8) were quite rare and they complicate the analysis of the search characteristics.

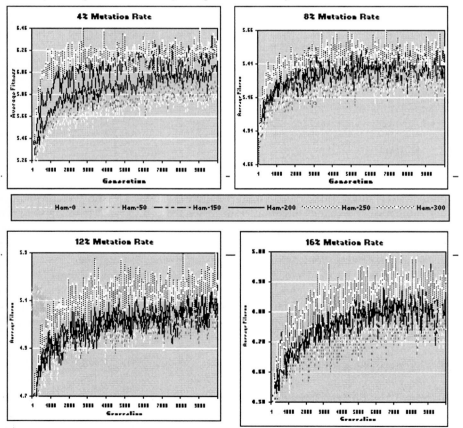

Figure 3   Average Population Fitness with Different Hamming Distances.

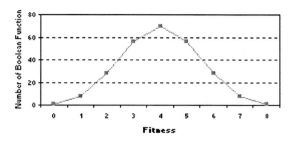

Figure 4   Fitness Distribution of Even-3-Parity Search Space.

6.1   Fitness 5 and 6 Search Space

With the presence of neutrality (hamming distance non-0 implementations), evolutionary search consists of two stages: neutral walk (the fitness of current winner remains 5) and the fitness improvement step (the fitness of current winner becomes 6). A neutral walk is a genetic drift process where both active and inactive genes undergo changes, although these changes do not produce fitness improvement. In Section 2.1, we have argued that the effect of active gene changes is exploitation while the effect of inactive gene changes is exploration. If the neutral walk can maintain the balance between exploitation and exploration, it is reasonable to believe that those gene changes will eventually lead to the fitness improvement step. In other words, for a genotype of fitness 5 to transform to become a genotype of fitness 6, adaptive *and* neutral mutations are required. The more the neutral walk can satisfy these mutations, the higher the probability of a genotype to reach the fitness improvement step.We test this hypothesis by investigating the relationship between the probability of success and the ratio of exploitation/exploration during the evolutionary search. The probability of success is the percentage of the genotypes with fitness 5 that successfully reach the fitness improvement step and are transformed into a fitness 6 genotype. The ratio of exploitation/exploration is defined as the number of active gene changes versus the number of inactive gene changes. We consider two such ratios in this study: one defined on the neutral walk and the other calculated from fitness improvement to the next fitness improvement. This information is calculated for various mutation rates. Figure 5 gives the results.

Figure 5(a) shows that this search space is very easy for the evolutionary algorithm to make the fitness improvement with most of the mutation rates and hamming distance thresholds. There are a few exceptions: hamming distance 0 with mutation rate 1%, 2%; hamming distance 50 with mutation rate 1%, 2%. (We ignore that of 99% success rate because they are too close to 100%). The hamming distance 0 implementation allows no neutral walk, i.e. a mutation operation has to transform a genotype of fitness 5 into a genotype of fitness 6 in one step. With low mutation rate, this can be quite difficult to achieve, hence the success rate is low. The same argument can be applied to the hamming distance 50 implementation.

An interesting question to ask is "why do other combinations of hamming distance and mutation rate generate high success rate?" We answer this question by analyzing the exploitation/exploration ratio during the neutral walk and at the fitness improvement step. Figure 5(b) shows that those runs with 100% success rates have the two ratios quite close to each other. For example, hamming distance 300 with mutation rate 10 generates an exploitation/exploration ratio of 0.43 at the fitness improvement step, i.e. for a genotype of fitness 5 to transform to become a genotype of fitness 6, the number of active genes changes versus the number of inactive changes is 0.43. The ratio provided by neutral walk is 0.40, which is very close to that is required for the successful transformation. This suggests that neutral walk has led the evolutionary search toward the fitness improvement step, hence enabled the genotype transformation to take place. We also examine the two combinations that have lower successful rates (hamming distance 50 with mutation rate 1% and 2%). In both cases, the two ratios are significantly different from each other. This suggests that neutral walk did not provide satisfactory adaptive/neutral mutations; hence evolutionary search fails to reach the fitness improvement step. These results endorse our hypothesis.

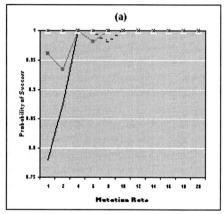
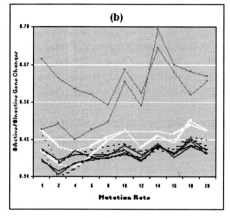

Figure 5   Fitness 5 and 6 search space.

6.2   Fitness 6 to 7 Search Space

The experimental results indicate that this search space is harder than the fitness 5 and 6 search space for most of the hamming distance implementations. Figure 6 (a) shows that only hamming distance 300 and 250 implementations still retain the 100% success rate across all mutation rates. The hamming distance 200 implementation only achieves 100% success for 6 of the 11 mutation rates. The success rate for hamming distance 150 implementation is about 95% across all mutation rates. In a similar way to that seen in the fitness 5 and 6 search space, hamming distance 50 and 0 implementations have better success rate when higher mutation rates are used. The lower the mutation rate, the lower the success rate. Once again, the exploitation/exploration ratios for neutral walk and for the fitness improvement step are very close to each other under the hamming distance 300 implementation. Across all mutation rates, the difference between the two ratios is about 0.009. A similar ratio difference is also exhibited in the hamming distance 250 implementation. These results, therefore, also

[4]   Harvey, I., Thompson, A.: Through the labyrinth evolution finds a way: a silicon ridge. In: Proceedings of First International Conference on Evolvable Systems: From Biology to Hardware, LNCS, Vol. 1259. Springer-Verlag (1996) 406-422.

[5]   Hinton, G. E., Nowlan, S. J.: How learning can guide evolution. Complex Systems, Vol. 1, (1987) 495-502.

[6]   Huynen, M. A., Stadler, P. F., Fontana, W.: Smoothness within ruggedness: the role of neutrality in adaptation. Proc. Natl. Acad. Sci. (USA) Vol. 93 (1996) 397-401.

[7]   Kimura, M.: Evolutionary Rate at the Molecular Level. Nature, Vol. 217 (1968) 624-626.

[8]   Kimura, M.: The neutral theory as a basis for understanding the mechanism of evolution and variation at the molecular level. In: Molecular Evolution, Protein Polymorphism and the Neutral Theory. Springer-Verlag, Berlin (1982) 3-56.

[9]   Kimura, M.: The Neutral Theory of Molecular Evolution. Cambridge Univ. Press, 1983.

[10]   Kimura, M.: Some recent data supporting the neutral theory. In: New Aspects of the Genetics of Molecular Evolution. Springer-Verlag, Berlin (1991) 3-14.

[11]   Koza, J. R.: Genetic Programming: On the Programming of Computers by Means of Natural Selection. MIT Press (1992).

[12]   Miller, J. F.: An empirical study of the efficiency of learning boolean functions using a cartesian genetic programming Approach. In: Proceedings of the First Genetic and Evolutionary Computation Conference (GECCO'99), Morgan Kaufmann, San Francisco, CA (1999) 1135-1142.

[13]   Miller, J. F., Thomson, P., Fogarty, T. C.: Designing electronic circuits using evolutionary algorithms, arithmetic circuits: a case study. In: Genetic Algorithms and Evolution Strategies in Engineering and Computer Science, Wiley, Chichester, UK (1998) 105-131.

[14]   Miller, J. F., Thomson, P.: Cartesian genetic programming. In: Proceedings of the Third European Conference on Genetic Programming (EuroGP2000). Lecture Notes in Computer Science, Vol. 1802, Springer-Verlag, Berlin (2000) 121-132.

[15]   Newman, M. E. J., and R. Engelhardt, R., Effects of neutral selection on the evolution of molecular species", Proc. Roy. Soc. London Series B Vol. 265 (1998) 1333-1338.

[16]   O'Neill, M., Ryan, C.: Under the hood of grammatical evolution. In: Proceedings of the First Genetic and Evolutionary Computation Conference (GECCO'99), Morgan Kaufmann, San Francisco, CA (1999) 1143-1148.

[17]   O'Neill, M., Ryan, C.: Genetic code degeneracy: implications for grammatical evolution and beyond. In: Proceedings of the 5th European Conference on Artificial Life, (1999).

[18]   Provine, W. B.: Sewall Wright and Evolutionary Biology. The University of Chicago Press, Chicago (1986).

[19]   Schwefel, H.P.: Kybernetische Evolution als Strategie der experimentellen Forschung in der Stromungstechnik. Diplomarbeit, Technische Universitat Berlin, 1965.

[20]   Vassilev, V. K., Miller J. F.: The advantages of landscape neutrality in digital circuit evolution. In: Proceedings of the 3rd International Conference on Evolvable Systems: From Biology to Hardware, Lecture Notes in Computer Science, Vol. 1801, Springer-Verlag, Berlin (2000) 252-263.

[21]   Yu, T. and Bentley, P.: Methods to evolve legal phenotypes. In: Proceedings of the Fifth International Conference on Parallel Problem Solving from Nature. Lecture Notes in Computer Science, Vol. 1498, Springer-Verlag, Berlin (1998) 280-291.

Polymorphism and Genetic Programming

Tina Yu

Chevron Information Technology Company
6001 Bollinger Canyon Road
San Ramon, CA 94583 U.S.A.
tiyu@chevron.com
http://www.addr.com/~tinayu

Abstract. Types have been introduced to Genetic Programming (GP) by researchers with different motivation. We present the concept of types in GP and introduce a typed GP system, PolyGP, that supports polymorphism through the use of three different kinds of type variable. We demonstrate the usefulness of this kind of polymorphism in GP by evolving two polymorphic programs (nth and map) using the system. Based on the analysis of a series of experimental results, we conclude that this implementation of polymorphism is effective in assisting GP evolutionary search to generate these two programs. PolyGP may enhance the applicability of GP to a new class of problems that are difficult for other polymorphic GP systems to solve.

1   Introduction

Types have been studied and implemented in many modern programming languages, e.g. Haskell, Ada and C++. The ability to support multiple types and to provide type checking for programs has made these languages more expressive and the execution of programs more efficient. Types are counterparts of programming languages.

Genetic Programming (GP) [5] automatically generates computer programs to solve specified problems. It does this by searching through a space of all possible programs for one that is nearly optimal in its ability to solve the given problem. The GP search algorithm is based on the model of natural evolution. In particular, three basic operations (selection, alteration and fitness evaluation) are applied iteratively to a population of programs. Similar to nature where the fittest would survive, the program which best solves the problem would emerge at the end of the GP search process.

The road from untyped to typed GP is led by two goals. Firstly, to enhance the applicability of GP by removing the "closure" requirement. Secondly, to assist GP searching for problem solutions using type information. Koza made the first attempt to introduce types to GP by extending GP with "constrained syntactic structures" when he realized that not all problems have solutions which can be represented in ways that satisfy the closure requirement [5]. Supporters of this argument [9,4] believe that it is important for GP to be able to handle multiple types and advocate excluding type-incorrect programs from the search space to speed up GP's evolutionary process. Another route to promote the use of types in GP is based on the idea that types provide inductive bias to direct GP search. For example, Wong and Leung included type information in a logic grammar to bias the selection of genetic operation

J. Miller et al. (Eds.): EuroGP 2001, LNCS 2038, pp. 218-233, 2001.

location during program evolution [10]. McPhee *et al.* also showed that a program representation which incorporates *function type* can bias genetic operations and benefit GP search on some problems [8].

These two paths, although with different purposes, are actually interrelated. Types exist in the real world naturally [2]. By allowing problems to be represented in their natural ways, an inductive bias is established which selects solutions based on criteria that reflect experience with similar problems.

In this paper, we first present the concept of types in GP by defining and differentiating *untyped*, *dynamically typed* and *strongly typed* GP. Next, the two different implementations of strongly typed GP, *monomorphic* GP and *polymorphic* GP, are discussed. We introduce our polymorphic GP system (PolyGP) and compare it with other polymorphic GP systems. This system is then used to evolve two polymorphic programs, nth and map, which represent a class of problems that we believe to be very difficult for other polymorphic GP system to evolve. We analyze a series of experimental results to evaluate the effectiveness of PolyGP polymorphism in assisting GP evolutionary search. Finally, we give our conclusions.

2   Types in Genetic Programming

In its traditional style, GP is not capable of distinguishing different types: the term *untyped* is used to refer to such a system. In the case when the programs manipulate multiple types and contain functions designed to operate on particular types, untyped GP leads to an unnecessarily large search space, which contains both type-correct and type-incorrect programs. To enforce type constraints, two approaches can be used: *dynamically typed* GP and *strongly typed* GP. In dynamically typed GP, type checking is performed at program *evaluation* time. In contrast, strongly typed GP performs type checking at program *generation* time. The computation effort required for these two different type checking methods is implementation dependent. It is not valid to claim that dynamic typing is more efficient than strong typing; nor vice versa. The details of these two type checking approaches are discussed in the following sections.

3   Dynamically Typed GP

Dynamic typing performs type checking when a program is evaluated to determine whether it is a solution, i.e. type-incorrect programs are not allowed to exist in the solution space. However, the search space may contain both type-correct and type-incorrect programs. Consequently, the size of the search space is bigger than that of the solution space (Figure 1).

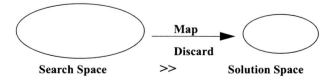

Figure 1   Search Versus Solution Space in Dynamically Typed GP.

The transformation of a type-incorrect into a type-correct program can be implemented using a "legal map" method [11]. For example, a value with an illegal type of "real" can be mapped into a value with legal type "integer". However, for more complex types such as list or matrix, a proper mapping scheme can be difficult to design. Montana implemented this dynamic typing approach in one of his experiments. When trying to add a 3-vector with a 4×2 matrix, the matrix is considered as an 8-vector, which is converted into a 3-vector by throwing away the last 5 entries. "The problem with such unnatural operations is that, while they may succeed in finding a solution for a particular set of data, they are unlikely to be part of a symbolic expression that can generalize to new data." [9].

Another way to implement dynamic typing is to discard type-incorrect programs. "The problem with this approach is that it can be terribly inefficient, spending most of its time evaluating programs that turn out to be illegal." [9]. In his experiments, Montana reported that within 50,000 programs in the initial population, only 20 are type-correct. Because of the complication involved with the mapping and discarding process, dynamic typing is not an ideal way to implement type checking in GP.

4   Strongly Typed GP

Strong typing performs type checking when a program is generated to be a member of a GP population, i.e. the search space is restricted to contain only type-correct programs. This is done through the "legal seeding" method (the initial population is seeded with solutions that do not conflict with the type constraints) and the "legal birth" method (alteration operators are designed such that they cannot generate type-incorrect programs) [11]. Consequently, the size of the search space is the same as that of the solution space (see Figure 2).

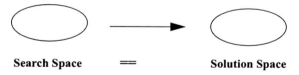

Search Space   ==   Solution Space

Figure 2   Search Versus Solution Space in Strongly Typed GP.

There are two ways of implementing strong typing in GP: *monomorphic GP* and *polymorphic GP*. Monomorphic GP uses monomorphic functions and terminals to generate monomorphic programs. In contrast, polymorphic GP can generate polymorphic programs using polymorphic functions and terminals. In the first instance, inputs and outputs of the generated program need to be of the specified types. In the latter case, the generated programs can accept inputs and produce outputs of more than one type. Polymorphic GP therefore can potentially generate more general solutions than those produced by monomorphic GP.

4.1   Monomorphic GP Systems

One can perceive Koza's untyped GP with closure requirement as a monomorphic GP; it is a single-type GP system. The first monomorphic GP system that supports multiple types is Montana's "basic" STGP [9]. In this system, types are atomic symbols and type compatibility is determined by simply checking whether the two types are the same or not. Later, Haynes *et al* implemented a similar monomorphic GP system (GPengine) to evolve cooperation strategies for a predator-prey pursuit problem [4].

4.2   Polymorphism through Type Variables

In PolyGP, polymorphism is implemented through the use of three different kinds of type variables. *Generic type variables* are used to specify the generated program can accept inputs of any type. For example, type[G1] (G1 is a generic type variable) is used to indicate that the input of nth program is a list of values with any type (see Section 5.2). Moreover, to enable the generated program to accept inputs of any type, the functions and terminals used to construct the programs have to be able to handle arguments of multiple types. This is specified using *dummy type variables*. For example, the argument of function head is of type[a] (a is a dummy type variable), which indicates that head can take a list of values of any type as input (see Section 5.2).

When a polymorphic function is selected to construct a program tree node, its dummy type variables have to be instantiated to known types. If the type of a dummy variable can't be determined, a *temporary type variable* is used. The temporary type variable can be instantiated to a different type, hence provides polymorphism during program evolution. With a type system that supports these three different kinds of type variables, the PolyGP system is able to generate generic programs while monomorphic GP can not.

On the surface level, it seems that PolyGP is simply a monomorphic GP system plus type variables. Indeed, when type variables are not utilized, PolyGP becomes a monomorphic GP system. However, the use of these type variables can impact the GP search space in ways that are not obvious to GP users. Misuse of these type variables can cause unnecessary overhead to the GP system. In [13], we have provided related information so that users can use PolyGP with or without type variables to suit their target problems.

4.3   Polymorphism through Generic Functions

Generic functions in Montana's STGP system [9] also provide a form of polymorphism. Generic functions are parameterized templates that have to be instantiated with actual values before they can be used to construct program tree nodes. The parameters can be type parameters, function parameters or value parameters. Generic functions with type parameters are polymorphic since the type parameters can be instantiated to many different type values.

However, the implementation of polymorphism in STGP is different from that of PolyGP in the following ways:

- It requires the generation of a type possibilities table;
- It uses a table-lookup mechanism to instantiate type variables;
- It does not provide a systematic way to support function types;
- It does not use *temporary type variables*, hence the system is monomorphic at program evolution time.

The detailed explanation of these differences is provided in Section 3.2.1 of [13].

4.4   Polymorphism through Subtyping

Unlike type variables and generic functions, where polymorphism is for an infinite number of types, subtyping supports polymorphism only for a finite number of types. Moreover, these types are related in a hierarchical manner. For example, a type A can have a subtype B which can have a subtype C. In this case, wherever type A may appear, its subtype B and C may appear. Polymorphism is for the 3 types (A, B, C) only. Haynes *et al.* implemented a polymorphic GP system that supports subtyping for a limited single inheritance type hierarchy (each type is allowed to have a maximum of one subtype and one supertype). They have used the system to solve a maximum clique problem [3].

The Evolutionary Computation Java (ECJ) system by Sean Luke used a set-based approach to support polymorphism: a type can be "compatible" with a set of types. He has used this mechanism to implement subtyping of multiple-inheritance: a type can have a set of subtypes and a set of supertypes. This polymorphic GP system has been used for an internal project at his university [7].

The unstructured nature of a set makes it suitable for implementing polymorphism for a group of types that are not related in a definable manner. Cardelli and Wegner classified this as ad-hoc polymorphism, which includes overloading and coercion [2]. We hope to see work using this kind of polymorphism with the ECJ system.

5   Experiments

To demonstrate the usefulness of the type-variables-polymorphism, we use the PolyGP system to generate two polymorphic programs, `nth` (which returns the n-th element of a list) and `map` (which applies a function to a list). Although simple, these two programs are appropriate because the two programs are generic to *any* type of inputs, which can be handled using generic type variables in our system:

```
nth ::  int->[ G1] ->G1

map ::  (G1->G2) ->[ G1] ->[ G2]
```

Subtyping GP systems (Section 4.4), which supports polymorphism to a finite number of types, can not be effective with this class of problems Although the generic function STGP system successfully generated the same two programs, it treated the function argument type of the `map` program in an ad-hoc manner. This system is therefore not a general solution to other similar problems. The PolyGP system, on the other hand, provides a systematic way of handling function types. It is therefore capable of dealing with the same class of problems. By generating these two programs, we show that PolyGP can enhance the applicability of GP to a class of problems that are very difficult for other polymorphic GP systems to solve.

Both `nth` and `map` are also recursive programs. To allow GP to evolve recursive programs, a simple method similar to that used in [1] is applied. In this method, the name of the program is included in the function set so that it can be used to construct program trees; hence making recursive calls. However, such implementation may also cause an evolved program to generate an infinite-loop, hence making the evaluation of such a program non-terminating. To handle this kind of error, a maximum number of recursive calls allowed in a program is specified (the length of the input list is used in this case). When this limit is reached, program evaluation halts and returns with a flag to indicate this error. Consequently, no partial credit is given to this kind of program.

Another kind of error that may occur during program evaluation is to apply the function `head` or `tail` to an empty list (which has an undefined value). When this error occurs during program evaluation, a default value is given and the evaluation of the program continues. In this way, partial solutions can be considered for partial credit. For example, a program which is expected to return the fifth element of the list may return the third element of the list due to this error. This program is given partial credit even though a non-optimal program is generated. The implementation details of these two error handling methods are described in [13].

5.1   Experimental Setup

The two kinds of error and their handling methods have complicated our experiments. In particular, it becomes unclear whether the ability of the PolyGP system to generate the two programs should be interpreted as the result of:

1. random sampling of the set of type-correct programs;
2. sampling by genetic operations in the set of type-correct programs that satisfy the two error constraints;
3. genetic operations guided by the fitness function toward a correct solution.

To allow us to make a determination, we have designed and implemented the following four experiments:

1. Programs are generated randomly, no genetic operation is applied.
2. Programs are generated randomly for the initial population. After that, new programs are generated by applying genetic operations on randomly selected programs.
3. Programs are generated randomly for the initial population. After that, new programs are generated by applying genetic operations on programs which are selected based on how well they satisfy the two error constraints. The correctness of the program outputs is not considered.
4. Programs are generated randomly for the initial population. After that, new programs are generated by applying genetic operations on programs which are selected based on a fitness function which evaluates both the correctness of the outputs and the satisfaction of the two error constraints.

The first experiment is conducted by random generation of 100,000 programs. We used the FULL method described in [5], where all program trees are grown into the maximum allowable depth. It has been argued that for most problems, the distribution of solutions in the search space is independent of the program length [6]. We hope this uniform program length tree generation approach will produce an unbiased performance.

For each of the second, third and fourth experiments, 10 runs are performed. This seems to be too small a sample size to be statistically meaningful. However, given that we used the same 10 random seeds for the three sets of experiments, we hope the results reflect more closely the different implementations of the experiments. To trace the performance of the entire run, each run continues until the end, even if a solution has been found.

In each set of the four experiments, the following data are recorded:

- The number of correct solutions found (first experiment) and the number of successful runs (other 3 experiments);
- The mean value of each component of the fitness function.

In terms of implementation, the three sets of GP experiments are basically the same except the fitness value used for selection. With the second experiment, a flat fitness (1.0) is given to every generated program (flatFitness). With the third experiment, the two error fitness values are used as the program's fitness for selection (errorFitness). With the fourth experiment, the combination of error fitness and output fitness is used as the program's fitness for selection (fullFitness).

The GP system uses a steady-state replacement with rank selection. In particular, programs in the population are ranked and the probability of a program to be selected is less than that of the next better program in the rank, based on the "parent scalar" parameter provided. The details of the implementation are described in [12].

5.2   The NTH Program

Problem Description: The nth program takes two arguments, an integer N and a list L. It returns the Nth element of L. If the value of N is less than 1, it returns the first element of L. If the value of N is greater than the length of L, it returns the last element of L.

Input Types: Input N has type int; input L has type [G1] .

Output Type: The output has type G1.

Terminal Set: {

```
        L:: [ G1] ,  N:: int,  one:: int}
```

Function Set: {

```
        if-then-else :: bool->a->a->a,
        head :: [ a] ->a,  tail :: [ a] ->[ a] ,
        length :: [ a] ->int,  gtr :: int->int->bool,
        less-eq :: int->int->bool,
        minus :: int->int->int,
        nth :: int->[ G1] ->G1}
```

Genetic Parameters: The population size is 3,000; parent scalar is 0.9965; maximum tree depth is 5; and crossover rate is 100%. Each run continues until 33,000 programs are generated (3,000 are created randomly and 30,000 are created by crossover).

5.2.1   Test Cases

Twelve test cases were used to evaluate the generated programs. Each test case gave N a different value from 0 to 11. The value L, however, is the same for all 12 test cases; it is a list containing the characters a to j. Table 1 lists the 12 test cases and their expected outputs.

5.2.2   Fitness Function

A generated program is evaluated with each of the 12 test cases, one at a time. The produced output is compared with the expected output to compute the fitness value for each test case according to equation 1:

Table 1: The 12 test cases for evolving the NTH program.

Case	N	L	output	Case	N	L	output
1	0	[a,b,c,d,e,f,g,h,i,j]	a	7	6	[a,b,c,d,e,f,g,h,i,j]	f
2	1	[a,b,c,d,e,f,g,h,i,j]	a	8	7	[a,b,c,d,e,f,g,h,i,j]	g
3	2	[a,b,c,d,e,f,g,h,i,j]	b	9	8	[a,b,c,d,e,f,g,h,i,j]	h
4	3	[a,b,c,d,e,f,g,h,i,j]	c	10	9	[a,b,c,d,e,f,g,h,i,j]	i
5	4	[a,b,c,d,e,f,g,h,i,j]	d	11	10	[a,b,c,d,e,f,g,h,i,j]	j
6	5	[a,b,c,d,e,f,g,h,i,j]	e	12	11	[a,b,c,d,e,f,g,h,i,j]	j

$$Fitness = 10 \cdot 2^{-d} - (10 \cdot rtError) - (10 \cdot reError) \qquad (1)$$

where d is the distance between the position of the expected value and the position of the value returned by the generated program; $rtError$ is 1 if there is an empty-list error; and $reError$ is 1 if there is a non-terminating recursion error. The value 10 is used to scale up the fitness values for better precision due to computational round up.

The first part of equation 1 indicates that a program which returns the value at the expected position receives a fitness 10. This fitness value decreases as the position of the returned value is farther away from the position of the expected value. If the returned value is not a part of the input list, this fitness is 0. When no error is encountered during program evaluation, a program can receive a maximum fitness value of 10 for each test case. The fitness of a program is the summation of the fitness for all 12 test cases, i.e. the maximum fitness of a program is 120.

5.2.3   Results

The first experiment, which randomly generates 100,000 type-correct programs, could not find a correct nth program. The average fitness is -121.266 where 7.342464 is the average output fitness; -41.9595 is the average empty-list error fitness and -86.6488 is the average recursion error fitness.

For the other three sets of experiments, only the one which applied genetic operations with full fitness (the fourth experiment) found correct nth programs. Within 10 runs, 4 of them found a solution. The probability of success is 40%. Moreover, all the successful runs found a solution before 12,000 programs were processed. The shortest program is given as the following. It's interesting to see the system uses (minus N N) to construct value 0.

```
if-then-else (less-eq (length (tail L)) (minus N N))
             (head L)
```

```
(if-then-else (gtr (minus N N) (minus one N))
        (nth (minus N one) (tail L))
        (head L)
```

5.2.4   Analysis

The fitness function in equation 1 specifies that an optimal solution not only has to produce the desired output but also has to satisfy two different constraints: a non-terminating error constraint and an empty-list error constraint. To meet the three criteria, the evolutionary process is directed toward different directions. Consequently, the seesaw of evolutionary pressure can favor either of the criteria.

In the fitness function, these three criteria are given equal importance (10 points each). However, the two error constraints are handled in ways which implicitly generated more weight for them. These effects can be illustrated in Table 2 where four categories are defined for a generated nth program when evaluated with a test case.

Table 2: The 4 categories of the NTH programs.

Program Errors	Output	Penalty	Fitness
non-terminating+empty-list	nothing	20	-20
non-terminating	nothing	10	-10
empty-list	a value	10	partialCredit-10
none	a value	0	calculatedFitness

The analysis shows that programs in the first two categories, which are non-terminating, have the lowest fitness values. Our steady-state implementation, which replaces the worst program in the population only when the new program has better fitness, makes them very unwelcome in the evolutionary process. They soon will be eliminated from the population pool. The evolution then starts to find programs which produce correct output and also satisfy the empty-list error constraint.

Our experimental results are consistent with this analysis. Using the fitness function in equation 1 to direct genetic operations (fullFitness), programs with recursion error were eliminated from the population very fast. After 6,000 programs were processed, the population contained no program with recursion error (see Figure 3(C))[1].

Between processing 6,000 and 8,000 programs, the average output fitness increased (see Figure 3(A)) while the average empty-list error fitness decreased (see Figure (B)), i.e. evolution was driven by the output fitness. After that, both output and empty-list fitness improved consistently. As a result, 4 of the 10 runs found a correct nth program.

When genetic operations were guided to evolve programs which only satisfy the two error constraints but not the output correctness (errorFitness), both the average empty-list and the recursion error fitness improve very fast. After 3,000 genetic operations, programs with either of the two errors were eliminated from the population (see

---

[1] With steady-state replacement, there is no concept of "generation". Hence, data are reported every 3,000 programs (the size of the population) processed.

Figure 3 (B) & (C)). Unfortunately, this "biased" selection also eliminated potential good programs from the population. As shown in Figure 3 (A), applying genetic operations randomly on the set of programs which satisfy the two error constraints does not improve output fitness (due to premature convergence). Consequently, no solution was found at the end of the 10 runs.

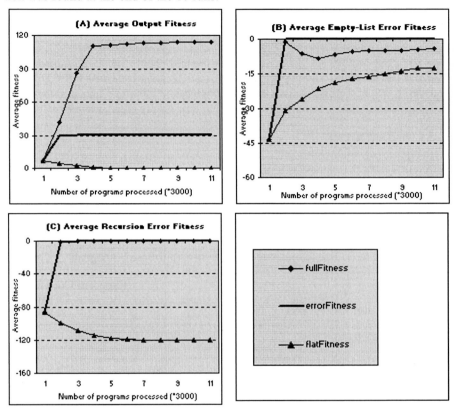

Figure 3   Experimental Results for the NTH program.

Without the guidance of a fitness function (flatFitness), genetic operations did not provide a consistent improvement of the solutions. Although the average empty-list error fitness increased (see Figure 3 (B)), the average output fitness and recursion error fitness decreased as the number of program processed increases (see Figure 3 (A) & (C)). Consequently, no solution was found at the end of the 10 runs.

5.3   The MAP Program

Problem Description: The map program takes inputs of two arguments, a function F and a list L. It returns the list obtained by applying F to each element of L.

Input Types: The input F has type G1 -> G2 and the input L has type [G1]

Output Type: The output has type [G2]

Terminal Set: {

L::[G1] ,nil::[a] ,F:: (G1->G2)}

Function Set: {

if-then-else :: bool->a->a->a,
F :: G1->G2, head :: [a] ->a,
tail :: [a] ->[a] , cons :: a->[a] ->[a] ,
null :: [a] ->bool,
map :: (G1->G2) ->[G1] ->[G2] }

Genetic Parameters: The population size is 5,000; parent scalar is 0.999; maximum tree depth is 5; and crossover rate is 100%. Each run terminates when 55,000 programs are generated (5,000 are created randomly and 50,000 are created by crossover).

5.3.1   Test Cases

Two test cases were used to evaluate the generated programs. The two test cases have different values for argument L: the first one is a list with 10 elements whose values were the characters A to J while the second one is an empty list. The function F, however, is the same for both test cases. It is a function which converts an alphabetic character into a number, i.e. A to 1, B to 2, C to 3 and so on. Table 3 lists these two test cases and their expected outputs.

Table 3: The 2 test cases for evolving the map program.

Case	F	L	Expected Output
1	atoi	[A,B,C,D,E,F,G,H,I,J]	[1,2,3,4,5,6,7,8,9,10]
2	atoi	[]	[]

5.3.2   Fitness Function

The fitness of a program is computed based on how close the return list is to the expected list. There are two elements in this criterion: 1) whether the returned list has the correct *length* and 2) whether the returned list has the correct *contents*. Equation 2 is the fitness function used to measure both elements for each test case.

$$Fitness = -2 \cdot \left|length(L_e) - length(L_r)\right| + \sum_{e \in L_e} 10 \cdot (2^{-dist(e, L_r)})$$

$$-(10 + 2 \cdot length(L_e)) \cdot rtError -(10 + 2 \cdot length(L_e)) \cdot reError \qquad (2)$$

where L_e is the expected list and L_r is the list returned by the generated program; $dist(e,L_r)$ is the distance between the position of e in the expected list and in the returned list. If e does not exist in L_r, i.e. $e \notin L_r$, this value is ∞. The *rtError* is 1 if there is an empty-list error. The *reError* is 1 if there is a non-terminating recursion error. Similar to equation 1, the value 10 is used to scale up the fitness value for better precision.

The first item in equation 2 measures whether the returned list has the same length as the expected list. Each discrepancy is penalized with a value of 2.

The second item in equation 2 measures whether the returned list has the same contents as the expected list. For each element in the expected list, the distance between its position in the expected list and in the returned list is measured. If the element is in the correct position in the returned list, a fitness value of 10 is given. This value decreases as the position of e in the returned list is farther away from the expected position. In the case that e does not exist in the returned list, this fitness is 0. The same measurement is applied to each element in the expected list. For the first test case, a program which generates a list with the correct length and contents would receive a fitness value of 100. For the second test case, a program which generates a list with the correct length and contents will receive a fitness value of 0.

The third and the fourth items in equation 2 measure whether an empty-list or a non-terminating error is encountered during program evaluation. The penalties of these two types of error are the same. It is proportionate to the length of the expected output list (the same as the length of the input list). This decision is due to the recursion limit being the length of the input list. It seems to be reasonable to penalize these two errors using the same criterion.

When no error is encountered during program evaluation, a program receives a maximum fitness value of 100 for the first test case and 0 for the second test case. The fitness of a program is the summation of the fitness for the two test cases, i.e. the maximum fitness of a program is 100.

5.3.3   Results

Similar to the results of the nth experiment, none of the randomly generated 100,000 programs is a correct map program. The average fitness is -82.6504 where -19.9724 is the average length fitness; 0.0976 is the average output fitness; -27.9946 is the average empty-list error fitness and -34.7787 is the average recursion error fitness.

Among the three sets of GP experiments, only those which applied genetic operations with the full fitness function found correct map programs. There are 3 such successful runs within 10 trials. The probability of success is thus 30%. Moreover, all the successful runs found a correct solution before 35,000 programs were processed. The shortest program is given as the following:

```
if-then-else  (null L)
              (head (cons nil nil))
              (cons (F (head L)) (map F (tail L))))
```

5.3.4   Analysis

The experimental results indicate that the map program is harder than the nth program for PolyGP to generate. Unlike the nth program where only one correct return value is required to get the maximum fitness, an optimal map program has to be able to process each of the 10 elements in the input list correctly. To meet this objective, one more criterion is added to the fitness function: the length discrepancy between the expected and the generated lists (see equation 2). Moreover, unlike that for the nth program, the fitness function for the map program gives different importance to the two objectives and the two constraints. In the first test case, 100 points are given to programs which return list with the correct contents; 20 points are given to programs which return lists with the correct length; 30 points are given to programs which produce no non-terminating error and 30 points are given to programs which produce no empty-list error. This is designed to direct GP searching for programs which return lists with the correct contents. In the second test case, the two objectives are not considered in the fitness function while the two constraints are each given 10 points of importance in the fitness function. It is obvious that the purpose of the second test case is to train GP to handle the empty list without producing any errors.

Additionally, the handling methods for the two errors during program evaluation generate another level of evolutionary pressures. Due to such a complicated fitness assignment and constraint handling pressure, the evolutionary process is directed toward many directions. Consequently, the generation of the correct map program is harder than the generation of the correct nth program.

To analyze the impact of these fitness assignments on the evolutionary process, we identify four categories for generated map programs when evaluated with the first test case (Table 4) and the second test case (Table 5)

Table 4: The 4 categories of map programs for the first test case.

Program Errors	Output	Error Penalty	Length Penalty	Fitness
non-terminating + empty-list	nothing	60	20	-80
non-terminating	nothing	30	20	-50
empty-list	a list	30	calculated penalty	partial credit - 30 - calculated penalty
none	a list	0	calculated penalty	calculated fitness - calculated penalty

Table 5: The 4 categories of map programs for the second test case.

Program Errors	Output	Error Penalty	Length Penalty	Fitness
non-terminating+empty-list	nothing	20	0	-20
non-terminating	nothing	10	0	-10
empty-list	empty list	10	0	-10
none	empty list	0	0	0

For both of the test cases, programs with non-terminating error are heavily discriminated in the population (the first and the second categories, with fitness values -100 and -60 respectively). Consequently, they would be eliminated from the population first. After that, evolution is a process of competition among programs to meet the three other criteria. The experimental results confirm our analysis. Using fitness defined in equation 2 to select programs for reproduction (fullFitness), the GP evolutionary process was dominated by recursion error fitness before 20,000 programs were processed (see Figure 4(D)). During this period of time, both the average output and length fitness also improved (see Figure 4 (A) and (B)). This indicates that programs without recursion error also produce more accurate outputs. The empty-list error fitness, however, did not increase consistently during this period of time. This result can be explained by the seesaw effect described in [11].

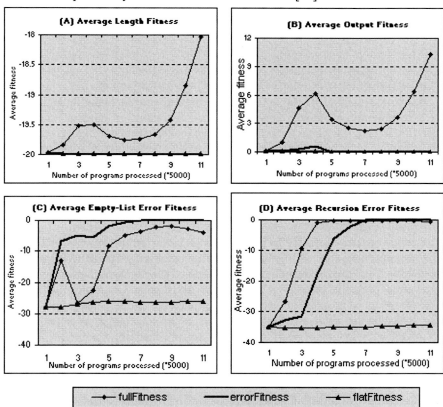

Figure 4   Experimental Results for the MAP program.

After most of the programs with recursion error were eliminated from the population, empty-list error fitness became the dominant factor to drive evolution. This was shown by the fast improvement of empty-list error fitness between the processing of 20,000 and 35,000 programs (see Fig 4(C)) and the decrease of both output and length fitness during this period of time (see Figure 4 (A) and (B)).

After 35,000 programs were processed, the population contained no program with recursion errors. Since the empty-list error fitness was reasonably good (-5), the evolution focused on improving output and length fitness. As shown in Figure 4 (A) and (B), their fitness values increased very fast. As a result, 3 of the 10 runs generated correct map programs.

When genetic operations were directed to evolve programs which satisfy the two error constraints (errorFitness), both the average empty-list and recursion fitness improved (see Figure 4 (C) and (D)). However, similar to the results of nth experiment, the average length and output fitness did not improve at all throughout the runs. Consequently, no solution was found at the end of the 10 runs. Applying genetic operations on randomly selected programs (flatFitness) did not generate better programs than those created using random search (initial population). Figure 4 (A), (B), (C) and (D) show that the four average fitness values stayed pretty much the same as the initial population throughout the run. Consequently, no solution was found at the end of the 10 runs.

6   Discussion

Based on the experimental results, we will make a determination of what has contributed to the success of the generation of the two polymorphic programs.

Random generation of 100,000 type-correct programs could not find a correct nth nor map program. Moreover, applying genetic operations on randomly selected programs did not provide better overall fitness than random search (initial generation). This can be explained by perceiving genetic operations as performing random search within the population. Instead of the whole search space of all possible solution to explore, genetic operations are restricted within the population. Such constraint has been shown to provide no advantage over random search for these two problems. Based on the results, we conclude that polymorphism alone (random sampling of the set of type-correct programs) can not generate correct nth nor map programs.

Genetic operations guided by a fitness function towards programs which satisfy error constraints have successfully eliminated all programs with these two errors from the population. This leads to the random application of genetic operations within the set of type-correct programs that satisfy the two error constraints. Unfortunately, this restricted set has reduced program diversity and prevented the improvement of population fitness. Based on the results, we conclude that nth and map programs can not be generated by the combination of polymorphism and error constraint handling.

Only when genetic operations are guided by a fitness function towards programs which not only satisfy the two error constraints but also generate correct output is the PolyGP system able to generate correct nth and map programs. This result indicates that the success of PolyGP in generating these two programs is due to the combination of polymorphism and GP evolutionary search. Polymorphism ensures that only type-correct programs are generated while GP evolutionary search promotes the programs which most satisfy the fitness function to emerge. Consequently, the two polymorphic programs are generated at the end of the GP search process.

7   Conclusions

We have presented the concept of types in GP and introduced a typed GP system, PolyGP, that provides polymorphism through the use of three different kinds of type variables. This implementation differs from others in that 1) polymorphism is for an infinite number of types, 2) polymorphism not only exists at program creation time but also at program evolution time and 3) polymorphism is extended to function type. This system is therefore strictly more powerful than other polymorphic GP systems.

The usefulness of this implementation is demonstrated by evolving two polymorphic programs (nth and map), which are in a class of programs we believe to be difficult for other polymorphic GP systems to evolve. We have purposely designed and implemented a series of experiments to assure that type-variable-polymorphism is indeed helpful to the GP evolutionary process. The experimental results confirm our hypothesis. PolyGP has enhance the applicability of GP to a new class of problems that are difficult for other polymorphic GP systems to solve.

Acknowledgments

I would like to thank the anonymous reviewers for their insightful comments. Thanks also to Wes Johnston for proof reading this work.

Bibliography

[1]   Brave, S.: Evolving recursive programs for tree search. In: *Advances in Genetic Programming II*. P. J. Angeline and K. E. Kinnear, Jr. (eds.), page 203-219. 1996.

[2]   Cardelli, L. and Wegner, P.: On understanding types, data abstraction, and polymorphism. In: *Computing Surveys*, Vol. 17:4, pages 471-522. 1985.

[3]   Haynes, T. D., Schoenefeld, D. A. and Wainwright, R. L.: Type inheritance in strongly typed genetic programming. In: *Advances in Genetic Programming II*, P. J. Angeline and K. E. Kinnear, Jr. (eds.), pages 359-376. 1996.

[4]   Haynes, T. D., Wainwright, R. L., Sandip, S. and Schoenefeld, D.: Strongly typed genetic programming in evolving cooperation strategies. In *Proceedings of the Sixth International Conference on Genetic Algorithms*, pages 271-278, 1995.

[5]   Koza, J. R.: *Genetic Programming: On the Programming of Computers by Means of Natural Selection*. MIT Press, Cambridge, MA. 1992.

[6]   Langdon, W. B.: Scaling of program fitness spaces. In: *Evolutionary Computation*, Vol. 7 No. 4, pages 399-428, 1999.

[7]   Luke, S.: personal communication, 2000.

[8]   McPhee, N. F., Hopper, N. J. and Reierson, M. L.: Impact of types on essentially typeless problems in GP. In: *Genetic Programming 1998: Proceedings of the Third Annual Conference.* pages 232-240. 1998.

[9]   Montana, D. J.: Strongly typed genetic programming. In: *Evolutionary Computation*, Vol. 3:2, pages 199-230. 1995.

[10]   M. L. Wong and K. S. Leung. An adaptive inductive logic programming system using genetic programming. *Evolutionary Programming IV: Proceedings of the Fourth Annual Conference on Evolutionary Programming.* pages 737-752, 1995.

[11]   Yu, T. and Bentley, P.: Methods to evolve legal phenotypes. In: *Proceedings of the Fifth International Conference on Parallel Problem Solving from Nature*. Lecture Notes in Computer Science, Vol. 1498, Springer-Verlag, Berlin, pages 280-291, 1998.

[12]   Yu, T. and Clack, C.: PolyGP: a polymorphic genetic programming system in haskell. In: *Proceedings of the Third Annual Genetic Programming Conference*, page 416-421, 1998.

[13]   Yu, T.: *An Analysis of the Impact of Functional Programming Techniques on Genetic Programming*, Phd Thesis, University College London, 1999.

Programmable Smart Membranes: Using Genetic Programming to Evolve Scalable Distributed Controllers for a Novel Self-Reconfigurable Modular Robotic Application

Forrest H Bennett III, Brad Dolin, and Eleanor G. Rieffel

FX Palo Alto Laboratory, Inc.
3400 Hillview Avenue, Bldg. 4, Palo Alto, CA 94304
{bennett,dolin,rieffel}@pal.xerox.com
http://www.fxpal.xerox.com/

Abstract. Self-reconfigurable modular robotics represents a new approach to robotic hardware, in which the "robot" is composed of many simple, identical interacting modules. We propose a novel application of modular robotics: the programmable smart membrane, a device capable of actively filtering objects based on numerous measurable attributes. Creating control software for modular robotic tasks like the smart membrane is one of the central challenges to realizing their potential advantages. We use genetic programming to evolve distributed control software for a 2-dimensional smart membrane capable of distinguishing objects based on color. The evolved controllers exhibit scalability to a large number of modules and robustness to the initial configurations of the robotic filter and the particles.

1 Introduction

A self-reconfigurable modular robot - fundamentally distinct from traditional robots - is composed of many simple, identical modules. Each module has its own power, computation, memory, motors, and sensors. The modules can attach to and detach from each other. Individual modules on their own can do little, but the robot, using the capabilities of the individual modules, can reconfigure itself to perform different tasks as needed.

Advantages of self-reconfigurable modular robots include physical adaptability to varying tasks and environments, robustness (since identical modules can replace each other in the event of failure), and economies of scale in the manufacturing process. Physical implementations of modular robots include CMU's I-cubes [23], USC-ISI's Spider Link Models [5], Dartmouth's Molecular Robots [13] and Crystalline Robots [21], MSU's Reconfigurable Adaptable Micro-Robot [22], Johns Hopkins University's Metamorphic Robots [19], as well as Xerox PARC's PolyBot [26], and Proteo robots [2].

J. Miller et al. (Eds.): EuroGP 2001, LNCS 2038, pp. 234–245, 2001.

We propose a novel application of modular robotics which fully exploits such advantages: the smart membrane. This device is an active, selective filter which can in principle distinguish objects based not only on size, but also on shape, color, angle of movement, and indeed any property which can be measured with small sensors, or computed with such information. The applications of a physical smart membrane implementation are determined by the scale on which it is built: At the macro scale, a smart membrane could be used for parts sorting, while at the nanometer scale, such a device could be useful for purifying substances and augmenting biochemical processes.

The problem of developing effective software for modular robotic applications like the smart membrane is recognized as one of the central challenges to the development of practical self-reconfigurable modular robots. The ultimate aim is to have the software completely decentralized and completely autonomous, so that tasks can be performed without reference to a central controller. Decentralized control takes advantage of the computational power of the individual modules and requires less communication bandwidth. All modules run the same program, but behave differently depending on individual sensor values, internal state, and messages received from nearby modules. The challenge is to design software that is robust to initial conditions, scales well as the number of modules increases, and acts at the local level but achieves useful global behavior.

We use genetic programming to evolve robust, scalable, distributed controllers for a simulated, 2-dimensional smart membrane capable of sorting particles based on color. The smart membrane's dimensions are flexible, as we discuss below, but a typical instantiation is around sixty modules across, and eight modules high. An arbitrary number of particles, the size of single modules and colored either blue or red, are placed above the artificial membrane. The modular robot then actively filters the particles - by pushing and pulling them, and creating temporary transport channels - so that the final configuration of the simulated world has all the red particles on top of the smart membrane, and all the blue particles below, with the membrane structure remaining reasonably intact.

2   Related Work

The smart membrane represents a novel application of modular robotics, and indeed the idea of a programmable filter is original for any implementation. Keller and Ferrari [11] provide a micro scale passive filter with sufficiently small holes to permit the passage of small desired biomolecules while at the same time preventing the passage of all larger molecules such as antibodies. A micromachined particle sorter was implemented by Koch et al. [12]. A nanometer scale active membrane was constructed [10] where the rate of water permeation through the membrane was controlled by pH levels and ionic strength. Drexler [6] gives a design for a unidirectional active molecule sorter capable of transporting specific molecules across a barrier. Drexler's sorter design was used as a component in the design of an artificial mechanical red blood cell [7], [8]. A membrane with porosity controlled by electroactive polymer actuators is described by Otero [18]. The smart membrane is unique in that its behavior can be determined by software, allowing for exceptional functional generality.

A small amount of centralized control software for modular robots has been developed. Casal and Yim [4] use a central controller for finding global strategies to achieve desired configurations. Global automated planning algorithms have been used for reconfiguring Crystalline Robots [21], [13]. Simulated annealing has been used to find near-optimal global methods for reconfiguring modular robots [20].

Almost no work has been done on developing decentralized control software for modular robots. Nearly all of such research has focused on hand-coding local rules for modular robotic tasks. Bonabeau, et al. [3] describe work in which local rules for reconfiguration of modular robots were hand-coded. Bojinov, et al. [2] hand-coded local control algorithms for a self-assembling robot made of rhombic dodecahedrons for two types of problems: reconfiguring in response to weight, and reconfiguring to grasp an object of unknown size and shape. Yim, et al. [25] hand-coded a local algorithm to enable the same kind of robot to reconfigure into any specified goal configuration. Kubica et al. hand-coded complex behaviors using local rules for robots which move by modular expansion and contraction [16], [17].

Bennett and Rieffel [1] were the first to automatically generate modular robot control software. They use genetic programming to evolve the control software for some simple modular robotic tasks. The tasks include locomotion of a group of modules through a crooked passage, cooperative propulsion of modules over a "slippery" bridge, and locomotion of a group of modules toward a goal. Their results exhibit robustness against module failures, changing environmental conditions, unknown environmental details, and varying initial conditions of the modular robots themselves.

3   Modular Robot Simulator

For our experiments, we wrote a simulator for the type of self-reconfigurable modular robot designed and built by Pamecha, et al. at Johns Hopkins University [19], Figure 1. We add sensing, communication, and processing capabilities that were not implemented in the modules built by Pamecha, et al.

Each square robot module occupies one grid location in the world. The state of a module includes its location, the most recent messages received from adjacent modules in each of eight directions, the values of its sensors, the values in its four memory locations, and its facing direction.

Directions are encoded as real values in $[0.0, 1.0)$, where direction 0.0 is the robot module's positive x-axis, and direction values increase going around counter clockwise. The direction values used by each robot module are local to that module's own frame of reference. The direction that a robot module is facing in the world is always direction 0.0 in the robot module's frame of reference. Direction 0.25 is 90 degrees to the left of where it is facing in the world, etc.

Fig. 1. Photograph of the physical hardware for two self-reconfigurable modules [19]. Reprinted by permission ASME

3.1   Movement

Robot modules are able to move exactly one grid location in one of four directions: east, north, west, and south. A robot module cannot move by itself; it can only move by sliding against an adjacent robot module.

To slide, a robot module can push itself against another robot module that is adjacent to it at 90 degrees from the direction of motion (Figure 2). Similarly, a robot module can pull against another robot module that is diagonally adjacent to it in the direction of motion. The pulling style of move is demonstrated in Figure 2 by considering step 2 as the initial configuration, and step 1 as the result of the move.

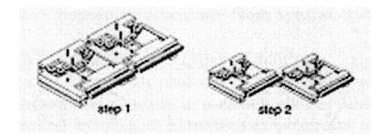

Fig. 2. Diagram of the basic single move operation for the style of self-reconfigurable robot module used for the smart membrane. Before the move, the two modules share a connected edge (step 1); after the move, the two modules are still connected at a shared corner (step 2) [19]. Reprinted by permission ASME

Robot modules can initiate two different types of moves to reconfigure the robot. A "single" move is the movement of a single robot module, and it succeeds if and only if that robot module is moving into an empty grid location and there is a module to push or pull against. A "line" move is the movement of an entire line of robot modules, and it succeeds if and only if the front-most module in the line is moving into an empty grid location, and there is a module to push or pull against. A line move can be initiated by any robot module in a line of robot modules.

3.2   Sensors

Each module has eight sensors for detecting other robot modules, and eight sensors for detecting walls and obstacles. Each module also has 8 color sensors which detect whether the object in the adjacent grid location in the current facing direction is red or blue. The eight directions for sensors are: 0.0 = east, 0.125 = northeast, 0.25 = north, 0.375 = northwest, 0.5= west, 0.625 = southwest, 0.75 = south, and 0.875 = southeast. A module's sensor readings are in units of intensity in [0.0, 1.0], where the intensity is the inverse of the distance to the thing sensed; zero means that the thing was not sensed at all, and one means that the thing was sensed in the immediately adjacent grid location.

4   The Smart Membrane Problem

In the training version of the problem, a single module-sized red or blue square, the "particle," is placed directly above the smart membrane. The membrane is required to reconfigure itself - pushing and pulling the particle, and creating temporary transport channels - so that the particle remain above the membrane, if red, or is moved to the bottom, if blue. In addition, the membrane itself must end up close to its initial position, though the individual modules within the membrane do not need to end up close to their original positions. After training, this behavior should generalize over a wide range of membrane sizes and particle positions.

4.1   Function Set

The following basic function set was used to evolve the control software for the smart membrane:

- (MoveSingle direction) causes the current robot module to move in the relative direction direction if it can move. This function returns true if the module is able to move, and false otherwise.
- (MoveLine direction) causes an entire line of robot modules to move in the relative direction direction if they can. The line of modules to move is the connected line of modules collinear with the current module in the relative direction direction of the current module. This function returns true if the line of modules is able to move, and false otherwise.

- (`Rotate direction`) rotates the robot module by the amount `direction`. This does not physically move the module, it merely resets the internal state of the robot module's internal facing direction. This function returns the value of direction.
- (`ReadMessage direction`) reads the real-valued message from the adjacent module (if any) that is location at the relative direction `direction` to the receiving module. The `direction` is interpreted mod 1, and then rounded to the nearest eighth to indicate one of the eight adjacent grid locations. This function returns the value of the message read.
- (`SendMessage message direction`) sends the real-valued message message from the sending module to an adjacent module (if any) in the direction `direction`, relative to the frame of reference of the sending module. The `direction` is interpreted as in `ReadMessage`. This function returns the value of the message sent.
- Functions (`ReadSensorSelf direction`), (`ReadSensorWall direction`), and (`ReadSensorParticle direction`) read the intensity value of the sensor for detecting another module, a wall, or a particle, respectively. Intensity is the inverse of the distance to the closest object of interest at the relative direction `direction`. The intensity is zero if there is no object of interest in that direction. This function returns the intensity value.
- (`IsBlue direction`), (`IsRed direction`) returns true if there is a blue or red particle, respectively, immediately next to this module in direction `direction`, and false otherwise.
- (`GetMemory index`) gets the current value of the robot module's memory numbered `index`. This function returns the value of the memory.
- (`SetMemory index value`) sets the value of the robot module's memory numbered `index` to `value`. This function returns `value`.
- (`ProgN arg1 arg2`) evaluates both `arg1` and `arg2`, and returns `arg1`. This function allows for sequential command execution.
- (`ProtectedDivide num denom`) divides `num` by `denom`, returning the result, or 1 if the operation results in an error or an infinite value.
- (`ProtectedModulus num denom`) calculates `num` modulus `denom`, returning the result, or 1 if the operation results in an error or an infinite value.
- (`And arg1 arg2`), (`If test arg1 arg2`), (`Less arg1 arg2`), with the usual definitions [15].

4.2   Terminal Set

The terminal set used to evolve the control software for the smart membrane includes only (`GetTurn`) and some numerical constants. (`GetTurn`) returns the current value of the "turn" variable, which is set to zero at the beginning of the simulation and is incremented each time all of the robot's modules are executed.

Six constant-valued terminals `0.0`, `0.25`, `0.5`, `0.75`, `1.0`, and `-1.0` are given. Program trees can use arithmetic to create other numerical values.

4.3   Fitness

Though the final smart membrane distributed control software generalizes to larger simulation worlds, the world used for fitness evaluation is a square with 10 units on a side. (The perimeter grid locations of the entire world contain wall boundary objects through which the robot modules cannot pass.)

The fitness for an individual program is calculated as a weighted average of the fitness in 24 simulation worlds. Each simulation world is initialized with the smart membrane's robot modules arranged in a vertically centered rectangle extending 8 units from the left wall to the right wall. In twelve of the worlds, the robotic smart membrane is of height three modules; in the other twelve, the membrane is of height four modules. At the beginning of each fitness evaluation, the values of the communication buffers and the values in all the robot's memory locations are initialized to zero. The facing direction of the modules is determined randomly for each world.

The fitness is computed by running a simulation of the robot's actions in each world. The simulation is run for 10 execution "turns." In each turn, the evolved program tree is executed once for each module. The order in which the modules' programs are executed is also determined randomly for each world, though the order remains constant over the 10 execution turns.

Each fitness world includes a single particle to be filtered, which is placed on top of the membrane. Particles are colored either blue or red. The membrane must filter the particles so that red particles remain above the filter, while blue particles are transported through the filter to end up below the membrane. An evenly distributed sample of possible horizontal positions for the particle is contained in the 24 fitness worlds. In six of the worlds, the particles that appears initially above the membrane is colored red, in which case the particles does not need to be moved at all. In the other 18 worlds, the particles that appears initially above the membrane is colored blue, so the membrane must transport the particles through the membrane to the other side.

The fitness is a weighted sum of two measurements, averaged over all turns: the location of the particle relative to the membrane, and the current absolute position of the membrane modules. The former term is given by the average offset in the vertical dimension of the modules from the particle. This value is normalized so that a score of 1 means that the membrane made no progress in moving the particle toward its correct final position, whereas a score of 0 means that the particle is either above or below the membrane, as appropriate. This term has the effect of making sure that each object is moved toward the appropriate final relative position.

The latter term is given by the average absolute displacement of each module from the horizontal central axis of the starting membrane position. This term penalizes the robot for failing to keep the original structure and position of the membrane intact, while the object is being filtered.

It was determined empirically that an effective setting of the weights was:

95(particle displacement) + 5(membrane distance from center).

This setting is fairly arbitrary, however, and other weights seemed to work as well. Note that the complexity of the task - and the difficulty of achieving a useful fitness gradient in initial generations - forced us to adopt this rather ad hoc fitness measure.

Parameters. The population size for this problem is 72,000 individuals. The crossover and mutation rates are 99%, and 1% respectively. Crossover and mutation select nodes with differential probability, depending on position within the tree. Leaf nodes have a 10% chance of being chosen for crossover, whereas internal nodes have an 89% chance. Leaf nodes have a 0.5% chance of mutation, as do internal nodes. We use the generational breeding model with tournament selection, and a tournament size of 7. Elitism is used, which insures that the most fit individual in each generation is cloned into the next generation. The method for creating program trees in generation 0 and in mutation operations is the "full" method [14]. The maximum depth for program trees in generation 0 is 5. The maximum depth for program trees created by crossover and mutation is 9. The maximum depth of subtrees created by mutation is 4. We use strongly typed genetic programming [9].

4.4   Parallelization

The population is divided into semi-isolated subpopulations called demes following Wright [24]. Breeding is panmictic within each deme, and rare between demes. The parallelization scheme is the distributed asynchronous island approach [15]. The communication topology between the demes is a toroidal grid with periodic boundary conditions. Each processor communicates only with its four nearest neighbors. At the end of each generation, 2% of the population is selected at random to migrate in each of the four cardinal directions.

5   Results

A working solution to this task emerged in generation 32 of the run. The solution was composed of 49 primitive function references and 32 real valued constants. The behavior of this solution is shown in Figure 3 for a single initial world condition at three points in time during the simulation. A string representation of the program tree is given by:

```
(ProtectedMod (SendMessage (If (IsBlue (ProtectedDiv 0.5 1.0)) (If
(Move -1.0) (ProtectedDiv 0.5 (Rotate (GetRegisterEntry
(SetRegisterEntry 0.5 0.25)))) 0.75) (Rotate (ProtectedDiv (Rotate
(ProtectedDiv (Rotate 0.25) (ReadSensorSelf 0.5))) (ProtectedMod
0.25 (SetRegisterEntry 0.75 0.0))))) (If (MoveOne (ProtectedDiv
(If (IsRed 0.25) (ReadSensorSelf 0.0) (GetRegisterEntry 0.5))
getTurn)) 0.0 0.75)) (SendMessage (If (IsBlue (ProtectedDiv
0.5 1.0)) (If (Move -1.0) (ProtectedDiv 0.25 (Rotate
```

```
(ReadSensorBrokenAlien -1.0))) (ReadSensorWall 0.75)) (Rotate
(ProtectedDiv (Rotate (ProtectedDiv (Rotate 0.25) (ReadSensorSelf
0.5))) (ProtectedMod 0.25 (SetRegisterEntry 0.75 0.0))))) (If
(MoveOne 0.0) 0.0 (ProgN 0.0 (GetRegisterEntry 0.0)))))
```

6 Generalization

Although this program was evolved in a 10x10 world, with membrane heights of
3 and 4, and one object filtered at a time, the same program successfully controls
much larger membranes which can filter multiple objects at the same time. For
example, the program functioned successfully when installed on each of the 496
robot modules in a 64x64 world, with a membrane height of eight modules and
six objects to be filtered (three red and three blue) spaced evenly along the top
of the membrane. An example of this out-of-sample generalization is shown in
Figure 4. The same program works just as well with intermediate numbers of
modules and particles, and with different particle placement (so long as there is
at least several modules of space between particles).

7 Conclusions and Future Work

We have demonstrated an effective means of evolving distributed control software for the smart membrane, a difficult modular robotic task. Furthermore, we
have demonstrated robustness of the evolved program to particle placement, and
scalability as the number of robot modules and particles increases.

We intend to extend this approach to a variety of modular robot types,
including three dimensional modules and modules that use non-sliding moves
such as compression and expansion moves [21]. We also intend to explore the
robustness of the smart membrane to failure of a small number of robot modules.

Additionally, we are currently investigating methods of evolving a smart
membrane capable of actively filtering objects based on other properties, like
size, shape, and pattern of movement. Because observation of these attributes
necessitates intermodular communication - a capability which has not yet been
exercised and proven - these tasks may prove significantly more challenging than
the filtering by color scenario.

Finally, we are currently implementing a co-evolutionary approach to evolving the smart membrane distributed control software and test worlds simultaneously. This approach will generate easy test worlds for early generation control
software fitness evaluation, which then become increasingly difficult as the controllers improve. The idea is to promote a co-evolutionary "arms race" in which
the control software is driven to continual improvement and increasing robustness, just as the test cases become more difficult and strive to exploit weaknesses
in the controllers.

Although an effective system for generating the test worlds needs to be implemented, along with a function for determining whether a membrane "succeeds"

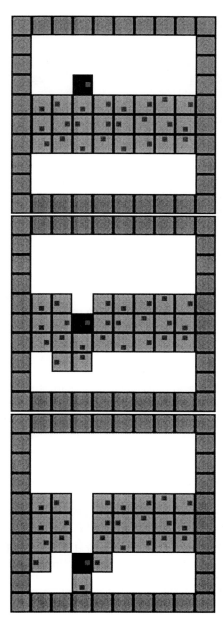

Fig. 3. This series shows the behavior of the evolved smart membrane control software on one test case. The leftmost scene shows the initial condition for the simulation, the middle scene shows an intermediate time step, and the rightmost scene shows the final configuration

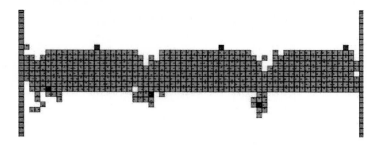

Fig. 4. This figure shows the final configuration of the evolved smart membrane control software on an out-of-sample world where the world size, depth of the membrane, width of the membrane, and number of foreign object to be sorted are all different from any of the worlds used in training. (The top and bottom of the world, devoid of modules, are not shown)

or "fails" in that given world, we hope that this approach will diminish the need to arbitrarily set weights and hand-design fitness functions capable of meaningfully guiding evolution when faced with consistently poor measured performance. We hope that such techniques will allow us to more autonomously evolve an even smarter smart membrane.

Acknowledgements

Many thanks to Tad Hogg and Arancha Casal for teaching us about modular robots and suggesting problem areas for us to work on, Wolfgang Polak for help in setting up the computing cluster and for conversations about modular robots, Zoe Abrams for her programming work and technical suggestions, Jeremy Kubica for his work in hand-coding some modular robotic algorithms and so helping us to debug the evolutionary technique, and Adil Qureshi for his Gpsys 1.1 Java genetic programming source code on which our system is based.

References

1. Bennett III, F.H, Rieffel, E.G.: Design of Decentralized Controllers for Self-Reconfigurable Modular Robots Using Genetic Programming. Proceedings of the 2nd NASA/DoD Workshop on Evolvable Hardware (2000) 43-52
2. Bojinov, H., Casal, A., Hogg, T.: Emergent Structures in Modular Self-Reconfigurable Ro-bots. IEEE Intl. Conf. on Robotics and Automation (2000) 1734-1741
3. Bonabeau, E., Dorigo, M., Theraulaz, G.: Swarm Intelligence: from Natural to Artificial Systems. Oxford Univ. Press (1999)
4. Casal, A., Yim, M.: Self-Reconfiguration Planning for a Class of Modular Robots. Proceedings of SPIE'99, Vol. 3839 (1999) 246-256
5. Castano, A., Chokkalingam, R., Will, P.: Autonomous and Self-sufficient Conro Modules for Reconfigurable Robots. Proceedings of the Fifth International Symposium on Distributed Autonomous Robotic Systems (DARS) (2000)

6. Drexler, K.E.: Nanosystems: Molecular Machinery, Manufacturing, and Computation. John Wiley & Sons, Inc. (1992)
7. Freitas Jr., R.A.: Respirocytes: High Performance Artificial Nanotechnology Red Blood Cells. NanoTechnology Magazine 2 (Oct. 1996) 1, 8-13 (8)
8. Freitas Jr., R.A.: Nanomedicine, Vol. 1: Basic Capabilities. Landes Bioscience (1999)
9. Haynes, T., Wainwright, R., Sen, S., Schoenfeld, D.: Strongly Typed Genetic Programming in Evolving Cooperation Strategies. Proceedings of the Sixth International Conference on Genetic Algorithms. Morgan Kaufmann (1995) 271-278
10. Ito, Y.: Signal-responsive Gating by a Polyelectrolyte Pelage on a Nanoporous Membrane. Nanotechnology, Vol. 9 No. 3, (Sep. 1998) 205-207
11. Keller, C.B., Ferrari, M.: Microfabricated Capsules for Immunological Isolation of Cell Transplants. US Patent No. 5,893,974 (13 Apr. 1999)
12. Koch, M., Schabmueller, C., Evans, A.G.R., Brunnschweiler, A.: A Micromachined Particle Sorter: Principle and Technology. Tech. Digest, Eurosensors XII, Southampton, UK, September 13-16 (1998)
13. Kotay, K., Rus, D., Vona, M., McGray, C.: The Self-Reconfiguring Robotic Molecule: Design and Control Algorithms. Proceeding of the 1998 International Conference on Intelligent Robots and Systems (1998)
14. Koza, J.R.: Genetic Programming: On the Programming of Computers by Means of Natural Selection. MIT Press (1992)
15. Koza, J.R., Bennett III, F.H, Andre, D., Keane, M.A.: Genetic Programming III: Darwinian Invention and Problem Solving. Morgan Kaufmann (1999)
16. Kubica, J., Casal, A., Hogg, T.: Agent-Based Control for Object Manipulation with Modular Self-reconfigurable Robots. Submitted to Intl. Joint Conf. on AI (2001)
17. Kubica, J., Casal, A., Hogg, T.: Complex Behaviors from Local Rules in Modular Self-Reconfigurable Robots. Submitted to IEEE ICRA (2001)
18. Otero, T.F.: EAP as Multifunctional and Biomimetic Materials. Smart Structures and Materials 1999: Electroactive Polymer Actuators and Devices 26-34
19. Pamecha, A., Chiang, C.J., Stein, D., Chirikjian, G.S.: Design and Implementation of Metamorphic Robots. Proceedings 1996 ASME Design Engineering Technical Conference and Computers and Engineering Conference (1996) 1-10
20. Pamecha, A., Ebert-Uphoff, I., Chirikjian, G.S.: Useful Metrics for Modular Robot Motion Planning, IEEE Transactions on Robots and Automation, Vol.13, No.4 (Aug. 1997) 531-545
21. Rus, D., Vona, M.: Self-Reconfiguration Planning with Compressible Unit Modules. IEEE Int. Conference on Robotics and Automation (1999)
22. Tummala, R.L., Mukherjee, R., Aslam, D., Xi, N., Mahadevan, S., Weng, J.: Reconfigurable Adaptable Micro-Robot. Proc. 1999 IEEE International Conference on Systems, Man, and Cybernetics (Oct. 1999)
23. Ünsal, C., Kiliccöte, H., Khosla, P.K.: A 3-D Modular Self-Reconfigurable Bipartite Robotic System: Implementation and Motion Planning. Submitted to Autonomous Robots Journal, special issue on Modular Reconfigurable Robots (2000)Wright, S.: Isolation by Distance. Genetics 28 (1943)114-138.
24. Wright, S.: Isolation by Distance. Genetics 28 (1943)114-138.
25. Yim, M., Lamping, J., Mao, E., Chase, J.G.: Rhombic Dodecahedron Shape for Self-Assembling Robots. Xerox PARC SPL TechReport P9710777 (1997)
26. Yim, M., Duff, D.G., Roufas, K.D.: PolyBot: a Modular Reconfigurable Robot. IEEE Intl. Conf. On Robotics and Automation (ICRA) (2000)

A GP Artificial Ant for Image Processing: Preliminary Experiments with EASEA

Enzo Bolis*, Christian Zerbi*, Pierre Collet†, Jean Louchet*, and Evelyne Lutton‡

*ENSTA	†Ecole Polytechnique	‡INRIA, projet FRACTALES
32 bd Victor	CMAPX/EEAAX	Rocquencourt, BP 105
F - 75739 Paris cedex 15	F - 91128 Palaiseau cedex	F - 78153 Le Chesnay cedex

Abstract. This paper describes how animat-based "food foraging" techniques may be applied to the design of low-level image processing algorithms. First, we show how we implemented the food foraging application using the EASEA software package. We then use this technique to evolve an animat and learn how to move inside images and detect high-gradient lines with a minimum exploration time. The resulting animats do not use standard "scanning + filtering" techniques but develop other image exploration strategies close to contour tracking. Experimental results on grey level images are presented.

1 Introduction

1.1 EASEA and Genetic Programming

EASEA [8] is a language dedicated to evolutionary algorithms. Its aim is to relieve the programmer of the painful chore of learning how to use evolutionary libraries and object-oriented programming by using the contents of a .ez source file written by the user. EASEA source files only need to contain the "interesting" parts of an evolutionary language, namely the fitness function, a specification of the crossover, the mutation, the initialisation of a genome plus a set of parameters describing the run. With this information, the EASEA compiler creates a complete C++ source file containing function calls to either the GALib [10] or EO [9] library, depending on the one that was installed by the user. Therefore, the minimum requirement necessary to write evolutionary algorithms is the capability of creating non-object-oriented functions, specific to the problem which needs to be solved.

In our case, the genetic programming involved to program artificial ants was implemented using a tree structure on which genetic operators were defined. The EASEA compiler converted the specification into a compilable C++ source file using GALib.

1.2 The Artificial Ant Problem, Animats, and Low-Level Image Processing

The Artificial Ant problem [18][15] considers the task of navigating an animat [25][28] gathering food scattered irregularly (e.g. using the Santa Fe trail) over a two-dimensional domain represented as a binary image. This problem, known as containing multiple levels of deception (GA-hard) [23], has often been used as a benchmark for Genetic Programming (GP). In the first part of this paper, we show an implementation of this problem using EASEA and following John Koza's implementation [18]. The animat's task is to detect all the food available in the image with the shortest possible path length. The output is a binary image showing the pixels detected by the animat.

J. Miller et al. (Eds.): EuroGP 2001, LNCS 2038, pp. 246-255, 2001.

In the second part of the paper, we propose an extension of this Animat methodology and genetic programming to automatically write low-level image processing tasks, without making any assumption about the exploration strategy used. The vast majority of low-level image processing algorithms uses standard, systematic image scanning and pipe-line data processing [14], which is not necessarily the most cost-effective solution (see Section 3). To this end, we use an animat fitted with simple sensors and actuators, able to move (from a position to one of its neighbours) inside the image and to see the values of its surrounding pixels, and optimise its internal program using genetic programming and a fitness function depending on the task to be performed (here, contour detection). The input is a natural grey level image: the animat's task is to find as many contour pixels as possible, using a minimal path length. Again, the output is a binary image showing the pixels the animat has detected.

The behavioural aspects of several different animat types have been studied [25] and linked to real-world behaviours in Biology [19][27][2], but as far as we know, only few applications to real image processing have been published. See [16,17] for crack detection with "image exploring agents".

2   Implementing a Food Foraging Process Using EASEA

2.1 Animat Functions

The topology used throughout this paper is 4-connexity. In other terms, the animat's axis may only have 4 possible orientations, and its elementary movements are rotations or one-step translation ahead. With regard to the animat functions, we followed Koza's definitions [18], but added specific sensors to our artificial ant, resulting in the following two classes of functions:

- animat's sensor functions:

  - if_food_ahead(): if there is food present in the pixel currently just ahead of the animat, the first argument is executed; else the second one is executed.
  - if_food_on_lf(), same if there is food on the front left side;
  - if_food_on_rg(), same if there is food on the front right side;
  - already_visited(), if the animat is on a pixel already visited, the first argument is executed; otherwise the second one is executed. An image-sized buffer is used to memorise pixels already visited.

- animat's actuator functions:

  - move(), moves the animat ahead;
  - left(), rotates the animat at a right angle counterclockwise;
  - right(), rotates the animat at a right angle clockwise;
  - progn2(action1, action2), the animat executes the actions 1 and 2 sequentially;
  - progn3(action1, action2, action3), the animat executes the actions 1, 2, 3 sequentially.

2.2 Initialising Trees

An ant's program is represented "à la Koza", with a genetic programming tree containing the previously described actions in its nodes. The population of trees is initialised randomly, with a maximum depth of 5. The maximum depth has been predetermined although we remarked that the trees are most often well balanced, thanks to the functions `progn2` and `progn3` which grow the tree both in depth and width.

2.3 Crossover

The two-parent crossover uses two independently chosen crossover sites for each parent. In order to limit crossover between leaves, if one of the sites is on a leaf, then this crossover will be done with a 30% probability. The total crossover probability is determined by the EASEA parameter `PCross`.

2.4 Mutation

Two types of mutation are introduced: leaf mutation and subtree mutation. leaf mutations (65% of total mutations) consist in randomly choosing a leaf, then replace it with a randomly chosen function. Subtree mutations (35% of total mutations) consist in randomly choosing two sites in the tree, then swapping the two corresponding subtrees. The total mutation probability is determined by the EASEA parameter `PMut`. These probability values have been determined experimentally.

2.5 Fitness Evaluation

As the primary goal is to find food, the quantity of food detected will be the main factor in the fitness function. However, it is also important to take into account the path complexity of the animat (measured by the number of elementary action steps) and the complexity of the genome. Appropriate weights A and B allow to control the relative impact of these factors.

$$fitness = (quantity\ of\ food\ found) - A \times (\#\ steps) - B \times (genome\ size)$$

The orders of magnitude are: $A = 10^{-2}$, $B = 10^{-4}$ (experimental values).

Additional constraints are taken into account by giving arbitrarily low values to the fitness if not satisfied:

- The `autonomy` parameter, which gives the maximum number of steps allowed without food.
- In order to prevent the animats from spinning around themselves, a credit of 4 rotations is given initially (in order to allow a complete 360° rotation and have a "panoramic sight") and the subsequent extra rotations are penalised. The rotation counter is reinitialised to −4 each time a `move` is executed.

The number of steps taken into account to calculate the fitness is fixed to a value *nsteps* which decreases during the first part of evolution (to eliminate those individuals trying to scan all the image without any clever strategy) from the parameter value `Operations_max` to `Operations_min`, then is raised again (to allow a more efficient selection of individuals able to find most of the existing food) back to `Operations_max`.

2.6 Results

The algorithm has been tested on three binary images with increasing difficulty (Fig.

1). With the first one, food has been placed continuously along a *Santa Fe* trail [18, 20]. The path in the second image was built by removing the food in the corners of the Santa Fe trail, thus resulting in a trail made of disconnected straight lines. In the third image, food is distributed with important gaps, or even on isolated pixels.

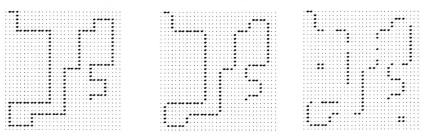

Image 1 : continuous Santa Fe trail.   Image 2 : Santa Fe trail   Image 3 : Santa Fe trail with
                                          with removed corners.   gaps and isolated food patches.

Figure 1: Binary test images used

The `autonomy` parameter has been fixed at 50 for the first data set, 100 for the 2nd, 150 for the 3rd one. Table 2 shows the best results we obtained on these data sets.

Terminal set	left, right, move
Function set	if_food_ahead, if_food_on_lf, if_food_on_rg, already_visited, progn2, progn3
Selection	ranking
Wrapper	program repeatedly executed for a fixed number of motion steps
Parameters	Pmut=0.4 (total), Pcross=0.9 (total)

Table 1: Main features of the GP

Image #	run #	food present	food found	motion steps	autonomy	nodes in animat	population	# generations
1	1	144	144	144	50	3	500	5
2	2	123	123	145	100	25	1000	5
2	3	123	123	145	100	10	2000	5
2	4	123	123	145	100	7	1000	25
3	5	105	91	701	150	31	8000	20
3	6	105	91	701	150	20	15000	10
3	7	105	105	423	150	21	10000	30

Table 2: Results obtained on binary test images

Runs 1-4 (on images 1 and 2) show that small populations and few generations are sufficient to get a satisfactory animat, however runs 3 and 4 illustrate the fact that larger populations or more generations help optimise the tree structure. Runs 5-7 (on image 3) show that on more difficult data, both large populations and large number of generations are necessary. The best code resulting from run 7 is given in Appendix A.

3   Contour Detection

3.1 Grey Level Images and Contour Detection

Contour detection in grey level images is a popular problem in image processing [1, 14]. While this problem may not always be as deceptive as the food foraging problem, its apparent similarity with the latter and the importance of its real-world applications led us to study the possibility of transposing the method presented in Section 2.

A contour in a grey level image is usually defined as a continuous line, whose points are local maxima of the image gradient norm. Most contour detection methods are based on standard image scanning. For each pixel a decision is taken, based e.g. on the first-order (and sometimes second order) grey level derivatives in the pixel's neighbourhood, or other characteristics like Hölder exponents [24]. Some approaches use contour tracking with local optimisation [14], or global optimisation methods [13], but most scan the image the usual way[1]. Among the few exceptions we can mention works on dynamic contour tracking and parallel algorithms developed for specific architectures. Our animat-based approach to contour detection does not make any assumption about the image exploration strategy that will be used.

3.2 Basic Animat Functions

The animat language primitives are similar to the ones used in the previous section. We have changed the perception functions, according to the new purposes of the application. We have replaced the `if_food_*` functions with the following ones:

- `if_contour_ah()`: if $|a - b|$ is greater than a fixed threshold, the first argument is executed; else the second one is executed;
- `if_contour_aw()`, same with $|c - f|$;
- `if_contour_af()`, same with $|d - e|$.

	d		e	
c	a		b	f
		↑ animat		

3.3 Genetic Operators

The mutation and crossover operators are the same as those used in the previous section. As in section 2, similar additional constraints have been added to the fitness function (rotation credit, number of steps).

3.4 Results

Here the fitness function will favour animats whose trajectory contains highly contrasted pixels. Thus the first term of the fitness function is now the number of pixels detected whose contrast is greater than a given threshold. With this fitness function applied to a classic Lena image we obtained the following results:

---

[1] The new generation of CMOS image sensors allows random pixel access, which is giving a new opportunity to vision systems not reading the pixels the linear way. The constraint of parallel image scanning is thus becoming more of a cultural than a technical constraint, and may encourage more costly calculations. A clever image exploration strategy may help get more efficient image processing algorithms, especially in embedded real-time applications.

Original B&W image (257×239)   Contours detected

Figure 2: "Lena" image and result found using the best animat obtained after 30 generations

It is worth noting that with a toroidal representation of the image, the genetic programming created an animat scanning the full image[2]. Some pixels are missed but it is interesting to remark that the system discovered by itself that image scanning is an efficient method not to miss contours.

Then, in order to avoid time-consuming full image scanning and get more efficient contour detectors, we replaced the first term of the fitness function with an expression including the number of detected contour pixels, the number of scanned pixels and the number of consecutive detections (in order to encourage continuous detection of contours). To test the improved fitness function, we have trained the genetic algorithm on the test images 1 and 2 shown on Fig. 3, obtaining quite efficient contour following algorithms:

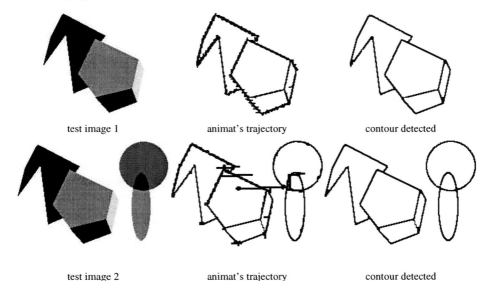

test image 1   animat's trajectory   contour detected

test image 2   animat's trajectory   contour detected

Figure 3: Synthetic test images and results

---

[2]   This is why we did not display the trajectory of the animat.

The change in exploration strategy comes essentially from the changes in the fitness function. We suppressed the constraint on path length which now becomes useless in the learning phase with the new fitness ($A = 0$). The resulting animat's program (given in Appendix C) is functionally equivalent to the following pseudo-C code:

```
if (contour ahead)
else turn right;        } first part
move;
move;
turn left;
if (contour ahead) {
  move;
  move;
}
else {                  } second part
  if (already visited) turn right;
  else {
    turn left;
    move;
    turn right;
  }
}
```

Code generated

A B C

↑

Relative positions of ant and pixels A, B, C

Some interesting remarks can be made on the simplified procedure. First of all, in this example, the functions `if_contour_aw` and `if_contour_af` are not used, showing that the analysis of the image can be done with the sole `if_contour_ahead` instruction.

If we now put the animat into an unexplored part of the picture without any contour pixel, and if we let pixels A, B and C be the three pixels in a straight line in front of the animat, executing the first part moves the animat two pixels to the right, to C. Only pixels A and C are tested as contour pixels. In the second part, the animat backtracks to pixel B using a `left-move-right` sequence, then gets the proper orientation for the following execution. All pixels on a line are tested unless an already visited position is reached during backtracking. Then, the animat turns right and starts analysing a perpendicular line. Other configurations may be analysed the same way.

4   Comments on Implementation

The project was first written using EASEA, which provided an easy implementation and efficient interfacing with GAlib. We then edited manually the resulting C++ code. Thanks to this method, we avoided all the effort of defining data and program structures, reading the GAlib documentation or writing calls to the GAlib library, and could concentrate into more specific issues like fine tuning the fitness function and genetic parameters. On the whole, EASEA allowed us a much faster and more efficient implementation.

5   Conclusion and Future Work

The aim of this paper is not to propose yet another "better" contour detection algorithm. We showed an example of how genetic programing is able to build from scratch, without using prior knowledge in image processing, a contour detection algorithm that gives results not competing but fairly comparable with those given by usual contour detectors [14]; perhaps more importantly, the experiment presented shows that EASEA can successfully evolve an artifical ant in a complex environment. The EASEA code generating the ant algorithm is available on the EASEA web site [8]. Genetic programming and EASEA can be an interesting alternative way to quickly and easily develop algorithms in image processing and in other application domains where previous resolution methods are not available.

Future extensions include:

- using several images for learning [20], in order to get a more robust algorithm,
- fitting the animat with an individual memory, e.g. of the average direction followed in the near past [25],
- giving the animat the ability of having a non-deterministic behaviour,
- using supervised learning,
- using an "ant colony" rather than a single animat, may allow cooperative behaviour (via direct cooperation or via pheromones).

References

[1] D. H. Ballard and C. M. Brown, *Computer Vision*, Prentice Hall, 1982.

[2] R. J. V. Bertin and W. A. van de Grind, *The Influence of Light-Dark Adaptation and Lateral Inhibition on Phototaxic Foraging: A Hypothetical Animal Study*, Pages 141-167, Adaptive Behavior, Volume 5, Number 2, Fall 1996.

[3] V. Cantoni, M. Ferretti, S. Levialdi, R. Negrini and S. Stefanelli, *Progress in Image Analysis and Processing*, World Scientific,1991.

[4] D. Cliff and S. Bullock, *Adding "Foveal Vision" to Wilson's Animat*, Pages 49-72, Adaptive Behavior, Volume 2, Number 1, Summer 1993.

[5] P. Collet, E. Lutton, M. Schoenauer, J. Louchet, *Take it EASEA,* Parallel Problem Solving from Nature VI, vol 1917, Springer pp 891-901, Paris, September 2000.

[6] R. J. Collins and D. R. Jefferson. *Antfarm: Towards simulated evolution* . In S. Rasmussen, J. Farmer, C. Langton and C. Taylor, editors, Artificial Life II, Reading, Massachusetts, Addison-Wesley, 1991.

[7] F. L. Crabbe, Michael G. Dyer, *Observation and Imitation: Goal Sequence Learning in Neurally Controlled Construction Animats: VI-MAXSON*, SAB 2000, Paris.

[8] EASEA (EAsy Specification of Evolutionary Algorithms) home page: http:// www-rocq.inria.fr/EASEA/

[9] EO (Evolutionary Objects) home page: http://geneura.ugr.es/~jmerelo/ EO.html

[10] GAlib home page: http://lancet.mit.edu/ga/

[11] P. Gaussier. *Autonomous Robots interacting with an unknown world,* Special Issue on Animat Approach to Control, Robotics and Autonomous Systems, 16, 1995.

[12] R. C. Gonzalez, R. E. Woods, *Digital Image Processing*, Wiley, 1992

[13] J. Ivins, J. Porrill, *Statistical Snakes: Active Region Models,* British Machine Vision Conference, York, Sep. 1994.

[14] R.C. Jain, R. Kasturi, B.G. Schunck, *Machine Vision*, McGraw-Hill, 1995.

[15] D. Jefferson, R. Collins, C. Cooper, M. Dyer, M. Flower, R. Korf, C. Taylor, A. Wang, Evolution as a theme in artificial life: the Genesys/Tracker system, Artificial life II, vol. X, Santa Fe Institute Studies in the Sciences of Complexity, Addison-Wesley, Feb. 1992, 549-578.

[16] M. Köppen, B. Nickolay, *Design of image exploring agent using genetic programming*, Proceedings of the 4th International Conference on Soft Computing, volume 2, pages 549--552, Fukuoka, Japan, 30 Sep - 5 Oct 1996, World Scientific, Singapore.

[17] M. Köppen, B. Nickolay, *Design of Image Exploring Agent using Genetic Programming*. Fuzzy Sets and Systems, Special Issue on Softcomputing, 103 (1999) 303-315.

[18] J. R. Koza, *Genetic Programming*, MIT Press 1992.

[19] J. R. Koza, J. Roughgarden and J. P. Rice, *Evolution of Food-Foraging Strategies for the Caribbean Anolis Lizard Using Genetic Programming*, Pages 171-199, Adaptive Behavior, Volume 1, Number 2, Fall 1992.

[20] I. Kuscu, *A genetic Constructive Induction Model*. In P. J. Angeline, Z. Michalewicz, M. Schoenauer, XinYao, and A. Zalzala, editors, Proceedings of the Congress on Evolutionary Computation , volume 1, pages 212-217, Mayflower Hotel, Washington D.C., USA, 6-9 July 1999. IEEE Press.

[21] W. B. Langdon, *Genetic Programming and Data Structures : Genetic Programming + Data Structures = Automatic Programming !*, Kluwer, 1998.

[22] W. B. Langdon and R. Poli, *Better Trained Ants for Genetic Programming*, Technical Report CSRP-98-12, April 1998, http://www.cs.bham.ac.uk/wbl.

[23] W. B. Langdon and R. Poli, *Why Ants are Hard*, Technical Report: CSRP-98-4, January 1998, http://www.cs.bham.ac.uk/wbl.

[24] J. Lévy Vehel, *introduction to the multifractal analysis of images*, in Fractal image encoding and analysis, Yuval Fischer ed., Springer Verlag, 1996.

[25] J. A. Meyer, A. Guillot, *From SAB90 to SAB94: Four Years of Animat Research*, Proceedings of Third International Conference on Simulation of Adaptive Behavior. Brighton, England, 1994.

[26] R. Moller, D. Lambrinos, R. Pfeifer, T. Labhart, and R. Wehner, *Modeling Ant Navigation with an Autonomous Agent*, From Animals to Animats 5, Proc. of the 5th Int. Conf. on Simulation of Adaptive Behavior, August 17-21, 1998, Zurich, Switzerland, edited by R. Pfeifer, B. Blumberg, J.-A. Meyer and S. W. Wilson.

[27] T. J. Prescott, *Spatial Representation for Navigation in Animats*, Adaptive Behavior, Volume 4, Number 2, Fall 1995, 85-123.

[28] S. W. Wilson, *Classifier systems and the animat problem*, Machine Learning 2 (1987), 199-228.

[29] S. W. Wilson, (1991). *The animat approach to AI* . In J. Meyer & S. W. Wilson (Eds), From Animals to Animats, Proceedings of the first International Conference on Simulation of Adaptive Behavior, Cambridge, MA: MIT Press, 15-21.

[30] M. Witkowski, *The Role of Behavioral Extinction in Animat Action Selection*, SAB 2000, Paris, 2000.

Appendix A: Best Code Generated in Food Pick-Up

```
|-+-PRG3    3 successive actions
 \_LEFT        turn left
|-+-IFOL    if food ahead on left
 |-+-PRG3     3 successive actions
  |-+-IAHR       if already visited         Steps: 423
   \_MOVE           move ahead              Food: 105 of 105
   \_RGHT           turn right              Current parameters:
  |-+-PRG3       3 successive actions       Max Operations: 850
   \_LEFT           turn left               Min Operations: 650
   \_MOVE           move ahead              Population size: 10000
   \_RGHT           turn right              Generations: 30
  \_MOVE         move ahead                 PMutation: 0.4
  |-+-IFOR    if food ahead on right        PCrossover: 0.9
   |-+-PRG2     2 successive actions        Replacement: 0.4
   \_MOVE           move ahead              Elapsed time: 199.33 seconds
   \_LEFT           turn left                 for 58184 evaluations.
  |-+-PRG3     3 successive actions
   \_MOVE           move ahead
   \_LEFT           turn left
   \_LEFT           turn left
 \_LEFT      turn left
```

Appendix B: Best Code Generated in Contour Detection (Lena Image)

```
|-+-PRG3    3 successive actions
 |-+-ICAH      if contrast (a-b)
  \__RGHT       turn right
  |-+-PRG2     2 succ. actions
   |-+-PRG3      3 succ. actions
    \__RGHT          turn right             Steps:    202970
    \__LEFT          turn left              Contour pixels:          2702
    \__RGHT          turn right             Pixel visited:           4599
   \__LEFT        turn left                 Current parameters:
  |-+-PRG2     2 successive actions         Max Operations : 203000
   |-+-PRG2      2 succ. actions            Min Operations : 180001
    \__MOVE          move ahead             Population size: 24952
    \__MOVE          move ahead             Generations: 33
   \__LEFT        turn left                 PMutation: 0.4
  |-+-ICAH     if contrast (a-b)            PCrossover: 0.9
   |-+-AHRE      if already here            Replacement: 0.4
    |-+-PRG3       3 suc. actions           Autonomy: 500000
     \__LEFT          turn left             Elapsed  time:  770.472  seconds  for
     \__MOVE          move ahead            157291 evaluations.
     \__RGHT          turn right
    \__RGHT        turn right
  |-+-PRG2     2 succ. actions
   |-+-ICAH      if contrast (a-b)
    \__LEFT          turn left
    \__MOVE          move ahead
   \__MOVE        move ahead
```

Appendix C: Best Code Generated in Contour Detection (Test 2)

```
|-+-PRG3    3 successive actions
 \__MOVE        move ahead
 |-+-ICAW    if contrast (c-f)
  |-+-AHRE      if already here
   |-+-ICAF        if contrast (d-e)        Steps:    41353
    \__RGHT           turn right            Contour pixels:          2378
    \__MOVE           move ahead            Pixel tested:            4178
   |-+-ICAF        if contrast (d-e)        Current parameters:
    \__LEFT           turn left             Max Operations : 90000
    \__LEFT           turn left             Min Operations : 60000
  |-+-ICAW       if contrast (c-f)          Population size: 20000
   \__MOVE          move ahead              Generations: 35
   \__RGHT          turn right              PMutation: 0.4
 |-+-ICAH    if contrast (a-b)              PCrossover: 0.9
  |-+-AHRE      if already here             Replacement: 0.4
   |-+-ICAF        if contrast (d-e)        Elapsed time: 959.262 seconds for
    \__LEFT           turn left             132147 evaluations.
    \__LEFT           turn left
   \__LEFT        turn left
  |-+-ICAF       if contrast (d-e)
   \__MOVE          move ahead
   \__MOVE          move ahead
```

Feature Extraction for the k-Nearest Neighbour Classifier with Genetic Programming

Martijn C.J. Bot

Vrije Universiteit, De Boelelaan 1081, 1081 HV Amsterdam
mbot@cs.vu.nl

Abstract. In pattern recognition the curse of dimensionality can be handled either by reducing the number of features, e.g. with decision trees or by extraction of new features.

We propose a genetic programming (GP) framework for automatic extraction of features with the express aim of dimension reduction and the additional aim of improving accuracy of the k-nearest neighbour (k-NN) classifier. We will show that our system is capable of reducing most datasets to one or two features while k-NN accuracy improves or stays the same. Such a small number of features has the great advantage of allowing visual inspection of the dataset in a two-dimensional plot.

Since k-NN is a non-linear classification algorithm[2], we compare several linear fitness measures. We will show the a very simple one, the accuracy of the minimal distance to means (mdm) classifier outperforms all other fitness measures.

We introduce a stopping criterion gleaned from numeric mathematics. New features are only added if the relative increase in training accuracy is more than a constant d, for the mdm classifier estimated to be 3.3%.

1 Introduction

For insurance companies, it would be interesting to determine the probability of a heart attack for setting the right price of a life insurance. In their application form, they ask about height and weight of persons. The degree of fatness, i.e. weight / height, might be an important indicator for this risk. This feature is not explicitly defined in the database however, only implicitly. It is conceivable that other, more complicated combinations of features are also good predictors. The process of finding these new, better features is called feature extraction.

Feature extraction is one of the key problems in pattern recognition and data-mining, since many databases contain large numbers of attributes, many of which have little to do with the classification variable. It is a process that is usually done by humans. We will demonstrate that genetic programming (GP)can successfully be used for automatic feature extraction. The tree structure of GP lends itself naturally for representing the new features.

The classification procedure is the k-nearest-neighbour (k-NN) algorithm [8]. This simple algorithm classifies a new example by measuring the "distance" to a number of other cases which are kept in memory. The class that the k-NN

J. Miller et al. (Eds.): EuroGP 2001, LNCS 2038, pp. 256–267, 2001.

predicts for this new example is that of the case which most resembles it, i.e. the one that has the smallest distance to it. Instead of taking the single nearest case, it is also possible to take a majority vote from the k nearest neighbours, hence the name. Distance can be measured in a variety of ways, but often the Euclidean distance is a good and simple measure.

Our aim is both to reduce the number of features and to increase the accuracy of k-NN on the new features. Feature reduction is achieved by looking at the relative gain in training accuracy of each additional feature. If this gain is smaller than a constant d, the last new feature isn't used and training stops. Otherwise, the GP will search for a new feature. For details on the estimation of d, see Section 3. Several fitness measures will be compared (see Subsection 3.4). We will see that huge reductions in number of features can be achieved, down to one or two features for most datasets with equally good or better accuracy. With one or two features it is possible to plot the data, thus allowing visual analysis. An extremely simple fitness measure (the accuracy of the Minimal Distance to Means classifier) will turn out to be the best.

For real life purposes it might be interesting to see how the new features found by the GP are calculated. This may say something about the importance of certain variables or about how different variables interact with respect to the output variable. We will demonstrate several discovered features.

The accuracy and reduction in number of features will be compared to that achieved by discriminant analysis [3] and principal component analysis[4].

In Section 2 some related work is described. In Section 3 more background is given about the system and about the way new features are extracted. In Section 4 the experimental setup is given. In Section 5 the results of the experiments are given and discussed. The conclusions are given in Section 6.

2   Related Work

Similar work has been done by Sherrah [11], who created a feature extraction system which uses evolutionary computation. His individuals are multi-trees, each tree encoding one feature. This means that the number of features is fixed beforehand. His system was not designed for k-NN however, but for less powerful classification techniques, such as the minimum distance to means classifier, the parallelepiped classifier and the Gaussian maximum likelihood classifier. He claims that "the classifiers must not be too powerful, otherwise they will do all the work of classification and there will be no pressure for EPrep [his system, MB] to evolve useful features" (page 104). Here we will show that the k-NN classifier can also successfully be combined with a genetic feature extraction system.

Raymer et al.[9] applied GP to improve k-NN performance without feature reduction. For each attribute, he evolved a tree which was a function of the attribute itself and zero or more constants, e.g. $2.1x^3 + 1.5x$. He applied this to one biochemistry database and claimed improvement over a similar system with a GA. No comparisons were made to other feature extraction algorithms.

Kotani et al.[5] have also applied genetic programming to feature extraction. They focus mainly on artificial datasets and on a acoustic diagnosis task, whereas we use real-life machine learning datasets. Their feature structure is unclear, but it probably allows only first- and second-order interactions between features, like in [1].

Masand et al.[7] used to GP to find additional features for one historical customer dataset used for predicting future customer behavior. They reported improved performance of C4.5 for this dataset.

Non-genetic approaches to feature extraction include work from Setiono and Liu[6, 10]. They use a neural network, the hidden layer of which encodes the new features. Performance of C4.5 on the new features is similar or better than that on the original data, while the trees are significantly smaller.

The procedure of extracting features from nominal, non-numeric data is called constructive induction. Zheng[12] compares four attribute types (conjunctive, disjunctive, M-of-N and X-of-N representations). Again, after feature extraction decision tree performance is better with smaller trees.

3   A Framework for Feature Extraction

3.1   Overview

The purpose of our research is to extract new features from the raw data. Some of the existing attributes are combined to form a new feature. We keep adding new features until a stopping criterion (Section 3.5) is met.

Our approach is a combination of greedy search and global search. The search is greedy because new features are added one by one and each new feature is the best that has been found so far. It is global because each new feature is searched for with evolutionary computation, which is by nature a global search technique.

3.2   Features

New features are constructed from the original variables by adding, subtracting, multiplying or dividing the original variables by constants and/or the other variables. Besides these operators, the Mean function has also been added which takes two or three inputs and returns their mean. The reason for the addition of this function is to make the trees more legible and possibly aid the GP in the search. The new features may be as simple as just one of the original variables or may be a complicated function of many variables and constants.

3.3   Course of Evolution

Individuals in the population are formulas that specify how a new feature should be calculated. For each additional feature, the GP is run. Suppose $n-1$ runs have already taken place. These previous $n-1$ runs have resulted in a new dataset of $n-1$ columns (the new features) plus the output column of the original data. In this run the nth column will be evolved.

The fitness score of an individual in the nth run is calculated as follows. First, for each training case the individual is "executed", i.e. the formula that is contained in the individual is calculated. The result of this is a new column that is (temporarily) added to the $n - 1$ previously added columns. The fitness of this new column is determined (see Subsection 3.4). After this calculation, the column that was added by this individual is removed again.

The usual GP evolution takes place for 10 generations. This would seem short, but experiments have indicated that more generations are not helpful. After those 10 generations, the best individual is taken. If the stopping criterion is met (see Subsection 3.5), the individual will not be used and the GP is terminated. Otherwise, the column of the individual is now definitely added to the $n - 1$ columns.

3.4   Fitness Measure

The most obvious fitness measure would be the accuracy of k-NN on the training data. Leave-one-out validation is performed for calculating this accuracy on all n columns. The distance measure is calculated on the $n - 1$ previously added features plus the new feature.

The disadvantage of this measure is that its execution time is super-linear in the number of training cases, which quickly becomes infeasible if the datasets become bigger. Therefore, we will compare two measures which take linear time in the number of training cases:

- Accuracy of the minimal distance to means (mdm) classifier. This is a very simple classification method, which calculates the mean of each class over all attributes and classifies each case by taking that mean which is closest.
- Parallelepiped classifier. This classifier builds a hyper-rectangle around all cases of each class. If a training case falls in only one hyper-rectangle, then that is its predicted class. If it falls in more than one hyper-rectangle, the class of which the centroid of the hyper-rectangle is closest, is taken.

3.5   Stopping Criterion

In order to know when to stop adding new features, a stopping criterion is needed. Our stopping criterion is based on the relative increase in training accuracy of the last new feature. If it is smaller than a constant d, the new feature is assumed not to be helpful enough (indeed, may be a cause of overtraining) and it is thrown away. Otherwise, the stopping criterion is not met, so the feature will be added and the GP continues searching for the next feature.

To illustrate our approach, let's look at Figure 1, where average training and validation accuracy of 10 runs on the Ecoli dataset is plotted for each additional feature. Clearly, after adding the fourth feature the GP can stop, because validation accuracy doesn't improve with additional features (in fact, it deteriorates). As we will in Section 5, the GP stops on average at 2.6 features, which is quite close to the optimal point. It is interesting to note that overtraining in the sense that validation accuracy drops after adding more features, does not occur. We observe that validation accuracy stays about the same, while training accuracy keeps improving. This means that the extra features are not harmful, but not helpful either.

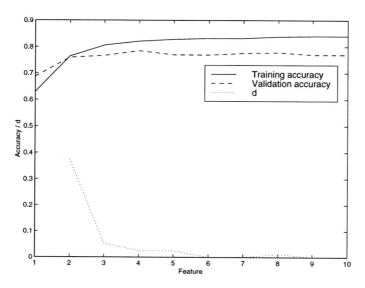

Fig. 1. Training and validation accuracy and relative increase in training accuracy (=d) for each additional feature, averaged over the 10 crossvalidation runs on the Ecoli dataset. Fitness measure was the mdm accuracy.

We have estimated the constant $\hat{d}$ by running 10 experiments on each of three randomly chosen databases. Those were Bupa, Ecoli and Pima. In each experiment, the GP was run to find 10 features. Of each additional feature, the validation accuracy is calculated. Since 10 fold crossvalidation was used, we have 30 experiments. For each of these experiments we determine d in the following way. First, we find the number of features f for which the accuracy of our classifier is highest (e.g., in the example above $f=4$). Then d is calculated from the formula:

$$d = \frac{t_f - t_{f-1}}{t_{f-1}}$$

where t_f is the training accuracy of the fth additional feature. It may happen that $f = 1$ (so the first feature has already done the job) – in such a situation d is not defined. Therefore, the final estimate of d is given by the formula:

$$\hat{d} = \frac{\sum(d|f > 1)}{\#(d|f > 1)}$$

3.6   Comparison Algorithms

The performance of the GP will be compared to the following algorithms:

- Discriminant analysis[3].
- Principal component analysis[4].
- The add-one algorithm. One by one, the best available variables are added until the improvement in training accuracy drops below its d.

4   Experiments

We used the GP system by Qureshi (GPSys)[1], which is written in Java.

The function set was $\{+, -, \times, /, \text{Mean2}, \text{Mean3}\}$. The terminal set was {Variable, Constant}. We used a tournament of size 7. Population size = 100. The number of generations = 10. Mutation rate = 10%. Maximum tree depth = 17. The initial population was created ramped half and half. We used steady state, elitist GP and 10-fold crossvalidation. k-NN has been performed with $k = 3$.

In the function set, there are two non-trivial functions, namely Mean2 and Mean3. These have been added in the hope of making the new features more legible. Mean2 is a function that takes two inputs and returns the mean of those. Mean3 does the same with three inputs.

The databases are from the Machine Learning Repository[2]. Only databases with no missing values and with numeric variables have been selected. It makes no sense to add or multiply symbolic variables. Some statistics of the datasets are given in Table 1. Note that the original Waves-dataset was much larger (5000 cases); we took a small random subset of it.

5   Results

The estimates of d (see Section 3.5) are given in Table 2. The values of d for k-NN, mdm, parallelepiped and PCA are quite consistent with each other, between 3% and 5%. The value of d for the add-one algorithm is quite high compared to the other values, but it turns out that a d of 0.04 results in almost exactly the same number of features and the same accuracy. Only with even smaller values of d does the number of features (and accuracy) change, validation accuracy generally getting worse. No value of d is optimal for all datasets, but these estimations prove to be a reasonable estimate. For some datasets, it is possible to get better performance by adding extra features or stopping earlier, but of course methodologically it is not allowed to take that number of features for which validation accuracy is optimal.

---

[1] http://www.cs.ucl.ac.uk/staff/A.Qureshi/gpsys.html
[2] http://www.ics.uci.edu/~mlearn/MLRepository.html

Table 1. Statistics of the datasets

Dataset	Nr cases	Nr variables	Nr classes
Australian	690	14	2
Bupa	345	6	2
Car	1728	5	4
Cmc	1473	9	3
Ecoli	337	7	8
German	1000	24	2
Glass	214	9	6
Ionosphere	351	34	2
Iris	150	4	3
Pima	768	8	2
Segmentation	2310	19	7
Sonar	198	60	2
Teaching	151	5	3
Waves	330	21	3
Wine	178	13	3
Yeast	1484	8	10

Table 2. Estimated values of d, see Section 3.5

Fitness measure	k-NN	Mdm	Parallelepiped	Add-one	PCA
$\hat{d}$	0.0332	0.0423	0.0437	0.1228	0.0474

In Tables 3 the results are given of the different fitness measures on all datasets. Clearly all fitness measure achieve a huge reduction in number of features, often down to only 1 or 2 features. This has the great advantage of allowing visual analysis of the dataset in a two-dimensional plot.

The mdm fitness measure achieves best performance. The fact that this classifier is so simple may actually be helpful here. The only way to optimize performance of the mdm classifier is to "pull apart" the cases in different classes so most cases of each class will be close to its mean. This is incidently also a good way to improve k-NN performance, since cases belonging to the same class will be closer together.

In Table 4, the performance is given of the comparison algorithms. In the first column the performance of the k-NN classifier is given after applying discriminant analysis on the data. The performance is on par with that of the GP with mdm fitness measure: on three datasets, the GP does better, on three others, it does worse and the rest is not statistically significantly different. Note that discriminant analysis does no feature reduction.

PCA is performed with our stopping criterion for good comparison. It does obviously much worse than the other algorithms.

The add-one algorithm performs worse than the GP in terms of accuracy. The reduction in features is larger: for all datasets it uses only one variable. Of course, for a human it would be interesting to see which one that is, but to just use one variable is clearly not enough.

The stopping criterion seems to work very well. In some preliminary runs, mdm was run for 10 features on all datasets. The resulting accuracy was slightly worse than with the stopping criterion, while of course the reduction in features is much less.

5.1 Evolved Features

To get an idea about the kind of features the GP evolves, we will look at some of the results of the 10 crossvalidation runs on the australian and the pima dataset with mdm training measure. For convenience, we will simplify the features.

Six of the 10 australian runs came up with the feature x_7. One run returned a linear combination of x_7 and x_{11}: $5.92(x_{11} + x_7) + 30.86$.

Two runs gave a second order interaction between x_7 and x_{11}:

$$(0.33x_{11} + 0.33x_7 + 0.50)^2$$

$$-1.41x_7 - 5.59x_{11} - 3.05x_7x_{11}$$

The most complicated feature was

$$\frac{x_7 - 7.29}{0.069(x_{11} + x_7) - 0.50}$$

The runs for most other datasets came up with much more complicated features. The three easiest(!) features on the pima dataset are given below. Clearly the GP "thinks" that the pima dataset requires higher order interactions than does the australian dataset.

$$(0.50x_1 + 3.13)(x_5 - 0.77)x_1^2$$

$$x_1(x_5 - 5.16)(x_1 + (x_1 - 1.34)(5.16 - x_1))$$

$$x_5\left(x_2 + \left(x_1 + x_5 + x_0\right)\left(x_5 + x_1\big((x_1 + x_5)(x_0 + x_1 + 2x_5)\big)\right)\right)$$

5.2 Timing

In Table 5 the average execution times of one run are given. All runs were on a 550 MHz Pentium III. Note that timing is sensitive to machine load, network traffic, etc. It is also dependent on the number of features evolved. The k-NN classifier is far slower than the other methods, due to its quadratic nature. The others are approximately equally fast.

Discriminant analysis is much faster than all these methods; typically the time between hitting the Enter key and the method being finished is not noticeable for a human (less than a second). On the small datasets the add-one algorithm is faster than all other algorithms, but it scales poorly to large datasets due to its non-linear training time.

In Figure 2 the average execution time of the mdm fitness measure divided by the number of features evolved is plotted as a function of the size of the datasets (number of cases). The non-linearness is caused by the validation of the best individual after each generation, which is done with the quadratic k-NN algorithm. For larger datasets, this may take a significant part of the total execution time. Deviations from the curves can be explained with differences in machine load, network traffic during the runs and in the size of the evolved features.

Table 3. Accuracy and standard deviation of k-NN on the original data; on the normalized original data; on the evolved features with k-NN, mdm and parallelepiped fitness. $\oplus$ and $\ominus$ mean statistically 95% better /worse with a paired t-test. Normalized original accuracy is tested w.r.t. non-normalized original accuracy. The GP performance is tested w.r.t. normalized original accuracy. In the columns called 'feat.' the average evolved number of features is given.

Dataset	Original accuracy	Orig. acc normalized	k-NN Accuracy	feat.	Mdm Accuracy	feat.	Parallelepiped Accuracy	feat.
Australian	59.1 9.8	81.2 $\oplus$ 4.0	83.1 6.89	1.0	82.5 10.01	1.0	80.3 10.25	1.2
Bupa	50.4 10.2	49.6 7.2	58.4 $\oplus$ 11.53	1.5	61.7 $\oplus$ 11.51	1.0	57.4 11.50	1.4
Car	81.1 5.6	84.6 $\oplus$ 4.5	79.1 $\ominus$ 8.36	1.0	73.1 $\ominus$ 8.81	1.2	81.5 10.49	2.9
Cmc	54.9 17.9	52.0 18.5	51.3 18.33	1.5	52.4 18.08	1.6	51.2 20.24	1.7
Ecoli	80.5 14.9	80.8 15.0	73.5 $\ominus$ 17.95	2.6	76.1 $\ominus$ 14.77	2.6	74.6 $\ominus$ 17.56	3.4
German	59.6 6.4	64.0 $\oplus$ 5.8	63.0 9.36	1.2	61.5 12.98	1.1	60.2 $\ominus$ 6.61	1.0
Glass	55.4 19.0	53.9 17.1	52.0 18.35	2.7	60.3 15.25	2.1	54.7 18.63	3.8
Ionosphere	74.9 9.2	74.9 9.6	80.0 6.48	1.3	83.1 $\oplus$ 8.51	1.3	76.9 12.97	1.6
Iris	92.7 6.6	92.7 6.6	94.1 7.88	1.0	95.3 7.04	1.0	92.5 7.32	1.0
Pima	66.7 8.7	70.2 $\oplus$ 4.3	69.5 6.92	1.2	68.9 7.08	1.0	70.8 7.89	1.0
Segm.	84.2 5.2	89.7 $\oplus$ 2.8	88.4 4.01	2.8	91.0 4.50	3.1	82.4 15.18	3.6
Sonar	69.9 18.5	71.8 19.6	72.2 19.08	2.3	75.5 18.83	1.3	74.2 18.34	2.4
Teaching	40.5 16.9	40.5 24.6	42.5 22.99	1.7	51.8 $\oplus$ 19.79	1.6	43.8 19.50	5.5
Waves	68.8 11.3	69.1 10.1	61.8 14.87	2.9	68.1 13.74	2.3	65.7 13.07	2.5
Wine	71.0 14.4	88.3 $\oplus$ 10.9	87.6 9.53	1.6	88.1 7.64	1.8	86.0 11.10	2.0
Yeast	48.0 6.2	48.8 5.9	41.9 $\ominus$ 8.66	2.8	46.2 $\ominus$ 4.89	3.9	41.9 $\ominus$ 5.40	3.6

6 Conclusion

Our system is capable of achieving huge reductions in the number of features, with equal of better accuracy of the k-NN classifier.

The GP performs best with mdm accuracy as fitness measure in terms of accuracy. On most datasets, one, two or three features are sufficient to attain equal or better k-NN accuracy than on the normalized original data. The fact that this classifier is so simple may actually be helpful here. The only way to optimize performance of the mdm classifier is to "pull apart" the class means so most cases of each class will be close to its mean. This is incidently also a good way to improve k-NN performance, since cases belonging to the same class will be close together.

Table 4. Performance of other techniques. The first column contains performance of k-NN after applying discriminant analysis on the data. The implementation in S-plus of discriminant analysis didn't work on two datasets, which is denoted as N/A. The second column contains PCA performance with our stopping criterion. The third column holds the performance of the Add-one algorithm (see Section 3.6). Paired t-tests were performed to compare performance with that of the GP with mdm fitness measure.

Dataset	Discr. analysis	PCA Accuracy		feat.	Add one Accuracy		feat.
Australian	81.3 7.5	58.12 ⊖	6.57	1.1	81.2	4.47	1.0
Bupa	59.0 10.4	50.71	13.02	1.8	51.8 ⊖	6.37	1.0
Car	86.8 ⊕ 3.9	62.97 ⊖	9.77	2.2	84.2 ⊕	4.42	1.0
Cmc	52.7 19.0	47.48 ⊖	20.31	1.8	51.4	18.39	1.0
Ecoli	79.9 14.6	56.23 ⊖	25.82	2.0	80.0	16.29	1.0
German	63.6 ⊕ 4.1	59.60	5.72	1.8	64.6	5.10	1.0
Glass	56.7 16.5	60.54	17.90	3.7	52.9	18.43	1.0
Ionosphere	N/A	66.00 ⊖	11.47	1.7	74.6 ⊖	10.35	1.0
Iris	89.3 9.5	85.33 ⊖	13.26	1.1	93.2	6.25	1.0
Pima	70.4 6.3	58.46 ⊖	13.83	2.0	70.5	4.79	1.0
Segmentation	N/A	71.21 ⊖	8.01	4.0	17.0 ⊖	4.95	1.0
Sonar	70.3 ⊖ 17.5	64.98	20.84	2.2	72.7	19.08	1.0
Teaching	37.9 ⊖ 23.4	40.29	16.32	1.1	45.9	23.58	1.0
Waves	54.8 ⊖ 7.9	36.97 ⊖	13.91	2.0	67.8	10.73	1.0
Wine	94.4 ⊕ 8.3	70.52 ⊖	18.85	2.0	89.9	9.60	1.0
Yeast	48.4 5.2	32.21 ⊖	4.20	3.7	49.0	5.85	1.0

Accuracy of the GP is similar to that of k-NN after discriminant analysis has been applied, but it is attained with much less features. Compared to the add-one algorithm, the GP is superior in accuracy.

The stopping criterion works very well, judging from the amount of feature reduction and the gain in accuracy. The estimated value of d is between 3 and 5% (depending on the fitness measure), meaning that if an extra feature doesn't improve training accuracy with more than this value, it is not added.

In terms of speed, discriminant analysis is easily the victor, but the GP with mdm does not do badly. As expected, using k-NN for training measure is both very slow and doesn't improve accuracy as well as does mdm.

Acknowledgements

We would like to thank Bart Craenen for his helpful suggestions regarding the stopping criterion.

Table 5. Average execution time of one run in seconds on a 550 MHz Pentium III. Note that timing is very sensitive to machine loads, type of pc, etc. and that it is also dependent on the number and size of features evolved.

Dataset	Knn	Mdm	Par.	Igain	Correlation	Add-one
Australian	2655	22	38	49	12	20
Bupa	345	11	10	10	9	1
Car	16939	86	218	80	45	64
Cmc	15320	73	154	52	39	36
Ecoli	1162	43	67	19	8	1
German	6182	36	64	44	29	107
Glass	481	19	49	13	5	1
Ionosphere	799	12	23	10	9	16
Iris	130	5	9	14	4	0
Pima	3699	24	42	29	17	7
Segmentation	58368	324	457	84	57	955
Sonar	405	7	171	6	5	11
Teaching	176	8	36	7	4	1
Waves	1189	20	31	12	3	7
Wine	236	8	14	9	4	1
Yeast	23414	309	473	77	36	62

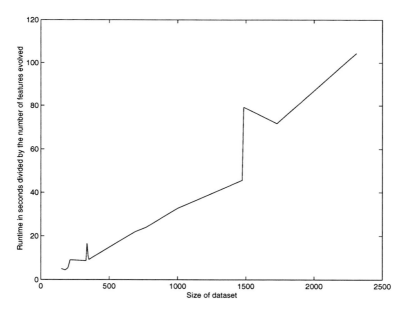

Fig. 2. Average execution time of one run with mdm divided by the number of features evolved as a function of the size of the datasets.

References

1. E.I. Chang and R.P. Lippman. Using genetic algorithms to improve pattern classification performance. In *Advances in Neural Information Processing Systems*, 1991.
2. J. Friedman, J. Bentley, and R. Finkel. An algorithm for finding best matches in logarithmic expected time. *ACM Transactions on Mathematical Software*, 3(3):209–226, 1977.
3. K. Fukunaga. *Introduction to Statistical Pattern Recognition.* Academic Press, New York, second edition, 1990.
4. J. Edward Jackson. *A User's Guide to Principal Components.* John Wiley & Sons, Inc, 1991.
5. M. Kotani, M. Nakai, and K. Akazawa. Feature extraction using evolutionary computation. In *CEC 1999*, pages 1230–1236, 1999.
6. H. Liu and R. Setiono. Feature transformation and multivariate decision tree induction. In *Discovery Science*, pages 279–290, 1998.
7. B. Masand and G. Piatetsky-Shapiro. Discovering time oriented abstractions in historical data to optimize decision tree classification. In P. Angeline and E. Kinnear Jr, editors, *Advances in Genetic Programming*, volume 2, pages 489–498. MIT Press, 1996.
8. T. Mitchell. *Machine Learning.* WCB/McGraw-Hill, 1997.
9. M. L. Raymer, W. F. Punch, E. D. Goodman, and L. A. Kuhn. Genetic programming for improved data mining: An application to the biochemistry of protein interactions. In *Proceedings GP 1996*, pages 375–380. MIT Press, 1996.
10. R. Setiono and H. Liu. Fragmentation problem and automated feature construction. In *Proc. 10th IEEE Int. Conf on Tools with AI*, pages 208–215, 1998.
11. J. Sherrah. *Automatic Feature Extraction for Pattern Recognition.* PhD thesis, University of Adelaide, South Australia, 1998.
12. Zijian Zheng. A comparison of constructive induction with different types of new attribute. Technical Report TR C96/8, Deakin University, Geelong, Australia, May 1996.

An Indirect Block-Oriented Representation for Genetic Programming

Eva Brucherseifer[1], Peter Bechtel[1], Stephan Freyer[2], and Peter Marenbach[1]

[1] Institute for Automatic Control
Landgraf-Georg-Str. 4, D-64283 Darmstadt, Germany
{eva,petbec,mali}@rt.e-technik.tu-darmstadt.de
http://www.rt.e-technik.tu-darmstadt.de
[2] BASF AG, Process Engineering Life Sciences
ZHV A015, 67056 Ludwigshafen
stephan.freyer@basf-ag.de

Abstract. When Genetic Programming (GP) is applied to system identification or controller design different codings can be used for internal
representation of the individuals. One common approach is a block-
oriented representation where nodes of the tree structure directly correspond to blocks in a block diagram. In this paper we present an indirect block-oriented representation, which adopts some aspects of the
way humans perform the modelling in order to increase the GP system's
performance. A causality measure based on an edit distance is examined
to compare the direct an the indirect representation. Finally, results from
a real world application of the indirect block-oriented representation are
presented.

1 Introduction

The aim of automation in process engineering is to enhance the reliability and
efficiency of production facilities. In order to achieve these goals computer based
simulations are helpful. For such simulations a model is required, which describes
the (dynamic) behaviour of the process of interest. In this context genetic programming can be applied to the generation of such a process model or to tasks
like controller design where a model is given and a system that stabilizes or
optimizes the process is to be found.

The choice of the right "genetic encoding" is of great importance to the
success of an evolutionary algorithm. First of all, it must guarantee that all
interesting phenotypes can be encoded. Furthermore, the way the solutions are
represented also effect the topology of the search space and therefore the fitness
landscape. A better representation can improve GP search similar to domain
specific or otherwise adapted genetic operators (Fogel and Ghozeil 1997).

The iterative strategy of evolutionary computation (EC) implies, that new
solutions always result from previous solutions by means of variation operators.
Therefore, the representation and the operators together should guarantee, that
an efficient search can be realized. For this, the genotype does not have to be

identical with the phenotype; an additional mapping even can make individuals smaller and improve search (O'Neill and Ryan 1999).

In this paper common codings for modelling or controller design, which is usually a task of symbolic regression, are discussed and a new indirect block-oriented representation is introduced. The different representations are then compared with regard to causality and potential efficiency. Finally, we present a successful application of the proposed coding to a real world problem.

2   GP Codings for Models or Controller

In order to construct a process model or a controller in mathematical form, the basic elements of mathematical expressions, i.e. operators, variables and coefficients, must be provided. The task of the evolutionary algorithms is to compose these modules to the most suitable process model.

In his fundamental work Koza (1990, pp. 37) introduced the term "symbolic regression" for the application of GP to the generation of mathematical expressions. The kind of coding Koza chose can be described as *direct equation-oriented representation*. It is *equation-oriented*, because the used function set and the terminals represent the elements of mathematical equations – numbers, variables and operators – and *direct*, because the format of the tree structure adopts the recursive parse tree structure used for numerical computations in digital computers.

Even though with these equation-oriented approaches first promising results were achieved, different codings are thinkable. Typically, for a given problem, domain specific standard approaches for models exist. A human modeller would try to utilize this knowledge by examining and extending these standard expressions rather than starting from scratch by using elementary operators like addition or multiplication for every process again. A tool for modelling or controller design should proceed in a similar way. Hence, in his recent work on controller design Koza *et al.* (2000) uses a block-oriented representation.

2.1   Direct Block-Oriented Representation

In a *direct block-oriented representation* as described in (Marenbach *et al.* 1996) the tree structure evolved by GP corresponds to the structure of a block diagram as it is widely used in control theory. The block diagram can either be in time or in frequency domain. Each node represents a block of the model. If two nodes of the tree structure are linked by a vertex this corresponds to a serial connection of the two blocks in the block diagram and is a signal path. So the signal flow in the block diagram is according to the direction from the leaves to the root of the tree structure.

As an example the block diagram in Fig. 1 (left) is represented by the tree structure depicted in Fig. 1 (right). The root of such a tree structure represents the output of the model, from which the model successively is processed to the inputs represented by the the leaves of the tree structure. An inner node defines a

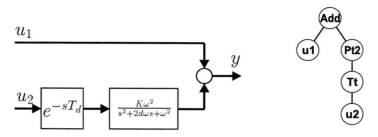

Fig. 1. Example of a model depicted as block diagram (left) and coded as tree structure (right).

block in the model with one output and at least one input. Models with multiple outputs (MIMO) can be represented by a corresponding number of trees assigned to each individual.

Special constructs in controller design are the feedback of signals or parallel signal paths (feedforward). These are realized by specialized blocks representing the input and the output of the feedback or feedforward loop.

In the equation-oriented representation parameters are nodes themselves and are constant. When complex blocks with various coefficients are used, you could represent these parameters as additional inputs to the blocks. Instead in the block-oriented representations coefficients within the blocks are separately adapted by classical parameter identification methods.

The GP tree shown in Fig. 1 results to the following differential equations with the coefficients K, ω and d:

$$\dot{x}_1(t) = x_2(t)$$
$$\dot{x}_2(t) = K u_x(t - T_d) - \omega^2 \dot{x}_1(t) + 2d\omega \dot{x}_2(t)$$
$$y(t) = u_1(t) + x_2(t)$$

These equations are used for the parameter identification and also for the simulation of the system in order to evaluate it.

The easiest form of this block-oriented representation would be the use of elementary mathematical elements (+,-,...) in time domain. This is equivalent to the equation-oriented representation, except that the parameters are not constant but can be changed by the parameter identification. Since the blocks used for the modelling can be configured the complexity of the modelling task can be varied and prior process knowledge can be implemented.

Earlier applications of this type of representation were described e. g. in (Bettenhausen and Marenbach 1995) or (Gray *et al.* 1996).

2.2   Indirect Block-Oriented Representation

Inspired by the work on so-called *cellular encoding* (Gruau 1994) we present an alternative coding for block diagrams. This time the tree structures evolved by GP describe how the block diagram is built rather than the structure itself. Therefore this coding is referred to as an *indirect block-oriented representation*.

The motivation for this new representation is the observation that when using conventional representations the variation of a tree involves very often a modification of the inputs as well. This does not reflect the way a human modeller works. He would more likely keep the inputs and vary only the system blocks instead. Another aspect is the low number of branching points. A human modeller would combinate several influences that operate in parallel by additive or multiplicative connections. In contrast the GP using direct block-oriented representation tends to build serial connections. Starting from these critical aspects the following indirect block-oriented representation was developed.

In the indirect block-oriented representation point-typing is used to distinguish between input defining branches and structure defining branches. The majority of nodes within an individual define its structure by either being a block of the block diagram, such as Pt2, or by defining the signal path, e. g. Add. So nodes either define the type of a block in the block diagram and are terminals or describe how the blocks are linked together and are part of the structure defining function set.

With each structure defining function that generates a new path within the block diagram one input defining branch is needed to specify a variable as input for the new path. As for the direct representation this variables can either be inputs to the overall model or even feedback of output variables defined by other trees within the same individual.

Two additional types of structure defining nodes are necessary to obtain the desired flexibility with the indirect representation: The structure defining function Serl generates two dummy nodes connected in serial and the terminal NOP simply replaces a dummy node by a connection.

In Fig. 2 an individual representing the model shown earlier in Fig. 1 is given as an example. New paths are always added as left branches, right branches

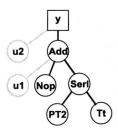

Fig. 2. Indirect block-oriented coding of the model in Fig. 1: structure defining nodes in black and input defining nodes in gray.

are the main path. Fig. 3 demonstrates step by step how the block diagram develops by subsequently interpreting the four levels of the tree structure. The dotted circles are place holders which are later replaced by the results from the referred subtrees. In the first level, there is only an output y with input u2 being the main path. Into this a new path is added by the block Add with u1 as input. Nop is part of the new path and Serl of the main path. In the fourth level the serial connection Serl is replaced by two input defining blocks, Tt and PT2. In the last step all placeholders are translated to the corresponding blocks of a blockdiagram.

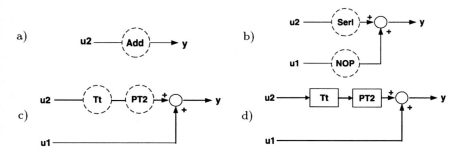

Fig. 3. Stepwise development of a block diagram with the help of dummy nodes according to the tree structure from Fig. 2.

3   Comparison of Both Representations

Search in EC is often described as a strategy of exploration and exploitation, which means that they combine local as well as global search mechanisms. Global search shall prevent from getting stuck in local optima too early. Local search on the other hand, is necessary to converge to an – global or local – optimum. In order to understand EC in more detail it is necessary to know which operation corresponds rather to a local or to a global search step respectively. Usually, one would expect that local search is performed by smaller changes of an individual and vice versa. However, as a consequence of the genotype to phenotype mapping in EC this is not necessarily true.

Rechenberg (1994, pp. 125) was the first to adopt the term *strong causality*, as it is known from physics, to the context of EC. Strong causality basically means that similar causes have similar effects. Whether these requirements can be fulfilled, is determined by the interaction of representation, fitness function and operators, because they define the topology of the search space, the roughness of the fitness landscape and the locomotion therein. At the same time causality reflects the ability to converge.

Early work on causality in GP can be found in (Iba and Sato 1992) and a more extensive analysis in (Rosca 1995). Rosca associates the existence of causality to an individuals possibility to survive in its genealogy. The focus of his work lies on the operators as well as the representations using Automatic Definition of Functions (ADF) and Hierarchical Genetic Programming (HGP).

Another method to determine causality is to correlate distances that are covered in the search space with change in fitness. In order to quantify the distance in GP it is necessary to define a measure for the similarity of tree structures. One common approach is the so-called edit distance of the traverses of two trees (e.g. O'Reilly 1997, Sendhoff *et al.* 1997). The edit distance measures the minimum number of insertions, deletions or replacements of nodes necessary to convert one individual into an other one and can be used for causality examinations in the field of GP. Igel (1998) proposed that the Levenshtein distance is an approximation of the edit distance of tree structures which can be computed easily.

Sendhoff *et al.* (1997) introduced a statistical causality measure to assess the ability to convergence of an evolutionary algorithm. It relates the differences of the genotypes and the resulting fitness differences when applying two variation operators on two individuals i and j. Considering the results of Igel (1998) and Sendhoff *et al.* (1997) we used the following statistical causality measure:

$$P(A|B) \quad \text{with} \quad A : (|\Delta F_i| < |\Delta F_j|) \quad B : (ld_i < ld_j) \quad i, j \in I\!N \quad (1)$$

If we have causal behaviour we expectfor a variation a smaller fitness difference $|\Delta F_i|$ for smaller Levenshtein distances ld_i. So a greater value of $P(A|B)$ indicates a higher causality probability[1], with a maximum of 1 and therefore a higher occurrence of causal operations.

In order to compare the block-oriented representations introduced above the modelling of two less complex processes was examined. In the first example the task was to model the kinetic rate expressions of the fermentation process of penicillin, using time series from a simplified simulation model (Bajpai and Reuß 1980) as training data for GP (further on referred to as process I). As a second example the statistic dependency of two quality measures of a chemical process on a set of up to 7 available process variables had to be found (process II). Because the focus of this section is to compare the applicability of the different representations the problem and the evolved solutions are not described in detail.

For GP we used a standard setup with standard recombination and mutation operators. Strategy parameters were chosen identically for both examples with exception of the generation size which was 50 for process I and 300 for process II.

The big number of individuals in process II (which is faster to compute) permites to have a more detailed look on the individuals in one generation. An interesting aspect can be seen in Fig. 4 showing the causality probability for three classes of individuals with high, medium and low fitness after variation for one typical run. There is a significant difference in the average of the causality probability for the different classes. Those individuals with medium fitness after their variation have a lower causality probability than the others. A reason for that might be that the change in fitness for these individuals is lower

---

[1] The probability of the counter event $P(\overline{A}|\overline{B})$, i. e. that the variation with the higher Levenshtein distance leads to higher fitness difference values, is implicitly taken into account, too.

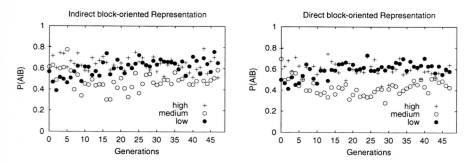

Fig. 4. Causality probabilities of process II separated in fitness classes of individuals, showing differences in causal behaviour.

than of the others for very large Levenshtein distances, which corresponds to non-causal behaviour. The higher causality measures for the class of individuals with lower fitness can be explained by the fact, that bigger structural changes often lead to models with very low assigned fitness because the numerical simulation failed. However, the most interesting result is that fitter individuals have a above-average causality probability. That means that the well-adapted individuals mainly result from causal variations.

In order to compare the overall performance of the block-oriented representations Table 1 lists the causality probability for both example processes obtained for the direct and indirect representation. Additionally, the respective values for

Table 1. Causality probabilities $P(A|B)$ obtained for both example processes using direct and indirect representation respectively compared to results of some standard GP problems, reported by (Igel 1998).

task	representation	$P(A|B)$	reference
dynamic process (I)	direct	0.59	
	indirect	0.62	
static process (II)	direct	0.54	
	indirect	0.58	
6-multiplexer	equation-oriented	0.41	(Igel 1998)
simple symbolic regression	equation-oriented	0.64	(Igel 1998)
artificial ant problem	special	0.41	(Igel 1998)

some common GP problems taken from (Igel 1998) are given. The table shows that the causality $P(A|B)$ of the block-oriented representations in the example processes are comparable to results from other problems. Generally, all computed values are higher than 0.5, which means that the search can be regarded as causal when using the block-oriented representations. Moreover, the causality is better when applying the indirect coding.

4   Real World Application of the Indirect Representation

As an example of a real world application, GP and the indirect representation discussed above was used for modelling of a fed-batch fermentation process. Such processes typically have a highly non-linear dynamic behaviour. For process development and optimization a simplified macroscopic description of this behaviour is desired, which cannot be derived from analytical reflections. The modelling of this process is a task of symbolic regression – an equation with parameters has to be found, that best fits the given data. The searched function can be written as differential equation or as block diagram, therefore the block-oriented representations can be used. Earlier work on similar processes using the direct representation can be found in (e.g. Marenbach *et al.* 1997, Freyer *et al.* 1998).

This example was part of an industrial project with the biotech company B.R.A.I.N. GmbH, Germany. Investigations took place in conjunction with the admission procedure of the biotechnical production of *mistletoe lectin* as active substance for cancer therapy. One important step of the whole synthesis is the fermentation of recombinant *Eschericha coli* bacteria. Aim of this work was to develop a simulation model of this fermentation in order to use it as a basis for process optimization.

For this fermentation two characteristic temporal phases have to be distinguished. During the first phase only cell growth but no product formation takes place. The second phase is initiated by induction of a promoter. After induction the cells start to form product while growth almost stops.

Only a few modelling approaches for this kind of processes are described in literature (e.g. Miao and Kompala 1992). Therefore, an reaction scheme was developed which is schematically depicted in Fig. 5. In order to describe the phase

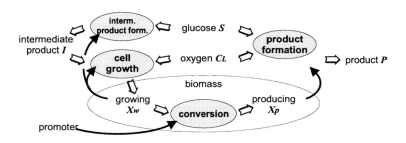

Fig. 5. Reactions considered for modelling.

transition it distinguishes between growing and producing biomass. Initially only growing biomass X_w exists which grows autocatalytically. The induction enables the conversion of X_w into producing biomass X_p. Due to the observation, that the growth continues after consumption of the main nutrient glucose, it was furthermore assumed that glucose is converted into a non-measured intermediate product I, that serves as additional basis for the growth.

Process measurements from 9 fermentations performed under varying conditions were available. Only the dissolved oxygen C_L was measured online. For biomass X, substrate (glucose) S and feed F offline determined values were used. For modelling with GP balance equations according to the scheme in Fig. 5 were provided as prior knowledge. The task for the GP system was to generate five kinetic expressions and all coefficients.

In Fig. 6 (top) the measured time courses of optical density – as a measurement for the total biomass $X = X_w + X_p$ – and of substrate for two fermentations are compared to the behaviour of the best model generated by GP. The stepwise

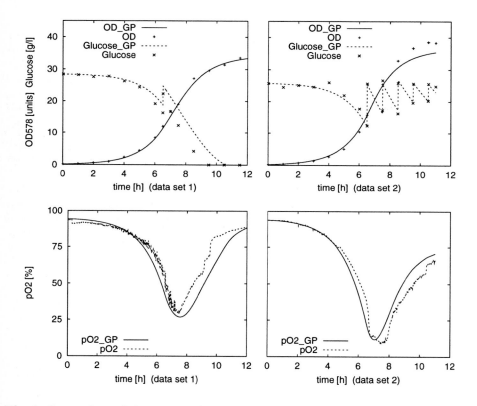

Fig. 6. Comparison of the measured optical density and glucose concentration (top) and of the dissolved oxygen (bottom) for the best model generated by GP for two different data sets (The data sets shown here were not used for training).

increases of the glucose concentration mark the time when the glucose feed occurred. The induction always took place with the first feed. In Fig. 6 (bottom), additionally, the dissolved oxygen is shown. The behaviour in all phases, i.e. before and after the induction and also after the glucose is consumed, approximates the measured data very good. However, for the acceptance of the model it is also important, that the curves of the non-measured variables are at least plausible. The time courses of the concentrations of growing and producing biomass as well as the intermediate are not shown here, but they lead to the same result that the model is realistic.

Finally, the aim of the application of GP for modelling is not only to reproduce an observed behaviour in an adequate manner, but also to obtain a transparent and understandable model. The tree structures for the five kinetics that were generated by GP are depicted in Fig. 7. The example of the specific growth rate μ (tree "mu1" in Fig. 7) demonstrates the possibility to interpret the results. The corresponding simplified mathematical formula would be

$$\mu = 0,70 \cdot \underbrace{\max\left\{0; (1 - \frac{X}{45,7})\right\}}_{X\text{-inhibition}} \cdot \left(\underbrace{\frac{C_L}{0,20 + C_L}}_{C_L\text{-limitation}} + \underbrace{\frac{I}{0,18 + I}}_{I\text{-limitation}}\right)$$

Within this expression three characteristic terms can be distinguished: inhibition of growth by high cell density as well as two limitations due to oxygen the intermediate respectively.

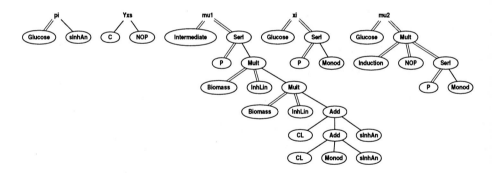

Fig. 7. Tree structure of the five kinetics as generated by GP.

The results described here were compared to earlier results obtained for similar problems using the direct coding. It was observed that the latter more often produces serial connected blocks. Overall it seems that the indirect representation forces GP to search in a way which is more similar to the strategy of a human expert. As a consequence the obtained models to an expert appear to be "more likely". Although this advantage cannot be measured it is of great importance for the acceptance of a model generated by GP.

5   Conclusion

In this paper we introduce a new indirect block-oriented representation for models or controller as an alternative to the direct coding commonly used for symbolic regression and block diagrams in GP. Results from the comparison of causality for both representations do not differ essentially. But they show a slight tendency for a superiority of the indirect approach. In a real world application, the biotechnical production process of misteltoe lectin, an accurate and compact solution could be found. This shows that the new indirect block-oriented representation supports the generation of useful and transparent models.

However, the success of the indirect representation in application suggests that for the analysis of GP further meaningful criteria for evaluation are to be found. Further investigation of the performance of GP will be conducted.

References

Bajpai, R. and Reuß, M. (1980). A mechanistic model for penicillin production. *J. Chem. Techn. Biotechn.* **30**, 332–344.

Bettenhausen, K. D. and Marenbach, P. (1995). Self-organizing modelling of biotechnological batch and fed-batch fermentations. In: *EUROSIM '95*. Elsevier Science Publishers B.V. Vienna, AT. pp. 445–450.

Fogel, D. B. and Ghozeil, A. (1997). A note on representation and variation operators. *IEEE Trans. on Evolutionary Computation* **1**(2), 159–161.

Freyer, S., Graefe, J., Heinzel, M. and Marenbach, P. (1998). Evolutionary generation and refinement of mathematical process models. In: *Eufit '98, 6th European Congress on Intelligent Techniques and Soft Computing, ELITE - European Laboratory for Intelligent Techniques Engineering*. Vol. III. Aachen, GER. pp. 1471–1475.

Gray, G. J., Murray-Smith, D. J., Li, Y. and Sharman, K. C. (1996). Nonlinear model structure identification using genetic programming. In: *Late Breaking Papers 1st Annual Conf. Genetic Programming (GP96)*. Stanford Bookstore. Stanford, CA. pp. 301–306.

Gruau, F. (1994). Neural Network Synthesis Using Cellular Encoding and the Genetic Algorithm. PhD thesis. Ecole Normale Supérieure de Lyon. France.

Iba, H. and Sato, T. (1992). Meta-level strategy learning for GA based on structured representation.. In: *Proc. 2nd Pacific Rim Int. Conf. on Artificial Intelligence*.

Igel, C. (1998). Causality of hierarchical variable length representations. In: *Proc. IEEE Int. Conf. on Evolutionary Computation*. IEEE Press. pp. 324–329.

Koza, J. (1990). Genetic programming: A paradigm for genetically breeding populations of computer programs to solve problems. Technical Report STAN-CS-90-1314. Computer Science Dept., Stanford University, CA.

Koza, J. R., Keane, M. A., Yu, J., Bennett III, F. H. and Mydlowec, W. (2000). Evolution of a controller with a free variable using genetic programming. In: *Genetic Programming, Proceedings of EuroGP'2000*. Vol. 1802 of *LNCS*. Springer-Verlag. Edinburgh. pp. 91–105.

Marenbach, P., Bettenhausen, K. D. and Freyer, S. (1996). Signal path oriented approach to generation of dynamic process models. In: *Proc. 1st Annual Conf. on Genetic Programming (GP96)*. The MIT Press. Stanford, CA. pp. 327–332.

Marenbach, P., Bettenhausen, K. D., Freyer, S., Nieken, U. and Rettenmaier, H. (1997). Data-driven structured modelling of a biotechnological fed-batch fermentation by means of genetic programming. *IMechE Proceedings I* **211**, 325–332.

Miao, F. and Kompala, D. S. (1992). Overexpression of cloned genes using recombinant Escherichia coli regulated by a T7 promoter: I. batch cultures and kinetic modeling. *Biotechnology & Bioengineering* **40**, 787–796.

O'Neill, M. and Ryan, C. (1999). Evolving multi-line compilable C programs. In: *Genetic Programming: Second European Workshop EuroGP'99*. Springer. Berlin. pp. 83–92.

O'Reilly, U.-M. (1997). Using a distance metric on genetic programs to understand genetic operators. In: *Late Breaking Papers 2nd Annual Conf. Genetic Programming (GP97)*. Stanford Bookstore. Stanford University, CA. pp. 199–206.

Rechenberg, I. (1994). *Evolutionsstrategie '94*. Verlag Frommann-Holzboog. Stuttgart.

Rosca, J. P. (1995). An analysis of hierarchical genetic programming. Technical Report 566. University of Rochester, Computer Science Department.

Sendhoff, B., Kreutz, M. and von Seelen, W. (1997). A condition for the genotype-phenotype mapping: Causality. In: *Proceedings of the Seventh International Conference on Genetic Algorithms*. Morgan Kauffmann Press. pp. 73–80.

Raising the Dead: Extending Evolutionary Algorithms with a Case-Based Memory

Jeroen Eggermont[1], Tom Lenaerts[2],
Sanna Poyhonen[3], and Alexandre Termier[4]

[1] Leiden Institute of Advanced Computer Science
Leiden University, The Netherlands
jeggermo@liacs.nl
[2] Computational Modeling Lab, Brussels Free University, Belgium
tlenaert@vub.ac.be
[3] Control Engineering Laboratory, Helsinki University of Technology, Finland
sanna.poyhonen@hut.fi
[4] Laboratoire de Recherche en Informatique, University of Paris XI, France
termier@lri.fr

Abstract. In dynamically changing environments, the performance of a standard evolutionary algorithm deteriorates. This is due to the fact that the population, which is considered to contain the history of the evolutionary process, does not contain enough information to allow the algorithm to react adequately to changes in the fitness landscape. Therefore, we added a simple, global case-based memory to the process to keep track of interesting historical events. Through the introduction of this memory and a storing and replacement scheme we were able to improve the reaction capabilities of an evolutionary algorithm with a periodically changing fitness function.

1 Introduction

Over the years evolutionary algorithms (EA) like genetic algorithms[Gol89,Mit97] or genetic programming[BNKF98,SLOA99] have been applied to a large number of problems. The major part of these problems were concerned with learning or optimisation in a static environment. A major characteristic of static environments is that the mapping between the solution encodings and their respective fitnesses is always the same. Once the optimal solution is evolved, it will always remain the optimal solution. This is opposed to biological evolution where the different players must evolve in a changing or dynamic environment. In other words the mappings between the solution encodings and their respective fitnesses changes over time.

We can distinguish two types of dynamic problems: periodic and non-periodic dynamic problems. The first type of problems presents an EA with recurring changes in the mapping between encoding and fitness. The second case is much more difficult since there is no recurring pattern in the fitness changes.

J. Miller et al. (Eds.): EuroGP 2001, LNCS 2038, pp. 280–290, 2001.

In this paper we will focus on the periodically changing functions and the performance of an EA in this changing fitness landscape. Moreover we will extend the EA with a simple, global case-based memory to improve its tracking capabilities. This technique can be combined with a genetic algorithm or genetic programming. Although both EAs can be used to examine the possibilities of a global case-based memory we will focus on a simple, standard genetic algorithm because of its simplicity and because we believe that the results obtained from this study will have a similar impact on genetic programming. We will prove this point in later work.

The content of this paper is as follows. In Section 2 we will discuss the context and provide the motivation for our algorithm. Then, in Section 3, we will describe an instance of the type of problems we used to perform experiments. Although only one problem instance is examined, the results can be extended to all similar instances. Afterwards we examine the abstract workings of our algorithm. In Section 5 we present the results. Finally, in Section 6, we discuss all results and elaborate on what we need to improve or investigate for periodic and non-period dynamic problems.

2   Context

Current literature contains two important research branches that form the context for this paper.

The first branch is the research in artificial co-evolution where the EA configuration is transformed into an interactive system. Research conducted by for instance D. Hillis and J. Paredis incorporates predator-prey interactions to evolve solutions for static problems[Hil92,Par97]. The EA configuration used to evolve a solution for these static problems is transformed to an interactive, co-evolutionary system to overcome the evaluation bottleneck of the EA. This evaluation bottleneck is caused by the number of the test-cases against which each individual has to be tested in order to find the optimal solution. In order to reduce the number of evaluations per individual they introduce a second population which contains a subset of the test cases (problems). These problems may evolve in the same fashion as the solutions. As a result their algorithm creates an arms-race between both populations, i.e. the population of problems evolves and tries to outsmart the population of solutions. A major problem in this co-evolutionary approach is memory[Par99]. The population of solutions tries to keep up with problems but its genetic memory is limited to the knowledge that is available in the population. If after a large number of generations the population of problems evolves back to an earlier genetic configuration there is a big chance that the population of solutions does not remember how it could win against those problems.

The second branch contains the work by for instance D. Goldberg and C. Ryan[GS87,Rya97]. Instead of creating a dynamic system, they investigate the performance of an EA on fitness functions which exhibit periodic changes in their fitness landscape. At certain time intervals the mapping between the solution encodings and their respective fitnesses changes. When using an EA, the algorithm will evolve towards the first temporary optimum. When the optimum changes the population is almost completely converged, depending on the length of time the optimum remains the same, and does not contain enough information to react swiftly to this change. Again the problem is memory. An example of this type of problems is used for our experiments and explained in Section 3.

Thus, to overcome the described memory problem, the EA has to be enhanced with some form of long-term memory since the population is not a sufficient memory by itself. As a result, the enhanced EA can use interesting solutions from the past in the search for a new optimum. This long-term memory can be introduced in different ways and can be classified into two groups depending on the level of incorporation: local and global (long-term) memory. Examples of local memory are D. Golbergs work on diploid genetic algorithms[GS87], C. Ryans work on polygenic inheritance[Rya97] and Paredis' LTFE paradigm which extends each individual with a memory containing information on its success at previous encounters of "prey"-problems[Par97]. An example of global memory is C. Rosins Hall of Fame (HOF) which he used in his research on co-evolution and game-playing[Ros97b]. This HOF stores individuals which were good in the past in order to remember how to play certain games in the future. A good survey on the application of EAs to dynamically changing fitness functions can be found in[Bra99]. In this paper we focus on a global long-term memory comparable to Rosins HOF and we will investigate the capabilities of this memory to track periodic changes in a fitness landscape.

3   Periodically Changing Problems

Table 1. The objects and associated weights and values for the 0-1 knapsack problem.

Object n°	Value	Weight	Object n°	Value	Weight
0	2	12	9	10	7
1	3	6	10	3	4
2	9	20	11	6	12
3	2	1	12	5	3
4	4	5	13	5	3
5	4	3	14	7	20
6	2	10	15	8	1
7	7	6	16	6	2
8	8	8			

As indicated in Section 1 we will focus on periodically changing fitness functions. A good example of such a function is the 0-1 knapsack problem adapted by D. Goldberg[GS87]. This problem requires us to make a selection from a number of items and put them in a knapsack which can only contain a particular number of elements. The number of elements which can be loaded into the knapsack is constrained by the weight of the items. Now, the goal of this problem is to put as many items as possible into the knapsack making sure that the maximum weight is not exceeded. To make this problem dynamic, D. Goldberg forced the maximum allowed weight to change after a fixed number of generations. In this particular problem the oscillations occur every 15 generations. Goldberg varied the maximum allowed weights between 80% and 50% of the total weight which corresponds to the weights 100 and 61 with the maximum fitnesses 87 and 71 respectively. The objects and their associated weights and values can be found in Table 1. The genotype of the evolutionary algorithm will be a binary string of length 17. Each position in this binary string can have the values 0 or 1. This value indicates whether or not the item that matches with this position is in the knapsack.

Goldberg used a simple genetic algorithm to perform his experiments. He demonstrated that the simple genetic algorithm is not able to track the changes in the 0-1 knapsack problem in an optimal way[GS87]. The population converges to the optimal genotype for the 80% constraint case but looses all meaning for the 50% case. The reason for this is that elements which are good for the 80% case are infeasible solutions for the 50% case. Which means that if the population is more or less converged to solutions for the 80% constraint all elements will encode a higher weight than is allowed for the 50% case. When the maximum allowed weight changes to 61, all previous solutions become infeasible since they try to store to much in the knapsack.

In order to better examine the possibilities of our global long-term memory we parameterised Goldbergs problem further. We conducted experiments varying: the number of allowed maximum weights and the order of the allowed maximum weights. Also, to keep things simple we use a genetic algorithm to perform our experiments.

1. The number of allowed maximum weights is varied to examine the scalability of our method. When it performs good on a function with two oscillating periods there is no guarantee that it will also perform well on one with three or four periods.
2. The order of the allowed maximum weights can vary to examine the importance of order on the performance of the global memory. It is possible that the order of the different fitness maxima has an influence on the performance of the evolutionary process. This could be due to the encoding of the genotype.

4   Incorporating a Case-Based Memory

In Section 2 we discussed that the problem of an EA in a dynamic environment is memory. To overcome the problem we incorporate a global case-based memory into the evolutionary process. The goal of this case-based memory is to collect information about the encountered optima during the evolutionary process.

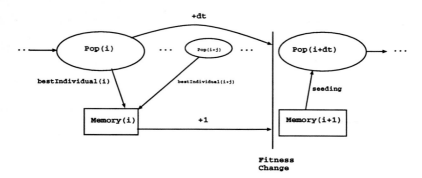

Fig. 1. Abstract representation of the new evolutionary process

The introduction of a case-based memory is actually a form of long-term elitism. Elitism forces the EA to maintain the best element of every generation so the current optimum will never be lost. In our case the case-based memory stores these elitists and reintroduces them when the time is right. We believe that this simple approach can improve the exploration capabilities of the EA when convergence has taken place.

In Figure 1 the entire process is visualised. At each generational step, the EA tries to optimise the current fitness function. After every attempt one or more individuals of that generation are added to the case-based memory. When a fitness change occurs, the elements of the case-based memory are re-evaluated and one or more of them are reintroduced in the population.

There are a number of primary decisions that need to be made. These primary decisions will influence the possibilities of the case-based memory. Especially, they will influence how advanced this memory will be.

1. *Which elements will be added to the case-based memory?* Currently, the decision was made to present the best element in a generation to the case-based memory. The best individual is added when it does not already exist in the memory. We only store the genotype and fitness information.
2. *What kind of structure will we use for the case-based memory?* In this paper we simply used a small population as representation for the case-based memory. In later work we will look further at alternative structures. As with the population, the case-based memory size is fixed. We use a strategy called the *least recently used* strategy (LRU) when removing elements from the case-based memory to add a new individual[SG98].
3. *How will the elements be reintroduced in the population?* Again we wanted to use a simple strategy to get a better understanding of the possibilities of the case-based memory. Two simple strategies, random and non-random replacement, will be compared to the standard genetic algorithm with elitism in the experiments. Random replacement just seeds the population with all the elements in the memory, i.e. if k is the number of elements in the memory, then those k elements replace k randomly chosen individuals in the

Table 2. Main parameters of the evolutionary algorithm.

Parameter	Value
Algorithm type	generational GA with elitism
Population size	150
Parent selection	Fitness proportionate selection
Stop condition	1000 generations
Mutation type	bit-flip mutation
Mutation probability	0.1
Crossover type	One-point crossover
Crossover probability	0.8

population. Non-random replacement removes the worst genotypes from the population and seeds the population with the better elements from the case-based memory. The best element in the memory is determined by evaluating the elements contained in the memory.

Next to these primary decisions, there are a number of secondary questions which require an answer.

1. *What will the size be of the case-based memory?* In order not to slow down the EA process the size of the case-based memory can not be to large. Since the elements also need re-evaluation. We decided to use a case-based memory with a maximum size of 10% of the population size. The maximum size is not always reached during the evolutionary process.
2. *When will we add the points to the case-based memory and when will we reintroduce the elements into the population?* In the knapsack problem we can easily use the case-based memory every 15 generations since there is a fitness change at those points. But in reality we do not know when the change will take place. So it could be wiser to use the case-based memory every generation. Further, we decided to reintroduce the individuals stored in the case-based memory every time the best fitness drops. This can occur at any point during the evolutionary process and does not have to occur every 15 generations.

5   Experiments

To evaluate the usefulness of the case-based memory we used the periodically changing 0-1 knapsack problem described in Section 3. As explained, we adapted the evaluation function to be able to vary the number of periods and the order of the periods. The EA we used was a standard genetic algorithm with elitism, but again, this could also be some genetic programming or other EA configuration.

The goal is to react as fast as possible to an oscillation. We will therefore examine the response time of the population through the performance of the best individual in the population. The response time is measured through the mean % tracking error. A tracking error is a value which measures the difference between the optimal fitness and the current best fitness. The entire population does not have to track the changing fitness landscape. Also, when calculating the mean % tracking error over all experiments, the standard deviation is important since a small standard deviation is better than a large one. A very small standard deviation shows that the algorithm is able to track the changing fitness function very closely.

In Table 2, the standard parameters for the experiments are described. For each experiments 100 separate runs were performed. For each run, the error resulting from the difference between the best individual in the population and the maximum fitness is collected and these values are used to calculate the mean % tracking error over all 100 runs. These tracking errors and standard deviations can be found in Table 3. In order to compare the tracking errors in a statistically correct way, we removed the trend from the error-data. Since we are only interested in the behaviour of the EA in tracking the changing optimum we calculated the mean % tracking error on the error values of the last 800 generations hence removing the evolutionary trend.

Table 3. Resullts for the dynamic 0-1 knapsack problem (example runs for the entries with * are shown in Figure 2, 3 and 4)

Periods (= max. weight)	Technique	Mean % track error	Stdev
{100, 61}*	SGA+elitism	3.7018	2.0452
	SGA+Mem(random)	0.0638	0.2503
	SGA+Mem(non-random)	0.0244	0.13
{61, 100}	SGA+elitism	2.5523	0.9930
	SGA+Mem(random)	0.0051	0.0504
	SGA+Mem(non-random)	0.0001	0.0007
{100, 61, 30}*	SGA+elitism	9.5358	0.7725
	SGA+Mem(random)	0.4566	0.4598
	SGA+Mem(non-random)	0.0706	0.1915
{30, 61, 100}	SGA+elitism	17.0504	2.8023
	SGA+Mem(random)	0.6467	0.7169
	SGA+Mem(non-random)	0.5725	0.7382
{100, 61, 30, 8}*	SGA+elitism	30.0398	1.27
	SGA+Mem(random)	5.0635	7.4957
	SGA+Mem(non-random)	4.0766	6.2624
{8, 30, 61, 100}	SGA+elitism	36.0144	2.0562
	SGA+Mem(random)	33.3807	6.7875
	SGA+Mem(non-random)	34.1175	7.7239

From the results in the table it is clear that, by introducing the case-based memory, the tracking capabilities of the standard genetic algorithm are dramatically improved. In order to compare the obtained results for the different EA

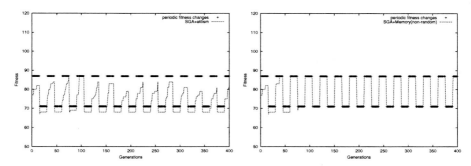

Fig. 2. Example run: Best fitness plot for the 2 periodic 0-1 knapsack problem (left: SGA, right: SGA+Mem(non-random))

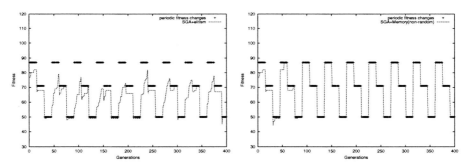

Fig. 3. Example run: Best fitness plot for the 3 periodic 0-1 knapsack problem (left: SGA, right: SGA+Mem(non-random))

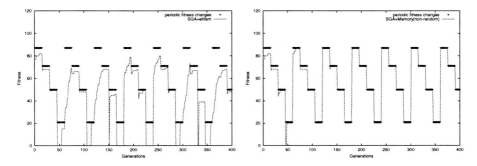

Fig. 4. Example run: Best fitness plot for the 4 periodic 0-1 knapsack problem (left: SGA, right: SGA+Mem(non-random))

configurations we used the student's t-test [Ros97a]. In Table 4 the results of this statistical test are reported.

Table 4. Results Student's t-test on the data in Table 3

	{100, 61}			{61, 100}			{100, 61, 30}		
	SGA	RAN	NRA	SGA	RAN	NRAN	SGA	RAN	NRAN
SGA	0	17.66	17.94	0	25.62	25.7	0	100.9	118.92
RAN	17.66	0	1.4	25.62	0	0.98	100.9	0	7.75
NRAN	17.94	1.4	0	25.7	0.98	0	118.92	7.75	0

	{30, 61, 100}			{100, 61, 30, 8}			{8, 30, 61, 100}		
	SGA	RAN	NRAN	SGA	RAN	NRAN	SGA	RAN	NRAN
SGA	0	56.71	56.86	0	32.85	40.63	0	3.71	2.37
RAN	56.71	0	0.72	32.85	0	1.01	3.71	0	0.72
NRAN	56.86	0.72	0	40.63	1.01	0	2.37	0.72	0

6   Conclusion and Future Work

Based on all the data we produced from the experiments we can conclude that the introduction of a simple case-based memory in an EA improves the performance of the algorithm in periodically changing environments. As one can see in Table 3 the mean % tracking error of the best individual in the population is much lower when using even this simple case-based memory. To verify whether or not there is a significant difference between the obtained results we performed the students t-test[Ros97a]. In Table 4 the results of this test are shown for every EA combination. From these resuls, we can conclude that the case-based memory approach is significantly better than the simple EA. Also, when examining the standard deviation values we see that the enhanced form of the EA tracks the periodical changes closer that the standard form. When comparing the random and non-random approach, the difference isn't significant anymore. But, these conclusions are not always true and it seems that the order of the optima is a crucial factor here, as can be seen in Table 3 for the experiment with periods {8, 30, 61, 100}. Also, the standard deviations for the last two experiments are much bigger than that of the standard genetic algorithm.

Although we now have information about the possibilities of a simple case-based memory for an EA some extra work has to be done. For instance, we also need to investigate what the influence is of the length between the fitness changes. The length between the fitness changes will determine how converged the population will be when the change occurs. We need to perform experiments on this to know how well our algorithm is able to seed the population with past information in order to increase the diversity required for the exploration of an EA. Further, since the size of the case-based memory is limited, it might be possible that, when the length between changes is much larger than the memory, we loose good information.

The case-based memory is now only used when a fitness change occurs. It might be useful to use the memory every generation since we do not always know when such a fitness change occurs. Also, the seeding and selection process are very simple strategies. Alternatives to these strategies have to be investigated and compared to the results and performance of the currently used EA configurations. Some work has already been conducted in this area but no real important results have surfaced yet.

Further, this simple memory can be extended with a meta-learner which tries to learn which elements are the most suited to seed the population. Such a meta-learner could be based on simple regression or some simple machine learning technique. As a result of extending the case-based memory with a meta-learner, we might be able to predict the best seed for future use.

As was mentioned in Section 1, next to periodically changing fitness functions there exist non-periodical ones. The case-based memory might also be useful in this context because it seeds the converged population with new information. Important will be how the population will be seeded and which information of the memory will be used. In this case, a meta-learner might come in handy since it would allow us to predict which individual improves the search process.

finally we need to incorporate the global case-based memory into other EAs in order to examine the generality of the solution.

Acknowledgement

The work presented in this paper was performed at the First COIL Summerschool at the University of Limerick. This summer-school lasted five days. The attendants were divided in groups and were assigned a problem which they had to solve with the techniques discussed in the first days. Our group was assigned the problem of dynamically changing fitness functions. This paper discusses our solution. Through this publication we would like to thank and congratulate the organisers, especially J. Willies and C. Ryan, for their excellent work. To implement the experiments we used the C++ library Evolutionary Objects[Mer,KMS]. Information on how to use the library was given by M. Keijzer who was also our supervisor at the summer-school. We want to thank him for the help and advice he gave us.

References

[BNKF98] W. Banzhaf, P. Nordin, R.E. Keller, and F.D. Francone. *Genetic Programming: an introduction.* Morgan Kauffman, 1998.

[Bra99]   J. Branke. Evolutionary approaches to dynamic optimization problems; a survey. *GECCO Workshop on Evolutionary Algorithms for Dynamic Optimization Problems*, pages 134–137, 1999.

290   Jeroen Eggermont et al.

[Gol89]   D. Goldberg. *Genetic Algorithms in Search, Optimization and Machine Learning*. Addison-Wesley, 1989.
[GS87]   D.E. Goldberg and R.E. Smith. Nonstationary function optimization using genetic algorithms with dominance and diploidy. *2nd International Conference on Genetic Algorithms*, pages 59–68, 1987.
[Hil92]   W. Hillis. Co-evolving parasites improve simulated evolution as an opimization procedure. *Artificial Life II*, pages 313–324, 1992.
[KMS]   M. Keijzer, J.J. Merlo, and M. Schoenauer, editors. *Evolutionary Objects*. http://sourceforge.net/projects/eodev/.
[Mer]   J.J. Merelo, editor. *EO Evolutionary Computation Framework*. http://geneura.ugr.es/~jmerelo/EO.html/.
[Mit97]   M. Mitchell. *An Introduction to Genetic Algorithms*. A Bradford Book, MIT Press, 3th edition, 1997.
[Par97]   J. Paredis. Coevolutionary algorithms. *The Handbook of Evolutionary Computation*, 1997.
[Par99]   J. Paredis. Coevolution, memory and balance. *International Joint Conference on Artificial Intelligence*, pages 1212–1217, 1999.
[Ros97a] W.A. Rosenkrantz. *Introduction to Probability and Statistics for Scientists and Engineers*. Mc. Graw-Hill, series in Probability and Statistics, 1997.
[Ros97b] C. Rosin. *Coevolutionary Search among Adversaries*. PhD thesis, University of California, San Diego, 1997.
[Rya97]   C. Ryan. Diploidy without dominance. *3rd Nordic Workshop on Genetic Algorithms*, pages 63–70, 1997.
[SG98]   A. Silberschatz and P. Galvin. *Operating System Concepts*. Wiley, 5 edition, 1998.
[SLOA99] L. Spector, W.B. Langdon, U.-M. O'Reilly, and P.J. Angeline, editors. *Advances in Genetic Programming*, volume 3. MIT Press, 1999.

Layered Learning in Genetic Programming for a Cooperative Robot Soccer Problem

Steven M. Gustafson[1] and William H. Hsu[2]

[1] ASAP Group, School of Computer Science & IT, University of Nottingham
Jubilee Campus, Nottingham, NG8 1BB, UK
smg@cs.nott.ac.uk
[2] Department of Computing and Information Sciences
Kansas State University, Manhattan, KS 66502, USA
bhsu@cis.ksu.edu

Abstract. We present an alternative to standard genetic programming (GP) that applies *layered learning* techniques to decompose a problem. GP is applied to subproblems sequentially, where the population in the last generation of a subproblem is used as the initial population of the next subproblem. This method is applied to evolve agents to play keepaway soccer, a subproblem of robotic soccer that requires cooperation among multiple agents in a dynnamic environment. The layered learning paradigm allows GP to evolve better solutions faster than standard GP. Results show that the layered learning GP outperforms standard GP by evolving a lower fitness faster and an overall better fitness. Results indicate a wide area of future research with layered learning in GP.

1 Introduction

For complex problems, such as robotic soccer [5][11], genetic programming (GP) may not be capable of finding a solution in its standard form. One reason is that the GP search space grows so large that it effectively leads to an intractable problem [17]. GP was previously used for robotic soccer to evolve teams of agents, but modifications were usually made to simplify the problem. Luke used GP to evolve high-level team strategies in [9], and Andre and Teller developed a fitness function based on human coaching principles of soccer in [1]. In a multiagent system (MAS) such as soccer, there is a definite hierarchy of behaviors that can be observed from human soccer. GP produces hierarchical programs by evolving and using automatically defined functions (ADF).

Koza gives a good description of ADFs and hierarchical programs in [7]. Hierarchical programs are evolved using ADFs to allow for code structure and code reuse. Rosca and Ballard, in [12], discuss ADFs and their importance in hierarchical programs. Although ADFs allow for the GP individuals to reuse evolved subprograms and develop solutions that have hierarchical code structure, they do not explicitly allow for *hierarchical learning* to take place. The distinction is that hierarchical learning describes a way in which behaviors are learned, not necessarily in how the code that represents them is structured. While code reuse

J. Miller et al. (Eds.): EuroGP 2001, LNCS 2038, pp. 291–301, 2001.

and program structure may help to overcome the inherent complexity of MAS problems, we suggest an approach for learning cooperative behaviors in a team-based MAS that is based upon primitive team objectives.

In many cases, teamwork can be made more tractable to learning, both in efficiency and in robustness of the performance element through a logical decomposition of the main problem [18]. For example, in the robotic soccer domain Stone and Veloso in [13] produce a very effective team of agents playing soccer by learning the overall task in a hierarchical manner. Tasks such as passing and kicking were learned before overall team strategies were learned. This technique of learning in layers is called *layered learning* and is formally described in [14]. It was applied with reinforcement learning for robotic soccer and the results indicated that layered learning may be a good adaptation for other machine learning methods such as GP.

To investigate layered learning in GP, the problem of learning keep-away soccer is chosen for its similarities to soccer and its properties of being a MAS problem. Also, keep-away soccer presents GP with a more reasonable search space than the full soccer problem and should allow for standard GP to find a solution so that comparisons can be made with the hybrid method of layered learning in GP.

Figure 1 is a screen capture of the visualization program used for the simulator built for keep-away soccer. The figure depicts the three offensive agents passing the ball in a counterclockwise motion (agent 3 passes the ball twice), with the trail of the ball denoted by the '-' character. The "*", "+", and ";" show the paths of other agents. The visualization was run for about 30 timesteps to collect the screen capture.

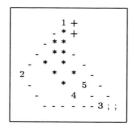

Fig. 1. Screen capture of simulator. 1,2, and 3 are offensive agents. 4 is the defender, and 5 is the ball. Ball moves from 3 to 1, 1 to 2, 2 to 3, and back towards 1.

Several variations exist for MAS and keep-away soccer can be categorized as multiagent learning with homogenous, noncommunicating agents [16]. This type of MAS problem requires robust solutions and is an interesting problem for research. A natural way to reduce complex, MAS problems, such as keep-away soccer, could prove to be useful for other MAS problems.

The keep-away soccer problem is described in Section 2, followed by a more detailed analysis of the application of layered learning to GP in Section 3. Section

4 describes experiments using an abstracted version of the TeamBots and Soc-cerServer robotic soccer simulator. Results are in Section 5 and research findings, conlusions, and future work follow.

2   Keep-Away Soccer

The RoboCup competition is an excellent testbed for MAS and are of inter-est to a wide variety of MAS research areas [4][3][19]. RoboCup competition occurs with real robots and in a simulation league, which presents several inter-esting challenges for researchers. Reinforcement learning, hierarchical sensing, neural networks, genetic programming, and a variety of hybrid combinations have been previously applied to the RoboCup simulation league [15][18] and real robot leagues. However, hand-coded and hybrid learning still outperform purely learned agent strategies. This poses a continuing challenge to researchers.

In keep-away soccer three offensive agents are located on a rectangular field with a ball and a defensive agent. The defensive agent is twice as fast moving as the offensive agents, and the ball can move, when passed, twice the speed of the defensive agent. This is similar to the predator-prey problem in [10] where more than one agent is required to solve the problem. The problem in keep-away soccer is to minimize the number of times the ball is turned over to the defender. A turnover occurs every time step that the defender is within one grid unit of the ball. Thus, the objective for offensive agents is to continously move and pass the ball to other offensive agents to keep the ball away from the defender and minimize turnovers.

Soccer, whether analyzing it as a human game or robotic game, can be broken down into subproblems of optimizing skills like ball control, passing, and moving. Keep-away soccer can be decomposed in the same manner. For the experiments here, we think of keep-away soccer as two layers of behaviors: passing accurately to other offensive agents with no defender agent present, and moving and passing with a defender to minimize the number of turnovers that occur in a game. The two layers of behaviors come from a human-like view of learning soccer, but are not heavily dependent on domain knowledge. These two types of behaviors are important to play good keep-away soccer, but these behaviors are not necessarily ways to measure the effectiveness of a team of agents who have just played keep-away soccer, which would be useful for finding a fitness function.

The layered learning application to GP is presented next, as we explain why keep-away soccer is a good test bed that illustrates its benefits.

3   Layered Learning

Applying the layered learning paradigm to a problem consists of breaking that problem into a bottom-up hierarchy of subproblems. When the subproblems are solved in order, where each previous subproblem's solution leads to the next subproblem's solution, the original problem is eventually solved. This type of hierarchical solution is different than the hierarchical solution ADFs propose to find, which focus on code reuse and structure, not on how subtasks are learned.

Problems that attempt to simulate human behaviors, such as robotic soccer and keep-away soccer, lend themselves well to a bottom-up decomposition. The reason for this is because human learning usually occurs in a bottom-up fashion of first learning the smaller tasks needed to solve a larger task. In fact, when the problem is of this type and we are already using a biologically motivated method like GP, it seems very natural to use a bottom-up decomposition of the problem that simulates human learning and allows GP to learn each one of the smaller problems.

Table 1 is a modified version of the table found in [14]. Each key principle of layered learning is correlated with a property of genetic programming for keep-away soccer showing why the application of layered learning is natural and possibly beneficial to this type of problem and solution.

Table 1. Key principles of layered learning and the GP keep-away soccer correlation.

Layered Learning	Genetic Programming
1. Learning from raw input is not tractable	$\Rightarrow$ MAS problems for GP are complex problems
2. A bottom-up decomposition is given	$\Rightarrow$ Human-like learning problems have a natural bottom-up decomposition
3. Learning occurs independantly at each level	$\Rightarrow$ GP applied to each layer is independent
4. The output of one layer feeds the next layer's input	$\Rightarrow$ The population in the last generation of one layer is the next layer's initial population

When we modify standard GP for layered learning, we need to decide what the learning objective at each layer is, i.e., the fitness at each layer that drives the search for ideal individuals. As seen in [9], using a single-objective fitness value often leads to the best performance, and is much easier than trying to define multi-objective fitness functions. While multiobjective fitness functions should allow GP to evolve more complex behaviors, it becomes difficult to decide what the multiobjective fitness should be and how important each fitness is to the solution. If one fitness is clearly more important than another, it is necessary to decide to what proportion that fitness is more important. While using a multi-objective fitness is a possibility, using a singule-objective fitness seems logical for layers of a layered learning system that represents a decomposition of a larger problem.

The last issue to address for layered learning in GP is that of transferring the population of the last generation of the previous layer to the initial population of the next generation. Because the ideal team will consist of individuals with high fitness on the coordinated MAS task, and in every population there are certain individuals that have a better fitness than others, we might want to copy that best individual many times to fill the initial population of the next layer. However, this duplication removes the diversity that was evolved from the previous layer, which seems counterintuitive, because the best individual may only be a suboptimal solution. Therefore, we propose two experiments with layered learning GP, one that duplicates the best individual and one that simply copies the entire population.

4   Experiments

Four initial experiments were chosen to investigate the performance of layered learning GP, standard GP (**SGP**), GP with ADFs (**ADFGP**), layered learning GP with the best individual duplicated to fill initial populations (**LL1GP**), and layered learning GP with the entire last population copied for the next initial population (**LL2GP**). SGP and ADFGP use the single fitness function of minimizing the number of turnovers that occur in a simulation. ADFGP allows each tree for kicking and moving to each have two additional trees that represent ADFs, where the first ADF can call the second ADF, and both have access to the full function set, as in SGP. LL1GP and LL2GP both have two layers, the first layer's fitness function is to maximize the number of accurate passes, and the second layer's fitness function is to minimize the number of turnovers.

Six variations of each experiment were developed that use standard GP parameter settings as described in [7] and vary the maximum generations allowed per run and the population size. Maximum generation values are 51 and 101, and population sizes of 1000, 2000, and 4000 are used. Six different runs are done for each type of experiment, SPG, ADFGP, LL1GP and LL2GP. The stopping criterion of each run is when an ideal fitness is found, a fitness equal to 0 or the maximum generation is reached. The genetic operators crossover and reproduction create 90 and 10 percent of the next generation, respectively. Tournament selection is used of size 7 with maximum depth 17. Table 2 summarizes the function set used and is similar to function sets used in [9] and [1]. Terminals are vectors, egocentric, or relative, to the agent whose tree is being evaluated, and all functions operate on and return vectors.

The GP system used was developed by Luke and is called Evolutionary Computation in Java [8] (ECJ). The simulator designed for keep-away soccer abstracts some of the low-level details of agents playing soccer from the Team-Bots [20] environment, which abstracts low-level details from the SoccerServer [2]. Abstractions of this type would allow the keep-away soccer simulator to be incorporated later to learn strategies for the TeamBots environment and the SoccerServer.

In the SoccerServer and TeamBots, players push the ball to maintain possession. To kick the ball, the player needs to be within a certain distance. For keep-away soccer, we eliminate the need for low-level ball possession skills and allow offensive agents to have possession of the ball. Once an agent has possession, possession is only lost when the ball is kicked, according to the evaluation of the agent's kick tree. Because we used vectors that have direction and magnitude, this implementation would allow for dribbling actions to be learned where the agent simply passes the ball a few units away. This abstraction greatly simplifies the problem and still allows for a wide range of behaviors to be learned.

At each simulation step that allow agents to act, if the agent has possession of the ball (i.e. the agent is on top of the ball in the grid) the agent's kick tree is evaluated. The kick tree evaluates to a vector that gives direction and distance to kick the ball. Otherwise, the agent's move tree is evaluated. Table 2 gives the terminals, functions, and their description.

For layered learning experiments, 40 percent of the maximum number of generations are spent in layer 1 learning accurate passing without a defender present. To evaluate accurate passes, we count the number of passes which are passed to a location that is within 3 grid units of another agent. The fitness is then $200 - passes$, 200 timesteps in a simulation and a fitness of 0 is best and 200 the worst. The remaining 60 percent of generations are spent in layer 2 with a fitness value based on the number of turnovers that occur with a defender present. The defender uses a hand coded stratey and always moves towards to the ball to cause a turnover.

Table 2. Keep-away soccer terminal (egocentric vectors) and function set

terminals	functions(args)	Description
defender	rotate90(1)	rotate current vector 90 degrees counter-clockwise
mate1	random(1)	new random magnitude between 0 and current value
mate2	negate(1)	negate vector magnitude
ball	div2(1)	divide vector magnitude by 2
	mult2(2)	multiply vector magnitude by 2
	vadd(2)	add two vectors
	vsub(2)	substract two vectors
	iflte(4)	if v1 < v2 then v3, else v4 (comparing magnitudes)

Each evaluation of an individual in the simulator takes 200 timesteps, where the ball can move on each step, the defender moves on every other step, and all offensive agents move together on every fourth timestep. The initial setup of the simulation places the defender agent in the middle of a 20 by 20 unit grid. The field is then partitioned into three sections, the top half and the bottom left and right halves. Offensive agents are placed randomly within those sections, one in each, and the ball is placed a few units from one of the offensive agents, chosen at random.

Early runs of the system resulted in local optima being achieved; the most common was all the offensive agents crowding the ball and preventing the defender from causing a turnover. To overcome this, the defender, if blocked from the ball, can move through an offensive agent without the ball by simply trading places with the agent if the two are within one unit on the grid. Each experiment was run 10 times and averages were taken across those runs. Running on a 16-processor 400 MHz Sun Ultra-Enterprise 10000 machine, evaluation of one generation took approximately 2 seconds for population size of 1000 and approximately 4-8 seconds for population size of 4000.

5   Results

The simplifications made to the problem allow SGP to find keep-away soccer agents with good fitness. For all experiments, the parameter of 101 generations always showed the best convergence and lowest fitness. For the remainder of the paper, we consider only that parameter setup.

ADFGP experiments converged to two clusters of fitnesses, one being better than SGP, and the other much worse. When observations of the individual size are accounted for, it appears that the bad cluster contains individuals with about half the number of nodes as individuals in the good cluster. Prefiltering ADFGP runs based on individual size may be appropriate to remedy this, but since we are not explicity studying ADFGP, we still use the averages here as this is only a hypothesized explanation of ADFGP. LL1GP, with duplicating the best individual from the previous layer, did much worse than SGP and ADFGP. LL2GP was competitive with SGP and ADFGP, remembering that the initial 40 generations are spent in layer 1 learning accurate passing.

These results do not highlight a strength or weakness of layered learning for GP, except that we can get nearly the same solutions with LL2GP as with SGP and ADFGP. However, when we look at the learning curve for best fitness per generation of layer 1 in LL2GP, we notice that convergence takes place in about 15 generations and settles to the same value for the rest of the run. This hints that perhaps we do not gain anything from running for a total of 40 generations. Two new experiments are then developed to test this hypothesis.

New layered learning GP, **nLL2GP** and **n2LL2GP**, are exactly the same as LL2GP, except that for nLL2GP the first layer is only run for 20 generations, and the second is run for 81. For n2LL2GP, the first layer is run for 10 generations and the second for 91. Figure 3 shows the learning curves for the new experiment, n2LL2GP, with the fitness of the last generation labeled. Figure 2 shows the same learning curves for SGP and ADFGP. We see a steeper drop in fitness in n2LL2GP, layer 2, and a better resulting fitness. The nLL2GP experiment showed some improvement, but not as much as n2LL2GP.

The same learning curves for mean fitness show that n2LL2GP, nLL2GP, SGP and ADFGP all produce the same values, approximately, with n2LL2GP being slightly better. These results suggest that a natural breakdown of the problem into subproblems, where GP solves each of the subproblems, could allow for a better overall fitness and a speed up in the learning over SGP. The standard deviation of the several runs of SGP, ADFGP, nLL2GP, n2LL2GP were 4.98, 17.45, 2.73 and 2.28 respectively, showing good stability for n2LL2GP. Table 3 gives some interesting values across all experiments. Note that individual size is the average number of nodes, where each node represents a function, terminal,

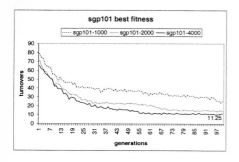 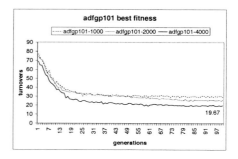

Fig. 2. Best fitness learning curve for SGP and ADFGP experiments

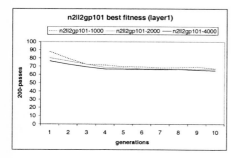 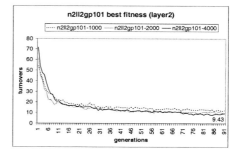

Fig. 3. Best fitness learning curve for n2LL2GP experiment. The left graph shows the learning of accurate passing in layer one, in 10 generations. The last generation is then transferred to layer 2, which is represented in the right graph where the minimizing of turnovers with a defender present is the objective.

or ADF call, of an individual in a generation. Figure 4 shows the learning curves for best fitness per generation and best generation so far in the run, where the n2LL2GP line only includes data for layer 2, omitting layer 1 that was attempting to maximize accurate passing.

Examining best-of-run individuals show the emergence of several behaviors, moving without the ball to avoid defenders, passing to open agents, and spreading out across the field, i.e. not crowding other agents or the ball. All the results highlight several other areas of interesting and worthwhile research with layered learning and keep-away soccer, and for other domains as well.

Table 3. Data for experiments with population size=4000, max generations=101, and averaged over 10 runs. Good-ADFGP represents the average of the 10 best runs selected from 20 runs of ADFGP.

	SGP	ADFGP	Good ADFGP	LL1GP	LL2GP	nLL2GP	n2LL2GP
best fit.gen.101	11.25	19.67	8.75	23.71	12.67	9.67	9.43
mean fit.gen.101	66.89	60.21	64.27	82.03	64.64	74.78	70.39
ave.ind.size gen.101	228.74	113.25	123.07	161.71	171.40	217.36	249.21
1st gen.fit.$\leq$ 20	33	62	22	101	55	31	26
best fit.run	9.0	16.56	6.83	19.29	9.0	7.32	5.78

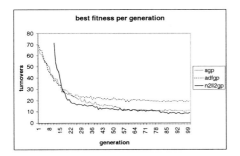 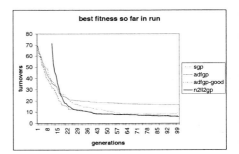

Fig. 4. The 'best fitness per generation graph' (left) compares the SGP, ADFGP and the n2LL2GP experiments for 101 generations and a population size of 4000. Because n2LL2GP spends the initial 10 generations learning accurate passing, only layer 2 is shown here, the layer for reducing the number of turnovers. The 'best fitness so far in run' (right) compares the same experiments with the addition of the Good-ADFGP experiment, the average of the best 10 out of 20 runs of ADFGP.

6   Conclusions

We showed that using layered learning for GP can evolve more fit individuals than standard GP. Additionally, layered learning GP allows for a natural decomposition of a large problem into subproblems. Each subproblem is then more easily solved with GP. The keep-away soccer problem is a good testbed for abstracting away the complexities of simulated soccer and allow for different GP methods to evolve good solutions for comparing methods. It is also an easily extended problem to the full game of soccer and transferred across platforms to other domains such as TeamBots and the SoccerServer from the simulator that was written here in ECJ.

Intuitively, we can liken our success with layered learning in GP with the success of human soccer teams. Successful teams are usually made up of players with unique strategies, where learning took place in a bottom-up fashion. The n2LL2GP experiment simulates this kind of behavior, where we attempt to minimize the number of generations needed per layer. The results indicate that it is beneficial to learn complex behaviors in a layered learning approach with GP, instead of standard GP, as it is easier to decide on fitness functions and natural to decompose the overall problem.

There are several extensions to this research that would be of interest. Developing a team for RoboCup competition using layered learning in GP would be a good way to test its ability more thoroughly. Studying other statistics about SGP, ADFGP, and n2LL2GP experiments could lead to other interesting conclusions, as would attempting to better optimize the number of generations needed in each layer. Diversity in populations is also an interesting issue, and whether layered learning promotes diversity. Other interesting modifications include developing heterogenous teams, adding additional lower and higher-level layers, and allowing ADFs in layered learning.

References

1. Andre, D., A. Teller. 1998. Evolving Team Darwin United. Lecture Notes in Artificial Intelligence: RoboCup-98: Robot Soccer World Cup II. vol 1604. Springer-Verlag.
2. Andre, D. et al. 1999. Soccerserver Manual. Ver. 4, Rev. 02. Available through the World-Wide Web at http://www.robocup.org.
3. Asada, M. et. al. 1999. Overview of RoboCup-98. Lecture Notes in Artificial Intelligence: RoboCup-98: Robot Soccer World Cup II. vol 1604. Springer-Verlag.
4. Kitano, H., Asada, M., Kuniyoshi, Y., Noda, I., Osawa, E. 1995. RoboCup: The Robot World Cup Initiative. In Proceedings of the IJCAI-95 Workshop on Entertainment and AI/ALife.
5. Kitano, H., et al. 1997. The RoboCup Synthetic Agent Challenge 97. In Proceedings of the IJCAI-97 Conference.
6. Koza, J.R. 1992. Genetic Programming: On the Programming of Computers by Means of Natural Selection. MIT Press.
7. Koza, J.R. 1994. Genetic Programming 2. MIT Press.
8. Luke, S. 2000. Issues in Scaling Genetic Programming: Breeding Strategies, Tree Generation, and Code Bloat. Ph.D. Dissertation, Department of Computer Science, University of Maryland, College Park, Maryland.
9. Luke, S. 1998. Genetic Programming Produced Competitive Soccer Softbot Teams for RoboCup97. In Proceedings of the Third Annual Genetic Programming Conference (GP98). J. Koza et al, eds. 204-222. San Fransisco: Morgan Kaufmann.
10. Luke, S. and L. Spector. 1996. Evolving Teamwork and Coordination with Genetic Programming. In Genetic Programming 1996: Proceedings of the First Annual Conference. J. Koza et al, eds. Cambridge: MIT Press. 141-149.
11. Matsubara, H., Noda, I., Hiraku, K. 1997. Learning of Coorperative actions in multi-agent systems: a case study of pass play in Soccer. In Adaption, Coevolution and Learning in Multiagent Systems: Papers from the 1996 AAAI Spring Symposium, pages 63-67, Menlo Park, CA. AAAI Press. AAAI Technical Report SS-96-01.
12. Rosca, J.P. and Ballard, D.H. 1994. Hierarchical Self-Orgainization in Genetic Programming. Proceedings of the Eleventh International Conference on Machine Learning. pp.251-258. Morgan Kaufmann Publishers, Inc.

13. Stone, P., Veloso M., Riley, P. 1999. The CMUnited-98 Champion Simulator Team. Lecture Notes in Artificial Intelligence: RoboCup-98: Robot Soccer World Cup II. vol 1604. Springer-Verlag.
14. Stone, P., Veloso, M. 2000. Layered Learning. Eleventh European Conference on Machine Learning (ECML-2000).
15. Stone, P., Veloso, M. 1998. A Layered Approch to Learning Client Behaviors in the RoboCup Soccer Server. Applied Artificial Intelligence (AAI), Volume 12.
16. Stone, P., Veloso, M. 2000. Multiagent Systems: A Survey from a Machine Learning Perspective. Autonomous Robots, volume 8, number 3.
17. Stone, P., Veloso, M. 1999. Team-Partitioned, Opaque-Transition Reinforcement Learning. Lecture Notes in Artificial Intelligence: RoboCup-98: Robot Soccer World Cup II. vol 1604. Springer-Verlag.
18. Tambe, M. 1997. Towards Flexible Teamwork. Journal of Artificial Intelligence Research, Volume 7, Pages 83-124.
19. Tambe, M., Adibi, J., Alonaizon, Y., Erdem, A., Kaminka, G., Marsella, S. and Muslea, I. 1999. Building agent teams using an explicit teamwork model and learning. Artificial Intelligence, volume 110, pages 215-240.
20. TeamBots software and documentation. Available through the World-Wide Web at http://www.teambots.org.

Linear-Tree GP and Its Comparison with Other GP Structures

Wolfgang Kantschik[1] and Wolfgang Banzhaf[1,2]

[1] Dept. of Computer Science, University of Dortmund, Dortmund, Germany
[2] Informatik Centrum Dortmund (ICD), Dortmund, Germany

Abstract. In recent years different genetic programming (GP) structures have emerged. Today, the basic forms of representation for genetic programs are tree, linear and graph structures. In this contribution we introduce a new kind of GP structure which we call Linear-tree. We describe the linear-tree-structure, as well as crossover and mutation for this new GP structure in detail. We compare linear-tree programs with linear and tree programs by analyzing their structure and results on different test problems.

1 Introduction of Linear-Tree GP

The representations of programs used in Genetic Programming can be classified by their underlying structure into three major groups: (1) tree-based [Koz92,Koz94], (2) linear [Nor94,BNKF98], and (3) graph-based [TV96] representations.

This paper introduces a new representation for GP programs. This new representation, named linear-tree, has been developed with the goal to give a program the flexibility to choose different execution paths for different inputs. For tree or linear based programs the interpreter usually executes the same nodes (functions) for each input. However, a program may contain many decisions and each decision may call another part of the program code. So the program flow of the linear-tree-program is more natural than linear or tree GP-programs, similar to the program flow of hand written programs.

In *linear-tree* GP each program $\mathcal{P}$ is represented as a tree. Each node in the tree has two parts, a *linear program* and a *branching node* (see Figure 1). The *linear program* will be executed when the node is reached during the interpretation of the program. After the linear program of a node is executed, a child node is selected according to the branching function of this node. If the node has only one child, this child will be executed. If the node has no child the execution of the program stops. During the interpretation only the nodes of one path through the tree, from the root node to a leaf will be executed.

The implementation of linear GP in our system represents a linear program as a variable length list of C instructions that operate on (indexed) variables or constants (see [BDKB98]). In linear GP all operations, e.g. a = b + 1.2, implicitly include an assignment of a variable. After a program has been executed its output

J. Miller et al. (Eds.): EuroGP 2001, LNCS 2038, pp. 302–312, 2001.

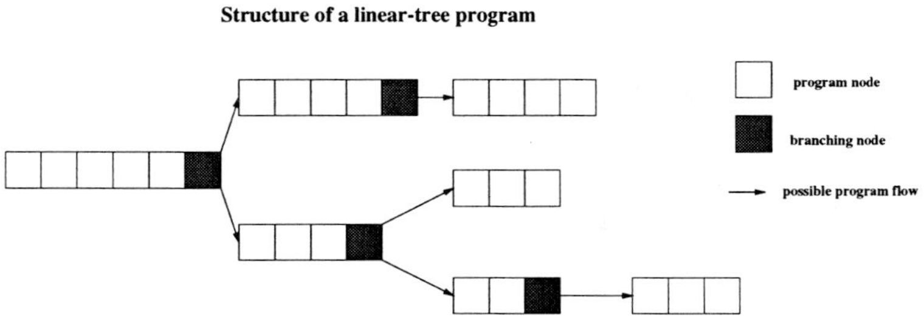

Structure of a linear-tree program

Fig. 1. Individual structure of a linear-tree representation.

value(s) are stored in designated variables. The *branching function* is also a C instruction that operates on the same variables as the linear program, but this function only reads these variables. Table 1 contains a collection of all branching functions. Figure 2 shows an example of a short linear program and a branching function for one node in a linear-tree.

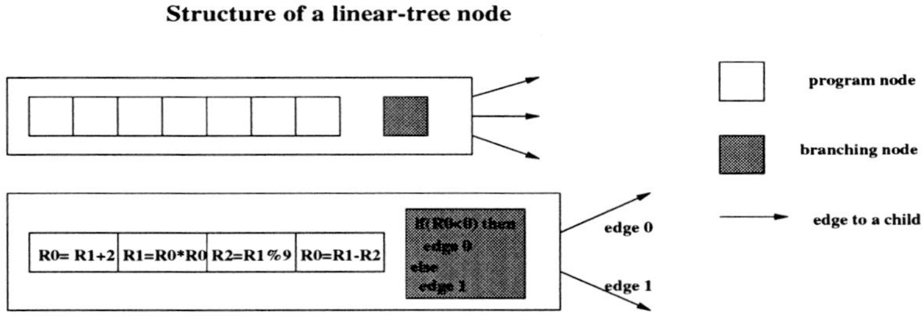

Structure of a linear-tree node

Fig. 2. The structure of a node in a linear-tree GP program (top) and an example node (bottom).

1.1   Recombination of Linear-Tree Programs

A crossover operation combines the genetic material of two parent programs by swapping certain program parts. The crossover for a linear-tree program can be realized in two ways. The first possibility is to perform the crossover like it is done in tree-based GP by exchanging subtrees (see [Ang97]). Figure 3 illustrates this tree-based recombination method. In each parent individual the crossover operator chooses a node randomly and exchanges the two corresponding subtrees. In our system, the crossover points are directed to inner nodes with a higher probability than to terminal nodes. We choose an inner node with a probability of 80 % and a terminal node with 20 % of the crossover operation. This values are also taken for the tree-based crossover in our tests.

Table 1. All the branching operators used in the runs described here.

branching operator	description of the operator
result < 0	If the result register is less than zero the left child is choosen else the right child.
result > 0	If the result register is greater than zero the left child is choosen else the right child.
result $== 0$	If the result register is equal zero the left child is choosen else the right child.
register $x <$ result	If the result register is less than register x the left child is choosen else the right child.
register $x >$ result	If the result register is greater than register x the left child else the right child.
register $x ==$ result	If the result register is equal register x the left child is choosen else the right child.

The second possibility is to perform linear GP crossover. Figure 4 illustrates the linear recombination method. A segment of random position and length is selected in each of the two parents for exchange. If one of the children exceeds the maximum length, crossover with equally sized segments will be performed.

For linear-tree programs we use both methods but only one at a time. The following algorithm for the recombination of linear-tree programs is applied for recombination:

procedure crossover (*ind1, ind2*)
1      $p_1 =$ a crossover point of *ind1*;
2      $p_2 =$ a crossover point of *ind1*;
3   *randProb* = random value between 0 and 1.;
4   **if** (*randProb* < *prob$_{xover}$*)
5   *depth1* = depth of *ind1* after potential crossover;
6   *depth2* = depth of *ind2* after potential crossover;
7   **if** (*depth1* < *depthMax* **and** *depth2* < *depthMax*)
8   perform a tree-based crossover with the given crossover points.;
9   **else**
10   perform linear crossover between the nodes p_1 and p_2;
11   **endif**
12   **else**
13   perform linear crossover between the nodes p_1 and p_2;
14   **endif**
end

In our tests the parameter *prob$_{xover}$*, which defines the probability whether the tree-based or linear crossover method is used, was set to the 50 %. We also tested the crossover operation with a probability of 10 % and 90 % (the results see Section 3.3).

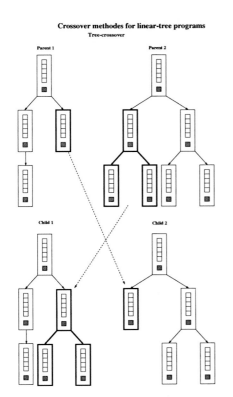

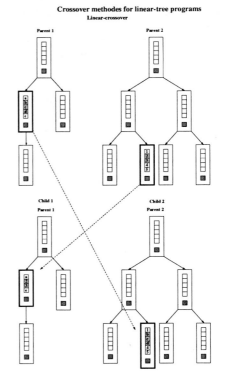

Fig. 3. Crossover-operation of two linear-tree programs using the tree-based crossover method. This crossover method exchanges two subtrees of the programs.

Fig. 4. Crossover-operation of two linear-tree programs using the linear-based crossover method. This crossover method is a two-point crossover, which exchanges a part of the linear-code between the nodes.

1.2 Mutation

The difference between crossover and mutation is that mutation operates on a single program only. After the recombination of the population a program is chosen with a given probability for mutation. The random mutation operator selects a subset of nodes randomly and changes either a node of a linear program, a branching function, or the number of outgoing edges. This version of the mutation operator does not generate new linear sequences. The altered program is then placed back into the population.

2 Test Problems

As test problems we use four different symbolic regression problems, the parity problem, and a classification problem to determine the effect of the linear-tree structure compared to other representation forms in GP. In Section 3 the results are presented. They show that the new representation performs better than both the linear and tree representations in most test cases.

2.1   Symbolic Regression

We use four different regression problems to test the linear-tree structure. In general, symbolic regression problems deal with the approximation of a set of n numeric input-output relations (x, y) by a symbolic function. The programs should produce an output as close as possible to y if the input is x. The fitness of an individual program p is defined here as the sum of the errors between all given outputs y (here one of the given functions $f(x)$) and the predicted outputs $p(x)$:

$$\text{fitness}(p) = \sum_{i=1}^{n} |p(x_i) - f(x_i)|.$$

The following functions are used as test problems:

- Sine with an input range $[0, 2\pi]$ and 20 fitness cases, chosen uniformly and including both endpoints.
- Sine with an input range $[0, 4\pi]$ and 40 fitness cases, chosen uniformly and including both endpoints.
- Rastrigin, $f(x) = x^2 - 5 * cos(2\pi * x)$, with an input range $[-4, 4]$ and 40 fitness cases.
- $f(x) = \frac{1}{2x} * sin(2x)$ with an input range $[-4, 4]$ and 40 fitness cases, the fitness case $f(0)$ is excluded from the sets of fitness cases.

All variants of GP have been configured with population size of 500 individuals, a maximum crossover and mutation rate of 100 %, and without adf's. This means that in one generation each individual is selected for a crossover and after the crossover each individual will be mutated by the mutation operator. All variants use the arithmetic operations $(+, -, *, /)$.

2.2   Non-regression Problems

For this paper we use the following two non-regression test problems:

- The 4-parity problem, a Boolean problem.
- The chain problem, a classification problem[BB01] Figure 5 visualises the two classes of the problem.

The task of the GP program for both problems is to find a relation that connects a given input x to the correct class, here $c \in 0, 1$, so the fitness cases are also an input-output tuple (x, c). The quality of the programs depends on its ability to find a generalised mapping from the input-output pairs (x, c) of the n fitness cases. The parity problem is a boolean problem though it can also interpreted as a classification problem.

All variants of GP have been configured with population size of 500 individuals, a maximum crossover and mutation rate of 100 %, and without adf's. For each problem we use different sets of operators; for the chain problem we use arithmetic operations $(+, -, *, /, \sin, \cos)$, for the 4-parity problem we use the following Boolean functions (not, or, and, nand, nor).

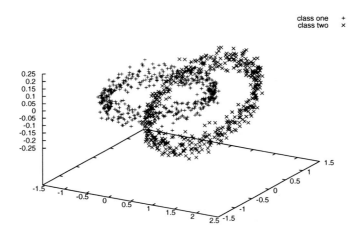

Fig. 5. This figure shows the both links of the chain, which represents the two classes of the problem [BB01]

3   Experimental Results

In this Section we describe the results of using the different GP structures on the six test problems from Section 2. All plots show the average fitness of the best individual. The average is calculated over 30 runs with the same parameter set. In all runs we used tournament selection with a tournament size of two and a population size of 500.

3.1   Difference between the Representations

Figure 6 and 7 show the development of the fitness values using the different structures for the sine problem with one and two periods respectively. Both plots exhibit the same ranking of the different GP structures. In both test cases the linear-structure is superior to the tree-structure and the new linear-tree-structure is superior to both structures. In Figure 7 we can see that the linear-tree-structure has not reached a stagnation phase even though the tree-structure has virtually reached a stagnation. The plot of Figure 8 shows the trend of the fitness values for the function $\frac{1}{2x} * sin(2x)$. Even for this function we get the same ranking for the three structures. The fitness differences are not as high as for the second sine problem, but this function can be approximated more easily by a polynomial than the sine problem with two periods.

The Rastrigin function is the first and only of our test problems that breaks the established ranking (see Figure 9). Here, a tree-structure is superior to the other program structures, but even here the linear-tree-structure shows better performance than the linear-structure.

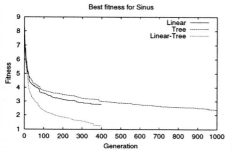

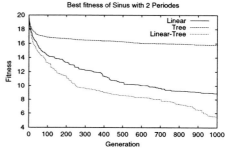

Fig. 6. The curves show the average fitness value of the sine function form 0 to 2π. Each curve is an average over 30 runs. Zero is the best fitness for a individual.

Fig. 7. The curves show the average fitness value of the sine function form 0 to 4π. Each curve is an average over 30 runs. Zero is the best fitness for a individual.

For the non-regression problems we obtain results similar to the regression problems. For both problems GP evolves individuals with linear-tree-structure which have better fitness values than with the other structures. Figure 10 shows the evolution of fitness values for the parity-4 problem. Only a few of the runs with the linear-tree-structure do not reach the optimal solution. The plot in Figure 11 shows the results for the chain problem (of Figure 5). For this problem the linear-tree-structure reaches the best results, but for the second time the tree-structure evolves individuals with a better fitness than the linear-structure.

3.2   Analysis of the Linear-Tree-Structure

After analyzing the individuals with the linear-tree-structure for the parity problem we saw that most programs did not make use of branching and executing different code for different inputs. Some individuals have copies of the same code at each node on the same level in the tree, so that each path through the

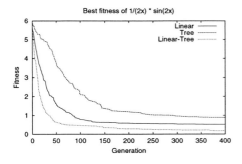

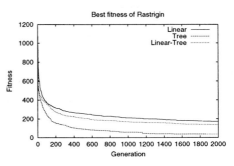

Fig. 8. The curves show the average fitness value of $\frac{1}{2x} * sin(2x)$ function. Each curve is an average over 30 runs. Zero is the best fitness for a individual.

Fig. 9. The curves show the average fitness value of the Rastrigin function. Each curve is an average over 30 runs.

linear-tree interprets the same code. Other individuals set the parameters for the branching functions in such a way that the result is always the same, and so the path through the individual is always identical. Whether the behavior of the structure during the evolution is a *bloat* phenomena [MM95,LP98] or not will be examined in future work.

Although there is no difference between a linear individual and a linear-tree individual in this case, evolution creates better individuals with the linear-tree-structure for this problem than with the other structures. The answer to this riddle seems to be the existence of *building blocks* [Hol75]. The structure of the linear-tree creates *natural blocks* of code, the nodes of a tree. The chance, then, for a good block or a sequence of blocks to survive a crossover is higher than in other structures. During around 50 % of crossover only subtrees will be exchanged, so *building blocks* can be passed on to other individuals.

Program analysis for the other problems reveal that in these problems individuals use the ability to branch through the code. Obviously, for some problems there is no need to exploit this ability and evolution circumvents the branching ability.

3.3   The Analysis of the Crossover-Operator

The crossover operator for linear-tree programs has two modes, in which genetic material can be exchanged (see Section 1.1). The first mode is the exchange of subtrees and the second mode is the exchange of linear sequences of nodes. During our tests we have set the probability to choose one of the modes to 50 % (parameter $prob_{xover}$). This means that 50 % of the crossover operations are linear crossover operations. The question is whether this parameter has a serious effect on the crossover performance and on evolution. We tested this question with values of 10 % and 90 % for $prob_{xover}$. We also tried changing the crossover operation so that line 10 is not executed in the crossover procedure if the tree-

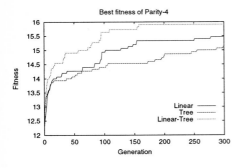

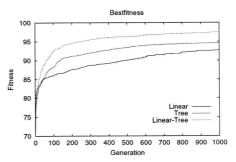

Fig. 10. Average fitness value of the parity 4 problem. Each curve is an average over 30 runs. The best fitness for this problem is 16. The linear-tree-structure shows the best results of the tree structures. In most runs it finds the optimal solution after 150 generations.

Fig. 11. Average fitness value of the chains classification problem. Each curve is an average over 30 runs. The best fitness is 100 for this problems, the fitness is the classification rate in percent.

based crossover was not allowed. This means if no tree-based crossover can take place no crossover will be performed.

For our first test to analyze the crossover-operator, we use the standard setting of our system, and we find no significant difference and this parameter has no real effect to the crossover operation. Because of our standard parameter setting after each crossover a mutation is performed. Therefore we performed a test series where mutation after the crossover operation was turned off. The results are shown in Figure 12. The test demonstrates that the gain of linear-based crossover is greater than that of the tree-based crossover for the linear-tree-programs. This plot shows also the result for the evolution without crossover, this curve shows how important mutation is for the evolution. Tree-based crossover makes big changes in the individual code compared to linear crossover and mutation. After a few hundred generations runs with a higher probability for linear-based crossover or mutation yield better results than runs with a high probability for tree based crossover. The linear crossover has the ability to make changes near the root node of the tree easily. Standard tree-based GP finds this very difficult[MH99] so this could also be a reason why linear crossover leads to better results.

4   Summary and Outlook

We tested the performance of linear-tree against other structures of GP programs. In all test cases the linear-tree-structure performed better than the linear-structure, and only in one test case the linear-tree-structure did perform worse than the tree-structure. From these tests we can say that the new structure has shown its advantage.

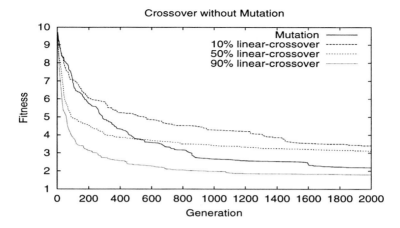

Fig. 12. Average fitness value of the sine function form 0 to 2π for the crossover operator with different values for the value $prob_{xover}$. For these results we use crossover without mutation. The curve 'mutation' is the result without a crossover operator. Each curve is an average over 30 runs.

We have observed that the structure of a GP individual makes a significant difference in the evolutionary process and the expressiveness of code. Good performance of a structure may be caused by the effect of building blocks [Hol75], which are the nodes in our linear-tree-structure. In order to clarify whether the good performance of the linear-tree-structure is a general phenomenon for genetic programming, more experiments have to be run on a variety of test problems, but the results achieved so far are strong evidence that the new structure may lead to better result for a range of problems. In future work we plan to extend tests to other problems and check different branching methods. We also have to examine in detail why the new structure leads to better results.

Acknowledgement

Support has been provided by the DFG (Deutsche Forschungsgemeinschaft), under grant Ba 1042/5-2.

References

[Ang97]   P.J. Angeline. Subtree crossover: Building block engine or macromutation? In *Genetic Programming 1997: Proceedings of the Second Annual Conference*, pages 9–17, San Francisco, CA, 1997. Morgan Kaufmann.

[BB01]   M. Brameier and W. Banzhaf. Evolving teams of mutiple predictors with Genetic Programming. Technical report, Universitt Dortmund SFB 531, 2001. Data available from the authors.

[BDKB98] M. Brameier, P. Dittrich, W. Kantschik, and W. Banzhaf. SYSGP - A C++ library of different GP variants. Technical Report Internal Report of SFB 531,ISSN 1433-3325, Fachbereich Informatik, Universität Dortmund, 1998.

[BNKF98] W. Banzhaf, P. Nordin, R. E. Keller, and F. D. Francone. *Genetic Programming – An Introduction On the Automatic Evolution of Computer Programs and its Applications*. Morgan Kaufmann, San Francisco und dpunkt verlag, Heidelberg, 1998.

[Hol75]   J. Holland. *Adaption in Natural and Artifical Systems*. MI: The University of Michigan Press, 1975.

[Koz92]   J. Koza. *Genetic Programming*. MIT Press, Cambridge, MA, 1992.

[Koz94]   J. Koza. *Genetic Programming II*. MIT Press, Cambridge, MA, 1994.

[LP98]   W. B. Langdon and R. Poli. Genetic programming bloat with dynamic fitness. In Wolfgang Banzhaf, Riccardo Poli, Marc Schoenauer, and Terence C. Fogarty, editors, *Proceedings of the First European Workshop on Genetic Programming*, volume 1391 of *LNCS*, pages 96–112, Paris, 14-15 April 1998. Springer-Verlag.

[MH99]   Nicholas Freitag McPhee and Nicholas J. Hopper. Analysis of genetic diversity through population history. In Wolfgang Banzhaf, Jason Daida, Agoston E. Eiben, Max H. Garzon, Vasant Honavar, Mark Jakiela, and Robert E. Smith, editors, *Proceedings of the Genetic and Evolutionary Computation Conference*, volume 2, pages 1112–1120, Orlando, Florida, USA, 13-17 July 1999. Morgan Kaufmann.

[MM95]   Nicholas Freitag McPhee and Justin Darwin Miller. Accurate replication in genetic programming. In L. Eshelman, editor, *Genetic Algorithms: Proceedings of the Sixth International Conference (ICGA95)*, pages 303–309, Pittsburgh, PA, USA, 15-19 July 1995. Morgan Kaufmann.

[Nor94]   J. P. Nordin. *A Compiling Genetic Programming System that Directly Manipulates the Machine code*. MIT Press, Cambridge, 1994.

[TV96]   A. Teller and M. Veloso. Pado: A new learning architecture for object recognition. In *Symbolic Visual Learning*, pages 81 –116. Oxford University Press, 1996.

Evolving Hand-Eye Coordination for a Humanoid Robot with Machine Code Genetic Programming

William B. Langdon[1] and Peter Nordin[2]

[1] Computer Science, University College, London
Gower Street, London, WC1E 6BT, UK
W.Langdon@cs.ucl.ac.uk
[2] Chalmers University of Technology, Institute of Physical Resource Theory
S-412 96 Göteborg, Sweden
nordin@fy.chalmers.se

Abstract. We evolve, using AIMGP machine code genetic programming, Discipulus, an approximation of the inverse kinematics of a real robotics arm with many degrees of freedom. Elvis is a bipedal robot with human-like geometry and motion capabilities — a humanoid, primarily controlled by evolutionary adaptive methods. The GP system produces a useful inverse kinematic mapping, from target 3-D points (via pairs of stereo video images) to a vector of arm controller actuator set points.

1 Introduction

Genetic programming moves a prototype humanoid robot's fingers to a designated position when given a pair of stereo images of the target from the robot's eyes. The robot is deliberately mechanically unsophisticated using uncalibrated inexpensive servos. Instead sophisticated adaptive control software is automatically created using evolutionary computation.

Section 2 explains the interest in humanoid robotics and the rational for the adaptive software approach. While Sect. 3 describes the robot in more detail and summarises previous results achieved with it. Section 4 describes these experiments, and Sects. 5 and 6 indicates the way forward. Finally, Sect. 7 summarises our results and gives our conclusions.

2 Background

The field of autonomous mobile robotics attracts an accelerating interest. Application areas are plentiful in both industry and academia, but an autonomous mobile robot system also demands high performance of both mechanical components and control software. The many degrees of freedom in a light mobile robot create new problem spaces in control and navigation where conventional methods often fall short. A relatively new and promising area for control of

J. Miller et al. (Eds.): EuroGP 2001, LNCS 2038, pp. 313–324, 2001.
© Springer-Verlag Berlin Heidelberg 2001

complex autonomous agents is *evolutionary algorithms*, which are inspired by the main adaptation method in nature — *natural selection*. Most challenging of all autonomous robots are robots that move using legs instead of wheels. Walking robots have very large potential in environments created for humans as well as in more natural terrain. The largest potential is associated with robots of human-like dimensions walking on two legs — *humanoid robots*. Man is the standard for almost all interactions in our world where most environments, tools and machines are adapted to the abilities, motion capabilities and geometry of humans. However, a bipedal humanoid robot demands extreme performance in everything from power supply to computer capacity and control algorithms, but if we succeed in building humanoids, it could be more efficient to control various machines by these robots than to rebuild all machines for direct computer control. It has been argued that humanoid robots could be the next dominating mechanical industry, as large as or larger than the auto industry. In the next section we briefly describe an evolutionary control architecture that will be the basis for several humanoid robotics experiments.

One of the most difficult control problems is approximating the *inverse kinematics* of a complex robot limb such as the arm. Finding a function which produces actuator settings for a desired point in 3-D space is difficult in an idealised model and a very hard problem in a real noisy environment. Below we have used a machine code GP system Discipulus™ [6] to evolve an approximate inverse kinematics function from real example data. The example data was produced with the Elvis robot using stereo cameras and a laser pointer.

3   The Elvis Humanoid

Elvis is a scale model of a full–size humanoid with a height of about 60 cm, built with 42 servos giving a high degree of freedom in legs, arms and hands, see Fig. 1. The robot will be guided by microphones, cameras and touch sensors. The imminent goals are to walk upright and to navigate through vision. Seven on board micro-controllers control the servos and sensors. Elvis is autonomous, with on board power supply and main processing unit but many experiments are mainly performed with connection to a host computer. Elvis can for instance walk fully autonomously. Elvis has some similarities with robots constructed at the University of Tokyo, but Elvis is intended to have on board control capabilities [4].

3.1   Software Architecture

The philosophy behind Elvis is that the software architecture should mainly build on evolutionary algorithms and specifically genetic programming. Evolution is thus used to induce programs, functions and symbolic rules for all levels of control [1, 3, 5]. Three hierarchical layers are used for control:

- Reactive Layer
- Model Building Layer
- Reasoning Layer

Fig. 1. The Elvis Humanoid Robot

Reactive Layer. The first layer is a reactive layer based on on-line evolution of machine code. This method assumes that all fitness feedback is obtained directly from the actual robot. The disadvantage is that the GP individuals spend most of their time waiting for feedback from the physical environment. This results in moderate learning speed, and the constant movement shortens the life-span of the hardware. The benefit of the method is its simplicity, and that the only constraints needed for the models being learned are that they should fulfil their task as a black box. This layer is used for reactive behaviours such as balancing.

Model Building Layer. To achieve higher learning speeds and more generic behaviour there is a second control layer that works with memories of past events. In this genetic reinforcement learning framework, the system tries to evolve a *model* of the underlying hardware system and problem. The model maps sensor inputs and actions to a predicted goodness or fitness value. The currently best model is then used to decide what action results in optimal predicted fitness given current sensor inputs. This layer allows the genetic programming system to run at full speed without having to wait for feedback from the environment; instead it fits the programs to memories of past events. The machine code genetic programming approach used is called Discipulus. (It self derived from Automatic Induction of Machine Code GP (AIMGP) [6]). AIMGP machine code is about 40 times faster than conventional GP systems due to the absence of any interpreting steps. In addition, the system is compact, which is beneficial when working on board a real robot. The model building layer is also used for basic control tasks.

Reasoning Layer. The third layer is a symbolic processing layer for higher "brain functions" requiring reasoning. The objective of this layer is to handle high level tasks such as navigation, safety, and energy supply. This layer is built on "genetic reasoning", a method where evolution is used as an inference engine, requiring less heuristics to guide the inference procedure [6].

Each of these layers consists of modules for various tasks such as balancing, walking and image processing. Some system functions are represented as several modules spanning different layers.

In the experiment described below we evolve an internal *model* for the inverse kinematics of Elvis' arm based on data from the vision system. This model works from the sensory data itself (twin video cameras) not some externally defined "perfect" 3-D co-ordinates and generates data directly usable by the robot's motors.

3.2   Experiments

Several experiments has been performed on Elvis:

- Balancing - evolution of functions for balance [9]
- Walking - evolution of efficient walking [10]
- Vision - evolution of 3-D vision [2]
- Navigation - evolution of plans [11]
- Audio orientation - evolution of stereo hearing [7,8]
- Manipulation - evolution of eye hand coordination for writing and the inverse kinematics experiment described here

4   Inverse Kinematics Experiment

In these experiments we demonstrate the evolution of eye hand coordination. That is, we show the robot's stereo vision can be used to drive the hand within the robot's field of vision.

While we intend to use the GP software architecture to allow the control system to adapt and incorporate online feedback, the camera hardware and MSwindows software system introduced considerable delays (on the order of 0.5 seconds). Since this is bigger than the time to move the arm, feedback via the twin cameras is not feasible with the existing setup. Therefore we were limited to solving the inverse kinematics problem for the robot's arm

The experiment consists of two parts. In the first (Sect. 4.2) the robot waves its hand about in front of its face in the manner of infant humans, while recording both the commands used to drive its hand and arm and the apparent location of its finger tip. In the second (Sect. 4.4) a stationary target is placed in front of the robot which then positions its finger tip as near to the target as possible using a collection of evolved functions. Section 4.5 gives our results, while Sect. 4.3 describes the GP system but first we start by describing the camera and system software.

4.1   Cameras and Image Processing

Since this is primarily an experiment in robot learning, the machine vision system was deliberately simple. The same system was used for both collection of training data and moving to the target. The robot was sat in a normal office albeit shielded from direct sun light. An omni directional red laser light source was attached to the index finger on the robot's right arm. An identical source was used to indicate the target. Both laser sources are spherical with a diameter of $1/8^{th}$inch (see Fig. 2). While this is mostly satisfactory, the mounting meant the laser was obscured, particularly from the right eye, when the hand was extended directly away from the face. Secondly care was needed to avoid picking up reflections of the laser from the metallic parts of the arm.

Fig. 2. Identical mountings were used for both finger tip and target lasers. A spherical translucent glass bead (light shading) is mounted directly in path of red light (dark shading) emitted by a solid state laser (short black rectangle). To shield the direct light and so reduce reflections, the whole is mounted inside a brass tube (approximately 6mm in diameter by 10mm in length).

The digital cameras were operated at a resolution of 160 by 120 pixels. Auto focus and auto exposure were suppressed. Instead the sensitivity of the cameras was manually adjusted so the laser source dominates the image, with almost all the background suppressed. The cameras were approximately parallel and 7cm apart.

The camera driver software allowed only one camera per PC computer. Therefore in these experiments each camera was attached via a high speed DSB (Digital Serial Bus) to a separate laptop PC, which communicated via TCP/IP running over UTP 10 Mhz Ethernet. (See Fig. 3). Nominally every 100 mS a C++ program scanned the camera image (looking only at the red component), discarded pixels whose brightness was below a manually controlled threshold and calculated the mean position of the remainder. The mean and number of bright pixels were sent to logging software via TCP/IP. In practise the data rate was just over 3 frames per second. The mean position was indicated by cross hairs on the laptop screen (by inverting blue and green intensity) and the bright pixels were similarly high lighted.

While the mean is robust and easy to calculate it is easily upset by outliers. Thus care was required to ensure the cameras and brightness threshold were set to eliminate all pixels except those due to the laser source. Potentially the apparent size of the target, as indicated by the number of pixels it occupies, could have been used by the GP programs, e.g. to calculate distance from the camera. However this data was not made available to GP.

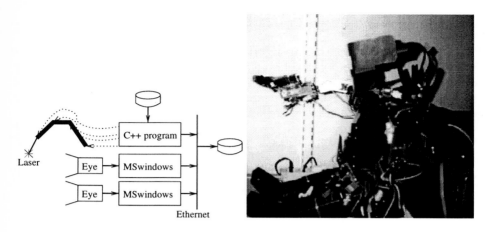

Fig. 3. Collection of Training Data. Data driven C++ program waves arm in front of robot's eyes. Both arm commands and apparent position of Laser are logged to disk.

4.2   Collection of Training Data

The servos are controlled via a C++ class library which drives a serial interface on one of the laptops. Up to eight microprocessor based controllers may be connected to a single serial line. Each microprocessor controls up to eight servos using timed analogue signals to specify their set point ($-2048\ldots2047$). In addition to electric motors, each servos contains integrated circuits to monitor the motors position and perform proportional control. The controller attempts to position the actuator to the given set point value. A time by which this should be achieved can also be specified. (It is actually implemented by each microprocessor). In these experiments, since they are not time critical, it was always set to one second, thus reducing the loading on the robot's mechanical systems. In other experiments the microprocessors are also used to relay sensor values back to the laptop.

A data driven C++ program was manually written to move the arm in three dimensions about in front of the robot, see Fig. 3. Note at this stage the control software need not be especially sophisticated all that the arm need do is wave about in front of both eyes. While waving the robots twin eyes record where its finger tip appears to be. Two avoid problems associated with delays and data skew between the two cameras the arm is move slowly and pauses every two seconds for the cameras to catch up. A time stamped file of arm servo commands and apparent finger tip positions was created.

Data was logged (at about 6 events per second) for twenty minutes, during which 287 arm commands (i.e. commands for the whole arm, each comprised of four servo set points) where sent. Off line the log was filtered to select only data where the finger tip was only visible to both cameras. This yielded 145 data points, which were used by Discipulus.

4.3   Use of Discipulus

Version 2.0 of the Discipulus machine code GP product was used to separately evolve a function for each of the robot's arm's servos. (Discipulus parameters are given in Table 1. Where parameter values are not given in Table 1, the default was used). Note the function is not from prescribed 3 dimensional coordinates but instead uses the stereo information from the cameras. I.e. each GP function is given two (X,Y) pairs, one from each camera and drives one of the arm's servos. The evolution of fitness in the four runs is given in Fig. 4, while Fig. 5 shows the match between the evolved function and the training data.

Table 1. Discipulus Parameters for Arm Servos

Objective:	Evolve a GP function from indicated target position to servo set point
Functions set:	FADD, Arithmetic (FABS FCHS FSQRT) Comparison (FCOMI) Condition (FCMOVB FCMOVNB JB JNB) Data transfer (FLD FXCH FLD) FDIV, No Exponentiation, FMUL, No rotate stack, FSUB, FCOS FSIN
Terminal set:	4 inputs 3 FPU registers 20 constants randomly chosen in $-100\ldots+100$
Fitness:	Squared error on 145 training examples. Each run independently fits its own servo data.
Selection:	steady state tournament
Pop Size:	5000
Max program:	256
Initial pop:	max size 80 (chose equally between inputs and constants)
Parameters:	50% crossover (Homologous 50%), 95% mutation (Block mutation rate 30%, Instruction mutation rate 30%, Instruction data mutation rate 40%)
Termination:	by hand after approx 1 hour (all completed at least 1,000,000 tournaments)

4.4   Demonstration

Another series of experiments were run to demonstrate the system. Here the robot was sat in front of another omni directional laser light source which indicated the target point. The apparent location of the target, i.e. as seen by both eyes, was fed into each of the GP functions whose output was connected to the corresponding servo, see Fig. 6. Thus the stereo effect between the two cameras was used to calculate the targets position in three dimensions and then the robot's arm was driven to this point, see Fig. 7. Note that the target's location is never explicitly calculated or represented in anyway. The evolved software only has its apparent location, as seen by the two cameras.

4.5   Results

The results (shown in Fig. 8) can be divided into two groups, successful ($\times$), when the arm was moved to within a few centimetres of the target laser or

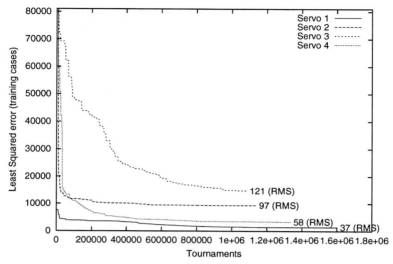

Fig. 4. Evolution of training error during the 4 Discipulus runs. Program with least error used to drive arm in Sect. 4.4.

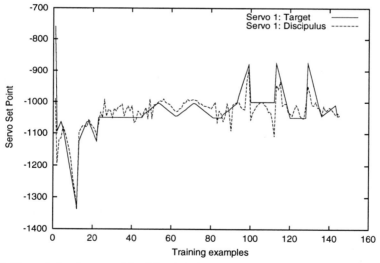

Fig. 5. Data fit by Servo 1 (shoulder joint) program with least error (see Fig. 4).

touching it and a smaller group where the arm was driven to points far from the target ($\square$). All but one such point ($\approx 17, -5$) can be explained as due to the target being in a position that was not used during the waving training sequence. All but one lie close to the face. Apart from not being within the training set, manoeuvring the hand into such locations may be difficult or infeasible due to the robot's geometry, the risk of collision between the hand and the head or collision between the arm and and other parts of the robot. In 60% of the ok

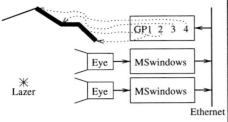

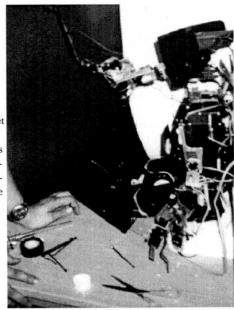

Fig. 6. GP driving robot arm. The robot's eyes feed the apparent position of the target (indicated by the laser) to 4 GP programs which together drive the arm to the laser.

Fig. 7. Robot finger tip (bright dot) driven by GP to target laser (bright dot on vertical mount).

cases, either the arm came into contact with the target or was within 1/2 cm of it. In the other 40% the finger tip was between 2.5 and 5.5 cm of the target. (Note both training and test points lie in three dimensional space, in Fig. 8 they have been projected into two dimensions).

5   Discussion

The approach of learning inverse kinematics, by having the robot watch its own limb movements, as infant humans do, has worked reasonably well. Yielding, in absence of online feed back, human like performance. The robot has learnt to cope with deficiencies of its vision system, such as spherical aberration.

To some extent Fig. 8 gives an overly pessimistic view. In fact over most of volume visible to both cameras and within reach of his right arm, Elvis could repeatedly position his arm within an inch of the target. This is about as well as people can do when not using their eyes as they move. Of this small error, only a small part comes from the inherent variability in the hardware, since, if given a fixed target, Elvis would move his fingers to within a few millimetres of the same point each time. Therefore a large part of the error must come from the evolved model. This may be due to not adequately fitting the available data or uncontrolled changes to the robot's environment between training and testing.

There are several ways to treat these small errors. Firstly they may be small enough so that for some applications, they don't matter. But since the hardware

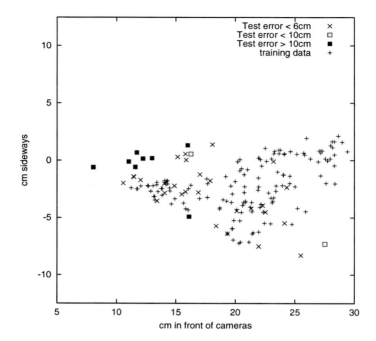

Fig. 8. Test results. Distance between target and finger tip when testing GP programs in Elvis (39 cases) are plotted in three ranges; successful ($\times$), small and large errors ($\square$). Most large errors correspond to regions without training data. They are mostly clustered very close to the face. 144 of the 145 training data are plotted ($+$).

can do better, it is defeatist for the software not to try. One approach would be better learning, or better control of the environment but this goes against the desire that the robot be both robust and adaptive. If we consider how people deal with the problem, we see immediate visual feedback is needed. People achieve fine positioning and control by looking at what they are doing as they do it. In Elvis' case this would mean dynamically tracking both the target and the hand. We feel this is within the reach of our GP system but some form of synchronisation (e.g. mirror based) between the eyes may be required and changes to the system software to get faster and more reliable response from the video system.

As has been mentioned, the cases of gross error arise at the extremes of the robot's vision. Where it is possible to place the target where it is literally impossible for the robot to reach. The approach of four separately evolved programs generalised well to data like that it had seen before and even to points outside the volume of the training data but at the very extremes of the visible area it failed to extrapolate. There is no particular reason to think other machine learning techniques, such as artificial neural networks, would have done better in these particular circumstances.

One immediate step would be to extend this to cover more degrees of freedom. E.g. head and neck movement (allowing target tracking [12]), two arms and then whole body movement. We suspect that fairly quickly as the task complexity rises, this demonstrated approach, would need to be augmented by the multi-layered approach described in Sect. 3.1.

6 Future Work

The final goal of our research project is to build a human-sized robot based on a plastic human skeleton to ensure geometric authenticity. The software architecture of Elvis will be used for the larger robots with small adjustments. The main objective of the skeleton based robot is a very light humanoid (60 Kilogrammes) with less sophisticated hardware compensated for by a more sophisticated adaptive control architecture. The full-size robot named Priscilla is now being constructed at Chalmers. Priscilla is based on pneumatics and some of the lower level controls for this is currently being evolved.

7 Summary and Conclusions

The Elvis humanoid robot is a very complex system both as far as hardware and software are concerned. It is unique in many ways: size, weight, degrees of freedom, possibility of autonomy and control method. Nevertheless Sect. 4.5 shows GP can control the movement of the arm to touch or lie within $1/2$ centimetres of a suitable target point in most cases.

Nature has shown that evolution is a very powerful tool for controlling complex systems in an adaptive way. Our hypothesis is that evolutionary systems such as genetic programming and AIMGP are very well suited for control of complicated systems. We have chosen to build the control architecture almost exclusively on evolutionary algorithms operating on a wide variety of tasks and using several different methods for evolution and representation. The experiments show some feasibility of this approach and we can conclude that evolutionary algorithms are broad enough for application to many AI related problems in humanoid control. Specifically we see in this experiment how GP can be used to evolve the inverse kinematics of a complex humanoid robot arm using a real robot. The results obtained are good enough for practical use in the control of Elvis.

We will use the experiences from Elvis for the construction of a full-size humanoid robot built on a plastic human skeleton.

Acknowledgements

Funded by in part by the Wennergren foundation, NUTEK and TFR. Peter Nordin gratefully acknowledges support from the Swedish Research Council for Engineering Sciences. Special thanks to Manne Kihlman and Marcus Tallhamn, who did excellent work in developing the hardware design for Elvis. Per Svensson, Björn Andersson, Rikard Karlsson, Thorbjörn Engdahl, Anders Eriksson and Christopher Graae have also made significant contributions to various parts of the project.

References

1. Banzhaf, W., Nordin, P., Keller, R. E., and Francone, F. D. (1997). Genetic Programming – An Introduction. On the automatic evolution of computer programs and its applications. Morgan Kaufmann, San Fransisco, and d-punkt, Heidelberg.
2. Christopher T.M. Graae, Peter Nordin and Mats Nordahl (2000) Stereoscopic Vision for a Humanoid Robot using Genetic Programming. Real-world applications of Evolutionary Computing, Edinburgh, *LNCS 1803*, Springer Verlag.
3. Husbands, P., Meyer, J-A, and Harvey, I. (1998) Evolutionary Robotics: a Survey of Applications and Problems. In Proceedings of the first European Workshop of Evolutionary Robotics, (EvoRobot98), volume 1468 of *LNCS*. Paris April 1998 (eds) Husbands, P., Meyer, J-A., Springer Verlag.
4. Kanehiro, F., Kagami, S., Inaba, M. and Inoue, M.(1994) A study on visually guided walking behaviors of remote-brained apelike robot. In Proceedings Japanese Society of Machinery, Annual Conference on Robotics and Mechatronics (ROBOMEC'94), pp. 197-202, 30 June - 1 July, 1994.
5. Koza, J. R. (1992). Genetic Programming: On the Programming of Computers by Means of Natural Selection. MIT Press, Cambridge, MA, USA.
6. Nordin, J.P. (1997), Evolutionary Program Induction of Binary Machine Code and its Application. Krehl Verlag, Muenster, Germany
7. Rikard Karlsson. Sound localization for a humanoid robot by means of genetic programming. Master's thesis, Complex Systems Group, Chalmers University of Technology, S-41296, Göteborg, Sweden, December 1998.
8. Rikard Karlsson, Peter Nordin, and Mats Nordahl. Sound localization for a humanoid robot using genetic programming. In Stefano Cagnoni, Riccardo Poli, George D. Smith, David Corne, Martin Oates, Emma Hart, Pier Luca Lanzi, Egbert Jan Willem, Yun Li, Ben Paechter, and Terence C. Fogarty, editors, *Real-World Applications of Evolutionary Computing*, volume 1803 of *LNCS*, pp. 65–76, Edinburgh, 17 April 2000. Springer-Verlag.
9. Nordin J. P., Nordahl M. (1999) ELVIS: An Evolutionary Architecture for a Humanoid Robot, In Proceeding of: Symposium on Artificial Intelligence (CIMAF99) Havana Cuba
10. Nordin J. P., Nordahl M. (1999) An Evolutionary Architecture For A Humanoid Robot, In Proceeding of: The Fourth International Symposium on Artificial Life and Robotics (AROB 4th 99) Oita Japan
11. Nordin J.P., Eriksson A., Nordahl M. (1999) Genetic Reasoning: Evolutionary Induction of Mathematical Proofs. In Proceeding of: Second European Workshop on Genetic Programming (EuroGP98), volume 1598 of *LNCS*, Springer Verlag
12. Simon Perkins. Evolving effective visual tracking through shaping. In Wolfgang Banzhaf, Jason Daida, Agoston E. Eiben, Max H. Garzon, Vasant Honavar, Mark Jakiela, and Robert E. Smith, editors, *Proceedings of the Genetic and Evolutionary Computation Conference*, volume 2, pp. 1156–1161, Orlando, Florida, USA, 13-17 July 1999. Morgan Kaufmann.

Adaption of Operator Probabilities in Genetic Programming

Jens Niehaus and Wolfgang Banzhaf

System Analysis, Computer Science Department
University of Dortmund, D-44221 Dortmund, Germany
{niehaus,banzhaf}@ls11.cs.uni-dortmund.de

Abstract. In this work we tried to reduce the number of free parameters within Genetic Programming without reducing the quality of the results. We developed three new methods to adapt the probabilities, different genetic operators are applied with. Using two problems from the areas of symbolic regression and classification we showed that the results in these cases were better than randomly chosen parameter sets and could compete with parameter sets chosen with empirical knowledge.

1 Introduction

One of the characteristics of Genetic Programming (GP) [10,5] is the enormous number of free parameters of the algorithm. As different problems require different parameter sets GP requires a lot of experience and knowledge on side of the user.

In this work we are trying to reduce the number of free parameters. Our aim is to find adaptive methods that result in solutions that are as good as the ones gained with the traditional algorithm and empirically established parameter sets. Furthermore the solutions found with our new methods should be better than those found with the traditional algorithm and randomly chosen parameter sets.

While adaption of parameters is common in other areas like Evolution Strategies [13,9] and Genetic Algorithms [8,3,4,14] there are only very few attempts with GP [1,15].

When we later apply GP to a new problem it will be possible to use this algorithm without preceding parameter studies, which always require a lot of time. At least it will be possible to get an initial parameter set, which can be used for further tweaking.

Every new method incorporated into the GP paradigm has to be compared with the traditional method. Besides that a feature might work well on some problems and not on others, the methods might need different parameter sets. Therefore, if one method seems to be better than another one, the reason might be either

J. Miller et al. (Eds.): EuroGP 2001, LNCS 2038, pp. 325–336, 2001.
© Springer-Verlag Berlin Heidelberg 2001

due to an advanced method or it could be due to a difference in quality of the parameter sets used. Our adaptive methods rule out the second reason.

During a run the algorithm creates new individuals by copying old individuals and applying genetic operators. As there are several operators one of them has to be chosen. We examined three different methods to decide which of the operators is applied in certain situations.

In Section 2 we present the GP-system used including the implemented genetic operators. Section 3 describes the new adaptive methods and Section 4 includes our experiments regarding two different problem domains and the corresponding results. The results are discussed in Section 5.

2   GGP and Genetic Operators

2.1   Graph Representation

We used our own GP-system called *GGP*, which is capable of solving problems modelled as acyclic digraphs. Each node of a graph represents one operation such as *ADD* or *MUL* and has a certain number of inputs and outputs, and sometimes additional parameters. All outputs of each node have to be connected with exactly one input of another node.

Opposite to other systems we use graphs as internal representation instead of trees [11] or arrays [12]. This way it is easy to extend the system for using cyclic graphs without any restrictions.

A problem is modelled within the graph. The node type *Input* takes the input values of the problem and propagates them via the outgoing edge to the next node. The fitness function is part of the graph, too. The fitness value of an individual represented by a graph is the sum of all values propagated to the *Output* nodes of the graph over all scenarios.

The node type *GP*, referred to as GP-node, stands for a subgraph created by the GP-system during evolution. The number of incoming and outgoing edges of a GP-subgraph is variable and depends on the surrounding graph. Traditional implementations of GP would call only this node an *individual* and the surrounding graph would be part of the GP program code. The approach *GGP* uses is far more flexible:

- The calculation of the fitness value is part of the graph. If the user wishes to use a method other than, for example, squared differences he just has to modify the graph and does not have to modify the GP-program.
- One graph can contain more than one GP-node. For traditional GP this would mean that one individual consists of more than one tree. Problems dealing with more than one input value could use a tree for each input for some kind of preprocessing and the results could be combined in another tree. To achieve this kind of behaviour with a traditional GP-system the user would have to modify the GP programm code.

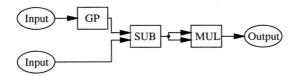

Fig. 1. A graph for symbolic regression

Figure 1 shows a graph used for symbolic-regression problems. For each scenario the first input takes the value from the function domain and the second input the value the function is supposed to calculate. The first value is used as input for the subgraph represented by the GP-node. The result of the calculation within the GP node is compared to the second input value. The fitness function is the sum of the squared differences over all scenarios.

In this work we allow only nodes with exactly one outgoing edge within the GP-subgraph. As the GP-node has only one *Output* node in our examples the contents of a GP-node can always be interpreted as a tree comparable to ordinary GP-systems.

During a run the number of nodes in a GP-subgraph within a GP-node is limited by a parameter the user has to choose at the beginning. The number of *Input* and *Output* nodes inside a GP-subgraph corresponds to the number of incoming and outgoing edges of the GP-node.

2.2 Genetic Operators

GGP includes one crossover operator and several mutation operators. Bear in mind that the operators modify only GP-subgraphs and not trees as in usual tree based GP. All the modifications result in acyclic graphs with all nodes of each GP-subgraph properly connected.

As each edge has one start and one ending the sum of all inputs of the nodes in a GP-subgraph must be the same as the number of outputs from these nodes making it impossible just to add or remove a node with a different number of inputs and outputs. Therefore most of the mutation operators modify subgraphs.

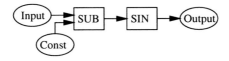

Fig. 2. An example graph

Figure 2 offers an example graph we use to explain the genetic operators described next.

1. We cannot remove the *Constant* node as it has no input but one output. The second input of the *SUB* node would not be connected afterwards. On the other hand it is possible to remove both the *Constant* node and the *SUB* node and to connect the *Input* node directly to the *Output* node. This mutation is called **delete path** as it removes the path between two nodes.
2. The opposite to **delete path** is the mutation operator **insert path.** As we are using only trees in this work the operation is reduced to the following: one edge of a GP-subgraph is split, a node with two inputs and one output is inserted, and the free input of this node gets connected to a newly inserted node with no incoming and one outgoing edge.[1]
3. The operator **insert node** inserts a node with one input and one output by splitting one existing edge.
4. As the name implies the operator **delete node** deletes a node with one input and one output by connecting the surrounding edges.
5. The operator **move node** moves a node with one input and one output to an adjacent position. For example the *SIN* node in Figure 2 could be moved to the position between *Input* and *SUB* node.
6. **Replace node** replaces a node with a different node with the same number of inputs and outputs. The *SUB* node in Figure 2 could be replaced by an *ADD* node.
7. **Subgraph crossover:** Given two individuals represented by two graphs with several GP-nodes each, one of the first individual's GP-subgraphs is replaced by the contents of the corresponding GP-node of the second individual. As our experiments use only models with one GP-node the operator is equivalent to replicating the first individual and we do not use it at all.

2.3   The Evolutionary Algorithm

GGP uses steady state tournament selection. There are always four individuals per tournament. The two winners overwrite the two losing individuals. Afterwards the new individuals will be mutated by one of the genetic operators. In the basic version of the algorithm the probabilities of the genetic operators are defined once at the beginning of a run. The sum of all probabilities must be smaller than or equal to one. As this work is about adapting these probabilities the next section will describe different methods to change the probabilities during runtime.

3   Different Methods of Adaption

We developed three new methods of adapting the probabilities of genetic operators and compared them to two static methods. Our aim was to find a method

---

[1] When we evolve graphs instead of trees the beginning of the new path can also be a node with two outputs and one input. The free input and output are inserted into another edge of the existing GP-subgraph. The operator also checks that the graph remains acyclic.

that is significantly better than randomly chosen static probabilities and not significantly worse than static probabilities that have empirically proved to result in good fitness values. We compare our results against the following methods without adaption:

Random Static Probabilities (RSP): Given n different genetic operators we compute an n-tuple $(p_1, ..., p_n)$ with $\sum_{i=1}^{n} p_i = 100$ and $p_1, ..., p_n \in \{0, 1, ..., 100\}$. Each of the $\frac{(n+99)!}{100!(n-1)!}$ possible tuples has the same probability of being chosen. The value of p_i represents the percentage of how often operator i is chosen for mutation.

Empirical Static Probabilities (ESP): During empirical tests some n-tuples have achieved significant better results than others. One of those was chosen.

Within all of the three following methods we calculate some values p_i, which represent the percentage of how often operator i is chosen for mutation. As the sum of all percentages might be smaller than 100 we introduce $p_0 = 100 - \sum_{i=1}^{n} p_i$ as the percentage for replication.

3.1   Population-Level Dynamic Probabilities (PDP)

The probabilities of the genetic operators are adapted based on the success rates of the operators.

- Twenty percent of all probabilities are shared equally distributed amongst all n genetic operators: $p_{all} = \lfloor \frac{20}{n} \rfloor$. This rule ensures that none of the probabilities can decrease to zero preventing the selection of the corresponding operator at a later time when its use is more suitable.
- To keep the next equation simple we introduce the ratio $r_i = \frac{success_i{}^2}{used_i}$ for each operator i where $used_i$ is the number how often operator i was applied and $success_i$ is the number how often these applications have lead to a fitness improvement compared to the parent individual.[2][3]
- For each operator p_i is computed using p_{all} and a scaled value of r_i: $p_i = p_{all} + \lfloor r_i \frac{(100 - np_{all})}{scale} \rfloor$ with $scale = \sum_{j=1}^{n} r_j$.

The name *'Population-level Dynamic Probabilities'* was chosen in reference to ANGELINE's categorisation of different classes for adaptive parameters. For an overview of other work on adaptive methods in Evolutionary Computation see [2].

---

[2] A squared value of success is used because a linear term always results in nearly equally distributed probabilities amongst the operators due to the unpleasant small success rate of genetic operators.

[3] To circumvent *division by zero*-errors $used_i$ is initialised with a value of one.

3.2   Fitness Based Dynamic Probabilities (FBDP)

Initial experiments have shown that different operators have different success rates depending on the fitness of their parent individual.

For each fitness improvement between a parent individual and the corresponding child the fitness of the parent and the operator used to achieve the improvement is stored in an array sorted by fitness values.

The probabilities are computed using the following method where twenty percent of all probabilities are again shared equally distributed amongst all n genetic operators: $p_{all} = \lfloor \frac{20}{n} \rfloor$.

- A probability of $p_{left} = 100 - \lfloor np_{all} \rfloor$ must be distributed among n operators.
- We create a set of p_{left} ($fitness, operator$)-tuples from the array containing all the fitness improvements with the corresponding genetic operators. The set consists of those p_{left} pairs whose fitness value is next to the fitness of the actual parent.
- p_i is the sum of p_{all} and the number of tuples in the set that use operator i.
- If there have not been p_{left} fitness improvements yet p_i is calculated as $p_i = \lfloor \frac{100}{n} \rfloor$.

This method works only for operators using one parent. With GP systems using two parents for one genetic operator the fitness of the individual with the higher impact on the offspring should be chosen to create the set of tuples. If the impact is uncertain one of the two fitness values of the parents should be chosen at random.

3.3   Individual-Level Dynamic Probabilities (IDP)

Each individual j has its own parameter set for operator probabilities. For each genetic operator i there is a variable cnt_j^i counting the unsuccessful attempts to improve fitness with this operator. A counter is reset if an application of the corresponding operator leads to a fitness improvement. The relation among the values of all counters of one individual is used to calculate the probabilities of the genetic operators.

- Again twenty percent of all probabilities are shared equally distributed among all n genetic operators: $p_{all} = \lfloor \frac{20}{n} \rfloor$.
- p_i is calculated using equation (1). The more often an operator has failed the smaller is p_i.

$$p_i = p_{all} + \left\lfloor \frac{(\max_{1 \le k \le n} cnt_j^k + 1 - cnt_j^i)(100 - n\, p_{all})}{n(\max_{1 \le k \le n} cnt_j^k + 1) - \sum_{k=1}^{n} cnt_j^k} \right\rfloor \quad (1)$$

– After a tournament is finished, a winning individual j is copied to the position of a losing individual k, and one of the operators is applied (based on p_i-values of the parent individual). Then the counter of the applied operator of the parent individual is updated. Afterwards all the counters of the parent j are propagated to the child individual k using equation (2).

$$cnt_k^i = \frac{1}{2}\left(cnt_j^i + \frac{1}{n}\sum_{l=1}^{n} cnt_j^l\right)$$ (2)

With equation (2) individuals can more easily adapt to new situations during a run. For example in a situation with one individual having a good fitness and one preferred operator, this individual might be the ancestor for a chain of descendants with slightly degrading fitness values. These individuals where all mutated with the same operator, which now seems to be a bad choice. Because of to equation (2), the difference between the probability of this operator and all the others will be reduced after each mutation so that the use of a different operator gets more probable soon.

For operators using two parents this method has to be extended. One way would be to propagate the smaller one of both values cnt_k^i from both of the parents but further research is needed on this topic.

4   Experiments and Results

This section studies the performance of the different methods introduced in Section 3 using a symbolic-regression and a classification problem. In both cases we used a population size of 100 individuals and a maximum number of 100,000 tournaments. With each problem and each method of adaption we tried four different values for the upper limit of nodes inside a GP-subgraph (40, 80, 100 and 140). For each of all possible combinations 60 runs were performed. As we only want to examine the influence of our methods on the solution we did not use advanced techniques such as ADFs or demes.

4.1   Symbolic Regression

We used GP to find a function $f : [0, 2\pi] \to \mathbb{R}$ that minimises the expression

$$\sum_{i=0}^{49}\left(f(\frac{6.3}{49}i) - \sin(\frac{6.3}{49}i)\right)^2 .$$ (3)

In other words we tried to evolve a sinus-function based on a training set of 50 equidistant points between 0 and 6.3. We used the graph shown in Figure 1. Table 1 lists all node types allowed in a GP-subgraph. The node type *Factor* scales the input by the value of its parameter. The output of the node type

Table 1. Nodes in GP-subgraph

Type	Inputs	Outputs	Params
ADD	2	1	0
SUB	2	1	0
MUL	2	1	0
DIV	2	1	0
Factor	1	1	1: $N(0,4)$
Const	0	1	1: $N(1,4)$
Inputval	0	1	0

Table 2. Average fitness of 60 runs

Nodes	RSP	ESP	PDP	FBDP	IDP
40	0.055	0.052	0.052	0.046	**0.045**
80	0.033	0.028	0.031	0.022	**0.022**
100	0.025	0.019	**0.012**	0.017	0.02
140	0.029	**0.01**	0.02	0.023	0.016

Inputval always has the same value as the *Input* node of the GP-subgraph. The GP-system uses the operators **insert path, delete path, replace node** and **delete node** as described in Section 2.2.

Table 2 shows the average fitness of 60 runs for each parameter set. All dynamic methods are in average better than RSP. With the exception of the experiments with GP-subgraphs with a maximum size of 140 nodes there were always two dynamic methods better than ESP.

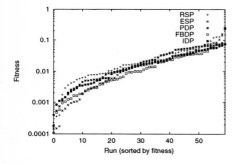

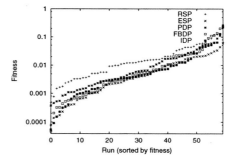

Fig. 3. Problem: Sinus, GP-subgraph with 80 nodes

Fig. 4. Problem: Sinus GP-subgraph with 140 nodes

Figures 3 and 4 show the results of all runs with a maximum of 80 and 140 nodes inside the GP-subgraph. Due to the similarity to Figure 3 the figures for 40 and 100 nodes are omitted.

For each GP-subgraph-size we did a KOLMOGOROV-SMIRNOV test [7] to find out whether the distributions of the fitness results for the alternative methods might differ. As the plots propose this is only true in a very few cases. With a confidence-level of 95 percent only the results of RSP seem to differ from all other methods in the 140 nodes case. For all other cases no hypothesis can be accepted or discarded.

4.2   Classification

The classification problem we used is shown in Figure 6. The data set consists of 1000 points and was taken from [6]. The corresponding graph is shown in Figure 5. The fitness was the error rate of an individual given in percent.

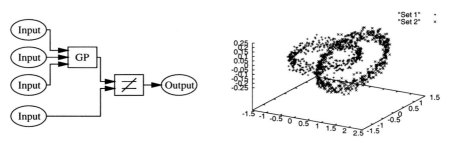

Fig. 5. Graph for classification

Fig. 6. The classification problem

Additional to the node types in Table 1 types called *SIN, COS* and *Threshold* were used, where *Threshold* has one parameter and sets the output to 1 if the parameter is smaller than the input value or -1 otherwise. Instead of *Inputval* we used the node type *Inputval2*. It uses a parameter to decide which input value of the GP-subgraph should be propagated to the output of the node.

The results are given in Table 3. Figures 7 and 8 show the results of the individual runs. The runs with 40 and 140 nodes within the GP-subgraph look similar to Figure 8 and are omitted.

Table 3. Average fitness of 60 runs

Nodes	RSP	ESP	PDP	FBDP	IDP
40	0.124	0.079	0.106	0.104	0.094
80	0.11	0.087	0.111	0.102	0.096
100	0.139	0.080	0.123	0.112	0.105
140	0.127	0.102	0.123	0.128	0.105

Table 4. Significant differences

Nodes	Methods
40, 80, 100:	RSP $\leftrightarrow$ ESP
40, 100, 140:	RSP $\leftrightarrow$ IDP
80, 100:	ESP $\leftrightarrow$ PDP
100:	ESP $\leftrightarrow$ FBDP

In both figures we see that the results of the adaptive methods lie between BSP and ESP. Of all the adaptive methods IDP seems to be most suited for this problem.

KOLMOGOROV-SMIRNOV tests offer some indicators that both ESP and IDP perform better than RSP. Table 4 lists the methods with different distributions at a confidence level of 95 percent.

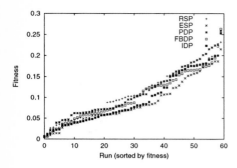

Fig. 7. Problem: Classification, GP-subgraph with 80 nodes

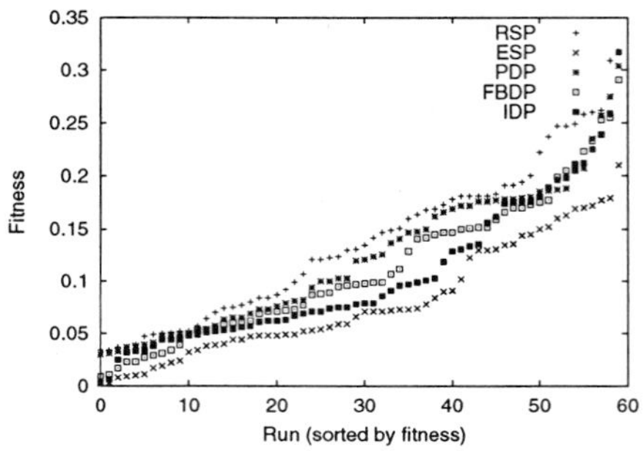

Fig. 8. Problem: Classification, GP-subgraph with 100 nodes

5   Discussion

The results given in Section 4 point out that the new methods seem to fulfil our aims.

Looking at the average fitness values the adaptive methods seem to be better than randomly chosen static parameter sets on both problems and even better than the empirically chosen parameter sets on the symbolic-regression task.

KOLMOGOROV-SMIRNOV tests show that our methods seem to be better than the randomly chosen parameter sets. As the distribution functions in both benchmarks chosen are not continuous the tests have to be taken with care because KOLMOGOROV-SMIRNOV tends to accept hypotheses for too long.

IDP seems to be the best of the three methods for adapting probabilities, at least for the benchmarks used. The reason for the differences might be explained as follows.

- PDP uses the same probabilities for all individuals. Those probabilities are based on all fitness improvements. Most of the successful mutations improve only the fitness of an individual relative to its parent but do not result in a new best fitness for the hole population. So the adaption might lead to a parameter set useful for improving fitness of average individuals without improving the fitness of the population.
- FBDP chooses probabilities based on the fitness of the parent. Therefore mutation of individuals with a good fitness does not interfere with mutation of those individuals with a worse fitness.
  The test results in Tables 2 and 3 show that the performance of FBDP decreases for large GP-subgraphs. The reason for this might be the following: On small GP-subgraphs individuals with a similar fitness tend to have a similar genotype (e.g. graph). As most operators can only be applied to certain positions in a graph it is quite possible that the mutation performed

is quite similar to those successful operations responsible for choosing this operator thus resulting in a fitness improvement. On bigger GP-subgraphs the chance to do a mutation completely unrelated to those responsible for choosing the probabilities grows, making a fitness improvement less probable.
– With IDP every individual has its own history of successful and unsuccessful mutation attempts. If an operator does not work for a certain individual it will not be used with it that much for later mutations. Other individuals, which might benefit from this operator, are not affected by this restriction.

6   Conclusion

In this contribution we have successfully applied new methods of parameter adaption to GP. In further studies we have to increase the number of runs to make the results statistically more significant, we have to validate the results using other problems and find methods to adapt other parameters such as population or GP-subgraph size.

References

1. P. J. Angeline: Adaptive and Self-adaptive Evolutionary Computations. In: M. Palaniswami, Y. Attikiouzel, R. Marks, D. Fogel and T. Fukuda (Eds.) *Computational Intelligence: A Dynamic System Perspective,* NJ: IEEE Press, 152–161, 1995
2. P. J. Angeline: Two Self-Adaptive Crossover Operators for Genetic Programming. In: P. Angeline, K. Kinnear (Eds.) *Advances in Genetic Programming II.* Cambridge, MA: MIT Press, 89–110, 1996
3. J. Arabas, Z. Michalewicz and J. Mulawka: GAVaPS – a Genetic Algorithm with Varying Population Size. In: *Procceedings of the First IEEE Conference on Evolutionary Computation.* Orlando, Florida: IEEE Press. 73–78, 1994
4. T. Bäck, A. E. Eiben and N. A. L. van der Vaart: An empirical study on GAs "without parameters". In: *Parallel Problem Solving from Nature - PPSN VI.* Berlin: Springer-Verlag, 315–324, 2000
5. Banzhaf, W., Nordin, P., Keller, R. E., Francone, F. D.: Genetic Programming: An Introduction. San Francisco, CA: Morgan Kaufmann, 1998
6. Brameier, M. and Banzhaf, W: Evolving Teams of Predictors with Genetic Programming. Technical Report, University of Dortmund, Computational Intelligence, Collaborative Research Center 531, 2001. To appear
7. W. J. Conover: Practical nonparametric statistics. New York: John Wiley & Sons, 309–314, 1971
8. L. Davis: Adapting Operator Probabilities in Genetic Algorithms. In: J. D. Schaffer (Ed.) *Procceedings of the Third International Conference on Genetic Algorithms and Their Applications.* San Mateo, CA: Morgan Kaufmann, 61–69, 1989
9. N. Hansen and A. Ostermeier: Adapting arbitrary normal mutation distributions in evolution strategies: The covariance matrix adaptation. In: *Proceedings of the 1996 IEEE International Conference on Evolutionary Computation.* 312–317, 1996

10. J. R. Koza: Genetic Programming: On the Programming of Computers by Natural Selection. Cambridge, MA: MIT Press, 1992
11. P. Marenbach and H. Pohlheim: Generation of Structured Process Models Using Genetic Programming. In: Fogarty, T. C. (Ed.) *Evolutionary Computing. Selected Papers,* volume 1143 of *Lecture Notes in Computer Science,* Berlin: Springer Verlag, 102–109, 1996
12. R. Poli: Some Steps Towards a Form of Parallel Distributed Genetic Programming. In: *The 1st Online Workshop on Soft Computing (WSC1).* http://www.bioele.nuee.nagoya-u.ac.jp/wsc1/, 1996
13. H.-P. Schwefel: Evolution and Optimum Seeking. New York: John Wiley & Sons, Inc., 1995
14. W. M. Spears: Adapting Crossover in Evolutionary Algorithms. In: R. Reynolds and D. B. Fogel (Eds.) *Procceedings of the Fourth Annual Conference on Evolutionary Programming.* MIT Press, 367-384, 1995
15. A. Teller and M. Veloso: PADO: A new learning architecture for object recognition. In: *Symbolic Visual Learning.* Oxford University Press, 81-116, 1996

Crossover in Grammatical Evolution:
The Search Continues

Michael O'Neill[1], Conor Ryan[1], Maarten Keijzer[2], and Mike Cattolico[3]

[1] Dept. Of Computer Science And Information Systems
University of Limerick, Ireland
{Michael.ONeill,Conor.Ryan}@ul.ie
[2] Danish Hydraulic Institute, Denmark, mak@dhi.dk
[3] Tiger Mountain Scientific, mike@tigerscience.com

Abstract. Grammatical Evolution is an evolutionary automatic programming algorithm that can produce code in any language, requiring as inputs a BNF grammar definition describing the output language, and the fitness function. The utility of crossover in GP systems has been hotly debated for some time, and this debate has also arisen with respect to Grammatical Evolution. This paper serves to continue an analysis of the crossover operator in Grammatical Evolution by looking at the result of turning off crossover, and by exchanging randomly generated blocks in a headless chicken-like crossover. Results show that crossover in Grammatical Evolution is essential on the problem domains examined. The mechanism of one-point crossover in Grammatical Evolution is discussed, resulting in the discovery of some interesting properties that could yield an insight into the operator's success.

1 Introduction

While crossover is generally accepted as an explorative operator in string based G.A.s [4] the benefit or otherwise of employing crossover in tree based Genetic Programming hasn't been fully established. Work such as [2] went as far as to dismiss GP as a evolutionary search method due to its use of trees, while [1] presented results which suggested that crossover in GP provides little benefit over randomly generating subtrees. Langdon and Francone et. al. have also addressed this issue, the former on tree based GP and the latter on linear structures, and have both introduced new crossover operators in an attempt to improve exploration [3] [7].

These exploit the idea of a homologous crossover that draws inspiration from the molecular biological crossover process. The principal exploited being the fact that in nature the entities swapping genetic material only swap fragments which belong to the same position and are of similar size, but which do not necessarily have the same functionality. This, it is proposed, will result in more productive crossover events, and results from both Langdon and Francone et. al. provide evidence to support this claim. A consequence arising from these conservative crossover operators is the reduction of the bloat phenomenon, occurring due to

J. Miller et al. (Eds.): EuroGP 2001, LNCS 2038, pp. 337–347, 2001.
© Springer-Verlag Berlin Heidelberg 2001

the fact that these new operators are less destructive [8]. As with many non-binary representations, it is often not clear how much useful genetic material is being exchanged during crossover, and thus not clear how much exploration is actually taking place.

Grammatical Evolution (GE) an evolutionary algorithm that can evolve code in any language, utilises linear genomes [9] [17]. As with GP systems, GE has come under fire for its seemingly destructive crossover operator, a simple one-point crossover inspired by GAs. Previously we have sought answers to questions such as how destructive one-point crossover operator is, and could the system benefit from a homologous-like crossover operator as proposed for tree-based GP, and the linear AIM GP [11]. Initial results suggested that this destructive behaviour did not transpire, at the beginning of runs results show that the number of crossover events that produce individuals which are better than those in the current population is very high. On average, this ratio remains relatively consistent throughout runs, which tells us that crossover is in fact a useful operator in recombining individuals effectively, rather than causing mass destruction. The idea of an homologous crossover has also been explored in the context of GE [11], but results demonstrated the superiority of the simple one-point crossover operator currently adopted.

We now continue the analysis of crossover in GE by turning off crossover, and by exchanging random blocks during crossover in a headless chicken-type crossover [1]. Before a description of our findings we firstly give an overview of GE and introduce the one-point crossover operator adopted.

2   Grammatical Evolution

Grammatical Evolution (GE) is an evolutionary algorithm that can evolve computer programs in any language. Rather than representing the programs as parse trees, as in standard GP [6], we use a linear genome representation. Each individual, a variable length binary string, contains in its codons (groups of 8 bits) the information to select production rules from a Backus Naur Form (BNF) grammar. BNF is a notation which represents a language in the form of production rules. It is comprised of a set of non-terminals which can be mapped to elements of the set of terminals, according to the production rules. An example excerpt from a BNF grammar is given below. These productions state that S can be replaced with any one of the non-terminals **expr**, **if-stmt**, or **loop**.

```
S ::= expr      (0)
    | if-stmt   (1)
    | loop      (2)
```

In order to select a rule in GE, the next codon value on the genome is generated and placed in the following formula:

$$Rule = Codon\ Integer\ Value$$

$$MOD$$

$$Number\ of\ Rules\ for\ this\ nonterminal$$

If the next codon integer value was 4, given that we have 3 rules to select from as in the above example, we get 4 MOD 3 = 1. S will therefore be replaced with the non-terminal if-stmt.

Beginning from the left hand side of the genome codon integer values are generated and used to select rules from the BNF grammar, until one of the following situations arise:

1. A complete program is generated. This occurs when all the non-terminals in the expression being mapped, are transformed into elements from the terminal set of the BNF grammar.
2. The end of the genome is reached, in which case the *wrapping* operator is invoked. This results in the return of the genome reading frame to the left hand side of the genome once again. The reading of codons will then continue unless an upper threshold representing the maximum number of wrapping events has occurred during this individual's mapping process. This threshold is currently set at ten events.
3. In the event that a threshold on the number of wrapping events has occurred and the individual is still incompletely mapped, the mapping process is halted, and the individual assigned the lowest possible fitness value.

GE uses a steady state replacement mechanism [16], such that, two parents produce two children, the best of which replaces the worst individual in the current population if the child has a greater fitness. The standard genetic operators of point mutation (applied at a probability of *pmut* (see Table 2) to each bit of the chromosome), and crossover (one point as outlined in Section 3) are adopted. It also employs a duplication operator that duplicates a random number of codons and inserts these into the penultimate codon position on the genome. A full description of GE can be found in [9].

3   The GE Crossover Operator

By default, GE employs a standard one point crossover operator as follows: (i) Two crossover points are selected at random, one on each individual (ii) The segments on the right hand side of each individual are then swapped. As noted in Section 1, it has been suggested that the cost of exploration via crossover is the possible destruction of building blocks. Indeed, there has been work which shows that a reason for the increase in bloat in many GP runs is to protect individuals from destructive crossover.

It is argued here that bloat occurs as a mechanism to prevent the disruption of functional parts of the individual arising from crossover events. To counteract the potentially destructive property of the crossover operator, and to indirectly reduce the occurrence of bloat, novel crossover operators have been developed [7][3]. Dubbed *homologous* crossover, these operators draw inspiration from the molecular biological process of crossover in which the chromosomes to crossover align, and common crossover points are selected on each individual (i.e. at the same locus), and typically a two point crossover occurs.

Results reported in [11] suggest that GE's one point crossover is not as damaging as has been suggested and appears to act as a global search operator throughout the duration of a run.

4   Experimental Approach

We wish to examine the strength of crossover in GE with a two pronged approach. Firstly, the probability of crossover will be set to zero, which effectively switches off the operator. Secondly, we will replace the standard one point crossover adopted with a headless chicken-type crossover. The headless chicken crossover operates by selecting crossover points as normal, but, instead of exchanging the blocks as is, new blocks are generated with a random bit generator.

For each experiment 50 runs were carried out on the Santa Fe ant trail and a symbolic regression problem [6]. Performance was ascertained by using a cumulative frequency of success measure. Tableau's describing the parameters and terminals are given in Tables 2 and 1, and the grammars for both problems are given in Appendix A and B.

5   Results

Results for the experiments can be seen in Figures 1 and 2. These graphs clearly demonstrate the damaging effects of the headless chicken crossover and switching crossover off completely. On the symbolic regression problem GE fails to find solutions in both of these cases, while on the Santa Fe ant trail the system's success rate falls off dramatically.

These results clearly demonstrate that the one point crossover operator is important to the effective operation of the system for the problems examined. Notice that mutation also makes a small difference to the success rate.

6   Discussion

The question arises then, as to why GE's one point crossover operator is so productive. If we look at the effect the operator plays on a parse tree representation of the programs undergoing crossover we begin to see more clearly the mechanism of this operator and it's search properties.

Table 1. Grammatical Evolution Tableau for Symbolic Regression

Objective :	Find a function of one independent variable and one dependent variable, in symbolic form that fits a given sample of 20 (x_i, y_i) data points, where the target function is the quartic polynomial $X^4 + X^3 + X^2 + X$
Terminal Operands:	X (the independent variable)
Terminal Operators	The binary operators $+, *, -$, and $/$ (protected division used) The unary operators Sin, Cos, Exp and Log
Fitness cases	The given sample of 20 data points in the interval $[-1, +1]$
Raw Fitness	The sum, taken over the 20 fitness cases, of the absolute error
Standardised Fitness	Same as raw fitness
Hits	The number of fitness cases for which the error is less than 0.01
Wrapper	Standard productions to generate C functions
Parameters	$Population = 500$, $Generations = 50$ $pmut = 0.01$, $pcross = 0.9$

Table 2. Grammatical Evolution Tableau for the Santa Fe Trail

Objective :	Find a computer program to control an artificial ant so that it can find all 89 pieces of food located on the Santa Fe Trail.
Terminal Operators:	left(), right(), move(), food_ahead()
Fitness cases	One fitness case
Raw Fitness	Number of pieces of food before the ant times out with 615 operations.
Standardised Fitness	Total number of pieces of food less the raw fitness.
Hits	Same as raw fitness.
Wrapper	Standard productions to generate C functions
Parameters	$Population = 500$, $Generations = 50$ $pmut = 0.01$, $pcross = 0.9$

When mapping a string to an individual, GE always works with the left most non-terminal. Thus, if one were to look at the individual's corresponding parse tree, one would see that the tree is constructed in a pre-order fashion. Furthermore, if the individual is over-specified, that is, has codons left over, they form a *tail*, which is, effectively, a stack of codons, as illustrated in Fig. 3.

If, during a crossover event, one tried to map the first half of the remaining string, the result not surprisingly, would usually be an incomplete tree. However, the tree would not be incomplete in the same manner as one taken from the middle of a GP crossover event. The pre-order nature of the mapping is such that the result is similar to that of Fig. 3 and Fig. 4. That is, the tree is left with a *spine* and several *ripple sites* from which one or more sub-trees, dubbed *ripple trees* are removed. This crossover behaviour, which is an inherent property of GE, was first noticed by [5] where they termed it *ripple crossover*.

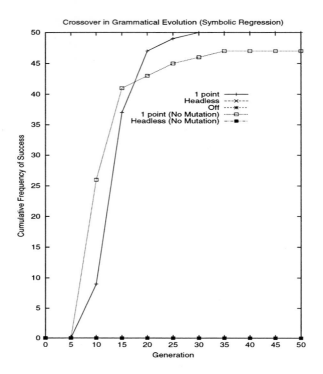

Fig. 1. A comparison of GE's performance on the symbolic regression problem is illustrated. When the headless chicken crossover is used the system fails to find solutions to this problem. This is also the case when crossover is switched off.

Each of the ripple trees is effectively dismantled and returned to the stack of codons in the individual's tail. Crossover then involves individuals swapping tails so that, when evaluating the offspring, the ripple sites on the spine will be filled using codons from the other parent.

There is no guarantee that the tail from the other parent will be of the same length, or even that it was used in the same place on the other spine. This means that a codon that represented which choice to make could suddenly be expected to make a choice from a completely different non-terminal, possibly even with a different number of choices. Fortunately, GE evaluates codons *in context*, that is, the exact meaning of a codon is determined by those codons that immediately precede it. Thus, we can say that GE codons have *intrinsic polymorphism*[5], as they can be used in any part of the grammar. Furthermore, if the meaning of one codon changes, the change "ripples" through all the rest of the codons. This means that a group of codons that coded a particular sub-tree on one spine can code an entirely different sub-tree when employed by another spine. The power of intrinsic polymorphism can even reach between the ripple trees, in that if one no longer needs all its codons, they are passed to the next

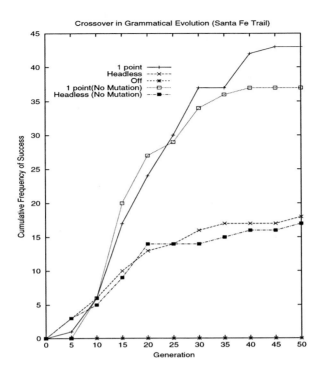

Fig. 2. A comparison of GE's performance on the Santa Fe ant trail can be seen. The graph clearly demonstrates the damaging effects of the headless chicken crossover and the case when crossover is switched off.

ripple tree and, conversely, if it now requires more codons, it can obtain them from its neighbouring ripple tree.

7   Conclusions and Future Work

We have previously demonstrated the ability of GE's one point crossover as an operator that exploits an exchange of blocks in a productive manner on the problem domains examined. Results presented here also show the detrimental effects of switching off crossover for GE on these problems, in one case crossover being essential to the generation of a correct solution.

A discussion on the mechanism of GE's one point crossover reveals an interesting *ripple* property when it's effect on parse trees is examined, providing a possible explanation as to why this operator may be so profitable for GE. Further investigations will be required in order to ascertain the usefulness of this *ripple* crossover mechanism. It is proposed that the key to the system is that it exchanges on average, half of the genetic material of the parents during each crossover, regardless of the size of the individuals. This is made possible by a

(a)   E ::== (+ E E) | (− E E) | (* E E) | (% E E) | X | Y

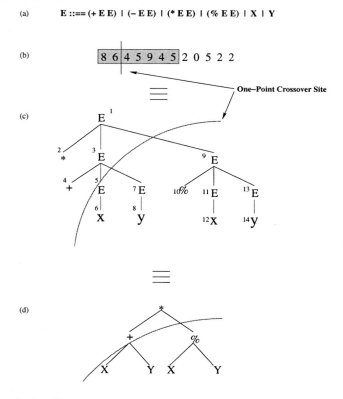

Fig. 3. The ripple effect of one-point crossover illustrated using an example GE individual represented as a string of codon integer values (b) and its equivalent derivation (c) and parse trees (d). The codon integer values in (b) represent the rule number to be selected from the grammar outlined in (a), with the part shaded gray corresponding to the values used to produce the trees in (c) and (d), the remaining integers are an intron. Fig. 4 shows the resulting spine with ripple sites and tails.

combination of the linear representation of the individuals and the property of intrinsic polymorphism, which permits any part of an individual's genome to legally be applied to any part of the grammar [5].

This paper also discuss the notion of spines, that is, the part of the tree that remains after crossover occurs. This could be the first step on the road to identifying a schema theorem for GE, as the system is clearly growing these rooted structures, in a manner similar to [10].

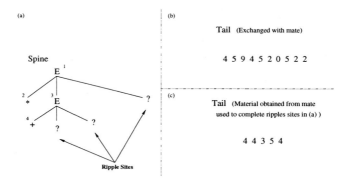

Fig. 4. Illustrated are the spine and the resulting ripple sites (a) and tails (b)(c) produced as a consequence of the one-point crossover in Fig. 3

References

1. Angeline, P.J. 1997. Subtree Crossover: Building block engine or macromutation? In *Proceedings of GP'97*, pages 9-17.
2. Collins, R. 1992. Studies in Artificial Life. PhD thesis. University of California, Los Angeles.
3. Francone F. D., Banzhaf W., Conrads M, Nordin P. 1999. Homologous Crossover in Genetic Programming. In *Proceedings of the Genetic and Evolutionary Computation Conference, GECCO 99*, pages 1021-1038.
4. Goldberg, David E. 1989. Genetic Algorithms in Search, Optimization and Machine Learning. Addison Wesley.
5. Keijzer M., Ryan C., O'Neill M., Cattolico M., Babovic V. 2001. Ripple Crossover in Genetic Programming. In *Proceedings of EuroGP 2001*.
6. Koza, J. 1992. *Genetic Programming*. MIT Press.
7. Langdon W.B. 1999. Size Fair and Homologous Tree Genetic Programming Crossovers. In *Proceedings of the Genetic and Evolutionary Computation Conference, GECCO 99*, pages 1092-1097.
8. Langdon W.B., Soule T., Poli R., and Foster J.A. 1999. The Evolution of Size and Shape. In *Advances in Genetic Programming Volume 3*, MIT Press 1999, pp 162-190.
9. O'Neill M. and Ryan C. 2001. Grammatical Evolution. *IEEE Trans. Evolutionary Computation*, 2001.
10. Justinian P. Rosca and Dana H. Ballard. 1999. Rooted-Tree Schemata in Genetic Programming, in *Advances in Genetic Programming 3*, Chapter 11, pp 243-271, 1999, MIT Press.
11. O'Neill M. and Ryan C. 2000. Crossover in Grammatical Evolution: A Smooth Operator? *Lecture Notes in Computer Science 1802, Proceedings of the European Conference on Genetic Programming*, pages 149-162. Springer-Verlag.
12. O'Neill M. and Ryan C. 1999. Genetic Code Degeneracy: Implications for Grammatical Evolution and Beyond. In *Proceedings of the Fifth European Conference on Artificial Life*.
13. O'Neill M. and Ryan C. 1999. Under the Hood of Grammatical Evolution. In *Proceedings of the Genetic & Evolutionary Computation Conference 1999*.

14. O'Neill M. and Ryan C. 1999. Evolving Multi-line Compilable C Programs. *Lecture Notes in Computer Science 1598, Proceedings of the Second European Workshop on Genetic Programming*, pages 83-92. Springer-Verlag.
15. Poli Riccardo, Langdon W.B. 1998. On the Search Properties of Different Crossover Operators in Genetic Programming. In *Proceedings of the Third annual Genetic Programming conference 1998*, pages 293-301.
16. Ryan C. and O'Neill M. 1998. Grammatical Evolution: A Steady State Approach. In *Late Breaking Papers, Genetic Programming 1998*, pages 180-185.
17. Ryan C., Collins J.J., and O'Neill M. 1998. Grammatical Evolution: Evolving Programs for an Arbitrary Language. *Lecture Notes in Computer Science 1391, Proceedings of the First European Workshop on Genetic Programming*, pages 83-95. Springer-Verlag.

A Symbolic Regression Grammar

$$N = \{expr, op, pre\_op\}$$
$$T = \{Sin, Cos, Exp, Log, +, -, /, *, X, ()\}$$
$$S = <expr>$$

And P can be represented as:

```
(1) <expr> ::= <expr> <op> <expr>      (A)
            | ( <expr> <op> <expr> )  (B)
            | <pre-op> ( <expr> )     (C)
            | <var>                   (D)


(2) <op> ::= + (A)
          | - (B)
          | / (C)
          | * (D)


(3) <pre-op> ::= Sin (A)
              | Cos (B)
              | Exp (C)
              | Log (D)


(4) <var> ::= X
```

B Santa Fe Trail Grammar

$$N = \{code, line, if - statement, op\}$$
$$T = \{left(), right(), move(), food\_ahead(), else, if, \{, \}, (,)\}$$
$$S = <code>$$

And P can be represented as:

```
(1) <code> :: =  <line>                  (A)
                 |<code><line>           (B)

(2) <line> :: =  <if-statement>          (A)
                 |<op>                    (B)

(3) <if-statement> :: = if(food_ahead()){<line>} else{<line>}

(5) <op> :: =     left()                 (A)
                | right()                 (B)
                | move()                  (C)
```

Computational Complexity, Genetic Programming, and Implications

Bart Rylander, Terry Soule, and James Foster

Initiative for Bioinformatics and Evolutionary Studies (IBEST)
Department of Computer Science, University of Idaho
Moscow, Idaho 83844-1014 USA
rylander@up.edu, {soule,foster}@csuidaho.edu

Abstract. Recent theory work has shown that a Genetic Program (GP) used to produce programs may have output that is bounded above by the GP itself [l]. This paper presents proofs that show that 1) a program that is the output of a GP or any inductive process has complexity that can be bounded by the Kolmogorov complexity of the originating program; 2) this result does not hold if the random number generator used in the evolution is a true random source; and 3) an optimization problem being solved with a GP will have a complexity that can be bounded below by the growth rate of the minimum length problem representation used for the implementation. These results are then used to provide guidance for GP implementation.

1 Introduction

Informally, computational complexity is the study of classes of problems based on the rate of growth of space, time, or other fundamental unit of measure as a function of the size of the input. It seeks to determine what problems are computationally tractable, and to classify problems based on their best possible convergence time over all possible problem instances and algorithms. A complexity analysis of a method of automatic programming such as a Genetic Algorithm (GA) or a GP seeks to answer another question as well. Namely, does the method in question, with all of its method-specific computational baggage, provide an advantage or disadvantage to solving a particular problem over all other methods. This is in contrast to a study that seeks to identify what features of a problem instance cause the method to converge more slowly, or a study that seeks to analyze the expected convergence time of the method itself.

To illustrate this difference, consider the well-known problem of Sort (i.e. given a list of n elements, arrange the list in some predefined manner). If there is only one element that is out of order then a particular algorithm may converge more quickly than if all the elements are out of order, as is the case with the algorithm Insertion Sort. An analysis based on problem instances is concerned with what features of the particular instance cause the convergence to occur more slowly (such as the number of elements being out of order). An analysis of the algorithm itself may come to the conclusion that Insertion Sort is $\in O(n^2)$. The *computational complexity* analysis is concerned with the complexity of the *problem* over all possible instances, sizes, and

J. Miller et al. (Eds.) : EuroGP 2001, LNCS 2038, pp. 348-360, 2001.

algorithms. In this case, the complexity of Sort is the complexity of the fastest *possible* algorithm for solving Sort, not just the fastest *known* algorithm.

By confining this analysis to the complexity of problems specifically when an evolutionary algorithm is applied, we can compare our findings with what is already known about the complexity of problems. In this way, we may be able to ascertain when best to apply evolutionary algorithms. This paper is a continuation of an ongoing effort to understand the computational complexity of problems specific to evolutionary algorithms. In particular, it is a report that provides proofs and analysis that describe the complexity of problems as they relate to GPs and the implications of these results.

GP is a biologically inspired method for evolving programs to solve particular prolems. In addition to evolving programs, GPs have been successfully used to optimize functions [2]. It is difficult to characterize the complexity of a problem specific to a method of programming. Holding all things constant, you measure what must change as the size of the input instance increases. It is even more difficult to describe the complexity of a problem that can be solved by a program that is *itself* the output of a program, as is the case with the typical GP. In general, this type of question cannot be answered. What *can* be done however, is to compare the information content of a program with the information content of its output and in this way provide a bound on the complexity of that output. This, in addition to an analysis for function optimization, is what will be described below.

2 Kolmogorov Complexity

Kolmogorov complexity analysis is uniquely suited for addressing this problem. It was created, among other reasons, to provide a way to evaluate objects statically. This section details some of the definitions and theorems of Kolmogorov complexity that are pertinent to this study.

Informally, the amount of information in a finite object (like a string) is the size in bits of the smallest program that, starting with a blank memory, outputs the string and then terminates. In the case of an infinite string, it is the smallest program that can continue to output the infinite series. As an example, consider pi. It is a provably infinite series. And yet, despite this infinity, it can be represented in much less than an infinite string. Another example is an infinite sequence of 1's. Though the sequence of 1's is infinite, a program to produce it can be written in far fewer bits. See Figure 1.

while(true){cout<<<"1";}

Fig. 1. Sample program to output an infinite series of 1's

By this type of measure, a number such as 9,857,384,002 is more complex than the number 10,000,000,000 even though the second number is larger than the first. This is because the amount of *information* contained in the first number is greater than that contained in the second. This *information* can be measured by the size of the program required to output it. This is the basis for scientific notation and, in a nutshell, is the basis for Kolmogorov complexity. Below is the formal definition for an object's Kolmogorov complexity.

Definition 1: $K_S(x) = \min \{|p|: S(p) = n(x)\}$. [3]

This says that the complexity of an object x, is the length of the minimum program p, using programming language (method) S, that can output x and then terminate. Other proofs, which can be found in [3], show that the complexity of an object is a property specific to that object, thus justifying dropping the subscripts and becoming:

$$K(x)=\min\{|p|:p=n(x)\}. \qquad (1)$$

A question that might be asked is whether K exists for every object. Though K is not computable, it does indeed exist for every string. Below is the Invariance Theorem (due to Solomonoff, Kolmogorov, and Chaitin) which states the existence of K. [3].

> **Theorem 1:** There exists a partial recursive function f_0, such that, for any other partial recursive function f, there is a constant c_f such that for all strings x,y, $K_{f0}(x|y) \leq K_f(x|y) + c_f$.

Again, though a more detailed description can be found elsewhere, for the purposes of our study we will provide a brief explanation before moving on. The above theorem is shown very closely to how it was originally presented, therefore some description of the symbols maybe helpful. y is included because it was easier to prove the complexity of an object x *given* an object y.   f is called the *interpreter* or *decoding* function that provides f(p,y)=x. In this case, f refers to the universal partial recursive function computed by a universal Turing machine *U*. Since any f_0 that satisfies the Invariance Theorem is optimal, we can fix a particular reference machine *U* with its associated partial recursive function f_0, and are justified in dropping the subscripts. We can then define the unconditional complexity $K(x|\varepsilon)$ where ε denotes the empty string ($|\varepsilon| = 0$). Consequently the complexity of x can be expressed as K(x).

In addition to the existence of K, Kolmogorov complexity theory also provides two important tools for our investigation. Firstly, some strings are incompressible (see **Theorem 2**). Secondly, random strings are themselves in this category.

> **Theorem 2:** If p(x) is defined as the shortest program for x, it is incompressible in the sense that there is a constant c > 0 such that for all strings x, $K(p(x)) \geq |p(x)| - c$.

This concludes a *very* brief presentation of some of the fundamental theorems of Kolmogorov complexity. The interested researcher is encouraged to read [3]. Those more interested in *this* particular study now have enough of a background to evaluate the meaningfulness of the research. In particular, for our study, these three points should be stressed:

1)   the length of the shortest program that produces an incompressible string is greater than or equal to (plus a constant) the string itself;

2) a random string is incompressible; and,
3) a shortest program is incompressible.

3 GP Complexity

The class of problems solvable by a GP can be grouped into two distinct subsets. The first group is the class of problems in which the GP is used to produce an output program that can be used to solve a desired problem. This is the class that GPs are typically associated with (evolutionary computation to produce programs). The second group is the class of optimization problems in which a GP is used to optimize the solution. In this case, the output of the GP is not a program but a solution to a particular problem. An example of this would be if a GP were used to solve an instance of the Maximum Clique problem. Though this is not how GPs are typically implemented, it has been shown that they are perhaps equally adept at optimizing functions [2].

3.1   GPs for Programs

For GPs that produce programs, the Kolmogorov complexity analysis is straightforward. Though it is impossible to classify the complexity of a problem that can be solved by the output program in advance, it *is* possible to relate the amount of information contained in the output program to the GP itself. By applying the theorems from Kolmogorov complexity, it can be shown that the complexity of the output program of a GP using a pseudo random number generator (PRNG) can be bound above by the GP itself.

> **Theorem 3:** For all strings x,y, if x is the shortest program that outputs y, that is $K(y)=|x|$, then $K(x) \geq K(y) + c$.
>
> **Proof:** Let x be the shortest program (by definition, incompressible) that outputs y. That is, $K(y) = |x|$. Suppose $K(y) > K(x)$. By substitution, $|x| > K(x)$, which is impossible since x was defined as incompressible.

   Though this proof applies to GPs it is not specific to them. It applies to any method for inductively producing programs and therefore should not be seen as a limitation only to GPs.
   A brief explanation may now be warranted.   By assuming that the GP x is a shortest program, we are only stating that in the best case, where x is a shortest program, the upper bound for the complexity of the output y is the length of x. It may well be that any *particular* implementation of a GP contains much extraneous code and is nowhere near the shortest program. This does not mean that the complexity of the output y is any greater. $K(x)$ still refers to the shortest program that can output x. And, $K(x)$ must still be greater than $K(y)$. So if the GP x is not a shortest program, then there must be a shorter program that can output x. This means that the complexity of the output y is even smaller. A simple diagram may be helpful.

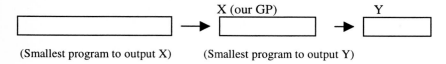

X (our GP)   Y

(Smallest program to output X)   (Smallest program to output Y)

Fig. 2. Diagram depicting that the smallest program to output *x* (our GP) must be larger than the smallest program (hopefully our GP *x*) to output *y* (our output program)

Though this proof applies to *any* method for inductively generating programs and is thus not reliant on any particular definition or implementation of GP, it may be instructional to describe exactly what constitutes the GP in reference to the complexity bound and what constitutes the output.

There are many types of GPs, and each implementation is relatively unique. Consequently a specific definition of a GP would not only be confining but also needlessly imply that the application of the proof is limited to that definition. We will instead provide an informal description of what is included in the GP. Essentially, it is all of the software required at execution time. In addition to the software written by the practitioner, all of the libraries used for implementation, the environment (if one is used), as well as the PRNG itself are included as part of the GP. The bound on the output is the Kolmogorov complexity of all of the software required for the GP implementation at execution time. If a more complex PRNG is used, the upper bound on the output will be greater. However, this does not mean that the output will necessarily be more complex. This only means that the upper bound is greater.

The output that is being bounded is the sum total of all of the individuals that are output, not just the final chosen program. To help explain this apparent paradox, think of a string of five 1's. Now think of a string of ten 1's. The shortest program that can output ten 1's is certainly not twice the length of the shortest program that can output five 1's. In fact, there is at most a constant difference in complexity. See Figure 3.

```
for(i=1;i<=5;i++)          for(i=1;i<=10;i++)
    cout<<'1';                 cout<<'1';
```

Fig. 3. Two *for-loops*, one that outputs five 1's and the other outputs ten 1's

But this proof only applies to GPs using a PRNG. This is because a *truly* random string is by definition incompressible. This leads to the following theorem.

Theorem 4: For all strings x, y, if x is a shortest length program that outputs y, and x uses a true random source for its generation of y, then:
1) K(x) is undefined during execution;
2) $K(y) \leq |y| + c$; (a well known Kolmogorov result)
3) K(y) can be > K(x) - random input.

Proof: Let K(x) = n, where x is a GP. Below is x

returnstring = "";

```
for i= 1 to n+1{
    get a random bit, b;
    returnstring += b;
}
return returnstring;
```

Since a random string is incompressible, $K(y) = n+1$. Therefore, $K(y) > K(x)$. Since it may be unknown how many times a GP will access a random bit, $K(GP)$ is undefined during execution.

These proofs give reason to pause when considering how best to implement a GP. Before we discuss this however, we must address the complexity of the optimization problems solvable by GPs.

3.2   GPs for Function Optimization

In addition to producing programs, GPs have often been used to optimize functions. To describe how to evaluate the complexity of a problem that can be solved by this sort of GP, it is necessary to examine the complexity of problems for GAs.

Since a GP is a GA designed for program discovery [4] it is possible to apply the methods developed for analyzing problems for GAs. Though GPs are typically written in a higher level language, it is easy to see that they can be implemented with strings composed of 1's and 0's, as is typical for GAs, and are in fact, converted to strings of 1's and 0's at execution. As such, it is clear that the problems solvable by GPs are a subset of the problems solvable by GAs. (The converse may also be true.) Consequently, we may introduce the theorems described for the complexity analysis of GA function optimization without a loss of specificity.

Essentially, the complexity of an optimization problem for a GA is bound above by the growth rate of the smallest representation [Minimum Chromosome Length - (MCL)] that can be used to solve the problem [5],[6],[7]. This is because the probabilistic convergence time will remain fixed as a function of the search space. All things held constant, the convergence time will grow as the search space grows. A brief, but more formal description is provided in the following definitions.

> **Definition 2:** For a problem P, and D_n the set of instances of P of size n, let $MCL(P,n)$ be the least l for which there is an encoding $e:S^l \rightarrow D_n$ with a domain dependent evaluation function g, where g and e are in FP (the class of functions computable in polynomial time).

That is, $MCL(P,n)$ measures the size of the smallest chromosome for which there is a polynomial time computable representation and evaluation function. The MCL *growth* rate can be used to bound the complexity of the problem for a GA. If a problem is in NPO, then the MCL growth rate will be no more than linear, since an NP algorithm can search a space which grows no more quickly than exponentially, and linear MCL growth implies exponential search space growth. Conversely, if MCL grows slowly enough, then the search space will be small enough to place the problem in PO. (PO and NPO are the optimization equivalents of P and NP, which are classes of decision problems.) In particular

Theorem 5: for any problem P, if $2^{MCL(P,n)} \in O(n^k)$ for some k, then P∈ PO.

It is currently unclear if the converse is true. However, if $2^{MCL(P,n)} \notin O(n^k)$ then the problem is most likely in NPG (the class of problems that take more than polynomial time for a GA to solve).

Definition 3: A problem P is in the class NPG if MCL(P,n)∈ O(n).

As an example, consider the problem of *Maximum 1's* (i.e. for a given string length n, find the maximum number of 1's that can be held in the string). This is possibly the easiest problem for a GA to implement. Simply let each bit position represent a possible 1. Then, for each chromosome, count the number of 1's to determine that chromosome's fitness. For a string of length 5, the maximum fitness for a chromosome is 5. As the problem instance size increases, the length of the chromosome increases. This means that the size of the search space doubles for every increase in instance size because the number of possible solutions is equivalent to the number 2 raised to the length of the chromosome, or 2^l.

Observe that regardless of the expected convergence time per instance size, the growth rate of the search space determines the complexity of the problem for the GA. As an example, imagine the GA will converge after examining 1/10 of the search space. If the search space doubles for every increase in instance size, the GA-complexity of the problem will be $(1/10)* 2^l$. This is clearly an exponential convergence time. The search space growth rate will dominate over every expected convergence rate regardless of how quickly a particular implementation can converge.

However, if the minimum chromosome length doesn't have to change *every* time the instance size increases, this indicates that the problem convergence and consequently the GA-complexity for the problem are *less* than exponential time. Note that with the problem *Maximum 1's* there is a smaller representation.

A representation can be created in which the maximum number of 1's in a string can be encoded in binary. This means that instead of 5 bits being required to represent a string of length 5, 3 bits will suffice (e.g. 101). The growth rate of the search space changes as well. Notice, for our new representation, we don't always have to increase the length of the chromosome. A 5 is encoded with 3 bits. Also, a 6 is encoded with 3 bits. Consequently, there is no change in convergence time when going from a string of length 5 to a string of length 6. In fact, our representation doesn't cause the chromosome length to increase until the instance size is increased from 7 to 8 (because 8 requires 4 bits, e.g. 1000). This fact alone suggests that the GA-complexity of *Maximum 1's* is some constant c times lg(x).

This prediction can be validated empirically. To conduct our study we employed a typical GA implementation strategy. We chose an arbitrarily fixed population of 10 chromosomes, single point crossover, and a fixed mutation rate of 1% per bit. There was 50% elitism thus providing a 50% survival rate for each generation. Selection was implemented randomly based on the chromosomes that survived.

It should be noted that the principle of measuring the growth rate of the minimum length representation can be used with *any* implementation, since what is actually being measured is the growth rate of the search space. Therefore it is not necessary to demonstrate the usefulness of this measure with *every* GA implementation.

Table 1. The average number of generations to converge per instance size of string length

String Length	4	8	16	32	64	512	32k	8m
Chrom. Length	3	4	5	6	7	10	16	23
Average Conver.	5	9	12	16	20	30	49	77

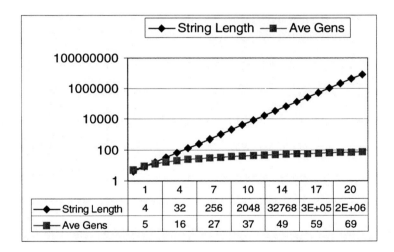

Fig. 4. A logarithmically scaled graph of the average convergence times for the Maximum 1's problem

We then let the GA run until all chromosomes had converged to the optimum solution. This was repeated 5000 times to produce an average convergence time for a given chromosome length. Then the problem instance was increased and the 5000 runs were repeated. This experiment tested the range of string lengths from 4 to 8,388,608. The length of the chromosomes ranged from 3 bits to 24 bits. See Table 1.

Since the chromosome itself grew at $\lg(x)$, this means that the convergence is in $O(\lg(x))$. It should be noted that this rate of convergence held for a very wide range. Consequently, unless it is possible to derive a smaller representation, we can assert from both experimental as well as theoretic evidence that the GA-complexity of

Maximum 1's is $\in O(lg(x))$. A graphical depiction of the convergence times over the entire range can be seen in Fig.4.

As can be seen, the convergence time is less than exponential. In fact, the convergence varied linearly with the chromosome length. This particular experiment had a convergence of roughly $3*|b(x)|$ (3 times the length in binary of x).

There is one further twist to applying this theory to GPs that optimize functions. Namely, GAs typically have fixed length chromosomes whereas GPs have no such bound. Consequently, the MCL problem complexity bound will actually be a lower bound for the problem when a GP is applied, since it assumes the GP will converge to an optimum solution with the minimum chromosome length, per instance size. This means that in the *best* case the complexity of an optimization problem for a GP will be the complexity of that problem for a GA. Since GPs have potentially infinite length chromosomes, it is impossible to establish an upper bound on their complexity without first bounding the length of the chromosomes. But trying to establish an upper bound for the complexity of a problem for a GP is relatively meaningless since it is the lower bound that will determine whether in fact such a method should be chosen for implementation in the first place. If in fact the lower bound shows that GP implementation would be beneficial, then inductive methods can be used to verify whether the lower bound is achieved [6].

This completes an introduction to the complexity analysis for problems that are solvable with GPs. However, though we can now define what the complexity of problems are when GPs are applied, there still must be guidance for GP implementation. Since GPs are in fact a very promising avenue of artificial intelligence theory, in light of these results, it seems appropriate to address how best to implement a GP. This will be discussed in the next section.

4   Implications to GP Design

Before exploring the implications of these results directly, it may be helpful to note that typical compressibility can serve as an approximation of Kolmogorov complexity [3]. Thus, it is reasonable to consider the GP as a compressed file and it's output as a compressed file. Our proofs indicate that the compressed output file must be smaller than the compressed GP, up to a constant factor.

Note that the output of the GP is not just the best program produced. The GP's output consists of all of the programs produced in all of the generations. In fact, convergence and the resulting redundancy in GP populations make them fairly compressible. Recall also that for this result the GP includes the GP itself, the PRNG, the training data, and any other code or data that is used in running the GP. As noted, some problems require a simulated environment for training the GP; this environment is also considered part of the GP for complexity measurements. However, any data or code used to *test* the final evolved programs are not considered part of the GP. This is because they do not influence the final program. They are only used for measurement. Thus, these results compare the compressed size of the GP, including training data etc. to the compressed size of all programs generated in all generations.

Another interesting point is that code bloat in GP appears to increase without limit in most cases [8][9]. Therefore, the Kolmogorov complexity of the ineffective code must converge over time to some fixed bound. However, we hypothesize that ineffective code will tend to converge toward the maximum possible Kolmogorov complexity, *appearing as random as possible*. Preliminary work has confirmed this hypothesis. It is interesting to speculate on whether the effective code in an evolved program approaches the maximum or the minimum possible Kolmogorov complexity for the target function. Both positions seem reasonable.

4.1   Large vs. Small Populations

There are several interesting and significant implications derivable from this result. First, there *must* be a limit to the advantages of larger populations and/or longer trials. The GP is finitely complex (in most cases, we will talk about infinitely complex GPs in a moment), therefore its output must also be finitely complex. Because the output complexity includes all individuals from all populations, producing more individuals through larger populations or longer runs must eventually stop producing new solutions because these solutions would necessarily increase the output complexity beyond the finite limit imposed by the GP.

This is not as limiting as it may appear however. First, we hope that our GPs will in fact converge, at which point they generally do not produce significantly new solutions or additional complexity. Second, the most complex solution possible is one that perfectly fits the training data. This introduces a natural limit to the output complexity. Therefore, a perfect solution is generally not desired as they often over-fit the training data and generalize poorly. Instead a simpler program that generalizes well is usually preferable.

4.2   Increasing Complexity

The above observations lead to a fairly intuitive relationship: *evolving more complex programs requires a more complex set of training data*. More complex training data often comes from having a more complex problem. Thus, the complexity of the solutions a GP can produce is *directly related to the complexity of the problem it is trying to solve*. Of course, this is only the potential complexity of the solution. The GP could produce much simpler solutions. This may be desired, for example, if they generalize well. Conversely, it could indicate that the GP is failing to solve the problem.

As an extreme case, very complex (i.e. incompressible) training data is random data. In this case the only perfect solution is to reproduce the training set entirely; i.e. evolve the same random data. Thus, a complex training set leads to complex solutions. Although GPs are not trained on random data, many systems include random noise in the training data. This noise actually increases the complexity of the total GP and thus increases the potential complexity of the generated solutions. Again, this additional allowed complexity may or may not be beneficial. Clearly a solution that is complex because it is fitting random noise is not desired.

A more practical example is evolving control programs for robots or other autonomous agents. Often the evolutionary process occurs in a relatively simple, simulated environment and the best programs are transferred to actual robots in the physical world.   However, because the training environment (the simulated environment) is simple it can only produce equally simple programs, which may not be capable of dealing with the complexities (such as noise) of the physical world. Thus, our results with Kolmogorov complexity prove that an oversimplified training environment can make it *impossible* to evolve a program complex enough to deal with more complex testing environments such as those found in the real world.   In contrast, programs that are trained in a real world environment are exposed to effectively infinite complexity (though some of this complexity may be filtered out by whatever sensory devices that are being used) and thus may produce programs of unlimited complexity.

4.3   Quantum GPs

Recently there has been interest in combining evolutionary techniques with quantum computers [10], [11], [12]. One unexplored advantage of this merger is that quantum computers have inherent *true* random number generators.   Because true random numbers are incompressible, the complexity of a GP executing on a quantum computer using true randomness is bounded below by the number of random numbers used. This is in contrast to the complexity of pseudo random numbers, which is fairly low and is fixed.

First, we note that a typical GP uses many random numbers, introducing a large amount of complexity (when the numbers are truly random).   Second, and more importantly, larger populations and longer runs both require additional random numbers. If the numbers are from a truly random source, then they introduce more complexity into the GP, making more complex solutions possible. Thus, indefinitely increasing the population size or number of generations *may* be useful when a true random number source (such as a quantum computer) is used.

4.4   Universal Genetic Program

Another potential alternative would be to develop a Universal Genetic Program (UGP).   As with Turing Machines (TM) each GP only seeks to evolve a single program for a specific problem. Conversely, with a Universal TM, the first part of the data that is read in is a description of a unique TM. The remainder of the data is the data that the selected TM will process. This can be done with GPs.

By creating a UGP, we have a single vehicle capable of evolving any program evolvable by a GP. To do this, we treat the first part of the data for the UGP as the *specification* (i.e. the "target" function) for a unique GP.   In this way, we can implement *any GP*. This does not eliminate the Kolmogorov complexity bound, rather it determines the *hidden constant* in the Kolmogorov complexity bound. This is because the bound is essentially a bound on the GP specification. Since the specification will come as data from the environment, which is infinite, the bound on the UGP will be initially infinite.

This idea is intuitive as well. It seems likely that the development of any form of intelligence is influenced *in the developmental stage* by the environment that effects it. Consequently, it seems hopeful that the development of a UGP may provide a meaningful next step in GP research.

5 Conclusions

This paper has provided a proof that the Komogorov complexity of the output of a GP using a PRNG can be bound above by the GP itself. It has also been shown that this result does not hold if the GP instead has access to a truly random source. An analysis of the complexity of problems solvable by a GP as optimizer has been presented. The implications of this have shown that an optimization problem's complexity can be bounded by measuring the growth rate of the minimum representation. We noted that this is essentially the same method used for analyzing GA problem complexity. This observation is important because GAs and GPs are clearly related. The main difference being that GP problem complexity is bounded *below* by the growth rate since GP chromosome length is dynamic during execution.

We have proposed that the complexity of the training data has a direct correlation to the complexity of the desired output. We have briefly explored the significance of employing a GP on a quantum computer and showed that there may be significant advantages to such an endeavor. Finally, we have suggested the development of a *Universal Genetic Program* (UGP) as perhaps an exciting new direction for GP research that does not adhere to complexity bounds of typical GPs.

There are many unanswered questions relating to this research. It is clear that there are several avenues from which to expand this work. One fruitful direction may be to determine how closely the actual implementations are bound to the theoretical projections. Another avenue for research may include the development of a UGP.

Acknowledgments

This research was funded in part by NSF EPS0080935, NIH F33GM20122-01, and NSA MDA 904-98-C-A894.

References

1.   Rylander,B.: On GP Complexity, Proceedings of the Genetic and Evolutionary Computation Conference Workshop Program (2000), pp. 309-311
2.   Soule, T., Foster, J., Dickinson, J.: Using Genetic Programming to Approximate Maximum Cliques, Proceedings Genetic Programming Conference (1998), pp. 400-405
3.   Li, M., Vitanyi, P.: Kolmogorov Complexity and its Applications, Handbook of Theoretical Computer Science Volume A. Algorithms and Complexity, pp. 189-254. The MIT Press, Cambridge, Massachusetts (1990)
4.   O'Reilly, U.: An Analysis of Genetic Programming, Doctoral Thesis, School of Computer Science, Carleton University, Ottawa, Ontario, Canada (1995), pp. 14
5.   Rylander, B., Foster, J.: GA-Hard Problems, Proceedings of the Genetic and Evolutionary Computation Conference (2000), pp. 367

6. Rylander, B., Foster, J.: Computational Complexity and Genetic Algorithms, Proceedings of the World Science and Engineering Society's Conference on Soft Computing (2001)
7. Rylander, B., Foster, J.: Genetic Algorithms, and Hardness, Proceedings of the World Science and Engineering Society's Conference on Soft Computing (2001)
8. Langdon, W., Soule, T., Poli, R., Foster, J.: The Evolution of Size and Shape, Advances in Genetic Programming Volume III, pp. 163-190. The MIT Press, Cambridge, Massachusetts (1999)
9. Soule, T., Foster, J., Dickinson, J.: Code Growth in Genetic Programming, Proceedings Genetic Programming Conference (1996), pp. 215-223
10. Rylander, B., Soule, T., Foster, J.: Quantum Genetic Algorithms, proceedings of the Genetic and Evolutionary Computation Conference (2000), pp. 373
11. Ge, Y., Watson, L., Collins, E.: Genetic Algorithms for Optimization on a Quantum Computer, Unconventional Models of Computation, Springer-Verlag, London (1998)
12. Narayan, A., Moore, M.: Quantum Inspired Genetic Algorithms, Technical Report 344, Department of Computer Science, University of Exeter, England (1998)

Genetic Programming for Financial Time Series Prediction

Massimo Santini and Andrea Tettamanzi

Polo Didattico e di Ricerca di Crema
Via Bramante, 65 – 26013 Crema (CR)
{santini,tettaman}@dsi.unimi.it

Abstract This paper describes an application of genetic programming to forecasting financial markets that allowed the authors to rank first in a competition organized within the CEC2000 on "Dow Jones Prediction". The approach is substantially driven by the rules of that competition, and is characterized by individuals being made up of multiple GP expressions and specific genetic operators.

1 Introduction

Predicting time-dependent phenomena is of great importance in various fields of real world problems [5]. One of these fields is trading in financial markets.

Evolutionary algorithms in general, and GP specifically, have been applied to financial time-series prediction by various authors since their beginning. Too many works have been produced recently on this task to be all cited here; applications range from trading model [13] or technical trading rule induction [1], to option pricing [2] and modeling of the dynamics underlying financial markets [4].

Approaches to time series prediction based on GP can be roughly classified into three strands:

- approaches which use GP or another evolutionary algorithm to optimize a neural network model of the time series [15,3,16];
- GP evolving some *ad hoc* structure representing in an indirect way knowledge or informations about the time series, such as decision trees [13];
- GP evolving an expression or simple program which computes future values of the time series based on a number of past values [14,12,11,10,7].

The approach we follow in this paper falls in this last strand.

As pointed out in [7], besides conducting an efficient exploration of the search space, with a population of models that adapt to market conditions, GP discovers automatically dependencies among the factors affecting the market and thus selects the relevant variables to enter the model. This may be an advantage with respect to more traditional, and popular, autoregressive statistical approaches such as ARCH, GARCH and the like [6].

This work originated from a (successful) attempt to predict the Dow Jones stock index, one of the challenges of a contest organized in the framework of the

J. Miller et al. (Eds.): EuroGP 2001, LNCS 2038, pp. 361–370, 2001.

"Congress on Evolutionary Computation" (CEC2000, La Jolla Marriott Hotel, La Jolla, California, USA, 16–19 July 2000). Some apparent peculiarities of our approach discussed later, are therefore mainly due to the rules of such competition.

The main original aspects of our work are the following:

- we evolve individuals made of several distinct expression, one for each time in the future we have to predict;
- we desing two specific genetic operators of crossover and mutation adapted to individuals of this form;
- since our objective was to predict a given realization of a time series (namely the daily closing values of the Dow Jones Industrial Average in a given period of time), we use the same data set both in the GP algorithm for training (i.e. computing the fitness) and for obtaining, from the best individual thus evolved, the prediction itself.

The work is organized as follows. In Section 2 we give the details of the challenge which influence some choices in our approach illustrated in Section 3. Finally, Section 4 reports the results of an empirical study of the behaviour of the algoritm both on a toy problem and on the target problem.

2   The Problem

While most time series prediction work found in the literature is on artificial functions, the "Dow Jones Prediction Competition" mentioned in the introduction was on real-world data: the Dow Jones Index.

The call for participation asked to submit by June 17, 2000 a Dow Jones prediction for the period from June 19 to June 30. That is, each contestant was required to send a file consisting of 10 real numbers each representing the forecast of the closing value of the Dow Jones index for such period.

Submissions were scored as follows: for each day, the difference between the prediced and real index at closing time was determined. The absolute values were discounted and summed up. For the first day, the discount factor was 1.0, for the second 0.9, for the third 0.8, and so forth. More precisely, the score was computed as

$$\sum_{t=1}^{10} \frac{11-t}{10} |x_t - \hat{x}_t| \tag{1}$$

where the x_t's denote the closing values of the index and the $\hat{x}_t$'s are the predictions. The rationale for this discounting is that forecasts for the near future are commonly considered easier that for the far future.

3   The Algorithm

To fix the notation, suppose we are given a time-series $x = (x_1, x_2, \ldots, x_T, x_{T+1}, \ldots, x_{T+h})$ for some *observation time* $T > 0$ and *horizon length* $h > 0$, together with some auxiliary time-series $\boldsymbol{x}^{(i)} = (x_1^{(i)}, x_2^{(i)}, \ldots, x_T^{(i)})$ for $1 \leq i \leq a$ (for some $a > 0$). Our *data set* is defined as $\boldsymbol{D} = \{\boldsymbol{x}^{(i)}, 0 \leq i \leq a\}$, where $\boldsymbol{x}^{(0)}$ is defined as $(x_1, x_2, \ldots, x_T)$ and $a = 0$ means that no auxiliary time-series are considered.

Our goal is to obtain a vector $\boldsymbol{e} = (e_1, e_2, \ldots, e_h)$ of expressions $e_j : \boldsymbol{D} \times \{1, \ldots, T\} \to \mathbf{R}$, such that the value $e_j(\boldsymbol{D}, T)$ is a *prediction* of x_{T+j}, for $1 \leq j \leq h$.

3.1   The Initial Structures

The expressions e_j are built from the *terminal set* of constants in $[-c, c] \subseteq \mathbf{R}$ and the *function set* $F = \{+, -, \times, /, \text{POW}, \text{SQRT}, \text{LOG}, \text{EXP}\} \cup \bigcup_{0 \leq i \leq a}\{\text{DATA}[i],$ $\text{DIFF}[i], \text{AVE}[i]\}$. First of all, notice that all the functions are "protected" in the sense that they return 0 if evaluated outside their domain of definition; the access to the data set is also "protected" in the sense that $x_k^{(i)}$ takes value 0 if $k < 1$ or $k > T$, for every $0 \leq i \leq a$. The functions $\{+, -, \times, /, \text{POW}, \text{SQRT}, \text{LOG}, \text{EXP}\}$ have their usual meaning, while the value of functions in $\bigcup_{0 \leq i \leq a}\{\text{DATA}[i], \text{DIFF}[i],$ $\text{AVE}[i]\}$, on input $\alpha \in \mathbf{R}$ and at time $0 \leq t \leq T$, is defined as follows:

$$\text{DATA}[i](\alpha, t) = x_{t-\lfloor|\alpha|\rfloor}^{(i)}$$

$$\text{DIFF}[i](\alpha, t) = x_t^{(i)} - x_{t-\lfloor|\alpha|\rfloor}^{(i)}$$

$$\text{AVE}[i](\alpha, t) = \frac{1}{1 + \lfloor|\alpha|\rfloor} \sum_{k=t-\lfloor|\alpha|\rfloor}^{t} x_k^{(i)}$$

Observe that according to the above definition, the value of each expression at any time $1 \leq t \leq T$ depends only on those value of past values in $\boldsymbol{D}$: more formally, if $\boldsymbol{D}_t = \{x_k^{(i)} : x_k^{(i)} \in \boldsymbol{D}, k \leq t\}$ we have that, for every $1 \leq t \leq T$, $e(\boldsymbol{D}, t) = e(\boldsymbol{D}_t, t)$.

For a fixed horizon length $h > 0$, the *population* consists of N *individuals* each one being a vector $\boldsymbol{e} = (e_1, e_2, \ldots, e_h)$ of expressions. The expressions are represented as strings of symbols in reverse Polish notation. The initial population is built by a procedure that generates independently each expression and individual [8]. To each element of the function set and to the constants of the terminal set is assigned a probability, each expression is then built recursively by selecting each function, or constant, according to such probabilities; if the depth (nesting level) of the expression exceeds a specified value m, then only constants are selected to ensure that every expression has at most a fixed depth.

3.2   Fitness

Since our goal is to obtain predictors for the values $(x_{T+1}, x_{T+2}, \ldots, x_{T+h})$, to evaluate the performance of such predictors we can use different notions of "distance" between the predicted and actual value.

Let $\delta : \mathbf{R} \times \mathbf{R} \rightarrow \mathbf{R}^+$ be a function measuring such distance, for instance $\delta(x,y) = (x-y)^2$ or $\delta(x,y) = |x-y|/|x|$. For a fixed δ, we define the mean error for the individual e at time $1 \leq t \leq T$ as

$$\varepsilon(e,t) = \frac{1}{h} \sum_{j=1}^{h} \delta(x_{t+j}, e_j(\boldsymbol{D}, t)),$$

hence, we define the mean error of individual e on the whole observation time as

$$f_s(e) = \frac{1}{T-h} \sum_{t=1}^{T-h} \varepsilon(e,t) = \frac{1}{h(T-h)} \sum_{t=1}^{T-h} \sum_{j=1}^{h} \delta(x_{t+j}, e_j(\boldsymbol{D}, t)).$$

Given that we choose positive valued δ, we have $f_s(e) \geq 0$ for every individual e, so that we can use $f_s(e)$ as the *standardized fitness*, $f_a(e) = (1 + f_s(e))^{-1}$ as *adjusted fitness* and $f(e) = f_a(e)/\sum_{\hat{e}} f_a(\hat{e})$ as *normalized fitness*.

3.3   Operations for Modifying Structures

Reproduction. For the reproduction we adopted two different approaches: fitness proportional, and truncation selection [9] whereby, for some ratio $0 < \rho_s < 1$, the new population is obtained replicating a suitable number of times the best $\lfloor N\rho_s \rfloor$ individuals of the previous generation. In the following, by $\rho_s = 0$ we mean that we choose the fitness proportional reproduction scheme.

Crossover. Following [8], we defined the crossover between two expression e, e' as the operation that selects at random two subexpressions, one in e and the other in e' and exchanges them. Then, the crossover between two individuals $e = (e_1, e_2, \ldots, e_h)$ and $e' = (e_1', e_2', \ldots, e_h')$ is defined as the operation performing the crossover between every pair of expressions e_j, e_j', for $1 \leq j \leq h$.

The individuals in the population are arranged in $N/2$ pairs and to each of these pairs, with a fixed probability $0 \leq p_c \leq 1$, the above crossover is applied.

Mutation. We defined the mutation of an individual as a crossover between two of its expressions chosen uniformly at random, or, with probability $1/2$, of an expression chosen uniformly at random from the individual and a new expression generated at random. Mutation is applied to every individual in the population with a fixed probability $0 \leq p_m \leq 1$.

4   Experiments

In order to assess the validity of our approach we selected a very simple test problem where the data are not actually stochastic but are generated by a completely specified, deterministic, law.

In that way, once we would be able to have the algorithm learn that law, we could rule out gross conceptual and implementation errors in our approach and then attack a more complex task such as predicting a financial time series.

4.1   Test Problem: Parabola

As a suitable law for our test problem we chose a parabola. More precisely, we let $x_k = k^2$ for $1 \leq k \leq T + h$; the parameters of the algorithm are set according to Table 1.

Table 1. Parameter setting for the parabola prediction.

Parameter	Explanation	Value
T	observation time	30
h	horizon length	5
N	population size	500
G	number of generations	200
m	expression max depth	5
δ	distance measure	$\lvert x - y \rvert / \lvert x \rvert$
ρ_s	selection ratio	0.1
p_c	crossover probability	0.2
p_m	mutation probability	0.01

We ran several experiments, collecting the maxmium and average adjusted fitness for every generation. Figure 1 shows the typical behaviour of these experiments where the above line represents the maximum adjusted fitness and the other represents the average.

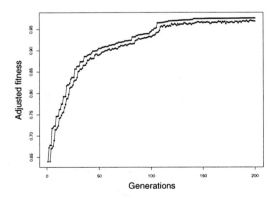

Figure 1. Graph of average and best adjusted fitness found by the algorithm after different numbers of generations, averaged over 40 runs (Parabola case).

In Figure 2 we plot the data versus the prediction: the line represent the data having coordinates (k, k^2) for $1 \leq k \leq T$, and the points represent the predictions, having coordinates $(k + j, e_j(\boldsymbol{D}, k))$ for $1 \leq k \leq T$ and $1 \leq j \leq h$.

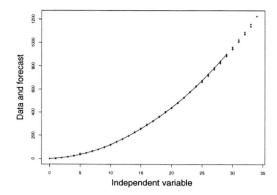

Figure 2. Graph of data versus the predictions found by the algorithm (Parabola case).

4.2   Predicting the Dow Jones

In adapting our algorithm to our main objective, we had to make several choices, which are discussed below.

Fitness. Since our aim was to win the "Dow Jones Prediction Competition", our first attempt in choosing δ was to mimic the score in Equation (1). However it was clear from the very first experiments that such a choice resulted in poor predictions apart from the first or second day in the future. This can be explained by the fact that the evolutionary algorithm found it more profitable to make a slight improvement in the first days than to make more important improvements in the farther future.

Indeed, experiments convinced us to use the relative error *without discount*, $\delta = |x - y|/|x|$. While the profound reason why this choice should give better results *even for the competition*, which uses a discounted score, is not clear and calls for a deeper investigation, nonetheless empirical evidence for this fact was overwhelming.

Observation Time. The challenge rules didn't place any constraint as to the observation time T so this was one of the parameters to fix. In principle, one would expect a longer T to give more accurate predictions, of course at the cost of a higher computational effort. However, a financial index like the Dow Jones shows a very marked nonstationary behaviour: exogenous factors can cause trend inversions, rallies, dips, etc.; too long an observation time T can cause the algorithm to be misled by the long-term behaviour, while we were interested in a short term prediction. For this reason, after some trial, we chose to fix $T = 116$ (which accounts for the period from January 1, 2000 up to July 17, 2000, the deadline for the challenge).

Algorithm Parameters. Some of the parameters showed no particular impact on the performance of the algorithm so, after some experiments, and following the relevant literature [8], they were set as follows: population size $N = 500$, expression (initial) max depth $m = 5$ and selection ratio $\rho_s = 1/10$.

Next we turned to study an appropriate value for the number of generations G. We ran several experiments whose results are summarized in Figure 3; it is clear from the figure that after 10 generations on average the fitness tends to stabilize so we set $G = 20$ to have a reasonable confidence to stop each run after the fitness has stabilized and no more improvements are expected.

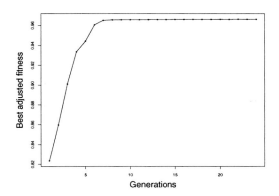

Figure 3. Graph of best adjusted fitness found by the algorithm after different numbers of generations, averaged over 40 runs (Dow Jones case).

The crossover probability p_c and the mutation probability p_m deserved a similar analysis; their effects are strongly correlated so we designed experiments to find the best combination of values for them. After plotting (see Figure 4) the best adjusted fitness after 20 generations, averaged over 20 runs, for (p_c, p_m) in the range of values usually found in the literature (that is for $p_c \in [0.4, 0.8]$ and $p_m \in [0, 0.4]$) we observe that no particular combination stood out as better than the others. So we simply set $p_c = 0.6$ and $p_m = 0.2$; we observe that this very high mutation probability is due to the fact that our mutation operator is indeed a crossover between distinct chromosomes of the same individual instead of a completely random perturbation.

The best values of the parameters determined through all the experiment discussed above are summarized in Table 2:

Results. Using the algorithm with parameters set as in Table 2, we took the best individual over 40 runs; Table 3 compares the actual closing values of the Dow Jones in the specified period against the predictions thus produced; in the last column is cumulated the score obtained by expresson in Equation (1).

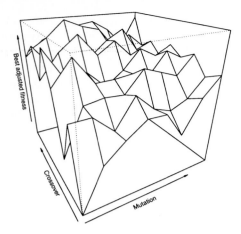

Figure 4. Graph of best adjusted fitness found by the algorithm for $p_c \in [0.4, 0.8]$ and $p_m \in [0, 0.4]$, averaged over 20 runs. Even though from the plot there appears to be a wide variation along the vertical axis, adjiusted fitness is comprised within the interval $[0.8126, 0.9671]$ (Dow Jones case).

Table 2. Parameter setting for the Dow Jones predicion.

Parameter	Explanation	Value
T	observation time	116
h	horizon length	10
N	population size	500
G	number of generations	20
m	expression max depth	5
δ	distance measure	$|x - y|/|x|$
ρ_s	selection ratio	0.1
p_c	crossover probability	0.6
p_m	mutation probability	0.2

5   Conclusion

There are already more than a dozen papers devoted to financial time series prediction using genetic programming in the literature; however, none of them approaches a problem formulated as in the Dow Jones Prediction competition. To be provocative, we could say that our work was on how to win a prediction competition rather than on how to actually predict the Dow Jones for investment or speculation purposes.

Nonetheless, we learned some lessons that might have some general value: at first, we thought that applying sophisticated statistical techniques such as ARCH, GARCH models, Markov processes and probabilistic learning, and using

Table 3. Results of the best predictor evolved by the algorithm for the "Dow Jones Prediction Competition".

Prediction	DowJones	Diff.	Disc. diff.	Score
10449.300	10557.80	108.5	108.5	108.5
10449.300	10435.20	14.1	12.69	121.19
10449.300	10497.70	−48.4	38.72	159.91
10417.374	10376.10	41.274	28.8918	188.8018
10476.400	10404.80	71.6	42.96	231.7618
10535.523	10542.99	−7.467	3.7335	235.4953
10435.246	10504.46	−69.214	27.6856	263.1809
10461.648	10527.79	−66.142	19.8426	283.0235
10418.607	10398.04	20.567	4.1134	287.1369
10421.874	10447.89	−26.016	2.6016	289.7385

evolutionary algorithms to fine tune their parameters would help us obtain high-quality results. In fact, it was not so, and eventually we resolved on using a pretty simple "pure" GP approach, where all non-standard enhancements are almost dictated by the terms of the problem.

The experiments demonstrated the adopted algorithm to be quite robust with respect to parameter settings. The variability between distinct runs with the same parameter setting was some order of magnitude larger than the variability between average performances of different parameter settings. We believe this to be a strength of the approach. Very good results were obtained by just running the algorithm as many times as it was possible after all the data needed were available and before the deadline for submission of results expired, and taking the highest fitness individual, which is a use of GP not too dissimilar in spirit from Monte Carlo methods.

References

1. F. Allen and R. Karjalainen. Using genetic algorithms to find technical trading rules. *Journal of Financial Economics*, 51(2):245–271, 1999.
2. N. K. Chidambaran, C. H. Jevons Lee, and J. R.Trigueros. An adaptive evolutionary approach to option pricing via genetic programming. In J. R. Koza, W. Banzhaf, K. Chellapilla, K. Deb, M. Dorigo, D. B. Fogel, M. H. Garzon, D. E. Goldberg, H. Iba, and R. Riolo, editors, *Genetic Programming 1998: Proceedings of the Third Annual Conference*, pages 38–41, University of Wisconsin, Madison, Wisconsin, USA, 22-25 July 1998. Morgan Kaufmann.
3. R. E. Dorsey and R. S. Sexton. The use of parsimonious neural networks for forecasting financial time series. *Journal of Computational Intelligence in Finance*, 6(1):24–31, 1998.
4. C. Dunis, editor. *Forecasting Financial Markets*. Wiley, 1996.
5. S. Andreas *et al. Time Series Prediction: Forecasting the future and understanding the past.* Addison-Wesley, 1994.

370   Massimo Santini and Andrea Tettamanzi

6. C. Gourieroux. *ARCH Models and Financial Applications*. Springer Verlag, 1997.
7. H. Iba and N. Nikolaev. Genetic programming polynomial models of financial data series. In *Proceedings of the 2000 Congress on Evolutionary Computation CEC00*, pages 1459–1466, La Jolla Marriott Hotel La Jolla, California, USA, 6-9 July 2000. IEEE Press.
8. J. R. Koza. *Genetic Programming*. MIT Press, Cambridge, MA, 1992.
9. H. Muehlenbein and D. Schlierkamp-Voosen. Analysis of selection, mutation and recombination in genetic algorithms. *Lecture Notes in Computer Science*, 899:142–??, 1995.
10. B. S. Mulloy, R. L. Riolo, and R. S. Savit. Dynamics of genetic programming and chaotic time series prediction. In John R. Koza, David E. Goldberg, David B. Fogel, and Rick L. Riolo, editors, *Genetic Programming 1996: Proceedings of the First Annual Conference*, pages 166–174, Stanford University, CA, USA, 28–31 July 1996. MIT Press.
11. M. Numata, K. Sugawara, S. Yamada, I. Yoshihara, and K. Abe. Time series prediction modeling by genetic programming without inheritance of model parameters. In M. Sugisaka, editor, *Proceedings 4th International Symposium on Artificial Life and Robotics*, B-Con Plaza, Beppu, Oita, Japan, 19-22 January 1999.
12. M. Numata, K. Sugawara, I. Yoshihara, and K. Abe. Time series prediction by genetic programming. In John R. Koza, editor, *Late Breaking Papers at the Genetic Programming 1998 Conference*, University of Wisconsin, Madison, Wisconsin, USA, 22-25 July 1998. Stanford University Bookstore.
13. M. Oussaidène, B. Chopard, O. V. Pictet, and M. Tomassini. Parallel genetic programming and its application to trading model induction. *Parallel Computing*, 23:1183–1198, 1997.
14. I. Yoshihara, T. Aoyama, and M. Yasunaga. GP-based modeling method for time series prediction with parameter optimization and node alternation. In *Proceedings of the 2000 Congress on Evolutionary Computation CEC00*, pages 1475–1481, La Jolla Marriott Hotel La Jolla, California, USA, 16–19 July 2000. IEEE Press.
15. B. Zhang, P. Ohm, and H. Mühlenbein. Evolutionary induction of sparse neural trees. *Evolutionary Computation*, 5(2):213–236, 1997.
16. B. T. Zhang. Forecasting high frequency financial time series with evolutionary neural trees: The case of hang-sheng stock market. In *Proceedings of ICAI'99*, 1999.

Active Handwritten Character Recognition Using Genetic Programming

Ankur Teredesai, J. Park, and Venugopal Govindaraju

Department of Computer Science
Center of Excellence for Document Analysis and Recognition
State University of New York at Buffalo, Buffalo, NY 14250, U.S.A.
{amt6,jaehwap,govind}@cedar.buffalo.edu
http://www.cse.buffalo.edu/amt6

Abstract. This paper is intended to demonstrate the effective use of genetic programming in handwritten character recognition. When the resources utilized by the classifier increase incrementally and depend on the complexity of classification task, we term such a classifier as active. The design and implementation of active classifiers based on genetic programming principles becomes very simple and efficient. Genetic Programming has helped optimize handwritten character recognition problem in terms of feature set selection. We propose an implementation with dynamism in pre-processing and classification of handwritten digit images. This paradigm will supplement existing methods by providing better performance in terms of accuracy and processing time per image for classification. Different levels of informative detail can be present in image data and our proposed paradigm helps highlight these information rich zones. We compare our performance with passive and active handwritten digit classification schemes that are based on other pattern recognition techniques.

1 Introduction

Active pattern recognition makes use of active heuristic function that adaptively determines the length of the feature vector as well as the features themselves used to classify an input pattern [8]. The classification stage in active pattern recognition outputs confidence and separability values. A post processing stage is used in decision making based on output of the classification stage. An iterative search method feeds sub images of finer resolution to the classification stage till the decision can be made with high enough confidence or the process times out. The dynamism of active methods is embedded in the way sub images are presented to the classifier to make better decisions. Passive methods use a pre-determined fixed dimension feature vector and are not adaptive. Fig 1 shows some of the handwritten digit images not recognized appropriately by such passive classifiers.

We propose to eliminate this iterative process of feeding sub images to the classifier and concentrate on schemes that will provide us with knowledge of areas

J. Miller et al. (Eds.): EuroGP 2001, LNCS 2038, pp. 371–379, 2001.
© Springer-Verlag Berlin Heidelberg 2001

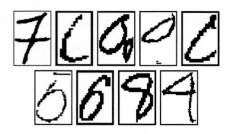

Fig. 1. Images with truth not being in top 2 choices of passive recognizers based on K-NN rule.

in the image having maximum separability information. One way to achieve this goal is to use only those features from the feature set that provide maximum separability. A second way is to generate a new set of features that represents the image data in a manner that provides a better classification accuracy. This is a two fold problem. One of designing a better classifier using given feature extraction methods. Two of designing a better feature set given the classification method and the a-priori knowledge associated with classes. Both these tasks are tightly coupled with each other and we propose to use genetic programming (GP) to decouple them.

By using GP, we have designed and developed techniques that can be suitably applied to the problem of recognition of handwritten digits and extend the taxonomy of feature selection algorithms to include GP as a class of its own.

There is an immense advantage in using GP to model problems in handwritten character recognition. The experiments conducted to design optimal classifiers are discussed in detail in section 4. Corresponding results are presented in section 5, and a comparative analysis of performance with respect to other techniques is also presented.

2   Related Work

In this section we consider the current state of research and recent developments in handwritten character recognition. We also present related research work in other fields like data mining, classical pattern recognition and evolutionary computation that has bearings on our research.

In Active Character Recognition most of the dynamism is involved in the classification stage. Features are hierarchically used to focus on smaller sub-images on each recursive pass till the classification process meets acceptance criteria. Our proposition is to introduce dynamism even at the feature extraction stage in the pre-processor. Once we obtain an optimal set of features that meets the classification criterion, we can redesign the pre-processor to extract only those features that are present in this set, thereby reducing resource utilization. Other advantages in the proposed research are the use of knowledge about separability issues at both the pre-processor and classifier stage to introduce further dynamic activity.

The Passive character recognizers use methods described in Favata et al[2]. These are classical methods which employ the paradigm *One Model Fits All*. The multi-resolution in feature space is obtained by the gradient, structural and concavity based features. The classifier is a K-Nearest Neighbor rule. Gradient captures the local shape of the character, structural features capture the relationships between stroke formation and concavity captures the global manner of character drawing. These recognizers assume a set of features and classification mechanism ad-hoc. They are built using the data given, and are then placed in their operational environment with no evolving training. Some systems like the adaptive resonance theory network learn as they perform. We can take a few lessons from these concepts.

The multi-layer perceptron model has the number of neurons, the layers and organization of the network, training parameters, etc. selected by the rule-of-thumb[1]. The architecture of the recognizer should be more flexible and self organizing because learning by weight modification in a fixed network topology can limit the classifier to a locally-optimal solution. The complexity of the problem may not be modeled favorably by the complexity of the network selected. The classification standards might be met, but there will always be a trade-off with learning time, network size and other issues. Efforts in [8] and [7] have discussed some of these issues. Moreover, the solution representation in our approach is far more comprehensible as compared to previously attempted methods.

The relation between data mining and genetic programming is explored in [3]. Simple classifier development using GP is noted in [4]. Main emphasis is again placed on the classification task and optimality of features sets is not explored. The penalty schemes discussed in [6] do not relate very well with our domain because the penalties assigned are not a function of the ability of the solution program to focus on the regions of maximum information pertinent to our application.

3   GeneARM- Genetic Active Recognition Methods

We now discuss the generic implementation of the new proposed method for improving recognition methods using the active recognition protocol discussed in[8]. The basic hierarchical restructuring of the image domain and gravity based recursive cognition are the major approaches that are being explored in the area of active pattern recognition today[9].

3.1   Apparatus Setup

Our strategy for evolving better classifiers using active recognition has the following GP components.

– Terminal Set :
This set is the actual variables of the problem, zero-argument functions and
random constants for the external nodes of the evolving computer program.
In pattern recognition the zero-argument functions are features. In our case
the features are derived from hierarchical feature extraction scheme discussed
in [9]. These features have been extracted in a coarse resolution and hier-

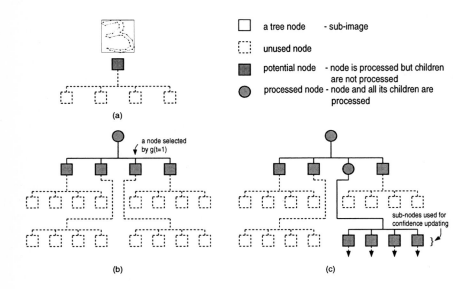

Fig. 2. Process representation of a typical image.

archically focus on smaller sub-images of the character on each recursive
pass. We use the following naming convention to label our features **F** then
sub-image number **1** and feature number **8** makes the label **F18**.See fig 2.
– Function Set :
These are selected from the mathematical operand set consisting of **+,-
,*,/,sin, cos, log, exp**.
The initial function set comprised of simple functions and in case of need,
we intended to increase the complexity of this set by adding more complex
functions to support the GP run. For the current set of experiments on digit
recognition this set was found adequate.
– Fitness measure :
This should be an evaluation strategy to measure the accuracy of the individuals generated during a run. The key idea was to focus on a suitable driving
function that helps us make the final solution dynamic in nature during the
testing phase. The raw fitness is calculated based on the number of correctly
classified training set samples. Each individual is assigned a penalty if the
accuracy is very poor.

- The Parameters for controlling the run :
  The parameters that need be included under this guideline are the selection mechanism for selection of programs depending on probability of fitness, how to specify probabilities for operations of genetic evolution like, reproduction, crossover, mutation, and other methods.
  Initially we used the defaults[5]. Certain variations on these parameters were later taken into consideration for better training time requirements. The performance of the classifiers generated with different parameters was not affected by the choice of these parameters even though the complexity of the classifiers produced differed greatly with change in parameters. Tournament selection with a size of 7 was a good selection parameter. Initial population size varied from 100 to 600 over different runs. Breeding was done in two phases, with crossover probability 0.8 and mutation probability 0.2. The maximum allowed depth of solution tree was 20.
- The termination criterion and result reporting :
  The termination criterion usually represent the combination of maximum number of runs and the optimal state of solution we desire.
  We experimented with various thresholds set for termination. Because we are in search of a globally optimal solution, it makes good sense to experiment with a wide range of termination criteria, as this can effect the time required to converge to a good solution and the complexity of the solution too.

3.2   Fitness Testing Phase

As noted in the previous section, we tested each individual generated in some quantitative terms. If we view the problem in terms of traditional neural network approach, we can say that one neural network program, is being tested on a set of images in the training set and the network is learning and so the program is evolving. In case of GP we have several hundred programs of varying architectures being evaluated on training images one after another.

In order to reduce the computational complexity of our approach, it is generally proposed to keep the training set of character images small in size. We experimented on both reduced training sets and large training sets. Then we evaluate each individual program generated by GP on these sets and measured the fitness. For the individual that performs best we can validate the performance by presenting a validation set to gain insight into the training effectiveness. The outcome of the fitness testing wrapper program can be one of the following :

- True Positive - Correct identification of a digit.
- True Negative - Correct identification of a non digit (noise) as a non digit.
- False Positive - Incorrect identification of a non digit as a digit.
- False Negative - Incorrect identification of a digit as non digit.
- Wrong Positive - Incorrect identification of a digit as a different digit.
- Right Negative - Correct identification of a digit as a digit but the digit is different from the one that the classifier is responsible for. We also term it as misfired true.

The standardized fitness is the sum, over all test cases, of the weighted errors produced by the program plus a penalty for lack of diversity[6]. The smaller the sum of the weighted errors and the penalty, the better is the fitness. The penalty aspect is very useful in ensuring that the search is not reduced to a random search in the solution space, but is rather an evolution towards the solution without explicit control on the movement in the solution space.

4   Experiments

As part of the effort to design optimal classifiers, we had to base our classifiers on a feature extraction scheme. Feature extraction based on quin or quad tree representation of the handwritten image is one such scheme that produces multilevel features[8]. Various levels of information are hierarchically processed at the feature extraction stage in this scheme. As shown in the figure Fig. 2, at each depth there are nine features extracted: four based on gradient, and five based on momentum. If we use the quin tree image representation as shown in figure 2 we note that there are four levels of resolution, each node being represented by a feature vector consisting of nine features.

- *Given the features used in Hierarchical Active Recognition Methods, we can design a strategy to help us focus directly at the level of detail for optimal separability.*

We adopted the following strategy for implementation :

- Use each of the levels mentioned below independently. As each level has complete information about the image, our classifiers are iteratively developed to check which level provides maximum separability of classes. It was found that classifiers that are relatively less complex and yet provide sound classification utilize features at all levels. This finding confirms our view that human vision utilizes information at different levels of visualization.
  - Type 1
    use F1 to F9 from level 1 to determine accuracy.
  - Type 2
    use F1 to F9 from level 2 to determine accuracy.
  - Type 3
    use F1 to F9 from level 3 to determine accuracy.
  - Type 4
    use F1 to F9 from all levels to determine accuracy.
- This way we can gradually use consolidated feature sets, which are features grouped together as a single feature vector. By using such feature vectors, we are able to focus on which level of visualization is important, and which features dominate at that level.
- Now that we have explained the way features are generated and utilized let us understand the way classifiers are developed in our scheme. The handwritten digit recognition problem is a 11 class problem. 10 classes of the digits 0 to 9 and the 11th class being the null class which represents noise or non-digits in the test set.

- In our implementation we train 10 different classifiers each to handle recognition of one digit. The output of these singleton class classifiers can be the digit each one is responsible for or the null class. It would be helpful to note that we do not split up the training set into class dominated sets where images from the class under consideration is given more presence. We train all the classifiers on the same complete training set that contains sample images from all classes in a heterogeneous mix. Our observation is that providing more samples of one class weakens the overall driver recognizer. Classifiers should not only be responsible for correctly identifying the classes they are trained for but should also be able to provide high separability with respect to other classes.
- Once optimum classifiers for all classes are trained, we combine these classifiers into a higher level wrapper called the classification driver. This driver is then the 10 class classifier which takes as input the test set and outputs the class of each of the incoming test image. Performance of this driver is measured in comparison to other classification schemes.
- At any given point, we maintain a pool of several possible digit classifiers for use in the driver. The simplicity of the solution in terms of number and level of features utilized is considered while ranking the suitability of the classifier to be a part of the classification driver.
- If more than one classifier fires for an incoming test image, there are two choices that can be set in the driver: one can either reject this image, or feed this image to a between-class classifier. A between-class classifier is a slightly more complex classifier that utilizes more information (features) to arbitrate between the classes that were fired in the first stage. For example, if for an incoming image of a handwritten digit '1' classifiers for digit 1 and 7 are fired, the driver can be set to either reject this image or it can be asked to provide a decision. If asked to provide a decision the driver presents the image to the between-class classifier for 1-7. This between-class classifier then makes the decision. We have provided both these options because our recognition strategy is active in nature such that resources utilized to make a decision should be incrementally increased in case of need. Complex classifiers should not be employed to make simple decisions.

5   Results and Discussion

We tested our system on various datasets including the NIST handwritten digit sets, and a more noisy CEDAR-Digit data set. The NIST data set consists of 159228 images in the training set, and 53300 images in the test set. The CEDAR-Digit data set is smaller in size with 7245 images in the training set and 2711 in the test set. This set consists of more noisy data with images that were incorrectly recognized or rejected even by the current recognizers based on K-Nearest Neighbor rule and neural networks. A sample of such images is seen in fig 1.

First let us present an analysis for a conventional passive classifier like GSC which is based on K-NN rule. When set of 12242 handwritten digit images were used as testing data, 540 images were rejected. A threshold of 0.4 was used on the confidence value of top choices (the confidence value ranges from 0 to 0.6 for the GSC). Among the accepted (12242-540) images, 60 were incorrect.

Accept rate = (12242-540)/12242 = 95.6 %

Error rate = 60/(12242-540) = 0.51% The results we obtained using our GP

Table 1. Results obtained during a GeneARM test run.

Class	Images	Correct	Incorrect	Mis-fired true	Correct (%)
0	5511	5373	138	20	97.5
1	5822	5665	157	30	97.3
2	5308	5143	165	12	96.9
3	5470	5311	159	17	97.1
4	5118	4949	169	15	96.7
5	4773	4639	134	12	97.2
6	5352	5207	145	22	97.3
7	5516	5317	199	28	96.4
8	5263	5047	216	11	95.9
9	5167	5043	124	34	97.6

based methodology are presented in table 1. Some sample classifier solutions for different digits are also presented below:

Solution for Digit 3

generation: 5   nodes : 20   depth : 5   hits : 5328/5470

accuracy : 97.1

Part of the solution tree : (+ (* (cos (- F04 F198)) (+ (cos (sin F02)) (exp F04)))
(* (cos (- F04 F198)) (cos (sin F02))))

Solution for Digit 5

generation: 17   nodes : 12   depth : 5   hits : 4639/4773

accuracy :97.2

Part of the solution tree : (+ (exp (sin (exp (* F217 F36))))) (exp (exp (* F78
F35))))

The features used in the first solution are **F04, F198, F02** suggesting that this implementation was able to recognize 97.1% of the presented test patterns using only 3 out of 9*31 = 279 total features. Another interesting fact is that the solution is very simple in expression and suggests that sub-image 0 and sub-image 19 accorded maximum separability in this case.The second solution is also relatively simple in expression. One observation that can be made from the second solution is that the solution space has a lot of variation in terms of features suggesting that GP is trying to focus on the key areas of separability and embeds them in individual solutions.

The way we set up these experiments helps us to implement a scheme of Automatic Feature Discovery whereby branches that occur frequently in good solution trees are stored as new features of higher information content. This enables us to gain intuitive knowledge about good features that combine together to produce composite features.

6 Conclusion

We demonstrated with our experiments that GP can be an excellent technique for feature discovery. The features that form the optimal feature set sometimes are embedded in repetitive structures or sub-trees. These sub-trees are repetitively expressed as a composite feature in good solution programs. Such sub-trees can be identified using Automatically Defined Functions and Modularity Identification schemes[6]. The heuristic that is used adaptively to determine the length of feature vectors in [8], was improved by making use of such structures in the pre-processing stage for classification.

A novel implementation of GP was attempted in the handwritten character recognition domain. The methodology adopted can be improved even further to achieve greater accuracy in classification of other data sets. A secondary classification stage can be implemented to handle those images that are not successfully recognized by the first stage by using pair wise discriminators.

References

1. R Duda and P Hart. *Pattern Classificaiton and Scene analysis.* Wiley International, 1973.
2. J Favata and G Srikantan. A multiple feature/resolution approach to handprinted digit and character recognition. *International Journal of Imageing Systems and Technology*, 7:304–311, 1996.
3. A Frietas. A genetic programming framework for two data mining tasks: Classification and generalized rule induction. In *Genetic Programming 1997: Proc. 2nd Annual Conference*, pages 96–101, Stanford University, July 1997. Morgan Kaufmann.
4. K Kinnear Jr. *Advances in Genetic Programming.* The MIT Press, 1994.
5. J Koza. *Genetic Programming: On the Programming of Computers by Means of Natural Selection.* MIT Press, 1992.
6. J Koza, F Bennett, D Andre, and M Keane. *Genetic Programming III.* Morgan Kaufmann Publishers, 1999.
7. G Miller, P Todd, and S Hegde. Designing neural networks using genetic algorithms. In *Proceedings of International Conference on Genetic Algorithms,*, pages 379–384, 1989.
8. J Park and V Govindaraju. Active character recognition using a *- like algorithm. In *Proceedings of Computer Vision and Pattern Recognition*, 2000.
9. J Park, V Govindaraju, and S Srihari. Ocr in a hierarchical feature space. *IEEE Transactions on Pattern Analysis and Machine Intelligence*, 22(4):400–407, April 2000.

Author Index

Subject Index

Lecture Notes in Computer Science

For information about Vols. 1–1933
please contact your bookseller or Springer-Verlag

Vol. 1972: A. Omicini, R. Tolksdorf, F. Zambonelli (Eds.), Engineering Societies in the Agents World. Proceedings, 2000. IX, 143 pages. 2000. (Subseries LNAI).

Vol. 1973: J. Van den Bussche, V. Vianu (Eds.), Database Theory – ICDT 2001. Proceedings, 2001. X, 451 pages. 2001.

Vol. 1974: S. Kapoor, S. Prasad (Eds.), FST TCS 2000: Foundations of Software Technology and Theoretical Computer Science. Proceedings, 2000. XIII, 532 pages. 2000.

Vol. 1975: J. Pieprzyk, E. Okamoto, J. Seberry (Eds.), Information Security. Proceedings, 2000. X, 323 pages. 2000.

Vol. 1976: T. Okamoto (Ed.), Advances in Cryptology – ASIACRYPT 2000. Proceedings, 2000. XII, 630 pages. 2000.

Vol. 1977: B. Roy, E. Okamoto (Eds.), Progress in Cryptology – INDOCRYPT 2000. Proceedings, 2000. X, 295 pages. 2000.

Vol. 1978: B. Schneier (Ed.), Fast Software Encryption. Proceedings, 2000. VIII, 315 pages. 2001.

Vol. 1979: S. Moss, P. Davidsson (Eds.), Multi-Agent-Based Simulation. Proceedings, 2000. VIII, 267 pages. 2001. (Subseries LNAI).

Vol. 1983: K.S. Leung, L.-W. Chan, H. Meng (Eds.), Intelligent Data Engineering and Automated Learning – IDEAL 2000. Proceedings, 2000. XVI, 573 pages. 2000.

Vol. 1984: J. Marks (Ed.), Graph Drawing. Proceedings, 2001. XII, 419 pages. 2001.

Vol. 1985: J. Davidson, S.L. Min (Eds.), Languages, Compilers, and Tools for Embedded Systems. Proceedings, 2000. VIII, 221 pages. 2001.

Vol. 1987: K.-L. Tan, M.J. Franklin, J. C.-S. Lui (Eds.), Mobile Data Management. Proceedings, 2001. XIII, 289 pages. 2001.

Vol. 1988: L. Vulkov, J. Waśniewski, P. Yalamov (Eds.), Numerical Analysis and Its Applications. Proceedings, 2000. XIII, 782 pages. 2001.

Vol. 1989: M. Ajmone Marsan, A. Bianco (Eds.), Quality of Service in Multiservice IP Networks. Proceedings, 2001. XII, 440 pages. 2001.

Vol. 1990: I.V. Ramakrishnan (Ed.), Practical Aspects of Declarative Languages. Proceedings, 2001. VIII, 353 pages. 2001.

Vol. 1991: F, Dignum, C. Sierra (Eds.), Agent Mediated Electronic Commerce. VIII, 241 pages. 2001. (Subseries LNAI).

Vol. 1992: K. Kim (Ed.), Public Key Cryptography. Proceedings, 2001. XI, 423 pages. 2001.

Vol. 1993: E. Zitzler, K. Deb, L. Thiele, C.A.Coello Coello, D. Corne (Eds.), Evolutionary Multi-Criterion Optimization. Proceedings, 2001. XIII, 712 pages. 2001.

Vol. 1995: M. Sloman, J. Lobo, E.C. Lupu (Eds.), Policies for Distributed Systems and Networks. Proceedings, 2001. X, 263 pages. 2001.

Vol. 1997: D. Suciu, G. Vossen (Eds.), The World Wide Web and Databases. Proceedings, 2000. XII, 275 pages. 2001.

Vol. 1998: R. Klette, S. Peleg, G. Sommer (Eds.), Robot Vision. Proceedings, 2001. IX, 285 pages. 2001.

Vol. 1999: W. Emmerich, S. Tai (Eds.), Engineering Distributed Objects. Proceedings, 2000. VIII, 271 pages. 2001.

Vol. 2000: R. Wilhelm (Ed.), Informatics: 10 Years Back, 10 Years Ahead. IX, 369 pages. 2001.

Vol. 2003: F. Dignum, U. Cortés (Eds.), Agent Mediated Electronic Commerce III. XII, 193 pages. 2001. (Subseries LNAI).

Vol. 2004: A. Gelbukh (Ed.), Computational Linguistics and Intelligent Text Processing. Proceedings, 2001. XII, 528 pages. 2001.

Vol. 2006: R. Dunke, A. Abran (Eds.), New Approaches in Software Measurement. Proceedings, 2000. VIII, 245 pages. 2001.

Vol. 2007: J.F. Roddick, K. Hornsby (Eds.), Temporal, Spatial, and Spatio-Temporal Data Mining. Proceedings, 2000. VII, 165 pages. 2001. (Subseries LNAI).

Vol. 2009: H. Federrath (Ed.), Designing Privacy Enhancing Technologies. Proceedings, 2000. X, 231 pages. 2001.

Vol. 2010: A. Ferreira, H. Reichel (Eds.), STACS 2001. Proceedings, 2001. XV, 576 pages. 2001.

Vol. 2013: S. Singh, N. Murshed, W. Kropatsch (Eds.), Advances in Pattern Recognition – ICAPR 2001. Proceedings, 2001. XIV, 476 pages. 2001.

Vol. 2015: D. Won (Ed.), Information Security and Cryptology – ICISC 2000. Proceedings, 2000. X, 261 pages. 2001.

Vol. 2018: M. Pollefeys, L. Van Gool, A. Zisserman, A. Fitzgibbon (Eds.), 3D Structure from Images – SMILE 2000. Proceedings, 2000. X, 243 pages. 2001.

Vol. 2020: D. Naccache (Ed.), Progress in Cryptology – CT-RSA 2001. Proceedings, 2001. XII, 473 pages. 2001

Vol. 2021: J. N. Oliveira, P. Zave (Eds.), FME 2001: Formal Methods for Increasing Software Productivity. Proceedings, 2001. XIII, 629 pages. 2001.

Vol. 2024: H. Kuchen, K. Ueda (Eds.), Functional and Logic Programming. Proceedings, 2001. X, 391 pages. 2001.

Vol. 2027: R. Wilhelm (Ed.), Compiler Construction. Proceedings, 2001. XI, 371 pages. 2001.

Vol. 2028: D. Sands (Ed.), Programming Languages and Systems. Proceedings, 2001. XIII, 433 pages. 2001.

Vol. 2029: H. Hussmann (Ed.), Fundamental Approaches to Software Engineering. Proceedings, 2001. XIII, 349 pages. 2001.

Vol. 2030: F. Honsell, M. Miculan (Eds.), Foundations of Software Science and Computation Structures. Proceedings, 2001. XII, 413 pages. 2001.

Vol. 2031: T. Margaria, W. Yi (Eds.), Tools and Algorithms for the Construction and Analysis of Systems. Proceedings, 2001. XIV, 588 pages. 2001.

Vol. 2034: M.D. Di Benedetto, A. Sangiovanni-Vincentelli (Eds.), Hybrid Systems: Computation and Control. Proceedings, 2001. XIV, 516 pages. 2001.

Vol. 2035: D. Cheung, G.J. Williams, Q. Li (Eds.), Knowledge Discovery and Data Mining – PAKDD 2001. Proceedings, 2001. XVIII, 596 pages. 2001. (Subseries LNAI).

Vol. 2038: J. Miller, M. Tomassini, P.L. Lanzi, C. Ryan, A.G.B. Tettamanzi, W.B. Langdon (Eds.), Genetic Programming. Proceedings, 2001. XI, 384 pages. 2001.